Letters from Switzerland and Travels in Italy

Johann Wolfgang von Goethe

Alpha Editions

This edition published in 2022

ISBN : 9789356718432

Design and Setting By
Alpha Editions
www.alphaedis.com
Email - info@alphaedis.com

LETTERS FROM SWITZERLAND.

When, a few years ago, the copies of the following letters were first made known to us, it was asserted that they had been found among Werther's papers, and it was pretended that before his acquaintance with Charlotte, he had been in Switzerland. We have never seen the originals: however we would not on any account anticipate the judgment and feelings of our readers; for whatever may be their true history, it is impossible to read them without sympathy.

PART THE FIRST.

How do all my descriptions disgust me, when I read them over. Nothing but your advice, your command, your injunction could have induced me to attempt anything of the kind. How many descriptions, too, of these scenes had I not read before I saw them. Did these, then, afford me an image of them,—or at best but a mere vague notion? In vain did my imagination attempt to bring the objects before it; in vain did my mind try to think upon them. Here I now stand contemplating these wonders, and what are my feelings in the midst of them? I can think of nothing—I can feel nothing,—and how willingly would I both think and feel. The glorious scene before me excites my soul to its inmost depths, and impels me to be doing; and yet what can I do—what do I? I set myself down and scribble and describe!—Away with you, ye descriptions—delude my friend—make him believe that I am doing something—that he sees and reads something.

Were, then, these Switzers free? Free, these opulent burghers in their little pent-up towns—free, those poor devils on their rocks and crags? What is it that man cannot be made to believe, especially when he cherishes in his heart the memory of some old tale of marvel? Once, forsooth, they did break a tyrant's yoke, and might for the moment fancy themselves free; but out of the carcase of the single oppressor the good sun, by a strange new birth, has hatched a swarm of petty tyrants. And so now they are ever telling that old tale of marvel: one hears it till one is sick of it. They formerly made themselves free, and have ever since remained free! and now they sit behind their walls, hugging themselves with their customs and laws—their philandering and philistering. And there, too, on the rocks, it is surely fine to talk of liberty, when for six months of the year they, like the marmot, are bound hand and foot by the snow.

Alas! how wretched must any work of man look, in the midst of this great and glorious Nature, but especially such sorry, poverty-stricken works as these black and dirty little towns—such mean heaps of stones and rubbish! Large rubble and other stones on the roofs too, that the miserable thatch may not be carried off from the top of them,—and then the filth, the dung, and the gaping idiots! When here you meet with man and the wretched work of his hands, you are glad to fly away immediately from both.

That there are in man very many intellectual capacities which in this life he is unable to develope, which therefore point to a better future, and to a more harmonious state of existence: on this point we are both agreed. But further than this I cannot give up that other fancy of mine, even though on account of it you may again call me, as you have so often done already, a mere enthusiast. For my part, I do think that man feels conscious also of corporeal qualities, of whose mature expansion he can have no hope in this life. This most assuredly is the case with "*flying.*" How strongly at one time used the clouds, as they drove along the blue sky, to tempt me to travel with them to foreign lands! and now in what danger do I stand, lest they should carry me away with them from the mountain peak as they sweep violently by. What desire do I not feel to throw myself into the boundless regions of the air—to poise over the terrific abyss, or to alight on some otherwise inaccessible rock. With what a longing do I draw deeper and deeper breath, when, in the dark blue depth below, the eagle soars over rocks and forests, or in company, and in sweet concord with his mate, wheels in wide circles round the eyrie to which he has entrusted his young. Must I then never do more than creep up to the summits? Must I always go on clinging to the highest rocks, as well as to the lowest plain; and when I have at last, with much toil, reached the desired eminence, must I still anxiously grasp at every holding place, shudder at the thought of return, and tremble at the chance of a fall.

Fancies and feelings.

With what wonderful properties are we not born,—what vague aspirations rise within us! How rarely do imagination and our bodily powers work in opposition! Peculiarities of my early boyhood again recur. While I am walking, and have a long road before me, my arms go dangling by my side, I often make a grasp, as if I would seize a javelin, and hurl it I know not at whom, or what; and then I fancy an arrow is shot at me which pierces me to the heart; I strike my hand upon my breast, and feel an inexpressible sweetness; and then after this I soon revert to my natural state. Whence comes this strange phenomenon,—what is the meaning of it? and why does it invariably recur under the same figures, in the same bodily movement, and with the same sensation?

I am repeatedly told that the people who have met me on my journey are little satisfied with me. I can readily believe it, for neither has any one of them contributed to my satisfaction. I cannot tell how it comes to pass, that society oppresses me; that the forms of politeness are disagreeable to me—that what people talk about does not interest me,—that all that they show to me is either quite indifferent, or else produces quite an opposite impression to what they expect. When I am shown a drawing or painting of any beautiful spot, immediately a feeling of disquiet arises within me which is utterly inexpressible. My toes within my shoes begin to bend, as if they would clutch the ground-a cramp-like motion runs through my fingers. I bite my lips, and I hasten to leave the company I am in, and throw myself down in the presence of the majesty of nature on the first seat however inconvenient. I try to take in the scene before me with my eye—to seize all its beauties, and on the spot I love to cover a whole sheet with scratches, which represent nothing exactly, but which, nevertheless, possess an infinite value in my eyes, as serving to remind me of the happy moment, whose bliss even this bungling exercise could not mar. What means, then, this strange effort to pass from art to nature, and then back again from nature to art: If it gives promise of an artist, why is steadiness wanting to me? If it calls me to enjoyment, wherefore, then, am I not able to seize it? I lately had a present of a basket of fruit. I was in raptures at the sight of it as of something heavenly,—such riches, such abundance, such variety and yet such affinity! I could not persuade myself to pluck off a single berry—I could not bring myself to take a single peach or a fig. Most assuredly this gratification of the eye and the inner sense is the highest and most worthy of man; in all probability it is the design of Nature, when the hungry and thirsty believe that she has exhausted herself in marvels merely for the gratification of their palate. Ferdinand came and found me in the midst of these meditations: he did me justice, and then said, smiling, but with a deep sigh, "Yes, we are not worthy to consume these glorious products of Nature; truly it were a pity. Permit me to make a present of them to my beloved?" How glad was I to see the basket carried off! How did I love Ferdinand—how did I thank him for the feeling he had excited in me—for the prospect he gave me? Aye, we ought to acquaint ourselves with the beautiful; we ought to contemplate it with rapture, and attempt to raise ourselves up to its height. And in order to gain strength for that, we must keep ourselves thoroughly unselfish—we must not make it our own, but rather seek to communicate it: indeed, to make a sacrifice of it to those who are dear and precious to us.

How sedulously are we shaped and moulded in our youth—how constantly are we then called on to lay aside now this, now that bad feeling! But what, in fact, are our so-called bad feelings but so many organs by means of which man is to help himself in life. How is not the poor child worried, in whom but a little spark of vanity is discovered! and yet what a poor miserable creature is the man who has no vanity at all. I will now tell you what has led me to make all these reflections. The day before yesterday we were joined by a young fellow, who was most disagreeable to me and to Ferdinand. His weak points were so prominent, his emptiness so manifest, and his care for his outward appearance so obvious, that we looked down upon him as far inferior to ourselves, yet everywhere he was better received than we were. Among other of his follies, he wore a waist-coat of red satin, which round the neck was so cut as to look like the ribbon of some order or other. We could not restrain our jokes at this piece of absurdity, but he let them all pass, for he drew a good profit from it, and perhaps secretly laughed at us. For host and hostess, coachman, waiter and chambermaid, and indeed not a few of our fellow-travellers, were taken in by this seeming ornament, and showed him greater politeness than ourselves. Not only was he always first waited upon, but, to our great humiliation, we saw that all the pretty girls in the inns bestowed all their stolen glances upon him; and then, when it came to the reckoning, which his eminence and distinction had enhanced, we had to pay our full shares. Who, then, was the fool in the game?—not he, assuredly.

Conventional education.

There is something pretty and instructive about the symbols and maxims which one here sees on all the stoves. Here you have the drawing of one of these symbols which particularly caught my fancy. A horse tethered by his hind foot to a stake is grazing round it as far as his tether will permit; beneath is written, "Allow me to take my allotted portion of food." This, too, will be the case with me, when I come home, and, like the horse in the mill, shall have to work away at your pleasure, and in return, like the horse here on the stove, shall receive a nicely-measured dole for my support. Yes, I am coming back, and what awaits me was certainly well worth all the trouble of climbing up these mountain heights, of wandering through these valleys, and seeing this blue sky—of discovering that there is a nature which exists by an eternal voiceless necessity, which has no wants, no feelings, and is divine, whilst we, whether in the country or in the towns, have alike to toil hard to gain a miserable subsistence, and at the same time struggle to subject everything to our lawless caprice, and call it liberty!

Aye, I have ascended the *Furca*—the summit of S. Gotthard. These sublime, incomparable scenes of nature, will ever stand before my eye. Aye,

I have read the Roman history, in order to gain from the comparison a distinct and vivid feeling what a thoroughly miserable being I am.

Never has it been so clear to me as during these last few days, that I too could be happy on moderate means—could be quite as happy as any one else, if only I knew a trade—an exciting one, indeed, but yet one which had no consequences for the morrow, which required nothing but industry and attention at the time, without calling for either foresight or retrospection. Every mechanic seems to me the happiest of mortals: all that he has to do is already settled for him, what he can do is fixed and known. He has not to rack his brains over the task that is set him; he works away without thinking, without exertion or haste, but still with diligence and pleasure in his work, like a bird building its nest, or a bee constructing its cells. He is but a degree above the beasts, and yet he is a perfect man. How do I envy the potter at his wheel, or the joiner behind his bench!

Tilling the soil is not to my liking—this first and most necessary of man's occupations is disagreeable to me. In it man does but ape nature, who scatters her seeds everywhere, whereas man would choose that a particular field should produce none but one particular fruit. But things do not go on exactly so—the weeds spring up luxuriantly—the cold and wet injures the crop, or the hail cuts it off entirely. The poor husbandman anxiously waits throughout the year to see how the cards will decide the game with the clouds, and determine whether he shall win or lose his stakes. Such a doubtful ambiguous condition may be right suitable to man, in his present ignorance, while he knows not whence he came, nor whither he is going. It may then be tolerable to man to resign all his labours to chance; and thus the parson, at any rate, has an opportunity, when things look thoroughly bad, to remind him of Providence, and to connect the sins of his flock with the incidents of nature.

An Adventure.

So then I have nothing to joke Ferdinand about! I too have met with a pleasant adventure. Adventure! why do I use the silly word? There is nothing of adventure in a gentle attraction which draws man to man. Our social life, our false relations, those are adventures, these are monstrosities and yet they come before us as well-known and as nearly akin to us, as Uncle and Aunt.

We had been introduced to Herr Tüdou, and we found ourselves very happy among this family—rich, open-hearted, good-natured, lively people, who in the society of their children, in comfort and without care, enjoy the good which each day brings with it—their property and their glorious neighbourhood. We young folks were not required, as is too often the case, in so many formal households, to sacrifice ourselves at the card-table, in order to humour the old. On the contrary, the old people, father, mother, and aunts, gathered round us, when for our own amusement, we got up some little games, in which chance, and thought, and wit, had their counteracting influence. Eleonora—for I must now at last mention her name—the second daughter—her image will for ever be present to my mind—a slim slight-frame, delicately chiselled features, a bright eye—a palish complexion, which in young girls of her age is rather pleasing than disagreeable, as being a sign of no very incurable a malady—on the whole, her appearance was extremely agreeable. She seemed cheerful and lively and every one felt at his ease with her. Soon—indeed I may venture to say at once,—at once, on the very first evening she made me her companion; she sat by my side, and if the game separated us a moment, she soon contrived to find her old place again. I was gay and cheerful—my journey, the beautiful weather, the country—all had contributed to produce in me an immoderate cheerfulness—aye, I might almost venture to say, a state of excitement. I derived it from everything and imparted it to everything; even Ferdinand seemed to forget his fair one. We had almost exhausted ourselves in varying our amusements when we at last thought of the "Game of Matrimony." The names of the ladies and of the gentlemen were thrown separately into two hats, and then the pairs were drawn out one by one. On each couple, as determined by the lot, one of the company whose turn it might happen to be, had to write a little poem. Every one of the party, father, mother, and aunts, were obliged to put their names in the hats; we cast in besides the names of our acquaintances, and to enlarge the number of candidates for matrimony, we threw in those of all the well-known characters of the literary and of the political world. We commenced playing, and the first pairs that were drawn were highly distinguished personages. It was not every one, however, who was ready at once with his verses. _She_, Ferdinand and myself, and one of the aunts who wrote very pretty verses in French—we soon divided among ourselves the office of secretary. The conceits were mostly good and the verses tolerable. Her's especially, had a touch of nature about them which distinguished them from all others; without being really clever they had a happy turn; they were playful without being bitter, and shewed good will towards every one. The father laughed heartily, and his face was lit up with joy when his daughter's verses were declared to be the best after mine. Our unqualified approbation highly delighted him,—we praised as men praise unexpected merit—as we praise an author who has bribed us. At last out came my lot, and chance had taken honourable care of me. It was no less a personage than the Empress of all the Russias, who was drawn to be my partner for life. The company laughed heartily at the match, and Eleonora maintained that the whole company must try their best to do honour to so eminent a consort. All began to try: a few pens were bitten to pieces; she was ready first, but wished to read last; the mother and the aunt could make nothing of the subject, and although the father was rather matter-of-fact, Ferdinand somewhat humorous, and the aunts rather reserved, still, through all you could see friendship and good-will. At last it came to her turn; she drew a deep breath, her ease and cheerfulness left her; she did not read but rather lisped it out—and laid it before me to read it to the rest. I was astonished, amazed. Thus does the bud of love open in beauty and modesty! I felt as if a whole spring had showered upon me all its flowers at once! Every one was silent, Ferdinand lost not his presence of mind. "Beautiful," he exclaimed, "very beautiful! he deserves the poem as little as an Empire." "If, only we have rightly understood it," said the father; the rest requested I would read it once more. My eyes had hitherto been fixed on the precious words, a shudder ran through me from head to foot, Ferdinand who saw my perplexity, took the paper up and read it. She scarcely allowed him to finish before she drew out the lots for another pair. The play was not kept up long after this and refreshments were brought in.

Shall I or shall I not? Is it right of me to hide in silence any thing from him to whom I tell so much—nay, all? Shall I keep back from you a great matter, when I yet weary you with so many trifles which assuredly no one would ever read but you who have taken so wonderful a liking for me? or shall I keep back anything from you because it might perhaps give you a false, not to say an ill opinion of me? No—you know me better than I even know myself. If I should do anything which you do not believe possible I could do, you will amend it; if I should do anything deserving of censure, you will not spare me,—you will lead me and guide me whenever my peculiarities entice me off the right road.

Art and nature.

My joy, my rapture at works of art when they are true, when they are immediate and speaking expressions of Nature afford the greatest delight to every collector, to every dilettante. Those indeed who call themselves connoisseurs are not always of my opinion; but I care nothing for their connoisseurship when I am happy. Does not living nature vividly impress itself on my sense of vision? Do not its images remain fixed in my brain?

Do not they there grow in beauty, delighting to compare themselves in turn with the images of art which the mind of others has also embellished and beautified? I confess to you that my fondness for nature arises from the fact of my always seeing her so beautiful, so lovely, so brilliant, so ravishing, that the similation of the artist, even his imperfect imitation transports me almost as much, as if it were a perfect type. It is only such works of art, however, as bespeak genius and feeling that have any charms for me. Those cold imitations which confine themselves to the narrow circle of a certain meagre mannerism, of mere painstaking diligence, are to me utterly intolerable. You see, therefore, that my delight and taste cannot well be riveted by a work of art, unless it imitates such objects of nature as are well known to me, so that I am able to test the imitation by my own experience of the originals. Landscape, with all that lives and moves therein—flowers and fruit-trees. Gothic churches,—a portrait taken directly from Nature, all this I can recognize, feel, and if you like, judge of. Honest W——— amused himself with this trait of my character, and in such a way that I could not be offended, often made merry with it at my expense. He sees much further in this matter, than I do, and I shall always prefer that people should laugh at me while they instruct, than that they should praise me without benefitting me. He had noticed what things I was most immediately pleased with, and after a short acquaintance did not hesitate to avow that in the objects that so transported me there might be much that was truly estimable, and which time alone would enable me to distinguish.

But I turn from this subject and must now, however circuitously, come to the matter which, though reluctantly, I cannot but confide to you. I can see you in your room, in your little garden, where, over a pipe of tobacco, you will probably break the seal and read this letter. Can your thoughts follow me into this free and motley world? Will the circumstances and true state of the case become clear to your imagination? And will you be as indulgent towards your absent friend as I have often found you when present?

Studies of the nude.

When my artistic friend became better acquainted with me, and judged me worthy of being gradually introduced to better pieces of art, he one day, not without a most mysterious look, took me to a case, which, being opened, displayed a Danæ, of the size of life, receiving in her bosom the golden shower. I was amazed at the splendour of the limbs—the magnificence of the posture and arrangement—the intense tenderness and the intellectuality of the sensual subject; and yet I did but stand before it in silent contemplation. It did not excite in me *that* rapture, *that* delight, *that* inexpressible pleasure. My friend, who went on descanting upon the merits of the picture, was too full of his own enthusiasm to notice my coldness, and was delighted with the opportunity this painting afforded him of pointing out the distinctive excellences of the Italian School.

But the sight of this picture has not made me happy—it has made me uneasy. How! said I to myself—in what a strange case do we civilized men find ourselves with our many conventional restraints! A mossy rock, a waterfall rivets my eye so long that I can tell everything about it—its heights, its cavities, its lights and shades, its hues, its blending tints and reflections—all is distinctly present to my mind; and whenever I please, comes vividly before me, in a most happy imitation. But of that masterpiece of Nature, the human frame—of the order and symmetry of the limbs, of all this I have but a very general notion—which in fact is no notion at all. My imagination presents to me anything but a vivid image of this glorious structure, and when art presents an imitation of it, to my eye it awakens in me no sensation and I am unable to judge of the merits of the picture. No, I will remain no longer in this state of stupidity. I will stamp on my mind the shape of man, as well as that of a cluster of grapes or of a peach-tree.

I sought an occasion and got Ferdinand to take a swim in the lake. What a glorious shape has my friend; how duly proportioned are all his limbs: what fulness of form; what splendour of youth! What a gain to have enriched my imagination with this perfect model of manhood! Now I can people the woods, the meadow, and the hills, with similar fine forms! I can see him as Adonis chasing the boar, or as Narcissus contemplating himself in the mirror of the spring.

But alas! my imagination cannot furnish, as yet, a Venus, who holds him from the chace, a Venus who bewails his death, or a beautiful Echo casting one sad look more on the cold corpse of the youth before she vanishes for ever! I have therefore resolved, cost what it will, to see a female form in the state that I have seen my friend.

When, therefore, we reached Geneva, I made arrangements in the character of an artist to complete my studies of the nude figure, and to-morrow evening my wish is to be gratified.

I cannot avoid going to-day with Ferdinand to a grand party. It will form an excellent foil to the studies of this evening. Well enough do I know those formal parties where the old women require you to play at cards with them, and the young ones to ogle with them; where you must listen to the learned, pay respect to the parson, and give way to the noble, where the numerous lights show you scarcely one tolerable form, and that one hidden and buried beneath some barbarous load of frippery. I shall have to speak

French, too,—a foreign tongue—the use of which always makes a man appear silly, whatever he may think of himself, since the best he can express in it is nothing but common place, and the most obvious of remarks, and that, too, only with stammering and hesitating lips. For what is it that distinguishes the blockhead from the really clever man but the peculiar quickness and vividness with which the latter discerns the nicer shades and proprieties of all that come before him, and expresses himself thereon with facility; whereas the former, (just as we all do with a foreign language,) is forced on every occasion to have recourse to some ready found and conversational phrase or other? To-day I will calmly put up with the sorry entertainment, in expectation of the rare scene of nature which awaits me in the evening.

My adventure is over. It has fully equalled my expectation—nay, surpassed it; and yet I know not whether to congratulate, or to blame myself on account of it.

PART THE SECOND.

Munster, October 3, 1797.

From Basle you will receive a packet containing an account of my travels up to that point, for we are now continuing in good earnest our tours through Switzerland. On our route to Biel we rode up the beautiful valley of the Birsch, and at last reached the pass which leads to this place.

> The valley of the Birsch.

Among the ridges of the broad and lofty range of mountains the little stream of the Birsch found of old a channel for itself. Necessity soon after may have driven men to clamber wearily and painfully through its gorges. The Romans in their time enlarged the track, and now you may travel through it with perfect ease. The stream, dashing over crags and rocks, and the road run side by side, and except at a few points, these make up the whole breadth of the pass which is hemmed in by rocks, the top of which is easily reached by the eye. Behind them the mountain chain rose with a slight inclination; the summits, however, were veiled by a mist.

Here walls of rock rise precipitously one above another; there immense strata run obliquely down to the river and the road-here again broad masses lie piled one over another, while close beside stands a line of sharp-pointed crags. Wide clefts run yawning upwards, and blocks, of the size of a wall, have detached themselves from the rest of the stony mass. Some fragments of the rock have rolled to the bottom; others are still suspended, and by their position alarm you, as also likely at any moment to come toppling down.

Now round, now pointed, now overgrown, now bare are the tops of these rocks among and high above which some single bald summit boldly towers, while along the perpendicular cliffs and among the hollows below, the weather has worn many a deep and winding cranny.

The passage through this defile raised in me a grand but calm emotion. The sublime produces a beautiful calmness in the soul which entirely possessed by it, feels as great as it ever can feel. How glorious is such a pure feeling, when it rises to the very highest, without overflowing. My eye and my soul were both able to take in the objects before me, and as I was pre-occupied by nothing, and had no false tastes to counteract their impression, they had on me their full and natural effect. When we compare such a feeling with that we are sensible of, when we laboriously harass ourselves with some trifle, and strain every nerve to gain as much as possible for it, and as it were, to patch it out, striving to furnish joy and aliment to the mind from its own creation; we then feel sensibly what a poor expedient, after all, the latter is.

A young man, whom we have had for our companion from Basle, said his feelings were very far from what they were on his first visit, and gave all the honour to novelty. I however would say, when we see such objects as these for the first time, the unaccustomed soul has to expand itself, and this gives rise to a sort of painful joy—an overflowing of emotion which agitates the mind, and draws from us the most delicious tears. By this operation the soul, without knowing it, becomes greater in itself, and is of course not capable of ever feeling again such a sensation, and man thinks in consequence that he has lost something, whereas in fact he has gained. What he loses in delight he gains in inward riches. If only destiny had bidden me to dwell in the midst of some grand scenery, then would I every morning have imbibed greatness from its grandeur, as from a lonely valley I would extract patience and repose.

After reaching the end of the gorge I alighted, and went back alone through a part of the valley. I thus called forth another profound feeling—one by which the attentive mind may expand its joys to a high degree. One guesses in the dark about the origin and existence of these singular forms. It may have happened, when and how it may,—these masses must, according to the laws of gravity and affinity, have been formed grandly and simply by aggregation. Whatever revolutions may subsequently have upheaved, rent and divided them, the latter were only partial convulsions, and even the idea of such mighty commotions gives one a deep feeling of the eternal stability of the masses. Time, too, bound by the everlasting law, has had here greater, here less, effect upon them.

Internally their colour appears to be yellowish. The air, however, and the weather has changed the surface into a bluish-grey, so that the original colour is only visible here and there in streaks and in the fresh cracks. The stone itself slowly crumbles beneath the influence of the weather, becoming rounded at the edges, as the softer flakes wear away. In this manner have been formed hollows and cavities gracefully shelving off, which when they have sharp slanting and pointed edges, present a singular appearance.

Vegetation maintains its rights on every ledge, on every flat surface, for in every fissure the pines strike root, and the mosses and plants spread themselves over the rocks. One feels deeply convinced that here there is nothing accidental; that here there is working an eternal law which, however slowly, yet surely governs the universe,—that there is nothing here from the hand of man but the convenient road, by means of which this singular region is traversed.

Geneva, October 27, 1779.

La Vallée de Joux.

The great mountain-range which, running from Basle to Geneva, divides Switzerland from France, is, as you are aware, named the Jura. Its principal heights run by Lausanne, and reach as far as Rolle and Nyon. In the midst of this summit ridge Nature has cut out—I might almost say washed out— a remarkable valley, for on the tops of all these limestone rocks the operation of the primal waters is manifest. It is called La Vallée de Joux, which means the Valley of the Rock, since Joux in the local dialect signifies a rock. Before I proceed with the further description of our journey, I will give you a brief geographical account of its situation. Lengthwise it stretches like the mountain range itself almost directly from south to north, and is locked in on the one side by Sept Moncels, and on the other by Dent de Vaulion, which, after the Dole, is the highest peak of the Jura. Its length, according to the statement of the neighbourhood, is nine short leagues, but according to our rough reckoning as we rode through it, six good leagues. The mountainous ridge which bounds it lengthwise on the north, and is also visible from the flat lands, is called the Black Mountain (Le Noir Mont). Towards the west the Risou rises gradually, and slopes away towards Franche Comté. France and Berne divide the valley pretty evenly between them; the former claiming the upper and inferior half, and the latter possessing the lower and better portion, which is properly called La Vallée du Lac de Joux. Quite at the upper part of the valley, and at the foot of Sept Moncels, lies the Lac des Rousses, which has no single visible origin, but gathers its waters from the numerous springs which here gush out of the soil, and from the little brooks which run into the lake from all sides. Out of it flows the Orbe, which after running through the whole of the French, and a great portion of the Bernese territory, forms lower down, and towards the Dent de Vaulion, the Lac de Joux, which falls on one side into a smaller lake, the waters of which have some subterraneous outlet. The breadth of the valley varies; above, near the Lac des Rousses it is nearly half a league, then it closes in to expand again presently, and to reach its greatest breath, which is nearly a league and a-half. So much to enable you better to understand what follows; while you read it, however, I would beg you now and then to cast a glance upon your map, although, so far as concerns this country, I have found them all to be incorrect.

October 24th. In company with a captain and an upper ranger of the forests in these parts, we rode first of all up Mont, a little scattered village, which much more correctly might be called a line of husbandmen's and vinedressers' cottages. The weather was extremely clear; when we turned to look behind us, we had a view of the Lake of Geneva, the mountains of Savoy and Valais, and could just catch Lausanne, and also, through a light mist, the country round Geneva, Mont Blanc, which towers above all the mountains of Faucigni, stood out more and more distinctly. It was a brilliant sunset, and the view was so grand, that no human eye was equal to it. The moon rose almost at the full, as we got continually higher. Through large pine forests we continued to ascend the Jura, and saw the lake in a mist, and in it the reflection of the moon. It became lighter and lighter. The road is a well-made causeway, though it was laid down merely for the sake of facilitating the transport of the timber to the plains below. We had been ascending for full three leagues before the road began gently to descend. We thought we saw below us a vast lake, for a thick mist filled the whole valley which we overlooked. Presently we came nearer to the mist, and observed a white bow which the moon formed in it, and were soon entirely enveloped in the fog. The company of the captain procured us lodgings in a house where strangers were not usually entertained. In its internal arrangement it differed in nothing from usual buildings of the same kind, except that the great room in the centre was at once the kitchen, the ante-room, and general gathering-place of the family, and from it you entered at once into the sleeping-rooms, which were either on the same floor with it, or had to be approached by steps. On the one side was the fire, which was burning on the ground on some stone slabs, while a chimney, built durably and neatly of planks, received and carried off the smoke. In the corner were the doors of the oven; all the rest of the floor was of wood, with the exception of a small piece near the window around the sink, which was paved. Moreover, all around, and over head on the beams a multitude of domestic articles and utensils were arranged in beautiful order, and all kept nice and clean.

October 26th.—This morning the weather was cold but clear, the meadows covered with hoar frost, and here and there light clouds were floating in the air. We could pretty nearly survey the whole of the lower valley, our house being situated at the foot of the eastern side of Noir Mont. About eight we set off, and in order to enjoy the sun fully, proceeded on the western side. The part of the valley we now traversed was divided into meadows, which, towards the lake were rather swampy. The inhabitants either dwell in detached houses built by the side of their farms, or else have gathered closer together in little villages, which bear simple names derived from their several sites. The first of those that we passed through was called "Le Sentier." We saw at a distance the Dent de Vaulion peeping out over a mist which rested on the lake. The valley grew broader, but our road now lay behind a ridge of rock which shut out our view of the lake, and then through another village called "Le Lieu." The mist arose, and fell off highly variegated by the sun. Close hereto is a small lake, which apparently has neither inlet nor outlet of its waters. The weather cleared up completely as we came to the foot of Dent de Vaulion, and reached the northern extremity of the great lake, which, as it turns westward, empties itself into a smaller by a dam beneath the bridge. The village just above is called "Le Pont." The situation of the smaller lake is what you may easily conceive, as being in a peculiar little valley which may be called pretty. At the western extremity there is a singular mill, built in a ravine of the rock which the smaller lake used formerly to fill. At present it is dammed out of the mill which is erected in the hollow below. The water is conveyed by sluices to the wheel, from which it falls into crannies of the rock, and being sucked in by them, does not show itself again till it reaches Valorbe, which is a full league off, where it again bears the name of the Orbe. These outlets (*entonnoirs*) require to be kept clear, otherwise the water would rise and again fill the ravine, and overflow the mill as it has often done already. We saw the people hard at work removing the worn pieces of the lime-stone and replacing them by others.

Dent de Vaulion.

We rode back again over the bridge towards "Le Pont," and took a guide for the Dent du Vaulion. In ascending it we now had the great Lake directly behind us. To the east its boundary is the Noir Mont, behind which the bald peak of the Dole rises up; to the west it is shut in by the mountain ridge, which on the side of the lake is perfectly bare. The sun felt hot: it was between eleven and twelve o'clock. By degrees we gained a sight of the whole valley, and were able to discern in the distance the "Lac des Rousses," and then stretching to our feet the district we had just ridden through and the road which remained for our return. During the ascent my guide discoursed of the whole range of the country and the lordships which, he said, it was possible to distinguish from the peak. In the midst of such talk we reached the summit. But a very different spectacle was prepared for us. Under a bright and clear sky nothing was visible but the high mountain chain, all the lower regions were covered with a white sea of cloudy mist, which stretched from Geneva northwards, along the horizon and glittered brilliantly in the sunshine. Out of it, rose to the east, the whole line of snow and ice-capt mountains acknowledging no distinction of names of either the Princes or Peoples, who fancied they were owners of them, and owning subjection only to one Lord, and to the glance of the Sun which was tinging them with a beautiful red. Mont Blanc, right opposite to us, seemed the highest, next to it were the ice-crowned summits of Valais and Oberland, and lastly, came the lower mountains of the Canton of Berne. Towards the west, the sea of mist which was unconfined to one spot; on the left, in the remotest distance, appeared the mountains of Solothurn; somewhat nearer those of Neufchatel, and right before us some of the lower heights of the Jura. Just below, lay some of the masses of the Vaulion, to which belongs the Dent, (tooth) which takes from it its name. To the west, Franche-Comté, with its flat, outstretched and wood-covered hills, shut in the whole horizon; in the distance, towards the north-west, one single mass stood out distinct from all the rest. Straight before us, however, was a beautiful object. This was the peak which gives this summit the name of a tooth. It descends precipitously, or rather with a slight curve, inwards, and in the bottom it is succeeded by a small valley of pine-trees, with beautiful grassy patches here and there, while right beyond it lies the valley of the Orbe (Val-orbe), where you see this stream coming out of the rock, and can trace, in thought, its route backwards to the smaller lake. The little town of Valorbe, also lies in this valley. Most reluctantly we quitted the spot. A delay of a few hours longer, (for the mist generally disperses in about that time), would have enabled us to distinguish the low lands with the lake—but in order that our enjoyment should be perfect, we must always have something behind still to be wished. As we descended we had the whole valley lying perfectly distinct before us. At Le Pont we again mounted our horses, and rode to the east side of the lake, and passed through l'Abbaye de Joux, which at present is a village, but once was a settlement of monks, to whom the whole valley belonged. Towards four, we reached our auberge and found our meal ready, of which we were assured by our hostess that at twelve o'clock it would have been good eating, and which, overdone as it was, tasted excellently.

The Dole.

Let me now add a few particulars just as they were told me. As I mentioned just now, the valley belonged formerly to the monks, who having divided it again to feudatories, were with the rest ejected at the Reformation. At present it belongs to the Canton of Berne, and the mountains around are the timber-stores of the Pays de Vaud. Most of the timber is private property, and is cut up under supervision, and then carried down into the plains. The planks are also made here into deal utensils of all kinds, and pails, tubs, and similar articles manufactured.

The people are civil and well disposed. Besides their trade in wood, they also breed cattle. Their beasts are of a small size. The cheese they make is excellent. They are very industrious, and a clod of earth is with them a great treasure. We saw one man with a horse and car, carefully collecting the earth which had been thrown up out of a ditch, and carrying it to some hollow places in the same field. They lay the stones carefully together, and make little heaps of them. There are here many stone-polishers, who work for the Genevese and other tradesmen, and this business furnishes occupation for many women and children. The houses are neat but durable, the form and internal arrangements being determined by the locality and the wants of the inmates. Before every house there is a running stream, and everywhere you see signs of industry, activity, and wealth. But above all things is the highest praise due to the excellent roads, which, in this remote region, as also in all the other cantons, are kept up by that of Berne. A causeway is carried all round the valley, not unnecessarily broad, but in excellent repair, so that the inhabitants can pursue their avocations without inconvenience, and with their small horses and light carts pass easily along. The air is very pure and salubrious.

View from the Dole.

26th Oct.—Over our breakfast we deliberated as to the road we should take on our return. As we heard that the Dole, the highest summit of the Jura, lay at no great distance from the upper end of the valley, and as the weather promised to be most glorious, so that we might to-day hope to enjoy all that chance denied us yesterday, we finally determined to take this route. We loaded a guide with bread and cheese, and butter and wine, and by 8 o'clock mounted our horses. Our route now lay along the upper part of the valley, in the shade of Noir Mont. It was extremely cold, and there had been a sharp hoar-frost. We had still a good league to ride through the part belonging to Berne, before the causeway which there terminates branches off into two parts. Through a little wood of pine trees we entered the French territory. Here the scene changed greatly. What first excited our attention was the wretched roads. The soil is rather stony; everywhere you see great heaps of those which have been picked off the fields. Soon you come to a part which is very marshy and full of springs. The woods all around you are in wretched condition. In all the houses and people you recognise, I will not say want, but certainly a hard and meagre subsistence. They belong, almost as serfs, to the canons of S. Claude; they are bound to the soil (*glebæ astricti*), and are oppressed with imposts (*sujets à la main-morte et au droit de la suite*), of which we will hereafter have some talk together, as also of a late edict of the king's repealing the droit de la suite, and inviting the owners and occupiers to redeem the main-morte for a certain compensation. But still even this portion of the valley is well cultivated. The people love their country dearly, though they lead a hard life, being driven occasionally to steal the wood from the Bernese, and sell it again in the lowlands. The first division is called the Bois d'Amant; after passing through it, we entered the parish of Les Rousses, where we saw before us the little Lake des Rousses and Les Sept Moncels,—seven small hills of different shapes, but all connected together, which form the southern limit of the valley. We soon came upon the new road which runs from the Pays de Vaud to Paris. We kept to this for a mile downwards, and now left entirely the valley. The bare summit of the Dole was before us. We alighted from our horses, and sent them on by the road towards S. Cergue while we ascended the Dole. It was near noon; the sun felt hot, but a cool south wind came now and then to refresh us. When we looked round for a halting-place, we had behind us Les Sept Moncels, we could still see a part of the Lac des Rousses, and around it the scattered houses of the parish. The rest of the valley was hidden from our eye by the Noir Mont, above which we again saw our yesterday's view of Franche-Comté, and nearer at hand southwards, the last summits and valleys of the Jura. We carefully avoided taking advantage of a little peep in the hill, which would have given us a glimpse of the country, for the sake of which in reality our ascent was undertaken. I was in some anxiety about the mist; however, from the aspect of the sky above, I drew a favourable omen. At last we stood on the highest summit, and saw with the greatest delight that to-day we were indulged with all that yesterday had been denied us. The whole of the Pays de Vaux and de Gex lay like a plan before us: all the different holdings divided off with green hedges like the beds of a parterre. We were so high that the rising and sinking of the landscape before us was unnoticeable. Villages, little towns, country-houses, vine-covered hills, and higher up still, where the forests and Alps begin, the cow-sheds mostly painted white, or some other light colour, all glittered in the sunshine. The mist had already rolled off from Lake Leman. We saw the nearest part of the coast on our side, quite clear; of the so-called smaller lake, where the larger lake contracts itself, and turns towards Geneva, which was right opposite to us, we had a complete view; and on the other side the country which shuts it in was gradually clearing. But nothing could vie with the view of the mountains covered with snow and glaciers. We sat down before some rocks to shelter us from the cold wind, with the sunshine fall upon us, and highly relished our little meal. We kept watching the mist, which gradually retired; each one discovered, or fancied he discovered, some object or other. One by one we distinctly saw Lausanne, surrounded with its houses, and gardens; then Bevay, and the castle of Chillon; the mountains, which shut out from our view the entrance into Valais, and extended as far as the lake; from thence the borders of Savoy, Evian, Repaille, and Tonon, with a sprinkling of villages and farm-houses between them. At last Geneva stood clear from the mist, but beyond and towards the south, in the neighbourhood of Monte Credo and Monte Vauche, it still hung immoveable. When the eye turned to the left it caught sight of the whole of the lowlands from Lausanne, as far as Solothurn, covered with a light halo. The nearer mountains and heights, and every spot that had a white house on it, could be closely distinguished. The guides pointed out a glimmering which they said was the castle of Chauvan, which lies to the left of the Neuberger-See. We were just able to guess whereabouts it lay, but could not distinguish it through the bluish haze. There are no words to express the grandeur and beauty of this view. At the moment every one is scarcely conscious of what he sees:—one does but recall the names and sites of well-known cities and localities, to rejoice in a vague conjecture that he recognizes them in certain white spots which strike his eye in the prospect before him.

And then the line of glittering glaciers was continually drawing the eye back again to the mountains. The sun made his way towards the west, and lighted up their great flat surfaces, which were turned towards us. How beautifully before them rose from above the snow the variegated rows of black rocks:—teeth,—towers,—walls! Wild, vast, inaccessible vestibules! and seeming to stand there in the free air in the first purity and freshness of their manifold variety! Man gives up at once all pretensions to the infinite, while he here feels that neither with thought nor vision is he equal to the finite!

Before us we saw a fruitful and populous plain. The spot on which we were standing was a high, bare mountain rock, which, however, produces a sort of grass as food for the cattle, which are here a great source of gain. This the conceited lord of creation may yet make his own:—but those rocks before his eyes are like a train of holy virgins which the spirit of heaven reserves for itself alone in these inaccessible regions. We tarried awhile, tempting each other in turn to try and discover cities, mountains, and regions, now with the naked eye, now with the telescope, and did not begin to descend till the setting sun gave permission to the mist,—his own parting breath,—to spread itself over the lake.

With sunset we reached the ruins of the fort of S. Cergue. Even when we got down in the valley, our eyes were still rivetted on the mountain glaciers. The furthest of these, lying on our left in Oberland, seemed almost to be melting into a light fiery vapour; those still nearer stood with their sides towards us, still glowing and red; but by degrees they became white, green, and grayish. There was something melancholy in the sight. Like a powerful body over which death is gradually passing from the extremities to the heart, so the whole range gradually paled away as far as Mont Blanc, whose ampler bosom was still covered all over with a deep red blush, and even appeared to us to retain a reddish tint to the very last,—just as when one is watching the death of a dear friend, life still seems to linger, and it is difficult to determine the very moment when the pulse ceases to beat.

This time also we were very loth to depart. We found our horses in S. Cergue; and that nothing might be wanting to our enjoyment, the moon rose and lighted us to Nyon. While on the way, our strained and excited feelings were gradually calmed, and assumed their wonted tone, so that we were able with keen gratification to enjoy, from our inn window, the glorious moonlight which was spread over the lake.

Geneva.

At different spots of our travels so much was said of the remarkable character of the glaciers of Savoy, and when we reached Geneva we were told it was becoming more and more the fashion to visit them, that the Count[1] was seized with a strange desire to bend our course in that direction, and from Geneva to cross Cluse and Salenche, and enter the valley of Chamouni, and after contemplating its wonderful objects, to go on by Valorsine and Trent into Valais. This route, however, which was the one usually pursued by travellers, was thought dangerous in this season of the year. A visit was therefore paid to M. de Saussure at his country-house, and his advice requested. He assured us that we need not hesitate to take that route; there was no snow as yet on the middle-sized mountains, and if on our road we were attentive to the signs of the weather and the advice of the country-people, who were seldom wrong in their judgment, we might enter upon this journey with perfect safety. Here is the copy of the journal of a day's hard travelling.

Cluse, in Savoy, Nov. 3, 1779.

To-day on departing from Geneva our party divided. The Count with me and a huntsman took the route to Savoy. Friend W. with the horses proceeded through the Pays de Vaud for Valais. In a light four-wheeled cabriolet we proceeded first of all to visit Hüber at his country-seat,—a man out of whom, mind, imagination and imitative tact, oozes at every pore,—one of the very few thorough men we have met with. He saw us well on our way, and then we set off with the lofty snow-capped mountains, which we wished to reach, before our eyes. From the Lake of Geneva the mountain-chains verge towards each other to the point where Bonneville lies, half way between the Mole, a considerable mountain, and the Arve. There we took our dinner. Behind the town the valley closes right in. Although not very broad, it has the Arve flowing gently through it, and is on the southern side well cultivated, and everywhere the soil is put to some profit. From the early morning we had been in fear of its raining some time at least before night, but the clouds gradually quitted the mountains, and dispersed into fleeces,—a sign which has more than once in our experience proved a favourable omen. The air was as warm as it usually is in the beginning of September, and the country we travelled through beautiful. Many of the trees being still green; most of them had assumed a brownish-yellow tint, but only a few were quite bare. The crops were rich and verdant; the mountains caught from the red sunset a rosy hue, blended with violet; and all these rich tints were combined with grand, beautiful, and agreeable forms of the landscape. We talked over much that was good. Towards 5 we came towards Cluse, where the valley closes, and has only one outlet, through which the Arve issues from the mountains, and by which also we propose to enter them to-morrow. We ascended a lofty eminence, and saw beneath us the city, partly built on the slightly inclined side of a rock, but partly on the flat portion of the valley. Our eyes ranged with pleasure over the valley, and sitting on the granite rocks we awaited the coming of night in calm and varied discourse. Towards seven, as we descended, it was not at all colder than it is usually in summer about nine. At a miserable inn (where, however, the people were ready and willing, and by their patois afforded us much amusement) we are now going, about ten o'clock, to bed, intending to set out early to-morrow, before the morning shall dawn.

Salenche, Nov. 4, 1779. *Noon.*

The cavern of the Col de Balme.

Whilst a dinner is being prepared by very willing hands, I will attempt to set down the most remarkable incidents of our yesterday's journey, which commenced with the early morning. With break of day we set out on foot from Cluse, taking the road towards Balme. In the valley the air was agreeably fresh; the moon, in her last quarter, rose bright before the sun, and charmed us with the sight, as being one which we do not often see. Single light vapours rose upwards from all the chasms in the rocks. It seemed as if the morning air were awakening the young spirits, who took pleasure in meeting the sun with expanded bosoms and gilding them in his rays. The upper heaven was perfectly clear; except where now and then a single cloudy streak, which the rising sun lit up, swept lightly across it. Balme is a miserable village, not far from the spot where a rocky gorge runs off from the road. We asked the people to guide us through the cave for which the place is famous. At this they kept looking at one another, till at last one said to a second, "Take you the ladder, I will carry the rope,— come, gentlemen." This strange invitation did not deter us from following then. Our line of descent passed first of all among fallen masses of limestone rock, which by the course of time had been piled up step by step in front of the precipitous wall of rock, and were now overgrown with bushes of hazel and beech. Over these you reach at last the strata of the rock itself, which you have to climb up slowly and painfully by means of the ladder and of the steps cut into the rock, and by help of branches of the nut-trees, which hung over head, or of pieces of rope tied to them. After this you find yourself, to your great satisfaction, in a kind of portal, which has been worn out of the rock by the weather, and overlooks the valley and the village below. We now prepared for entering the cave; lighted our candles and loaded a pistol which we proposed to let off. The cave is a long gallery, mostly level and on one strand; in parts broad enough for two men to walk abreast, in others only passable by one; now high enough to walk upright, then obliging you to stoop, and sometimes even to crawl on hands and feet. Nearly about the middle a cleft runs upwards and forms a sort of a dome. In one corner another goes downwards. We threw several stones down it, and counted slowly from seventeen to nineteen before it reached the bottom, after touching the sides many times, but always with a different echo. On the walls a stalactite forms its various devices; however it is only damp in a very few places, and forms for the most part long drops, and not those rich and rare shapes which are so remarkable in Baumann's cave. We penetrated as far as we could for the water, and as we came out let off our pistol, which shook the cave with a strong but dull echo, so that it boomed round us like a bell. It took us a good quarter of an hour to get out again, and on descending the rocks, we found our carriage and drove onwards. At Staubbachs-Art we saw a beautiful waterfall; neither its height was very great nor its volume very large, and yet it was extremely interesting, for the rocks formed around it, as it were, a circular niche in which, its waters fell, and the pieces of the limestone as they were tumbled one over another formed the most rare and unusual groups.

We arrived here at mid-day, not quite hungry enough to relish our dinner, which consisted of warmed fish, cow beef, and very stale bread. From this place there is no road leading to the mountains that is passable for so stately an equipage as we have with us; it therefore returns to Geneva, and I now must take my leave of you, in order to pursue my route a little further. A mule with my luggage will follow us as we pick our way on foot.

Chamouni, Nov. 4, 1779.
Evening, about 9 o'clock.

It is only because this letter will bring me for awhile nearer to yourself that I resume my pen; otherwise it would be better for me to give my mind a little rest.

We left Salenche behind us in a lovely open valley; during our noonday's rest the sky had become overcast with white fleecy clouds, about which I have here a special remark to make. We had seen them on a bright day rise equally fine, I if not still finer, from the glaciers of Berne. Here too it again seemed to us as if the sun, had first of all attracted the light mists which evaporated from the tops of the glaciers, and then a gentle breeze had, as it were, combed the fine vapours, like a fleece of foam over the atmosphere. I never remember at home, even in the height of summer, (when such phenomena do also occur with us,) to have seen any so transparent, for here it was a perfect web of light. Before long the ice-covered mountains from which it rose lay before us; the valley began to close in; the Arve was gushing out of the rock; we now began to ascend a mountain, and went up higher and higher, with the snowy summits right before us. Mountains and old pine forests, either in the hollows below or on a level with our track, came out one by one before the eye as we proceeded. On our left were the mountain-peaks, bare and pointed. We felt that we were approaching a mightier and more massive chain of mountains. We passed over a dry and broad bed of stones and gravel, which the watercourses tear down from the sides of the rocks, and in turn flow among and fill up. This brought us into an agreeable valley, flat, and shut in by a circular ridge of rocks, in which lies the little village of Serves. There the road runs round some very highly variegated rocks, and takes again the direction towards the Arve. After crossing the latter you again ascend; the masses become constantly more imposing, nature seems to have begun here with a light hand, to prepare her enormous creations. The darkness grew deeper and deeper as we approached the valley of Chamouni, and when at last we entered it, nothing but the larger masses were discernible. The stars came out one by one, and we noticed above the peaks of the summits right before us, a light which we could not account for. Clear, but without brilliancy, like the milky way, but closer, something like that of the Pleiades; it rivetted our attention until at last, as our position changed, like a pyramid illuminated by a secret light within, which could best be compared to the gleam of a glow-worm, it towered high above the peaks of all the surrounding mountains, and at last convinced us that it must be the peak of Mont Blanc. The beauty of this view was extraordinary. For while, together with the stars which clustered round it, it glimmered, not indeed with the same twinkling light, but in a broader and more continuous mass, it seemed to belong to a higher sphere, and one had difficulty in thought to fix its roots again in the earth. Before it we saw a line of snowy summits, sparkling as they rested on the ridges covered with the black pines, while between the dark forests vast glaciers sloped down to the valley below.

My descriptions begin to be irregular and forced; in fact, one wants two persons here, one to see and the other to describe.

Here we are in the middle village of the valley called "Le Prieuré," comfortably lodged in a house, which a widow caused to be built here in honour of the many strangers who visited the neighbourhood. We are sitting close to the hearth, relishing our Muscatel wine from the Vallée d'Aost far better than the lenten dishes which were served up to our dinner.

Nov. 5, 1779. Evening.

To take up one's pen and write, almost requires as great an effort as to take a swim in the cold river. At this moment I have a great mind to put you off, by referring you to the description of the glaciers of Savoy, given by that enthusiastic climber Bourritt.

Invigorated however by a few glasses of excellent wine, and by the thought that these pages will reach you much sooner than either the travellers or Bourritt's book, I will do my best. The valley of Chamouni, in which we are at present, lies very high among the mountains, and, from six to seven leagues long, runs pretty nearly from south to north. The characteristic features which to my mind distinguish it from all others, are its having scarcely any flat portion, but the whole tract, like a trough, slopes from the Arve gradually up the sides of the mountain. Mont Blanc and the line of mountains which runs off from it, and the masses of ice which fill up the immense ravines, make up the eastern wall of the valley, on which, throughout its entire length, seven glaciers, of which one is considerably larger than the others, run down to the bottom of the valley.

The Ice-Lake.

The guides whom we had engaged to show us to the ice-lake came to their time. One was a young active peasant, the other much older, who seemed to think himself a very shrewd personage, who had held intercourse with all learned foreigners, well acquainted with the nature of the ice-mountains, and a very clever fellow. He assured us that for eight and twenty years,—so long had he acted as guide over the mountains,—this was the first time that his services had been put in requisition so late in the year—after All Saints' Day, and yet that we might even now see every object quite as well as in June. Provided with wine and food we began to ascend Mont Anvert, from which we were told the view of the ice-lake would be quite ravishing. Properly I should call it the ice-valley or the ice-stream; for looking at it from above, the huge masses of ice force themselves out of a deep valley in tolerable smoothness. Right behind it ends a sharp-pointed mountain, from both sides of which waves of ice run frozen into the principal stream. Not the slightest trace of snow was as yet to be seen on the rugged surfaces, and the blue crevices glistened beautifully. The weather by degrees became overcast, and I saw grey wavy clouds, which seemed to threaten snow, more than it had ever yet done. On the spot where we were standing is a small cabin, built of stones, loosely piled together as a shelter for travellers, which in joke has been named "The Castle of Mont Anvert." An Englishman, of the name of Blaire, who is residing at Geneva, has caused a more spacious one to be built at a more convenient spot, and a little higher up, where, sitting by a fire-side, you catch through the window a view of the whole Ice-Valley. The peaks of the rocks over against you, as also in the valley below, are very pointed and rugged. These jags are called needles, and the Aiguille du Dru is a remarkable peak of this kind, right opposite to Mont Anvert. We now wished to walk upon the Ice Lake itself, and to consider these immense masses close at hand. Accordingly we climbed down the mountain, and took nearly a hundred steps round about on the wave-like crystal cliffs. It is certainly a singular sight, when standing on the ice itself, you see before you the masses pressing upwards, and divided by strangely shaped clefts. However, we did not like standing on this slippery surface, for we had neither come prepared with ice-shoes, nor with nails in our usual ones; on the contrary, those which we ordinarily wore had become smooth and rounded with our long walk; we, therefore, made our way back to the hut, and after a short rest were ready for returning. We descended the mountain, and came to the spot where the ice-stream, step by step, forces its way to the valley below, and we entered the cavern, into which it empties its water. It is broad, deep, and of the most beautiful blue, and in the cave the supply of water is more invariable than further on at the mouth, since great pieces of ice are constantly melting and dissolving in it.

On our road to the Auberge we passed the house where there were two Albinos,—children between twelve and fourteen, with very white complexions, rough white hair, and with red and restless eyes like rabbits. The deep night which hangs over the valley invites me to retire early to bed, and I am hardly awake enough to tell you, that we have seen a tame young ibex, who stands out as distinctly among the goats as the natural son of a noble prince from the burgher's family, among whom he is privately brought up and educated. It does not suit with our discourses, that I should speak of anything out of its due order. Besides, you do not take much delight in specimens of granite, quartz, or in larch and pine trees, yet, most of all, you would desire to see some remarkable fruits of our botanising. I think I am stupid with sleep,—I cannot write another line.

Chamouni, Nov. 6, 1776. Early.

Content with seeing all that the early season allows us to see, we are ready to start again, intending to penetrate as far as Valais to-day. A thick mist covers the whole valley, and reaches half way up the mountains, and we must wait and see what sun and wind will yet do for us. Our guide purposes that we should take the road over the Col-de-Balme, a lofty eminence, which lies on the north side of the valley towards Valais, from the summit of which, if we are lucky, we shall be able to take another survey of the valley of Chamouni, and of all its remarkable objects.

Whilst I am writing a remarkable phenomenon is passing along the sky. The mists which are shifting about, and breaking in some places, allow you through their openings as through skylights, to catch a glance of the blue sky, while at the same time the mountain peaks, which rising above our roof of vapour, are illuminated by the sun's rays. Even without the hope it gives of a beautiful day, this sight of itself is a rich treat to the eye.

We have at last obtained a standard for judging the heights of the mountains. It is at a considerable height above the valley, that the vapour rests on the mountains. At a still greater height are clouds, which have floated off upwards from the top of the mist, and then far above these clouds you see the summits glittering in the sunshine.

It is time to go. I must bid farewell to this beautiful valley and to you.

* * *

Martinac, in Valais,
Nov. 6, 1779. Evening.

We have made the passage across without any mishap, and so this adventure is over. The joy of our good luck will keep my pen going merrily for a good half hour yet.

Having packed our luggage on a mule, we set out early (about 9,) from Prieuré. The clouds shifted, so that the peaks were now visible and then were lost again; at one moment the sun's rays came in streaks on the valley, at the next the whole of it was again in shade. We went up the valley, passing the outlet of the ice-stream, then the glacier d'Argentière, which is the highest of the five, the top of it however was hidden from our view by the clouds. On the plain we held a counsel, whether we should or not take the route over Col de Balme, and abandon the road over Valorsine. The prospect was not the most promising; however, as here there was nothing to lose and much perhaps to gain, we took our way boldly towards the dark region of mists and clouds. As we approached the Glacier du Tour, the clouds parted, and we saw this glacier also in full light. We sat down awhile and drank a flask of wine, and took something to eat. We now mounted towards the sources of the Arve, passing over rugged meadows and patches scantily covered with turf, and came nearer and nearer to the region of mists, until at last we entered right into it. We went on patiently for awhile till at last as we got up higher, it began again to clear above our heads. It lasted for a short time, so we passed right out of the clouds, and saw the whole mass of them beneath us spread over the valley, and were able to see the summits of all the mountains on the right and left that enclosed it, with the exception of Mont Blanc, which was covered with clouds. We were able to point them out one by one, and to name them. In some we saw the glaciers reaching from their summits to their feet, in others we could only discern their tracks, as the ice was concealed from our view by the rocky sides of the gorges. Beyond the whole of the flat surface of the clouds, except at its southern extremity, we could distinctly see the mountains glittering in the sunshine. Why should I enumerate to you the names of summits, peaks, needles, icy and snowy masses, when their mere designations can furnish no idea to your mind, either of the whole scene or of its single objects?

Col de Balme.

It was quite singular how the spirits of the air seemed to be waging war beneath us. Scarcely had we stood a few minutes enjoying the grand view, when a hostile ferment seemed to arise within the mist, and it suddenly rose upwards and threatened once more to envelope us. We commenced stoutly ascending the height, in the hope of yet awhile escaping from it, but it outstripped us and enclosed us on all sides. However, perfectly fresh, we continued to mount, and soon there came to our aid a strong wind, blowing from the mountain. Blowing over the saddle which connected two peaks, it drove the mist back again into the valley. This strange conflict was frequently repeated, and at last, to our joy, we reached the Col de Balme. The view from it was singular, indeed unique. The sky above the peaks was overcast with clouds; below, through the many openings in the mist, we saw the whole of Chamouni, and between these two layers of cloud the mountain summits were all visible. On the east we were shut in by rugged mountains, on the west we looked down on wild valleys, where, however, on every green patch human dwellings were visible. Before us lay the valley of Valais, where at one glance the eye took in mountains piled in every variety of mass one upon another, and stretching as far as Martinac and even beyond it. Surrounded on all sides by mountains which, further on towards the horizon, seemed continually to multiply and to tower higher and higher, we stood on the confines of Valais and Savoy.

Some contrabandists, who were ascending the mountains with their mules, were alarmed at seeing us, for at this season they did not reckon on meeting with any one at this spot. They fired a shot to intimate that they were armed, and one advanced before the rest to reconnoitre. Having recognised our guide and seen what a harmless figure we made, he returned to his party, who now approached us, and we passed one another with mutual greetings.

The wind now blew sharp, and it began to snow a little as we commenced our descent, which was rough and wild enough, through an ancient forest of pines, which had taken root on the faces of the gneiss. Torn up by the winds, the trunks and roots lay rotting together, and the rocks which were loosened at the same time were lying in rough masses among them.

At last we reached the valley where the river Trent takes its rise from a glacier, and passing the village of Trent, close upon our right, we followed the windings of the valley along a rather inconvenient road, and about six reached Martinac, which lies in the flatter portion of the Valais. Here we must refresh ourselves for further expeditions.

Martinac, Nov. 6, 1779.
Evening.

Just as our travels proceed uninterruptedly, so my letters one after another keep up my conversation with you. Scarcely have I folded and put aside the conclusion of "Wanderings through Savoy," ere I take up another sheet of paper in order to acquaint you with all that we have further in contemplation.

It was night when we entered a region about which our curiosity had long been excited. As yet we have seen nothing but the peaks of the mountains, which enclose the valley on both sides, and then only in the glimmering of twilight. We crept wearily into our auberge, and saw from the window the clouds shifting. We felt as glad and comfortable to have a roof over our heads, as children do when with stools, table-leaves and carpets, they construct a roof near the stove, and therein say to one another that outside "it is raining or knowing," in order to excite a pleasant and imaginary shudder in their little souls. It is exactly so with us on this autumnal evening in this strange and unknown region.

> Valais.

We learn from the maps that we are sitting in the angle of an elbow, from which the smaller part of Valais, running almost directly from south to north, and with the Rhone, extends to the lake of Geneva, while the other and the larger portion stretches from west to east, and goes up the Rhone to its source, the Furca. The prospect of riding through the Valais is very agreeable, our only anxiety is how we are to cross over into it. First of all, with the view of seeing the lower portion, it is settled that we go to-morrow to S. Maurice, where we are to meet our friend, who with the horses has gone round by the Pays de Vaud. To-morrow evening we think of being here again, and then on the next day shall begin to go up the country. If the advice of M. de Saussure prevails, we shall perform the route to the Furca on horseback, and then back to Brieg over the Simplon, where, in any weather, the travelling is good over Domo d'Osula, Lago Maggiore, Bellinzona, and then up Mount Gotthard. The road is said to be excellent, and everywhere passable for horses. We should best prefer going over the Furca to S. Gotthard, both for the sake of the shorter route, and also because this detour through the Italian provinces was not within our original plan, but then what could we do with our horses; they could not be made to descend the Furca, for in all probability the path for pedestrians is already blocked up by the snow.

With regard to the latter contingency, however, we are quite at our ease, and hope to be able, as we have hitherto done, to take counsel, from moment to moment, with circumstances as they arise.

The most remarkable object in this inn is a servant-girl, who with the greatest stupidity gives herself all the airs of one of our would-be delicate German ladies. We had a good laugh, when after bathing our weary feet in a bath of red wine and clay, as recommended by our guide, we had in the affected hoyden to wipe them dry.

Our meal has not refreshed us much, and after supper we hope to enjoy our beds more.

S. Maurice, Nov. 7, 1779.
Nearly Noon.

On the road it is my way to enjoy the beautiful views, in order that I may call in one by one my absent friends, and converse with them on the subject of the glorious objects. If I come into an inn it is in order to rest myself, to go back in memory and to write something to you, when many a time my overstrained faculties would much rather collapse upon themselves, and recover their tone in a sort of half sleep.

This morning we set off at dawn from Martinac; a fresh breeze was stirring with the day, and we soon passed the old castle which stands at the point where the two arms of Valais make a sort of Y. The valley is narrow, shut in on its two sides by mountains, highly diversified in their forms, and which without exception are of a peculiar and sublimely beautiful character. We came to the spot where the Trent breaks into the valley around some narrow and perpendicular rocks, so that one almost doubts whether the river does not flow out of the solid rock itself. Close by stands the old bridge, which only last year was greatly injured by the stream, while not far from it lie immense masses of rock, which have fallen very recently from the mountains and blocked up the road. The whole group together would make an extremely beautiful picture. At a short distance from the old bridge a new wooden one has been built, and a new road been laid down to it.

The water-fall of Pisse Vache.

We were told that we were getting near the famous water-fall of Pisse Vache, and wished heartily for a peep at the sun, while the shifting clouds gave us a good hope that our wish would be gratified. On the road we examined various pieces of granite and of gneiss, which with all their differences seem, nevertheless, to have a common origin. At last we stood before the waterfall, which well deserves its fame above all others. At a considerable height a strong stream bursts from a cleft in the rock, falling downward into a basin, over which the foam and spray is carried far and wide by the wind. The sun at this moment came forth from the clouds, and made the sight doubly vivid. Below in the spray, wherever you go, you have close before you a rainbow. If you go higher up, you still witness no less singular a phenomenon. The airy foaming waves of the upper stream of water, as with their frothy vapour, they come in contact with the angle of vision at which the rainbow is formed, assume a flame-like hue, without giving rise to the pendant form of the bow, so that at this point you have before you a constantly varying play of fire.

We climbed all round, and sitting down near it, wished we were able to spend whole days and many a good hour of our life on this spot. Here too, as in so many other places during our present tour, we felt how impossible is was to enjoy and to be fully impressed with grand objects on a passing visit.

We next came to a village where there were some merry soldiers, and we drank there some new wine. Some of the same sort had been set before us yesterday. It looked like soap and water; however, we had rather drink it than their sour "this year's" and "two years' old" wine. When one is thirsty nothing comes amiss.

We saw S. Maurice at a distance; it lies just at the point where the valley closes in, so much as to cease to be anything more than a mere pass. Over the city, on the left, we saw a small church with a hermitage close to it, and we hope to have an opportunity yet of visiting them both.

We found in the inn a note from our friend, who has stopped at Bec, which is about three quarters of a league from this place; we have sent a messenger to him. The Count is gone out for a walk to see the country before us. I shall take a morsel to eat, and then set out towards the famous bridge and the pass.

After 1 o'clock.

I have at last got back from the spot where one could be contented to spend whole days together, lounging and loitering about without once getting tired, holding converse with oneself.

If I had to advise any one as to the best route into Valais, I should recommend the one from the Lake of Geneva up the Rhone. I have been on the road to Bec over the great bridge, from which you step at once into the Bernese territory. Here the Rhone flows downwards, and the valley near the lake becomes a little broader. As I turned round again I saw that the rocks near S. Maurice pressed together from both sides, and that a small light bridge, with a high arch, was thrown boldly across from them over the Rhone, which rushes beneath it with its roaring and foaming stream. The numerous angles and turrets of a fortress stands close to the bridge, and a single gateway commands the entrance into Valais. I went over the bridge back towards S. Maurice, and even beyond it, in search of a view which I had formerly seen a drawing of at Huber's house, and by good luck found it.

The count is come back. He had gone to meet the horses and mounting his grey had outstripped the rest. He says the bridge is so light and beautiful that it looks like a horse in the act of leaping a ditch. Our friend too is coming, and is quite contented with his tour. He accomplished the distance from the Lake of Geneva to Bec in a few days, and we are all delighted to see one another again.

Martinac, towards 9.

We were out riding till late at night, and the road seemed much longer returning than going, as in the morning, our attention had been constantly attracted from one object to another. Besides I am for this day, at least, heartily tired of descriptions and reflections; however, I must try hastily to perpetuate the memory of two beautiful objects. It was deep twilight when on our return we reached the waterfall of the Pisse Vache. The mountains, the valley, and the heavens themselves were dark and dusky. By its greyish tint and unceasing murmur you could distinguish the falling stream from all other objects, though you could scarcely discern the slightest motion. Suddenly the summit of a very high peak glowed just like molten brass in a furnace, and above it rose a red smoke. This singular phenomenon was the effect of the setting sun which illuminated the snow and the mists which ascended from it.

Sion, Nov. 8, 1779.
about 3 o'clock.

From Martinac to Sion.

This morning we missed our way riding, and were delayed in consequence, three hours at least. We set out from Martinac before dawn, in order to reach Sion in good time. The weather was extraordinarily beautiful, only that the sun being low in the heavens was shut out by the mountains, so that the road, as we passed along, was entirely in the shade. The view, however, of the marvellously beautiful valley of Valais brought up many a good and cheerful idea. We had ridden for full three hours along the high road with the Rhone on our left, when we saw Sion before us; and we were beginning to congratulate ourselves on the prospect of soon ordering our noon-day's meal, when we found that the bridge we ought to cross had been carried away. Nothing remained for us, we were told by the people who were busy repairing it, but either to leave our horses and go by a foot-path which ran across the rocks, or else to ride on for about three miles, and then cross the Rhone by some other bridges. We chose the latter; and we would not suffer any ill-humour to get possession of us, but determined to ascribe this mischance to the interposition of our good genius, who intended to take us a slow ride through this interesting region with the advantage of good day-light. Everywhere, indeed, in this narrow district, the Rhone makes sad havoc. In order to reach the other bridges we were obliged, for more than a league and a half, to ride over sandy patches, which in the various inundations are constantly shifting, and are useful for nothing but alder and willow beds. At last we came to the bridges, which were wretched, tottering, long, and composed of rotten timbers. We had to lead our horses over one by one, and with extreme caution. We were now on the left side of the Valais and had to turn backwards to get to Sion. The road itself was for the most part wretched and stony; every step, however, opened a fresh view, which was well worth a painting. One, however, was particularly remarkable. The road brought us up to a castle, below which there was spread out the most lovely scene that we had seen in the whole road. The mountains nearest to us run down on both sides slantingly to the level ground, and by their shape gave a kind of perspective effect to the natural landscape. Beneath us was the Valais in its entire breadth from mountain to mountain, so that the eye could easily take it in; the Rhone, with its ever varying windings and bushy banks was flowing past villages, meadows, and richly cultivated highlands; in the distance you saw the Castle of Sion, and the various hills which begin to rise behind it; the farthest horizon was shut in, amphitheatre like, with a semicircular range of snow-capped mountains which, like all the rest of the scene, stood glittering in the sun's meridian splendour. Disagreeable and rough was the road we had to ride over; we therefore enjoyed the more, perhaps, the still tolerably green festoons of the vines which over-arched it. The inhabitants, to whom every spot of earth is precious, plant their grape-vines close against the walls which divide their little holdings from the road, where they grow to an extraordinary thickness, and by means of stakes and trellises are trained across the road so as almost to form one continuous arbour. The lower grounds were principally meadows: in the neighbourhood of Sion, however, we notice? some tillage. Towards this town the scenery is extremely diversified by a variety of hills, and we wished to be able to make a longer stay in order to enjoy it. But the hideousness of the town and of the people fearfully disturb the pleasant impression which the scenery leaves. The most frightful goitres put me altogether out of humour. We cannot well put our horses any further to-day, and therefore we think or going on foot to Seyters. Here in Sion the inn is disgusting, and the whole town has a dirty and revolting appearance.

Seyters, Nov. 8, 1779.
Night.

Sion-Seyters.

As evening had begun to fall before we set out from Sion, we reached here at night, with the sky above us clear and starry. We have consequently lost many a good view—that I know well. Particularly we should have liked to have ascended to the Castle of Tourbillon, which is at no great distance from Sion; the view from it must be uncommonly beautiful. A guide whom we took with us skilfully guided us through some wretched low lands, where the water was out. We soon reached the heights, and had the Rhone below us on our right. By talking over some astronomical matters we shortened our road, and have taken up our abode here with some very worthy people, who are doing their best to entertain us. When we think over what we have gone through, so busy a day, with its many incidents and sights, seems almost equal to a whole week. I begin to be quite sorry that I have neither time nor talent to sketch at least the outlines of the most remarkable objects; for that would be much better for the absent than all descriptions.

Seyters, Nov. 9, 1779.

Before we set out I can just bid you good morning. The Count is going with me to the mountains on the left, towards Leukerbad; our friend will, in the meantime, stay here with the horses, and join us to-morrow at Leuk.

Leukerbad, Nov. 9, 1779.
At the Foot of Mount Gemmi.

In a little wooden house where we have been friendlily received by some very worthy people, we are sitting in a small, low room, and trying how much of to-day's highly interesting tour can be communicated in words. Starting from Seyters very early we proceeded for three leagues up the mountains, after having passed large districts laid waste by the mountain torrents. One of these streams will suddenly rise and desolate an extent of many miles, covering with fragments of rock and gravel the fields, meadows, and gardens, which (at least wherever possible) the people laboriously set to work to clear, in order within two generations, perhaps, to be again laid waste. We have had a grey day, with every now and then a glimpse of sunshine. It is impossible to describe how infinitely variegated the Valais here again becomes; the landscape bends and changes every moment, cooking around you all the objects seem to lie close together, and yet they are separated by great ravines and hills. Generally we had had the open part of the valley below us, on the right, when suddenly we came upon a spot which commanded a most beautiful view over the mountains.

In order to render more clear what it is I am attempting to describe, I must say a few words on the geographical position of the district in which we are at present. We had now for three hours been ascending the mountainous region which separates Valais from Berne. This is, in fact, the great track of mountains which runs in one continuous chain from the Lake of Geneva to Mount S. Gothard, and on which, as it passes through Berne, rest the great masses of ice and snow. Here *above* and *below* are but the relative terms of the moment. I say, for instance, beneath me lies a village—and in all probability the level on which it is built is on a precipitous summit, which is far higher above the valley below, than I am above it.

As we turned an angle of the road and rested awhile at a hermitage, we saw beneath us, at the end a lovely green meadowland, which stretched along the brink of an enormous chasm, the village of Inden, with its white church exactly in the middle of the landscape, and built altogether on the slope of the hill-side. Beyond the chasm another line of meadow lands and pine forests went upwards, while right behind the village a vast cleft in the rocks ran up the summit. On the left hand the mountains came right down to us, while those on our right stretched far away into the distance, so that the little hamlet, with its white church, formed as it were the focus towards which the many rocks, ravines, and mountains all converged. The road to Inden is cut out of the precipitous side of the rock, which, on your left going to the village, lines the amphitheatre. It is not dangerous although it looks frightful enough. It goes down on the slope of a rugged mass of rocks, separated from the yawning abyss on the right, by nothing but a few poor planks. A peasant with a mule, who was descending at the same time as ourselves, whenever he came to any dangerous points caught his beast by the tail, lest the steep descent should cause him to slip, and roll into the rocks below. At last we reached Inden. As our guide was well known there, he easily managed to obtain for us, from a good-natured dame, some bread and a glass of red wine, for in these parts there are no regular inns.

We now ascended the high ravine, behind Inden, where we soon saw before us the Gemmiberg (of which we had heard such frightful descriptions), with Leukerbad at its foot, lying between two lofty, inaccessible, snow-covered mountains, as if it were in the hollow of a hand. It was three o'clock, nearly, when we arrived there, and our guide soon procured us lodgings. There is properly no inn even here, but in consequence of the many visitors to the baths at this place, all people have good accommodations. Our hostess had been put to bed the day before, but her husband with an old mother and a servant girl, did very creditably the honours of the house. We ordered something to eat, and went to see the warm springs, which in several places burst out of the earth with great force, and are received in very clean reservoirs. Out of the village, and more towards the mountains, there are said to be still stronger ones. The water has not the slightest smell of sulphur, and neither at its source nor in its channel does it make the least deposit of ochre or of any other earth or mineral, but like any other clear spring water it leaves not the slightest trace behind it. As it comes out of the earth it is extremely hot, and is famous for its good qualities. We had still time for a walk to the foot of the Gemmi, which appeared to us to be at no great distance. I must here repeat a remark that has been made so often already; that when one is surrounded with mountain scenery all objects appear to be extremely near. We had a good league to go, amongst fragments of rock which had fallen from the heights, and over gravel brought down by the torrents, before we reached the foot of the Gemmi, where the road ascends along the precipitous crags. This is the only pass into the canton of Berne, and the sick have to be transported along it in sedan chairs.

If the season did not bid us hasten onwards, in all probability we might make an attempt to-morrow to ascend this remarkable mountain; as it is, however, we must content ourselves with the simple view of it. On our return we saw the clouds brewing, which in these parts is a highly interesting sight. The fine weather we have hitherto enjoyed has made us forget almost entirely that it is in November that we are; besides too, as they foretold us in Berne, the autumn here is very delightful. The short days, however, and the clouds which threaten snow, warn us how late it is in the year. The strange drift which has been agitating them this evening was singularly beautiful. As we came back from the foot of the Gemmi, we saw light mists come up the ravine from Inden, and move with great rapidity. They continually changed their direction, going now forwards, now backwards, and at last, as they ascended, they came so near to Leukerbad that we saw clearly that we must double our steps if we would not before nightfall be enveloped in the clouds. We reached our quarters, however, without accident, and whilst I write this it is snowing in earnest. This is the first fall of snow that we have yet had, and when we call to mind our warm ride yesterday, from Martinach to Sion, beneath the vine-arbours, which were still pretty thick with leaves, the change does appear sudden indeed. I have been standing some time at the door, observing the character and look of the clouds, which are beautiful beyond description. It is not yet night, but at intervals the clouds veil the whole sky and make it quite dark. They rise out of the deep ravines until they reach the highest summits of the mountains; attracted by these they appear to thicken, and being condensed by the cold they fall down in the shape of snow. It gives you an inexpressible feeling of loneliness to find yourself here at this height, as it were, in a sort of well, from which you scarcely can suppose that there is even a footpath to get out by, except down the precipice before you. The clouds which gather here in this valley, at one time completely hiding the immense rocks, and absorbing them in a waste impenetrable gloom, or at another letting a part of them be seen like huge spectres, give to the people a cast of melancholy. In the midst of such natural phenomena the people are full of presentiments and forebodings. Clouds—a phenomenon remarkable to every man from his youth up—are, in the plain countries, generally looked upon at most as something foreign—something super-terrestrial. People regard them as strangers, as birds of passage, which, hatched under a different climate, visit this or that country for a moment or two in passing—as splendid pieces of tapestry wherewith the gods part off their pomp and splendour from human eyes. But here, where they are hatched, man is inclosed in them from the very first, and the eternal and intrinsic energy of his nature feels itself at every nerve moved to forebode and to indulge in presentiments.

To the clouds, which, with us even produce these effects, we pay little attention; moreover as they are not pushed so thickly and directly before our eyes, their economy is the more difficult to observe. With regard to all such phenomena one's only wish is to dwell on them for a while, and to be able to tarry several days in the spots where they are observable. If one is fond of such observations the desire becomes the more vivid the more one reflects that every season of the year, every hour of the day, and every change of weather produces new phenomena which we little looked for. And as no man, not even the most ordinary character, was ever a witness, even for once, of great and unusual events, without their leaving behind in his soul some traces or other, and making him feel himself also to be greater for this one little shred of grandeur, so that he is never weary of telling the whole tale of it over again, and has gained at any rate a little treasure for his whole life; just so is it with the man who has seen and become familiar with the grand phenomena of nature. He who manages to preserve these impressions, and to combine them with other thoughts and emotions, has assuredly a treasury of sweets wherewith to season the most tasteless parts of life, and to give a pervading relish to the whole of existence.

I observe that in my notes I make very little mention of human beings. Amid these grand objects of nature, they are but little worthy of notice, especially where they do but come and go. I doubt not but that on a longer stay we should meet with many worthy and interesting people. One fact I think I have everywhere observed; the farther one moves from the highroad and the busy marts of men, the more people are shut in by the mountains, isolated and confined to the simplest wants of life, the more they draw their maintenance from simple, humble, and unchangeable pursuits: so much the better, the more obliging, the more friendly, unselfish, and hospitable are they.

Leukerbad, Nov. 10, 1779.

We are getting ready by candle-light, in order to descend the mountain again as soon as day breaks. I have had rather a restless night. Scarcely had I got into bed before I felt as if I was attacked all over with the nettle rash. I soon found, however, that it was a swarm of crawling insects, who, ravenous of blood, had fallen upon the new comer. These insects breed in great numbers in these wooden houses. The night appeared to me extremely long, and I was heartily glad when in the morning a light was brought in.

We have not much time to spare; however, before we set out, I will give you an account of the remarkable breaking up of our company, which has here taken place, and also of the cause of it. We set out from Leukerbad with daybreak this morning, and had to make our way over the meadows through the fresh and slippery snow. We soon came to Inden, where, leaving above us on our right the precipitous road which we came down yesterday, we descended to the meadow lands along the ravine which now lay on our left. It is extremely wild and overgrown with trees, but a very tolerable road runs down into it. Through the clefts in the rock the water which comes down from Leukerbad has its outlets into the Valais. High up on the side of the hill, which yesterday we descended, we saw an aqueduct skilfully cut out of the rock, by which a little stream is conducted from the mountain, then through a hollow into a neighbouring village.

Leuk.

Next we had to ascend a steep height, from which we soon saw the open country of Valais, with the dirty town of Valais lying beneath us. These little towns are mostly stuck on the hill sides; the roofs inelegantly covered with coarsely split planks, which within a year become black and overgrown with moss; and when you enter them, you are at once disgusted, for everything is dirty; want and hardship are everywhere apparent among these highly privileged and free burghers.

We found here our friend, who brought the unfavourable report that it was beginning to be injudicious to proceed further with the horses. The stables were everywhere small and narrow, being built only for mules or sumpter horses; oats too were rarely to be procured; indeed he was told that higher up among the mountains there were none to be had. Accordingly a council was held. Our friend with the horses was to descend the Valais and go by Bee, Bevay, Lausanne, Freiburg, and Berne, to Lucerne, while the Count and I pursued our course up the Valais, and endeavoured to penetrate to Mount Gotthard, and then through the Canton of Uri, and by the lake of the Forest Towns, likewise make for Lucerne. In these parts you may anywhere procure mules, which are better suited to these roads than horses, and to go on foot invariably proves the most agreeable in the end. Our friend is gone, and our portmanteaus packed on the back of a mule, and so we are now ready to set off and make our way on foot to Brieg. The sky has a motley appearance, still I hope that the good luck which has hitherto attended us, and attracted us to this distant spot, will not abandon us at the very point where we have the most need of it.

Of to-day's expedition I have little to tell you, unless you would like to be entertained with a long circumstantial account of the weather. About 11 o'clock we set off from Leuk., in company with a Suabian butcher's boy, who had run away hither, and had found a place where he served somewhat in the capacity of Hanswurst (Jack-Pudding), and with our luggage packed on the back of a mule, which its master was driving before him. Behind us, as far as the eye could reach, thick snow clouds, which came driving up the lowlands, covered everything. It had really a threatening aspect. Without expressing my fears I felt anxious lest, even though right before us it looked as clear as it could do in the land of Goshen, the clouds might nevertheless overtake us, and here, perhaps in the territory of the Valais, shut in on both sides by mountains, we might be covered with the clouds, and in one night snowed up. Thus whispered alarm which got possession almost entirely of one ear; at the other good courage was speaking in a confident tone, and reproving me for want of faith, kept reminding me of the past, and called my attention to the phenomena of the atmosphere before us. Our road went continually on towards the fine weather. Up the Rhone all was clear, and as a strong west wind kept driving the clouds behind us, it was little likely that they would reach us.

The following was the cause of this. Into the valley of Valais there are, as I have so often remarked already, many ravines running down from the neighbouring mountain-chains, which fall into it like little brooks into a great stream, as indeed all their waters flow off into the Rhone. Out of each of these openings rushes a current of wind, which has been forming in the inner valleys and nooks of the rocks. When now the principal drift of the clouds up the valley reaches one of these ravines, the current of the wind does not allow the clouds to pass, but contends with them, and with the wind which is driving them, and thus detains them, and disputes with them for whole hours the passage up the valley. This conflict we often witnessed, and when we believed we should surely be overtaken by the clouds, an obstacle of this kind would again arise, and after we had gone a good league, we found they had scarcely stirred from the spot.

Brieg.

Towards evening the sky was uncommonly beautiful. As we arrived at Brieg, the clouds got there almost as soon as we did; however, as the sun had set, and a driving east wind blew against them, they were obliged to come to a halt, and formed a huge crescent from mountain to mountain across the valley. The cold air had greatly condensed them, and where their edge stood out against the blue sky, it presented to the eye many beautiful, light, and elegant forms. It was quite clear that they were heavy with snow; however, the fresh air seemed to us to promise that much would not fall during the night.

Here we are in a very comfortable inn, and what greatly tends to make us contented, we have found a roomy chamber with a stove in it, so that we can sit by the fire-side and take counsel together as to our future travels. Through Brieg runs the usual road to Italy over the Simplon; should we, therefore, give up our plan of going over the Furca to Mont S. Gothard, we shall go with hired horses and mules to Domo d'Ossula, Margozro, pass up Lago Maggiore, and then to Bellinzona, and then on to S. Gotthard, and over Airolo to the monastery of the Capuchins. This road is passable all the winter through, and is good travelling for horses; however, to our minds it is not very inviting, especially as it was not in our original plan, and will not bring us to Lucerne till five days after our friend. We wish rather to see the whole of the Valais up to its extreme limit, whither we hope to come by to-morrow evening, and, if fortune favours, we shall be sitting by about the same time next day in Realp, in the canton of Uri, which is on Mont Gotthard, and very near to its highest summit. If we then find it impossible to cross the Furca, the road back to this spot will still be open to us, and then we can take of necessity the route which of free choice we are disinclined to.

You can well believe that I have here closely examined the people, whether they believe that the passage over the Furca is open, for that is the one idea with which I rise up, and lie down to sleep, and occupy myself all day long. Hitherto our route may be compared to a march to meet an enemy, and now it is as if we were approaching to the spot where he has entrenched himself, and we must give him battle. Besides our mule two horses are ordered to be ready by the evening.

Munster, Nov. 11, 1779.
Evening, 6 o'clock.

Again we have had a pleasant and prosperous day. This morning as we set out early and in good time from Brieg our host, when we were already on the road said, "If the mountain (so they call the Furca here,) should prove too fearful, you can easily come back and take another route." With our two horses and mule we soon came upon some pleasant meadows, where the valley becomes so narrow that it is scarcely some gun-shots wide. Here are some beautiful pasture lands, on which stand large trees, while pieces of rock lie scattered about which have rolled down from the neighbouring mountains. The valley gradually grows narrower, and the traveller is forced to ascend along the side of the mountain, having the while the Rhone below him in a rugged ravine on his left. Above him, however, the land is beautifully spread out; on the variously undulating hills are verdant and rich meadows and pretty hamlets, which, with their dark-brown wooden houses, peep out prettily from among the snow. We travelled a good deal on foot, and we did so in turns to accommodate one another. For although riding is safe enough, still it excites one's alarm to see another riding before you along so narrow a track, and on so weak an animal, and just on the brink of so rugged a precipice; and as too there are no cattle to be seen on the meadows, (for the people here shut them all up in sheds at this season,) such a region looks lonely, and the thought that one is continually being hemmed in closer and closer by the vast mountains, fills the imagination with sombre and disagreeable fancies, enough to make you fall from your seat, if you are not very firm in the saddle. Man is never perfectly master of himself. As he lives in utter ignorance of the future, as indeed what the next moment may bring forth is hidden from him, consequently, when anything unusual falls beneath his notice, he has often to contend with involuntary sensations, forebodings, and dream-like fancies, at which shortly afterwards he may laugh outright, but which at the decisive moment are often extremely oppressive.

The legend of S. Alexis.

In our noonday quarters we met with some amusement. We had taken up our lodgings with a woman in whose house everything looked neat and orderly. Her room, after the fashion of the country, was wainscotted, the beds ornamented with carving; the cupboards, tables, and all the other little repositories which were fastened against the walls or to the corners, had pretty ornaments of turner's work or carving. From the portraits which hung around the room, it was easy to see that several members of the family had devoted themselves to the clerical profession. We also observed a collection of bound books over the door, which we took to be the endowment of one of these reverend personages. We took down the Legends of the Saints, and read it while our meal was preparing. On one occasion of our hostess entering the room, she asked us if we had ever read the history of S. Alexis? We said no, and took no further notice of her question, but went on reading the chapter we each had begun. When, however, we had sat down to table, she placed herself by our sides, and began again to talk of S. Alexis. We asked her whether he was the patron saint of herself, or of her family; which she denied, affirming at the same time, however, that this saintly person had undergone so much for the love of God, that his history always affected her more than any other's. When she saw that we knew nothing about him, she began to narrate to us his history. "S. Alexis," she said, "was the son of noble, rich, and God-fearing parents in Rome, and in the practice of good works he delighted to follow their example, for they did extraordinary good to the poor. All this, however, did not appear enough to Alexis; but secretly in his own heart he devoted himself entirely to God's service, and took a vow to Christ of perpetual virginity. When, then, in the course of time, his parents wished to marry him to a lovely and amiable maiden, he did not oppose their will. When, however, the marriage ceremony was concluded, instead of retiring to his bed in the nuptial chamber, he went on board a vessel which he found ready to sail, and with it passed over to Asia. Here he assumed the garb of a wretched mendicant, and became thereby so thoroughly disguised that the servants of his father who had been sent after him failed to recognise him. Here he posted himself near the door of the principal church, invariably attending the divine services, and supporting himself on the alms of the faithful. After two or three years various miracles took place, betokening the special favour of the Almighty. The bishop heard a voice in the church, bidding him to summon into the sacred temple that man whose prayer was most acceptable to God, and to keep him by his side while he celebrated divine worship. As the bishop did not at once know who could be meant, the voice went on to point out to him the beggar, whom, to the great astonishment of the people, he immediately fetched into the church. The saintly Alexis, embarrassed by having the attention of the people directed towards himself, quietly and silently departed thence, also on ship-board, intending to proceed still further in foreign lands. But by a tempest and other circumstances he was compelled to land in Italy. The saint seeing in all this the finger of God, was rejoiced to meet with an opportunity of exercising self-denial in the highest degree. He therefore set off direct for his native town, and placed himself as a beggar at the door of his parents' house. With their usual pious benevolence did they receive him, and commanded one of their servants to furnish him with lodging in the castle and with all necessary sustenance. This servant, annoyed at the trouble he was put to, and displeased with his master's benevolence, assigned to this seeming beggar a miserable hole under some stone steps, where he threw to him, as to a dog, a sorry pittance of food. The saint instead of suffering himself to be vexed thereat, first of all thanked God sincerely for it in his heart, and not only bore with patient meekness all this which he might easily have altered, but with incredible and superhuman fortitude, endured to witness the lasting grief of his parents and his wife for his absence. For he heard his much-loved parents and his beautiful spouse invoke his name a hundred times a day, and pray for his return, and he saw them wasting their days in sorrow for his supposed absence." At this passage of her narrative our good hostess could not refrain her tears, while her two daughters, who during the story had crept close to her side, kept steadily looking up in their mother's face. "But," she continued, "great was the reward which the Almighty bestowed on his constancy, giving him, at his death, the greatest possible proofs of his favour in the eyes of the faithful. For after living several years in this state, daily frequenting the service of God with the most fervent zeal, he at last fell sick, without any particular heed being given to his condition by any one. One morning shortly after this, while the pope was himself celebrating high mass, in presence of the emperor and all the nobles, suddenly all the bells in the whole city of Rome began to toll as if for the passing knell of some distinguished personage. Whilst every one was full of amazement, it was revealed to the pope that this marvel was in honour of the death of the holiest person in the whole city, who had but just died in the house of the noble Patrician.—The father of Alexis being interrogated, thought at once of the beggar. He went home and found him beneath the stairs quite dead. In his folded hands the saintly man clutched a paper, which his old father sought in vain to take from him. He returned to the church and told all this to the emperor and the pope, who thereupon, with their courtiers and clergy, set off to visit the corpse of the saint. When they reached the spot, the holy father took it without difficulty out of the hands of the dead man, and handed it to the emperor, who thereupon caused it to be read aloud by his chancellor. The paper contained the history of the saint. Then you should have seen the grief of his parents and wife, which now became excessive, to think that they had had near to them a son and husband so dear; for whom there was nothing too good that they would not have done; and then too to know how ill he had been treated! They fell upon his corpse and wept so bitterly that there was not one of the bystanders who could refrain from tears. Moreover, among the multitude of the people who gradually flocked to the spot, there were many sick, who were brought to the body and by its touch were made whole."

The legend of S. Alexis.

Our fair story-teller affirmed over and over again, as she dried her eyes, that she had never heard a more touching history, and I too was seized with so great a desire to weep that I had the greatest difficulty to hide and to suppress it. After dinner I looked out the legend itself in Father Cochem, and found that the good dame had dropped none of the purely human traits of the story, while she had clean forgotten all the tasteless remarks of this writer.

We keep going continually to the window watching the weather; and are at present very near offering a prayer to the winds and clouds. Long evenings and universal stillness are the elements in which writing thrives right merrily, and I am convinced that if, for a few months only, I could contrive, or were obliged, to stay at a spot like this, all my unfinished dramas would of necessity be completed one after another.

We have already had several people before us, and questioned them with regard to the pass over the Furca; but even here we have been unable to gain any precise information, although the mountain is only two or three leagues distant. We must, however, rest contented, and we shall set out ourselves at break of day to reconnoitre, and see how destiny will decide for us. However, in general, I may be disposed to take things as they go, it would, I must confess, be highly annoying to me if we should be forced to retrace our steps again. If we are fortunate we shall be by to-morrow evening at Realp or S. Gotthard, and by noon the next day among the Capuchins at the summit of the mountain. If things go unfortunately we nave two roads open for a retreat. Back through the whole of Valais, and by the well-known road over Berne to Lucerne; or back to Brieg, and then by a wide detour to S. Gotthard. I think in this short letter I have told you that three times. But in fact it is a matter of great importance to us. The issue will decide which was in the right, our courage, which gave us a confidence that we must succeed, or the prudence of certain persons who were very earnest in trying to dissuade us from attempting this route. This much, at any rate, is certain, that both prudence and courage must own chance to be over them both. And now that we have once more examined the weather, and found the air to be cold, the sky bright, and without any signs of a tendency to snow, we shall go calmly to bed.

Munster, Nov. 12, 1776.
Early. 6 o'clock.

We are quite ready, and all is packed up in order to set out from hence with the break of day. We have before us two leagues to Oberwald, and from there the usual reckoning makes six leagues to Realp. Our mule is to follow us with the baggage as far as it is possible to take him.

Realp, Nov. 12, 1779.
Evening.

We reached this place just at nightfall. We have surmounted all difficulties, and the knots which entangled our path have been cut in two. Before I tell you where we are lodged, and before I describe to you the character of our hosts, allow me the gratification of going over in thought the road that we did not see before us without anxiety, and which, however, we have left behind us without accident, though not without difficulty. About seven we started from Munster, and saw before us the snow-covered amphitheatre of mountain summits, and took to be the Furca, the mountain which in the background stood obliquely before it. But as we afterwards learned, we made a mistake; it was concealed from our view by the mountains on our left and by high clouds. The east wind blew strong and fought with some snow-clouds, chasing the drifts, now over the mountains, now up the valley. But this only made the snow drifts deeper on the ground, and caused us several times to miss our way; although shut in as we were on both sides, we could not fail of reaching Oberwald eventually. About nine we actually got there, and dropping in at an auberge, its inmates were not a little surprised to see such characters appearing there this time of the year. We asked whether the pass over the Furca were still practicable, and they answered that their folk crossed it for the greater part of the winter, but whether we should be able to get across they could not tell. We immediately sent to seek for one of these persons as a guide. There soon appeared a strong thick-set peasant, whose very look and shape inspired confidence. With him we immediately began to treat: if he thought the pass was practicable for us, let him say so; and then take one or more comrades and come with us. After a short pause he agreed, and went away to get ready himself and to fetch the others. In the meantime we paid our muleteer the hire of his beast, since we could no longer make any use of his mule; and having eaten some bread and cheese and drank a glass of red wine, felt full of strength and spirits, as our guide came back, followed by another man who looked still bigger and stronger than himself, and seeming to have all the strength and courage of a horse, he quickly shouldered our portmanteau. And now we set out, a party of five, through the village, and soon reached the foot of the mountain, which lay on our left, and began gradually to ascend it. At first we had a beaten track to follow which came down from a neighbouring Alp; soon, however, this came to an end, and we had to go up the mountain side through the snow. Our guides, with great skill, tracked their way among the rocks, around which the usual path winds, although the deep and smooth snow had covered all alike. Next our road lay through a forest of pines, while the Rhone flowed beneath us in a narrow unfruitful valley. Into it we also, after a little while, had to descend, and by crossing a little foot-bridge we came in sight of the glacier of the Rhone. It is the hugest we have as yet had so full a view of. Of very great breadth, it occupies the whole saddle of the mountain, and descends uninterruptedly down to the point where, in the valley, the Rhone flows out of it. At this source the people tell us it has for several years been decreasing; but that is as nothing compared with all the rest of the huge mass. Although everything was full of snow, still the rough crags of ice, on which the wind did not allow the snow to lie, were visible with their glass blue fissures, and you could see clearly where the glacier ended and the snow-covered rock began. To this point, which lay on our left, we came very close. Presently we again reached a light foot-bridge over a little mountain stream, which flowed through a barren trough-shaped valley to join the Rhone. After passing the glacier, neither on the right, nor on the left, nor before you, was there a tree to be seen, all was one desolate waste; no rugged and prominent rocks-nothing but long smooth valleys, slightly inclining eminences, which now, in the snow which levelled all inequalities, presented to us their simple unbroken surfaces. Turning now to the left we ascended a mountain, sinking at every step deep in the snow. One of our guides had to go first, and boldly treading down the snow break the way by which we were to follow.

The passage over the Furca.

It was a strange sight, when turning for a moment your attention from the road, you directed it to yourself and your fellow travellers. In the most desolate region of the world, in a boundless, monotonous wilderness of mountains enveloped in snow, where for three leagues before and behind, you would not expect to meet a living soul, while on both sides you had the deep hollows of a web of mountains, you might see a line of men wending their way, treading each in the deep footsteps of the one before him, and where, in the whole of the wide expanse thus smoothed over, the eye could discern nothing but the track they left behind them. The hollows as we left them lay behind us gray and boundless in the mist. The changing clouds continually passed over the pale disc of the sun, and spread over the whole scene a perpetually moving veil. I am convinced that any one who, while pursuing this route, allowed his imagination to gain the mastery, would even, in the absence of all immediate danger, fall a victim to his own apprehensions and fears. In reality, there is little or no risk of a fall here; the great danger is from the avalanches, when the snow has become deeper than it is at present, and begins to roll. However our guide told us that they cross the mountains throughout the winter, carrying from Valais to S. Gotthard skins of the chamois, in which a considerable trade is here carried on. But then to avoid the avalanches, they do not take the route that we did, but remain for some time longer in the broad valley, and then go straight up the mountain. This road is safer, but much more inconvenient. After a march of about three hours and a-half, we reached the saddle of the Furca, near the cross which marks the boundary of Valais and Uri. Even here we could not distinguish the double peak from which the Furca derives its name. We now hoped for an easier descent, but our guides soon announced to us still deeper snow, as we immediately found it to be. Our march continued in single file as before, and the foremost man who broke the path often sank up to his waist in the snow. The readiness of the people, and their light way of speaking of matters, served to keep up our courage; and I will say, for myself, that I have accomplished the journey without fatigue, although I cannot say that it was a mere walk. The huntsman Hermann asserted that he had often before met with equally deep snow in the forests of Thuringia, but at last he could not help bursting out with a loud exclamation, "The Furca is a ————."

A vulture or lammergeier swept over our heads with incredible rapidity: it was the only living thing that we had met with in this waste. In the distance we saw the mountains of the Ursi lighted up with the bright sunshine. Our guides wished to enter a shepherd's hut which had been abandoned and snowed up, and to take something to eat, but we urged them to go onwards, to avoid standing still in the cold. Here again is another groupe of valleys, and at last we gained an open view into the valley of the Ursi.

The capuchins at Realp.

We now proceeded at a shorter pace, and after travelling about three leagues and a-half from the Cross, we saw the scattered roofs of Realp. We had several times questioned our guides as to what sort of an inn, and what kind of wine we were likely to find in Realp. The hopes they gave us were anything but good, but they assured us that the Capuchins there, although they had not, like those on the summit of S. Gotthard, an hospice, were in the habit of entertaining strangers. With them we should get some good red wine, and better food than at an inn. We therefore sent one of our party forwards to inform the Capuchins of our arrival, and to procure a lodging for us. We did not loiter long behind, and arrived very soon after him, when we were received at the door by one of the fathers—a portly, good-looking man. With much friendliness of manner he invited us to enter, and at the threshold begged that we would put up with such entertainment they could alone offer, as at no time and least of all at this season of the year, were they prepared to receive such guests. He therefore led us into a warm room, and was very diligent in waiting upon us, while we took off our boots, and changed our linen. He begged us once for all to make ourselves perfectly at home. As to our meat, we must, he said, be indulgent, for they were in the middle of their long fast, which would last till Christmas-day. We assured him that a warm room, a bit of bread, and a glass of red wine would, in our present circumstances, fully satisfy all our wishes. He procured us what we asked for, and we had scarcely refreshed ourselves a little, ere he began to recount to us all that concerned the establishment, and the settlement of himself and fellows on this waste spot. "We have not," he said, "an hospice like the fathers on Mont S. Gotthard,—we are here in the capacity of parish priests, and there are three of us. The duty of preaching falls to my lot; the second father has to look after the school, and the brother to look after the household." He went on to describe their hardships and toils; here, at the furthest end of a lonely valley, separated from all the world, and working hard to very little profit. This spot, like all others, was formerly provided with a secular priest, but an avalanche having buried half of the village, the last one had run away, and taken the pix with him, whereupon he was suspended, and they, of whom more resignation was expected, were sent there in his place.

In order to write all this I had retired to an upper room, which is warmed from below by a hole in the floor; and I have just received an intimation that dinner is ready, which, notwithstanding our luncheon, is right welcome news.

About 9.

The fathers, priests, servants, guides and all, took their dinner together at a common table; the brother, however, who superintended the cooking, did not make his appearance till dinner was nearly over. Out of milk, eggs, and flour he had compounded a variety of dishes, which we tasted one after another, and found them all very good. Our guides, who took a great pleasure in speaking of the successful issue of our expedition, praised us for our uncommon dexterity in travelling, and assured us that it was not every one that they would have undertaken the task of being guides to. They even confessed also that this morning, when their services were required, one had gone first to reconnoitre, and to see if we looked like people who would really go through all difficulties with them; for they were particularly cautious how they accompanied old or weak people at this time of the year, since it was their duty to take over in safety every one they had once engaged to guide, being bound in case of his falling sick, to carry him, even though it should be at the imminent risk of their own lives, and if he were to die on the passage, not to leave his body behind. This confession at once opened the flood-gates to a host of anecdotes, and each in turn had his story to tell of the difficulties and dangers of wandering over the mountains amidst which the people had here to live as in their proper element, so that with the greatest indifference they speak of mischances and accidents to which they themselves are daily liable. One of them told a story of how, on the Candersteg, on his way to Mount Gemmi, he and a comrade with him (he is mentioned on every occasion with both Christian and surname) found a poor family in the deep snow, the mother dying, her boy half dead, and the father in that state of indifference which verges on a total prostration of intellect. He took the woman on his back, and his comrade her son, and thus laden, they had driven before them the father, who was unwilling to move from the spot.

The Capuchins at Realp.

During the descent of Gemmi the woman died on his back, but he brought her dead as she was to Leukerbad. When we asked what sort of people they were, and what could have brought them at such a season into the mountains, he said they were poor people of the canton of Berne, who, driven by want, had taken to the road at an unseasonable period of the year, in the hope of finding some relations either in Valais or the Italian canton, and had been overtaken by a snow-storm. Moreover, they told many anecdotes of what had happened to themselves during the winter journeys over the Furca with the chamois-skins, on which expeditions, however, they always travelled in companies. Every now and then our reverend host would make excuses for the dinner, and we redoubled our assurances that we wished for nothing better. We also found that he contrived to bring back the conversation to himself and his own matters, observing that he had not been long in this place. He began to talk of the office of preaching, and of the dexterity that a preacher ought to have. He compared the good preacher to a chapman who cleverly puffs his wares, and by his pleasant words makes himself agreeable to his customers. After dinner he kept up the conversation, and, as he stood with his left hand leaning on the table, he accompanied his remarks with his right, and while he discoursed most eloquently on eloquence, appeared at the moment as if he wished to convince us that he himself was the dexterous chapman. We assented to his observations, and he came from the lecture to the thing itself. He panegyrized the Roman Catholic religion. "We must," he said, "have a rule of faith; and the great value of it consists in its being fixed, and as little liable as possible to change, We," he said, "had made Scripture the foundation of our faith, but it was insufficient. We ourselves would not venture to put it into the hands of common men: for holy as it is, and full as every leaf is of the Spirit of God, still the worldly-minded man is insensible of all this, and finds rather perplexities and stumbling-blocks throughout. What good can a mere layman extract from the histories of sinful men, which are contained therein, and which the Holy Ghost has there recorded for the strengthening of the faith of the tried and experienced children of God? What benefit can a common man draw from all this, when he is unable to consider the whole context and connection? How is such a person to see his way clear out of the seeming contradictions which occasionally occur?—out of the difficulties which arise from the ill arrangement of the books, and the differences of style, when the learned themselves find it so hard, and while so many passages make them hold their reason in abeyance? What ought we therefore to teach? A rule of faith founded on Scripture, and proved by the best of commentaries? But who then is to comment upon the Scripture? Who is to set up this rule? I, perhaps, or some other man? By no means. Every man has his own way of taking and seeing things, and represents them after his own ideas. That would be to give to the people as many systems of doctrines as there are are heads in the world, and to produce inexplicable confusion as indeed had already been done. No, it remains for the Holy Church alone to interpret Scripture to determine the rule of faith by which the souls of men are to be guided and governed. And what is the church? It is not any single supreme head, or any particular member alone. No! it is all the holiest, most learned, and most experienced men of all times, who, with the co-operation of the Holy Spirit, have successively combined together in building up that great, universal, and agreeing body, which has its great councils for its members to communicate their thoughts to one another, and for mutual edification; which banishes error, and thereby imparts to our holy religion a certainty and a stability such as no other profession can pretend to, and gives it a foundation and strengthens it with bulwarks which even hell itself cannot overthrow. And just so is it also with the text of the sacred scriptures. We have," he said, "the Vulgate, moreover an approved version of the Vulgate, and of every sentence a commentary which the church itself has accredited. Hence arises that uniformity of our teaching which surprises every one. Whether," he continued, "you hear me preaching in this most remote corner of the world, or in the great capital of a distant country are listening to the dullest or cleverest of preachers, all will hold one and the same language; a Catholic Christian will always hear the same doctrine; everywhere will he be instructed and edified in the same manner. And this it is which constitutes the certainty of our faith; which gives us the peace and confidence by which each one in life holds sure communion with his brother Catholics, and at death can calmly part in the sure hope of meeting one another again."

In his speech, as in a sermon, he let the subjects follow in due order, and spoke more from an inward feeling of satisfaction that he was exhibiting himself under a favourable aspect than from any bigotted anxiety for conversion. During the delivery he would occasionally change the arm he rested upon, or draw them both into the arms of his gown, or let them rest on his portly stomach; now and then he would, with much grace, draw his snuff-box out of his capote, and after using it replace it with a careless ease. We listened to him attentively, and he seemed to be quite content with our way of receiving his instructions. How greatly amazed would he have been if an angel had revealed to him, at the moment, that he was addressing his peroration to a descendant of Frederick the Wise.

November 13, 1779.
Among the Capuchins, on the summit of Mont S. Gotthard,
Morning, about 10 o'clock.

> Mount S. Gotthard.

At last we have fortunately reached the utmost limits of our journey. Here it is determined we shall rest awhile, and then turn our steps towards our dear fatherland. Very strange are my feelings here, on this summit, where four years ago I passed a few days with very different anxieties, sentiments, plans, and hopes, and at a very different season of the year, when, without any foreboding of my future fortunes, but moved by I know not what, I turned my back upon Italy, and ignorantly went to meet my present destiny. I did not even recognise the house again. Some time ago it was greatly injured by an avalanche, and the good fathers took advantage of this opportunity, and made a collection throughout the canton for enlarging and improving their residence. Both of the two fathers who reside here at present are absent, but, as I hear, they are still the same that I met four years ago. Father Seraphin, who has now passed fourteen years in this post is at present at Milan, and the other is expected to-day from Airolo. In this clear atmosphere the cold is awful. As soon as dinner is over I will continue my letter; for, I see clearly we shall not go far outside the door.

After dinner.

It becomes colder and colder; one does not like to stir from the stove. Indeed it is most delightful to sit upon it, which in this country, where the stoves are made of stone-tiles, it is very easy to do. First of all, therefore, we will tell you of our departure from Realp, and then of our journey hither.

Yesterday evening before we retired to our beds, the good father would shew us his sleeping cell, where everything was in nice order, in a very small space. His bed, which consisted of a bag of straw, with a woollen coverlid, did not appear to us to be anything very meritorious, as we ourselves had often put up with no better. With great pleasure and internal satisfaction he showed us everything—his bookcase and all other things. We praised all that we saw, and parting on the best terms with each other, we retired for the night. In furnishing our room, in order that two beds might stand against one wall, both had been made unusually small. This inconvenience kept me long awake, until I thought of remedying it by placing four chairs together. It was quite broad daylight before we awoke this morning. When we went down we found nothing but happy and friendly faces. Our guides, on the point of entering upon their return over yesterday's beautiful route, seemed to look upon it as an epoch, and as a history with which hereafter they would be able to entertain other strangers, and as they were well paid the idea of an adventure became complete in their minds. After this we made a capital breakfast and departed.

Our road now lay through the valley of the Uri, which is remarkable as having, at so great an elevation, such beautiful meadows and pasturage for cattle. They make here a cheese which I prefer to all others. No trees, however, grow here. Sally bushes line all the brooks, and on the mountains little shrubs grow thickly together. Of all the countries that I know, this is to me the loveliest and most interesting,—whether it is that old recollections make it precious to me, or that the perception of such a long chain of nature's wonders excites within me a secret and inexpressible feeling of enjoyment. I take it for granted that you bear in mind that the whole country through which I am leading you is covered with snow, and that rock and meadow alike are snowed over. The sky has been quite clear, without a single cloud; the hue far deeper than one is accustomed to see in low and flat countries, and the white mountain ridges, which stood out in strong contrast to it, were either glittering in the sunshine, or else took a greyish tint in the shade.

In a hour and a half we reached Hôpital,—a little village within the canton of Uri, which lies on the road to S. Gotthard. Here at last I regained the track of my former tour. We entered an inn, and though it was as yet morning, ordered a dinner, and soon afterward began to ascend the summit. A long train of mules with their bells enlivened the whole region. It is a sound which awakens all one's recollections of mountain scenery. The greater part of the train was in advance of us, and with their sharp iron shoes had pretty well cut up the smooth icy road. We also saw some labourers who were employed in covering the slippery ice with fresh earth, in order to render it passable. The wish which I formerly gave utterance to, that I might one day be permitted to see this part of the world under snow, is now at last gratified. The road goes up the Reuss as it dashes down over rocks all the way, and forms everywhere the most beautiful waterfalls. We stood a long while attracted by the singular beauty of one which in considerable volume was dashing over a succession of dark black rocks.

Here and there in the cracks, and on the flat ledges pieces of ice had formed, and the water seemed to be running over a variegated black and white marble. The masses of ice glistened like veins of crystal in the sun, and the water flowed pure and fresh between them.

Mount S. Gotthard.

On the mountains there is no more tiresome a fellow-traveller than a train of mules; they have so unequal a pace. With a strange instinct they always stop a while at the bottom of a steep ascent, and then dash off at a quick pace up it, to rest again at the top. Very often too they will stop at the level spots which do occur now and then, until they are forced on by the drivers or by other beasts coming up. And so the foot passenger, by keeping a steady pace, soon gains upon them, and in the narrow road has to push by them. If you stand still a little while to observe any object, they in their turn will pass by you, and you are pestered with the deafening sound of their bells, and hard brushed with their loads, which project to a good distance on each side of them. In this way we at last reached the summit of the mountain, which you can form some idea of by fancying a bald skull surrounded with a crown. Here one finds oneself on a perfect flat surrounded with peaks. Far and near the eye falls on nothing but bare and mostly snow-covered peaks and crags.

It is scarcely possible to keep oneself warm, especially as they have here no fuel but brushwood, and of that too they are obliged to be very sparing, as they have to fetch it up the mountains, from a distance of at least three leagues, for at the summit, they tell us, scarcely any kind of wood grows. The reverend father is returned from Airolo, so frozen that on his arrival he could scarcely, utter a word. Although here the Capuchins are allowed to clothe themselves a little more comfortably than the rest of their order, still their style of dress is by no means suited for such a climate as this. All the way up from Airolo the road was frozen perfectly smooth, and he had the wind in his face; his beard was quite frozen, and it was a long while before he recovered himself. We had some conversation together on the hardships of their residence here; he told us how they managed to get through the year, their various occupations, and their domestic circumstances. He could speak nothing but Italian, and so we had an opportunity of putting to use the exercises in this language which we had taken during the spring. Towards evening we went for a moment outside the house-door that the good father might point out to us the peak which is considered to be the highest summit of Mont Gotthard; but we could scarcely endure to stay out a very few minutes, so searching and pinching was the cold. This time, therefore, we shall remain close shut up within doors, and shall have time enough before we start to-morrow, to travel again in thought over all the most remarkable parts of this region.

A brief geographical description will enable you to understand how remarkable the point is at which we are now sitting. S. Gothard is not indeed the highest mountain of Switzerland; in Savoy, Mont Blanc has a far higher elevation and yet it maintains above all others the rank of a king of mountains, because all the great chains converge together around him, and all rest upon him as their base. Indeed; if I do not make a great mistake, I think I was told at Berne, by Herr Wyttenbach, who, from its highest summit, had seen the peaks of all the others, that the latter all leaned towards it. The mountains of Schweitz and Unterwalden, joined by those of Uri range from the north, from the east those of the Grisons, from the south those of the Italian cantons, while from the east, by means of the Furca, the double line of mountains which enclose Valais, presses upon it. Not far from this house, there are two small lakes, one of which sends forth the Ticino through gorges and valleys into Italy, while from the other, in like manner, the Reuss proceeds till it empties itself in the Lake of the Forest towns.[2] Not far from this spot are the sources of the Rhine, which pursue an easterly course, and if then we take in the Rhone which rises at the foot of the Furca and runs westward through Valais, we shall find ourselves at the point of a cross, from which mountain ranges and rivers proceed towards the four cardinal points of heaven.

[1] The Duke Charles Augustus of Weimar, who travelled under the title of Count of....

[2] Lake Lucerne.

TRAVELS IN ITALY

I TOO IN ARCADIA!

FROM CARLSBAD TO THE BRENNER.

Ratisbon, September 4, 1786.

As early as 3 o'clock in the morning I stole out of Carlsbad, for otherwise I should not have been allowed to depart quietly. The band of friends who, on the 28th of August, rejoiced to celebrate my birthday, had in some degree acquired a right to detain me. However, it was impossible to stay here any longer. Having packed a portmanteau merely, and a knapsack, I jumped alone into a post-chaise, and by half past 8, on a beautifully calm but foggy morning, I arrived at Zevoda. The upper clouds were streaky and fleecy, the lower ones heavy. This appeared to me a good sign. I hoped that, after so wretched a summer, we should enjoy a fine autumn. About 12, I got to Egra, under a warm and shining sun, and now, it occurred to me, that this place had the same latitude as my own native town, and it was a real pleasure to me once more to take my midday meal beneath a bright sky, at the fiftieth degree.

On entering Bavaria one comes at once on the monastery of Waldsassen, with the valuable domain of the ecclesiastical lords, who were wise sooner than other men. It lies in a dish-like, not to say cauldron-like hollow, in beautiful meadow-land, inclosed on all sides by slightly ascending and fertile heights. This cloister also possesses property in the neighbouring districts. The soil is decomposed slate-clay. The quartz, which is found in this mineral formation, and which does not dissolve nor crumble away, makes the earth loose and extremely fertile. The land continues to rise until you come to Tirschenreuth, and the waters flow against you, to fall into the Egra and the Elbe. From Tirschenreuth it descends southwards, and the streams run towards the Danube. I can form a pretty rapid idea of a country as soon as I know by examination which way even the least brook runs, and can determine the river to whose basin it belongs. By this means, even in those districts which it is impossible to take a survey of, one can, in thought, form a connection between lines of mountains and valleys. From the last-mentioned place begins an excellent road formed of granite. A better one cannot be conceived, for, as the decomposed granite consists of gravelly and argillaceous earths, they bind excellently together, and form a solid foundation, so as to make a road as smooth as a threshing floor. The country through which it runs looks so much the worse; it also consists of a granite-sand, lies very flat and marshy, and the excellent road is all the more desirable. And as, moreover, the roads descend gradually from this plane, one gets on with a rapidity that strikingly contrasts with the general snail's pace of Bohemian travelling. The inclosed billet will give you the names of the different stages. Suffice it to say, that on the second morning I was at Ratisbon, and so I did these twenty-four miles[1] and a half in thirty-nine hours. As the day began to dawn I found myself between Schwondorf and Begenstauf, and I observed here a change for the better in the cultivation of the land. The soil was no longer the mere debris of the rock, but a mixed alluvial deposit. The inundation by which it was deposited must have been caused by the ebb and flood, from the basin of the Danube into all the valleys which at present drain their water into it. In this way were formed the natural bolls (*pölder*), on which the tillage is carried on. This remark applies to all lands in the neighbourhood of large or small streams, and with this guide any observer may form a conclusion as to the soils suited for tillage.

Ratisbon.

Ratisbon is, indeed, beautifully situated. The country could not but invite men to settle and build a city in it, and the spiritual lords have shown their judgment. All the land around the town belongs to them; in the city itself churches crowd churches, and monastic buildings are no less thick. The Danube reminds me of the dear old Main. At Frankfort, indeed, the river and bridges have a better appearance; here, however, the view of the northern suburb, Stadt-am-hof, looks very pretty, as it lies before you across the river.

Immediately on my arrival I betook myself to the College of the Jesuits, where the annual play was being acted by the pupils. I saw the end of the opera, and the beginning of the tragedy. They did not act worse than many an unexperienced company of amateurs, and their dresses were beautiful, almost too superb. This public exhibition also served to convince me still more strongly of the worldly prudence of the Jesuits. They neglect nothing that is likely to produce an effect, and contrive to practise it with interest and care. In this there is not merely prudence, such as we understand the term abstractedly; it is associated with a real pleasure in the matter in hand, a sympathy and a fellow feeling, a taste, such as arises from the experience of life. As this great society has among its members organ builders, sculptors, and gilders, so assuredly there are some who patronise the stage with learning and taste; and just as they decorate their churches with appropriate ornaments, these clear-sighted men take advantage of the world's sensual eye by an imposing theatre.

To-day I am writing in latitude forty-nine degrees. The weather promises fair, and even here the people complain of the coldness and wet of the past summer. The morning was cool, but it was the beginning of a glorious and temperate day. The mild atmosphere which the mighty river brings with it is something quite peculiar. The fruits are nothing very surprising. I have tasted, indeed, some excellent pears, but I am longing for grapes and figs.

My attention is rivetted by the actions and principles of the Jesuits. Their churches, towers, and buildings, have a something great and perfect in their plan, which imposes all beholders with a secret awe. In the decoration, gold, silver, metal, and polished marble, are accumulated in such splendour and profusion as must dazzle the beggars of all ranks. Here and there one fails not to meet with something in bad taste, in order to appease and to attract humanity. This is the general character of the external ritual of the Roman Catholic Church; never, however, have I seen it applied with so much shrewdness, tact, and consistency, as among the Jesuits. Here all tends to this one end; unlike the members of the other spiritual orders, they do not continue an old worn-out ceremonial, but, humouring the spirit of the age, continually deck it out with fresh pomp and splendour.

A rare stone is quarried here into blocks. In appearance it is a species of conglomerate; however, it must be held to be older, more primary, and of a porphyritic nature. It is of a greenish color, mixed with quartz, and is porous; in it are found large pieces of very solid jasper, in which, again, are to be seen little round pieces of a kind of Breccia. A specimen would have been very instructive, and one could not help longing for one; the rock, however, was too solid, and I had taken a vow not to load myself with stones on this journey.

[1] A German mile is exactly equal to four English geographical, and to rather more than four and a quarter ordinary miles. The distance in the text may, therefore, he roughly set down as one hundred and four miles English. [A. J. W. M.]

Munich, September 6, 1786.

At half past 12, on the 5th of September, I set off for Ratisbon. At Abbach the country is beautiful, while the Danube dashes against limestone rocks as far as Saal. The limestone, somewhat similar to that at Osteroda, on the Hartz, close, but, on the whole, porous. By 6 A.M. I was in Munich, and, after having looked about me for some twelve hours, I will notice only a few points. In the Sculpture Gallery I did not find myself at home. I must practise my eye first of all on paintings. There are some excellent things here. The sketches of Reubens from the Luxembourg Gallery caused me the greatest delight.

Here, also, is the rare toy, a model of Trajan's Pillar. The material Lapis Lazuli, and the figures in gilt. It is, at any rate, a rare piece of workmanship, and, in this light, one takes pleasure in looking at it.

In the Hall of the Antiques I soon felt that my eye was not much practised on such objects. On this account I was unwilling to stay long there, and to waste my time. There was much that did not take my fancy, without my being able to say why. A *Drusus* attracted my attention; two Antonines pleased me, as also did a few other things. On the whole, the arrangement of the objects was not happy, although there is an evident attempt to make a display with them, and the hall, or rather the museum, would have a good appearance if it were kept in better repair and cleaner. In the Cabinet of Natural History I saw beautiful things from the Tyrol, which, in smaller specimens, I was already acquainted with, and, indeed, possessed.

Munich-Mittelwald.

I was met by a woman with figs, which, as the first, tasted delicious. But the fruit in general is not good considering the latitude of forty-eight degrees. Every one is complaining here of the wet and cold. A mist, which might well be called a rain, overtook me this morning early before I reached Munich. Throughout the day the wind has continued to blow cold from off the Tyrolese mountains. As I looked towards them from the tower I found them covered, and the whole heavens shrouded with clouds. Now, at setting, the sun is shining on the top of the ancient tower, which stands right opposite to my window. Pardon me that I dwell so much on wind and weather. The traveller by land is almost as much dependent upon them as the voyager by sea, and it would be a sad thing if my autumn in foreign lands should be as little favoured as my summer at home.

And now straight for Innspruck. What do I not pass over, both on my right and on my left, in order to carry out the one thought which has become almost too old in my soul.

Mittelwald, September 7, 1786.

It seems as if my guardian-spirit had said "Amen" to my "Credo," and I thank him that he has brought me to this place on so fine a day. My last postilion said, with a joyous exclamation, it was the first in the whole summer. I cherish in quiet my superstition that it will long continue so; however, my friends must pardon me if again I talk of air and clouds.

As I started from Munich about 5 o'clock, the sky cleared up. On the mountains of the Tyrol the clouds stood in huge masses. The streaks, too, in the lower regions did not move. The road lies on the heights over hills of alluvial gravel, while below one sees the Isar flowing slowly. Here the work of the inundations of the primal oceans become conceivable. In many granite-rubbles I found the counterparts of the specimens in my cabinet, for which I have to thank Knebel.

The mists from the river and the meadows hung about for a time, but, at last, they, too, dispersed. Between these gravelly hills, which you must think of as extending, both in length and breadth, for many leagues, is a highly beautiful and fertile region like that in the basin of the Regen. Now one comes again upon the Isar, and observe, in its channel, a precipitous section of the gravel hills, at least a hundred and fifty feet high. I arrived at Wolfrathshausen and reached the eight-and-fortieth degree. The sun was scorching hot; no one relies on the fine weather; every one is complaining of the past year, and bitterly weeping over the arrangements of Providence.

And now a new world opened upon me. I was approaching the mountains which stood out more and more distinctly.

Benedictbeuern has a glorious situation and charms one at the first sight. On a fertile plain is a long and broad white building, and, behind it, a broad and lofty ridge of rocks. Next, one ascends to the Kochel-see, and, still higher on the mountains, to the Walchen-see. Here I greeted the first snow-capt summit, and, in the midst of my admiration at being so near the snowy mountains, I was informed that yesterday it had thundered in these parts, and that snow had fallen on the heights. From these meteoric tokens people draw hopes of better weather, and from this early snow, anticipate change in the atmosphere. The rocks around me are all of limestone, of the oldest formation, and containing no fossils. These limestone mountains extend in vast, unbroken ranges from Dalmatia to Mount St. Gothard. Hacquet has travelled over a considerable portion of the chain. They dip on the primary rocks of the quartz and clay.

The road up the Brenner.

I reached the Wallen-see about half past 4. About three miles from this place I met with a pretty adventure. A harper came before me with his daughter, a little girl, of about eleven years, and begged me to take up his child. He went on with his instrument; I let her sit by my side, and she very carefully placed at her feet a large new box. A pretty and accomplished creature, and already a great traveller over the world. She had been on a pilgrimage on foot with her mother to Maria Einsiedel, and both had determined to go upon the still longer journey to S. Jago of Compostella, when her mother was carried off by death, and was unable to fulfil her vow. It was impossible, she thought, to do too much in honor of the Mother of God. After a great fire, in which a whole house was burnt to the lowest foundation, she herself had seen the image of the Mother of God, which stood over the door beneath a glass frame-image and glass both uninjured—which was surely a palpable miracle. All her journeys she had taken on foot; she had just played in Munich before the Elector of Bavaria, and altogether her performances had been witnessed by one-and-twenty princely personages. She quite entertained me. Pretty, large, hazel eyes, a proud forehead, which she frequently wrinkled by an elevation of the brows. She was natural and agreeable when she spoke, and especially when she laughed out loud with the free laugh of childhood. When, on the other hand, she was silent, she seemed to have a meaning in it, and, with her upper lip, had a sinister expression. I spoke with her on very many subjects, she was at home with all of them, and made most pertinent remarks. Thus she asked me once, what tree one we came to, was. It was a huge and beautiful maple, the first I had seen on my whole journey. She narrowly observed it, and was quite delighted when several more appeared, and she was able to recognize this tree. She was going, she told me, to Botzen for the fair, where she guessed I too was hastening. When she met me there I must buy her a fairing, which, of course, I promised to do. She intended to put on there her new coif which she had had made out of her earnings at Munich. She would show it to me beforehand. So she opened the bandbox and I could not do less than admire the head-gear, with its rich embroidery and beautiful ribbons.

Over another pleasant prospect we felt a mutual pleasure. She asserted that we had fine weather before us. For they always carried their barometer with them and that was the harp. When the treble-string twanged it was sure to be fine weather, and it had done so yesterday. I accepted the omen, and we parted in the best of humours, and with the hope of a speedy meeting.

On the Brenner, September 8, 1786,
Evening.

Hurried, not to say driven, here by necessity, I have reached at last a resting-place, in a calm, quiet spot, just such as I could wish it to be. It has been a day which for many years it will be a pleasure to recall. I left Mittelwald about 6 in the morning, and a sharp wind soon perfectly cleared the sky. The cold was such as one looks for only in February. But now, in the splendour of the setting sun, the dark foreground, thickly planted with fig-trees, and peeping between them the grey limestone rocks, and behind all, the highest summit of the mountain covered with snow, and standing out in bold outline against the deep blue sky, furnish precious and ever-changing images.

One enters the Tyrol by Scharnitz. The boundary line is marked by a wall which bars the passage through the valley, and abuts on both sides on the mountains. It looks well: on one side the rocks are fortified, on the other they ascend perpendicularly. From Seefeld the road continually grew more interesting, and if from Benedictbeuern to this place it went on ascending, from height to height, while all the streams of the neighbouring districts were making for the Isar, now one caught a sight over a ridge of rocks of the valley of the Inn, and Inzingen lay before us. The sun was high and hot, so that I was obliged to throw off some of my coats, for, indeed, with the varying atmosphere of the day, I am obliged frequently to change my clothing.

At Zierl one begins to descend into the valley of the Inn. Its situation is indescribably beautiful, and the bright beams of the sun made it look quite cheerful. The postilion went faster than I wished, for he had not yet heard mass, and was anxious to be present at it at Innspruck, where, as it was the festival of the Nativity of the Virgin Mary, he hoped to be a devout participant. Accordingly, we rattled along the banks of the Inn, hurrying by Martinswand, a vast, precipitous, wall-like rock of limestone. To the spot where the Emperor Maximilian is said to have lost himself, I ventured to descend and came up again without a guide, although it is, in any case, a rash undertaking.

Innsbruck-Meteorology.

Innsbruck is gloriously situated in a rich, broad valley, between high rocks and mountains. Everybody and everything was decked out in honour of the Virgin's Nativity. At first I had some wish to stop there, but it promised neither rest nor peace. For a little while I amused myself with the son of my host. At last the people who were to attend to me came in one by one. For the sake of health and prosperity to the flocks, they had all gone on a pilgrimage to Wilden, a place of worship on the mountains, about three miles and a half from the city. About 2 o'clock, as my rolling carriage divided the gay, merry throng, every one was in holiday garb and promenade.

From Innsbruck the road becomes even still more beautiful; no powers of description can equal it. The most frequented road, ascending a gorge which empties its waters into the Inn, offers to the eye innumerable varieties of scenery. While the road often runs close to the most rugged rocks—indeed is frequently cut right through them—one sees the other side above you slightly inclining, and cultivated with the most surprising skill. On the high and broad-ascending surface lie valleys, houses, cottages, and cabins, whitewashed, glittering among the fields and hedges. Soon all changed; the land becomes available only for pastime, until it, too, terminates on the precipitous ascent. I have gained some ideas for my scheme of a creation; none, however, perfectly new and unexpected. I have also dreamed much of the model I have so long talked about, by which I am desirous to give a notion of all that is brooding in my own mind, and which, in nature itself, I cannot point out to every eye.

Now it grew darker and darker; individual objects were lost in the obscurity; the masses became constantly vaster and grander; at last, as the whole moved before me like some deeply mysterious figure, the moon suddenly illuminated the snow-capt summits; and now I am waiting till morning shall light up this rocky chasm in which I am shut up on the boundary line of the north and south.

I must again add a few remarks on the weather, which, perhaps, favours me so highly, in return for the great attention I pay to it. On the lowlands one has good or bad weather when it is already settled for either; on the mountains one is present with the beginning of the change. I have so often experienced this when on my travels, or walks, or hunting excursions, I have passed days and nights between the cliffs in the mountain forests. On such occasions, a conceit occurred to me, which I give you as nothing better, but which, however, I cannot get rid of, as indeed, generally, such conceits are, of all things, most difficult to get rid of. I altogether look upon it as a truth, and so I will now give utterance to it, especially as I have already so often had occasion to prove the indulgence of my friends.

When we look at the mountains, either closely or from a distance, and see their summits above us at one time glittering in the sunshine, at another enveloped in mist, swept round with strong clouds, or blackened with showers, we are disposed to ascribe it all to the atmosphere, as we can easily with the eye see and discern its movements and changes. The mountains, on the other hand, with their glorious shapes lie before our outward senses immoveable. We take them to be dead because they are rigid, and we believe them to be inactive because they are at rest. For a long while, however, I cannot put off the impulse to ascribe, for the most part, to their imperceptible and secret influence the changes which are observable in the atmosphere. For instance, I believe that the mass of the earth generally, and, therefore, also in an especial way its more considerable continents do not exercise a constant and invariable force of attraction, but that this attractive force manifests itself by a certain pulse which, according to intrinsic, necessary, and probably also accidental, external causes, increases or decreases. Though all attempts by other objects to determine this oscillation may be too limited and rude, the atmosphere furnishes a standard both delicate and large enough to test their silent operations. When this attractive force decreases never so little, immediately the decrease in the gravity and the diminished elasticity of the air indicates this effect. The atmosphere is now unable to sustain the moisture which is diffused throughout it either chemically or mechanically; the clouds lower, and the rain falls and passes to the lowlands. When, however, the mountains increase their power of attraction, then the elasticity of the air is again restored, and two important phenomena result. First of all, the mountains collect around their summits vast masses of clouds; hold them fast and firm above themselves like second heads, until, as determined by the contest of electrical forces within them, they pour down as thunder-showers, rain or mist, and then, on all that remains the electricity of the air operates, which is now restored to a capacity of retaining more water, dissolving and elaborating it. I saw quite clearly the dispersion of a cloudy mass of this kind. It was hanging on the very highest peak; the red tints of the setting sun still illuminated it. Slowly and slowly pieces detached themselves from either end. Some fleecy nebulæ were drawn off and carried up still higher, and then disappeared, and in this manner, by degrees, the whole mass vanished, and was strangely spun away before my eyes, like a distaff, by invisible hands.

Meteorology-Vegetation.

If my friends are disposed to laugh at the itinerant meteorologist and his strange theories, I shall, perhaps, give them more solid cause for laughter by some other of my remarks, for I must confess that, as my journey was, in fact, a flight from all the unshapely things which tormented me in latitude 51°, I hoped, in 48°, to meet with a true Goshen. But I found myself disappointed; for latitude alone does not make a climate and fine weather, but the mountain-chains—especially such as intersect the land from east to west. In these, great changes are constantly going on, and the lands which lie to the north have most to suffer from them. Thus, further north, the weather throughout the summer was determined by the great Alpine range on which I am now writing. Here, for the last few months, it has rained incessantly, while a south-east or south-west wind carried the showers north-wards. In Italy they are said to have had fine weather, indeed, a little too dry.

And now a few words on a kindred subject—the vegetable world, which, in so many ways, depends on climate and moisture, and the height of the mountain-ranges. Here, too, I have noticed no remarkable change, but still an improvement. In the valley before Innspruck, apples and pears are abundant, while the peaches and grapes are brought from the Welsh districts, or, in other words, the Southern Tyrol. Near Innspruck they grow a great deal of Indian corn and buck wheat, which they call *blende*. On the Brenner I first saw the larch, and near Schemberg the pine. Would the harper's daughter have questioned me about them also?

As regards the plants, I feel still more how perfect a tyro I am. Up to Munich I saw, I believed, none but those I was well accustomed to. In truth, my hurried travelling, by day and night, was not favorable to nicer observation on such objects. Now, it is true, I have my *Linnæus* at hand, and his Terminology is well stamped on my brain; but whence is the time and quiet to come for analysing, which, if I at all know myself, will never become my forte? I, therefore, sharpen my eye for the more general features, and when I met with the first Gentiana near the Walchensee, it struck me that it was always near the water, that I had hitherto noticed any new plants.

What made me still more attentive was the influence which the altitude of the mountain region evidently had on plants. Not only did I meet there with new specimens, but I also observed that the growth of the old ones was materially altered. While in the lower regions branches and stalks were stronger and more sappy, the buds stood closer together, and the leaves broader; the higher you got on the mountains the stalks and branches became more fragile, the buds were at greater intervals, and the leaves thinner and more lanceolate. I noticed this in the case of a Willow and of a Gentiana, and convinced myself that it was not a case of different species. So also, near the Walchensee, I noticed longer and thinner rushes than anywhere else.

The limestone of the Alps, which I have as yet travelled over, has a greyish tint, and beautiful, singular, irregular forms, although the rock is divisible into blocks and strata. But as irregular strata occur, and the rock in general does not crumble equally under the influence of the weather, the sides and the peaks have a singular appearance. This kind of rock comes up the Brenner to a great height. In the region of the Upper Lake I noticed a slight modification. On a micaceous slate of dark green and grey colours, and thickly veined with quartz, lay a white, solid limestone, which, in its detritus, sparkled and stood in great masses, with numberless clefts. Above it I again found micaceous slate, which, however, seemed to me to be of a softer texture than the first. Higher up still there was to be seen a peculiar kind of gneiss, or rather a granitic species which approximated to gneiss, as is in the district of Ellbogen. Here at the top, and opposite the Inn, the rock is micaceous slate. The streams which come from the mountains leave deposits of nothing but this stone, and of the grey limestone.

Geology—My fellow travellers.

Not far from here must be the granitic base on which all rests. The maps show that one is on the side of the true great Brenner, from which the streams of a wide surrounding district take their rise.

The following is my external judgment of the people. They are active and straightforward. In form they are pretty generally alike: hazel, well-opened eyes; with the women brown and well-defined eyebrows, but with the men light and thick. Among the grey rocks the green hats of the men have a cheerful appearance. The hats are generally ornamented with ribbons or broad silk-sashes, and with fringes which are prettily sewn on. On the other hand, the women disfigure themselves with white, undressed cotton caps of a large size, very much like men's nightcaps. These give them a very strange appearance; but abroad, they wear the green hats of the men, which become them very much.

I have opportunity of seeing the value the common class of people put upon peacock's feathers, and, in general, how every variegated feather is prized. He who wishes to travel through these mountains will do well to take with him a lot of them. A feather of this kind produced at the proper moment will serve instead of the ever-welcome "something to drink."

Whilst I am putting together, sorting, and arranging these sheets, in such a way that my friends may easily take a review of my fortunes up to this point, and that I may, at the same time, dismiss from my soul all that I have lately thought and experienced, I have, on the other hand, cast many a trembling look on some packets of which I must give a good but brief account. They are to be my fellow travellers; may they not exercise too great an influence on my next few days.

I brought with me to Carlsbad the whole of my MSS. in order to complete the edition of my works, which Goschen has undertaken. The unprinted ones I had long possessed in beautiful transcripts, by the practised hand of Secretary Vögel. This active person accompanied me on this occasion, in order that I might, if necessary, command his dexterous services. By this means, and with the never-failing co-operation of Herder, I was soon in a condition to send to the printer the first four volumes, and was on the point of doing the same with the last four. The latter consisted, for the most part, of mere unfinished sketches, indeed of fragments; for, in truth, my perverse habit of beginning many plans, and then, as the interest waned, laying them aside, had gradually gained strength with increasing years, occupations, and duties.

As I had brought these scraps with me, I readily listened to the requests of the literary circles of Carlsbad, and read out to them all that before had remained unknown to the world, which already was bitter enough in its complaints that much with which it had entertained itself still remained unfinished.

The celebration of my birthday consisted mainly in sending me several poems in the name of my commenced but unfinished works. Among these, one was distinguished above the rest. It was called the *Birds*. A deputation of these happy creatures being sent to a true friend earnestly entreat him to found at once and establish the kingdom so long promised to them. Not less obvious and playful were the allusions to my other unfinished pieces, so that, all at once, they again possessed a living interest for me, and I related to my friends the designs I had formed, and the entire plans. This gave rise to the expression of wishes and urgent requests, and gave the game entirely into Herder's hands, while he attempted to induce me to take back these papers, and, above all, to bestow upon the *Iphigenia* the pains it well deserved. The fragment which lies before me is rather a sketch than a finished piece; it is written in poetical prose, which occasionally falls into a sort of Iambical rhythm, and even imitates other syllabic metres. This, indeed, does great injury to the effect unless it is read well, and unless, by skilful turns, this defect is carefully concealed. He pressed this matter on me very earnestly, and as I concealed from him as well as the rest the great extent of my intended tour, and as he believed I had nothing more in view than a mountain trip, and as he was always ridiculing my geographical and mineralogical studies, he insisted I should act much wiser if, instead of breaking stones, I would put my hand to this work. I could not but give way to so many and well-meant remonstrances; but, as yet, I have had no opportunity to turn my attention to these matters. I now detach *Iphigenia* from the bundle and take her with me as my fellow-traveller into the beautiful and warm country of the South. The days are so long, and there will be nothing to disturb reflection, while the glorious objects of the surrounding scenery by no means depress the poetic nerve; indeed, assisted by movement and the free air, they rather stimulate and call it forth more quickly and more vividly.

FROM THE BRENNER TO VERONA.

Trent, morning of the 11th Sept.

After full fifty hours, passed in active and constant occupation, I reached here about 8 o'clock yesterday evening, and soon after retired to rest, so that I now find myself in condition to go on with my narrative. On the evening of the 9th, when I had closed the first portion of my diary, I thought I would try and draw the inn and post-house on the Brenner, just as it stood. My attempt was unsuccessful, for I missed the character of the place; I went home therefore in somewhat of an ill-humor. Mine host asked me if I would not depart, telling me it was moon-light and the best travelling. Although I knew perfectly well that, as he wanted his horses early in the morning to carry in the after-crop (*Grummet*), and wished to have them home again in time for that purpose, his advice was given with a view to his own interest, I nevertheless took it, because it accorded with my own inclination. The sun reappeared, the air was tolerable, I packed up, and started about 7 o'clock. The blue atmosphere triumphed over the clouds, and the evening was most beautiful.

Trent.

The postilion fell asleep, and the horses set off at a quick trot down-hill, always taking the well-known route. When they came to a village they went somewhat slower. Then the driver would wake up, and give them a fresh stimulus, and thus we descended at a good pace with high rocks on both sides of us, or by the banks of the rapid river Etsch. The moon arose and shed her light upon the massive objects around. Some mills, which stood between primæval pine-trees, over the foaming stream, seemed really everlasting.

When, at 9 o'clock, I had reached Sterzingen, they gave me clearly to understand, that they wished me off again. Arriving in Mittelwald, exactly at 12 o'clock, I found everybody asleep except the postilion, and we were obliged to go on to Brixen, where I was again taken off in like manner, so that at the dawn of day I was in Colman. The postilions drove so fast that there was neither seeing nor hearing, and although I could not help being sorry at travelling through this noble country with such frightful rapidity; and at night, too, as though I was flying the place, I nevertheless felt an inward joy, that a favorable wind blew behind me, and seemed to hurry me towards the object of my wishes. At day-break I perceived the first vineyard. A woman with pears and peaches met me, and thus we went on to Teutschen, where I arrived at 7 o'clock, and then was again hurried on. After I had again travelled northwards for a while, I at last saw in the bright sunshine the valley where Botzen is situated. Surrounded by steep and somewhat high mountains, it is open towards the south, and sheltered towards the north by the Tyrolese range. A mild, soft air pervaded the spot. Here the Etsch again winds towards the south. The hills at the foot of the mountain are cultivated with vines. The vinestocks are trained over long but low arbourwork; the purple grapes are gracefully suspended from the top, and ripen in the warmth of the soil, which is close beneath them. In the bottom of the valley, which for the most part consists of nothing but meadows, the vine is cultivated in narrow rows of similar festoons, at a little distance from each other, while between grows the Indian corn, the stalks of which at this time are high. I have often seen it ten feet high. The fibrous' male blossom is not yet cut off, as is the case when fructification has ceased for some time.

I came to Botzen in a bright sunshine. A good assemblage of mercantile faces pleased me much. Everywhere one sees the liveliest tokens. An existence full of purpose, and highly comfortable. In the square some fruit-women were sitting with round fiat baskets, above four feet in diameter, in which peaches were arranged side by side, so as to avoid pressure. Here I thought of a verse, which I had seen written on the window of the inn at Ratisbon:

> Comme les pêches et les melons
> Sont pour la bouche d'un Baron,
> Ainsi les verges et les bâtons
> Sont pour les fous, dit Salomon.

It is obvious that this was written by a northern baron, and no less clear is it that if he were in this country, he would alter his notions.

At the Botzen fair a brisk silk-trade is carried on. Cloths are also brought here, and as much leather as can be procured from the mountain districts. Several merchants, however, came chiefly for the sake of depositing their money, taking orders, and opening new credits. I felt I could have taken great delight in examining the various products that were collected here; but the impulse, the state of disquiet, which keeps urging me from behind, would not let me rest, and I must at once hasten from the spot. For my consolation, however, the whole matter is printed in the statistical papers, and we can, if we require it, get such instructions from books. I have now to deal only with the sensible impressions, which no book or picture can give. In fact, I am again taking interest in the world, I am testing my faculty of observation, and am trying how far I can go with my science and my acquirements, how far my eye is clear and sharp, how much I can take in at a hasty glance, and whether those wrinkles, that are imprinted upon my heart, are ever again to be obliterated. Even in these few days, the circumstance that I have had to wait upon myself, and have always been obliged to keep my attention and presence of mind on the alert, has given me quite a new elasticity of intellect. I must now busy myself with the currency, must change, pay, note down, write, while I formerly did nothing but think, will, reflect, command, and dictate.

Botzen—Trent.

From Botzen to Trent the stage is nine leagues and runs through a valley, which constantly increases in fertility. All that merely struggles into vegetation on the higher mountains, has here more strength and vitality; the sun shines with warmth, and there is once more belief in a Deity.

A poor woman cried out to me to take her child into my vehicle, as the hot soil was burning its feet. I did her this little service out of honour to the strong light of heaven. The child was strangely decked out, but I could get nothing from it in any way.

The Etsch flows more gently in these parts, and it makes broad deposits of gravel in many places. On the land, near the river and up the hills, the planting is so thick and close, that one fancies one thing will suffocate the other. It is a regular thicket of vineyards, maize, mulberry trees, apples, pears, quinces, and nuts. The danewort (*Attig*) thrives luxuriantly on the walls. Ivy with solid stems runs up the rocks, on which it spreads itself; the lizards glide through the interstices, and whatever has life or motion here, reminds one of the most charming works of art. The braided top-knots of the women, the bared breasts and light jackets of the men, the fine oxen which you see driven home from market, the laden asses,—all combine to produce one of Heinrich Roos's animated pictures. And when evening draws on, and through the calmness of the air, a few clouds rest upon the mountains, rather standing than running against the sky, and, as immediately after sunset, the chirp of the grasshoppers begins to grow loud, one feels quite at home in the world, and not a mere exile. I am as reconciled to the place as if I were born and bred in it, and had now just returned from a whaling expedition to Greenland. Even the dust, which here as in our fatherland often plays about my wheels, and which has so long remained strange to me, I welcome as an old friend. The bell-like voice of the cricket is most piercing, and far from unpleasant. A cheerful effect is produced, when playful boys whistle against a field of such singers, and you almost fancy that the sound on each side is raised by emulation. The evening here is perfectly mild no less than the day.

If any one who lived in the South, or came from the South, heard my enthusiasm about these matters, he would consider me very childish. Ah, what I express here, I long ago was conscious of, while ruffling under an unkindly sky; and now I love to experience as an exception the happiness which I hope soon to enjoy as a regular natural necessity.

Trent, the evening of the 10th Sept.

I have wandered about the city, which has an old, not to say a very primitive look, though there are new and well-built houses in some of the streets. In the church there is a picture in which the assembled council of the Jesuits is represented, listening to a sermon delivered by the general of the order. I should like to know what he is trying to palm upon them. The church of these fathers may at once be recognised from the outside by pilasters of red marble on the façade. The doors are covered by a heavy curtain, which serves to keep off the dust. I raised it, and entered a small vestibule. The church itself is parted off by an iron grating, but so that it can be entirely overlooked. All was as silent as the grave, for divine service is no longer performed here. The front door stood open, merely because all churches must be open at the time of Vespers.

Trent.

While I stood considering the architecture, which was, I found, similar to other Jesuit churches, an old man stepped in, and at once took off his little black cap. His old faded black coat indicated that he was a needy priest. He knelt down before the grating, and rose again after a short prayer. When he turned round, he said to himself half-aloud: "Well, they have driven out the Jesuits, but they ought to have paid them the cost of the church. I know how many thousands were spent on the church and the seminary." As he uttered this he left the spot, and the curtain fell behind him. I, however, lifted it again, and kept myself quiet. He remained a while standing on the topmost step, and said: "The Emperor did not do it; the Pope did it." With his face turned towards the street, so that he could not observe me, he continued: "First the Spaniards, then we, then the French. The blood of Abel cries out against his brother Cain!" And thus he went down the steps and along the street, still talking to himself. I should conjecture he is one who, having been maintained by the Jesuits, has lost his wits in consequence of the tremendous fall of the order, and now comes every day to search the empty vessel for its old inhabitants, and, after a short prayer, to pronounce a curse upon their enemies.

A young man, whom I questioned about the remarkable sights in the town, showed me a house, which is called the "Devil's house," because the devil, who is generally too ready to destroy, is said to have built it in a single night, with stones rapidly brought to the spot. However, what is really remarkable about the house, the good man had not observed, namely, that it is the only house of good taste that I have yet seen in Trent, and was certainly built by some good Italian, at an earlier period. At 5 o'clock in the evening I again set off. The spectacle of yesterday evening was repeated, and at sun-set the grasshoppers again began to sing. For about a league the journey lies between walls, above which the grape-espaliers are visible. Other walls, which are not high enough, have been eked out with stones, thorns, &c., to prevent passengers from plucking off the grapes. Many owners sprinkle the foremost rows with lime, which renders the grapes uneatable, but does not hurt the wine, as the process of fermentation drives out the heterogeneous matter.

Evening of September 11.

I am now at Roveredo, where a marked distinction of language begins; hitherto, it has fluctuated between German and Italian. I have now, for the first time, had a thoroughly Italian postilion, the inn-keeper does not speak a word of German, and I must put my own linguistic powers to the test. How delighted I am that the language I have always most loved now becomes living—the language of common usage.

Torbole, 12th September (after dinner).

How much do I wish that my friends were with me for a moment to enjoy the prospect, which now lies before my eyes.

I might have been in Verona this evening but a magnificent natural phenomenon was in my vicinity—Lake Garda, a splendid spectacle, which I did not want to miss, and now I am nobly rewarded for taking this circuitous route. After 5 o'clock I started from Roveredo, up a side valley, which still pours its waters into the Etsch. After ascending this, you come to an immense rocky bar, which you must cross in descending to the lake. Here appeared the finest calcareous rocks for pictorial study. On descending you come to a little village on the northern end of the lake, with a little port, or rather landing-place, which is called Torbole. On my way upwards I was constantly accompanied by fig-trees, and, descending into the rocky atmosphere, I found the first olive-tree full of fruit. Here also, for the first time, I found as a common fruit those little white figs, which the Countess Lanthieri had promised me.

A door opens from the chamber in which I sit into the court-yard below. Before this I have placed my table, and taken a rough sketch of the prospect. The lake may be seen for its whole length, and it is only at the end, towards the left, that it vanishes from our eyes. The shore, which is inclosed on both sides by hill and mountain, shines with a countless number of little hamlets.

After midnight the wind blows from north to south, and he who wishes to go down the lake must travel at this time, for a few hours before sunset the current of air changes, and moves northward. At this time, the afternoon, it blows strongly against me, and pleasantly qualifies the burning heat of the sun. Volkmann teaches me that this lake was formerly called "Benacus," and quotes from Virgil a line in which it was mentioned:

"Fluctibus et fremiter resonans, Benace, marino."

This is the first Latin verse, the subject of which ever stood visibly before me, and now, in the present moment, when the wind is blowing stronger and stronger, and the lake casts loftier billows against the little harbour, it is just as true as it was hundreds of years ago. Much, indeed, has changed, but the wind still roars about the lake, the aspect of which gains even greater glory from a line of Virgil's.

The above was written in a latitude of 45° 50'.

I went out for a walk in the cool of the evening, and now I really find myself in a new country, surrounded by objects entirely strange. The people lead a careless, sauntering life. In the first place, the doors are without locks, but the host assured me that I might be quite at ease, even though all I had about me consisted of diamonds. In the second place, the windows are covered with oiled paper instead of glass. In the third place, an extremely necessary convenience is wanting, so that one comes pretty close to a state of nature. When I asked the waiter for a certain place, he pointed down into the court-yard: "Qui, abasso puo servirsi!" "Dove?" asked I. "Da per tutto, dove vuol," was the friendly reply. The greatest carelessness is visible everywhere, but still there is life and bustle enough. During the whole day there is a constant chattering and shrieking of the female neighbors, all have something to do at the same time. I have not yet seen an idle woman.

Lago Di Garda.

The host, with Italian emphasis, assured me, that he felt great pleasure in being able to serve me with the finest trout. They are taken near Torbole, where the stream flows down from the mountains, and the fish seeks a passage upwards. The Emperor farms this fishery for 10,000 gulden. The fish, which are large, often weighing fifty pounds, and spotted over the whole body to the head, are not trout, properly so called. The flavour, which is between that of trout and salmon, is delicate and excellent.

But my real delight is in the fruit.—in the figs, and in the pears, which must, indeed, be excellent, where citrons are already growing.

Evening of September 13.

At 3 o'clock this morning I started from Torbole, with a couple of rowers. At first the wind was so favorable that we put up a sail. The morning was cloudy but tine, and perfectly calm at day-break. We passed Limona, the mountain-gardens of which, laid out terrace-fashion, and planted with citron-trees, have a neat and rich appearance. The whole garden consists of rows of square white pillars placed at some distance from each other, and rising up the mountain in steps. On these pillars strong beams are laid, that the trees planted between them may be sheltered in the winter. The view of these pleasant objects was favored by a slow passage, and we had already passed Malsesine when the wind suddenly changed, took the direction usual in the day-time, and blew towards the north. Rowing was of little use against this superior power, and, therefore, we were forced to land in the harbour of Malsesine. This is the first Venetian spot on the eastern side of the lake. When one has to do with water we cannot say, "I will be at this or that particular place to-day." I will make my stay here as useful as I can, especially by making a drawing of the castle, which lies close to the water, and is a beautiful object. As I passed along I took a sketch of it.

Sept. 11th.

The wind, which blew against me yesterday, and drove me into the harbour of Malsesine, was the cause of a perilous adventure, which I got over with good humour, and the remembrance of which I still find amusing. According to my plan, I went early in the morning into the old castle, which having neither gate nor guard, is accessible to everybody. Entering the court-yard, I seated myself opposite to the old tower, which is built on and among the rocks. Here I had selected a very convenient spot for drawing;—a carved stone seat in the wall, near a closed door, raised some three or four feet high, such as we also find in the old buildings in our own country.

An incident at Malsesine.

- 74 -

I had not sat long before several persons entered the yard, and walked backwards and forwards, looking at me. The multitude increased, and at last so stood as completely to surround me. I remarked that my drawing had excited attention; however, I did not allow myself to be disturbed, but quietly continued my occupation. At last a man, not of the most prepossessing appearance, came up to me, and asked me what I was about. I replied that I was copying the old tower, that I might have some remembrance of Malsesine. He said that this was not allowed, and that I must leave off. As he said this in the common Venetian dialect, so that I understood him with difficulty, I answered, that I did not understand him at all. With true Italian coolness he took hold of my paper, and tore it, at the same time letting it remain on the pasteboard. Here I observed an air of dissatisfaction among the by-standers; an old woman in particular said that it was not right, but that the podestà ought to be called, who was the best judge of such matters. I stood upright on the steps, having my back against the door, and surveyed the assembly, which was continually increasing. The fixed eager glances, the good humoured expression of most of the faces, and all the other characteristics of a foreign mob, made the most amusing impression upon me. I fancied that I could see before me the chorus of birds, which, as Treufreund, I had often laughed at, in the Ettersburg theatre. This put me in excellent humour, and when the podestà came up with his actuary, I greeted him in an open manner, and when he asked me why I was drawing the fortification, modestly replied, that I did not look upon that wall as a fortification. I called the attention of him and the people to the decay of the towers and walls, and to the generally defenceless position of the place, assuring him that I thought I only saw and drew a ruin.

I was answered thus: "If it was only a ruin, what could there be remarkable about it?" As I wished to gain time and favour, I replied very circumstantially, that they must be well aware how many travellers visited Italy, for the sake of the ruins only, that Rome, the metropolis of the world, having suffered the depredations of barbarians, was now full of ruins, which had been drawn hundreds of times, and that all the works of antiquity were not in such good preservation as the amphitheatre at Verona, which I hoped soon to see.

The podestà, who stood before me, though in a less elevated position, was a tall man, not exactly thin, of about thirty years of age. The flat features of his spiritless face perfectly accorded with the slow constrained manner, in which he put his questions. Even the actuary, a sharp little fellow, seemed as if he did not know what to make of a case so new, and so unexpected. I said a great deal of the same sort; the people seemed to take my remarks good naturedly, and on turning towards some kindly female faces, I thought I could read assent and approval.

When, however, I mentioned the amphitheatre at Verona, which in this country, is called the "Arena," the actuary, who had in the meanwhile collected himself, replied, that this was all very well, because the edifice in question was a Roman building, famed throughout the world. In these towers, however, there was nothing remarkable, excepting that they marked the boundary between the Venetian domain and Austrian Empire, and therefore *espionage* could not be allowed. I answered by explaining at some length, that not only the Great and Roman antiquities, but also those of the Middle-Ages were worth attention. They could not be blamed, I granted, if, having been accustomed to this building from their youth upwards, they could not discern in it so many picturesque beauties as I did. Fortunately the morning sun, shed the most beautiful lustre on the tower, rocks, and walls, and I began to describe the scene with enthusiasm. My audience, however, had these much lauded objects behind them, and as they did not wish to turn altogether away from me, they all at once twisted their heads, like the birds, which we call "wry necks" (Wendehälse), that they might see with their eyes, what I had been lauding to their ears. Even the podestà turned round towards the picture I had been describing, though with more dignity than the rest. This scene appeared to me so ridiculous that my good humour increased, and I spared them nothing—least of all, the ivy, which had been suffered for ages to adorn the rocks and walls.

The actuary retorted, that this was all very good, but the Emperor Joseph was a troublesome gentleman, who certainly entertained many evil designs against Venice; and I might probably have been one of his subjects, appointed by him, to act as a spy on the borders.

"Far from belonging to the Emperor," I replied, "I can boast, as well as you, that I am a citizen of a republic, which also governs itself, but which is not, indeed, to be compared for power and greatness to the illustrious state of Venice, although in commercial activity, in wealth, and in the wisdom of its rulers, it is inferior to no state in Germany. I am a native of Frankfort-on-the-Main, a city, the name and fame of which has doubtless reached you."

An incident at Malsesine.

"Of Frankfort-on-the-Main!" cried a pretty young woman, "then, Mr. Podestà, you can at once see all about the foreigner, whom I look upon as an honest man. Let Gregorio be called; he has resided there a long time, and will be the best judge of the matter."

The kindly faces had already increased around me, the first adversary had vanished, and when Gregorio came to the spot, the whole affair took a decided turn in my favor. He was a man upwards of fifty, with one of those well-known Italian faces. He spoke and conducted himself like one, who feels that something foreign is not foreign to him, and told me at once that he had seen service in Bolongari's house, and would be delighted to hear from me something about this family and the city in general, which had left a pleasant impression in his memory. Fortunately his residence at Frankfort had been during my younger years, and I had the double advantage of being able to say exactly how matters stood in his time, and what alteration had taken place afterwards. I told him about all the Italian families, none of whom had remained unknown to me. With many particulars he was highly delighted, as, for instance, with the fact that Herr Alessina had celebrated his "golden wedding,"[2] in the year 1774, and that a medal had been struck on the occasion, which was in my possession. He remembered that the wife of this wealthy merchant was by birth a Brentano. I could also tell him something about the children and grand-children of these families, how they had grown up, and had been provided for and married, and had multiplied themselves in their descendants.

When I had given the most accurate information about almost everything which he asked, his features alternately expressed cheerfulness and solemnity. He was pleased and touched, while the people cheered up more and more, and could not hear too much of our conversation, of which—it must be confessed—he was obliged to translate a part into their own dialect.

At last he said: "Podestà, I am convinced that this is a good, accomplished, and well-educated gentleman, who is travelling about to acquire instruction. Let him depart in a friendly manner, that he may speak well of us to his fellow-countrymen, and induce them to visit Malsesine, the beautiful situation of which is well worthy the admiration of foreigners. I gave additional force to these friendly words by praising the country, the situation, and the inhabitants, not forgetting to mention the magistrates as wise and prudent personages."

This was well received, and I had permission to visit the place at pleasure, in company with Master Gregorio. The landlord, with whom I had put up, now joined us, and was delighted at the prospect of the foreign guests, who would crowd upon him, when once the advantages of Malsesine were properly known. With the most lively curiosity he examined my various articles of dress, but especially envied me the possession of a little pistol, which slipped conveniently into the pocket. He congratulated those who could carry such pretty weapons, this being forbidden in his country under the severest penalties. This friendly but obtrusive personage I sometimes interrupted to thank my deliverer. "Do not thank me," said honest Gregorio, "for you owe me nothing. If the Podestà had understood his business, and the Actuary had not been the most selfish man in the world, you would not have got off so easily. The former was still more puzzled than you, and the latter would have pocketed nothing by your arrest, the information, and your removal to Verona. This he rapidly thought over, and you were already free, before our dialogue was ended."

Towards the evening the good man took me into his vineyard, which was very well situated, down along the lake. We were accompanied by his son, a lad of fifteen, who was forced to climb the trees, and pluck me the best fruit, while the old man looked out for the ripest grapes.

While thus placed between these two kindhearted people, both strange to the world, alone, as it were, in the deep solitude of the earth, I felt, in the most lively manner, as I reflected on the day's adventure, what a whimsical being Man is—how the very thing, which in company he might enjoy with ease and security, is often rendered troublesome and dangerous, from his notion, that he can appropriate to himself the world and its contents after his own peculiar fashion.

Towards midnight my host accompanied me to the barque, carrying the basket of fruit with which Gregorio had presented me, and thus, with a favorable wind, I left the shore, which had promised to become a Læstrygonicum shore to me.

[2] The fiftieth anniversary of a wedding-day is so called in Germany. Trans.

Lago Di Garda.

And now for my expedition on the lake. It ended happily, after the noble aspect of the water, and of the adjacent shore of Brescia had refreshed my very heart. On the western side, where the mountains cease to be perpendicular, and near the lake, the land becomes more flat, Garignano, Bojaco, Cecina, Toscolan, Maderno, Verdom, and Salo, stand all in a row, and occupy a reach of about a league and a half; most of them being built in long streets. No words can express the beauty of this richly inhabited spot. At 10 o'clock in the morning I landed at Bartolino, placed my luggage on one mule and myself on another. The road went now over a ridge, which separates the valley of the Etsch from the hollow of the lake. The primæval waters seem to have driven against each other from both sides, in immense currents, and to have raised this colossal dam of gravel. A fertile soil was deposited upon the gravel at a quieter period, but the labourer is constantly annoyed by the appearance of the stones on the surface. Every effort is made to get rid of them, they are piled in rows and layers one on another, and thus a sort of thick wall is formed along the path. The mulberry-trees, from a want of moisture, have a dismal appearance at this elevation. Springs there are none. From time to time puddles of collected rain-water may be found, with which the mules and even their drivers quench their thirst. Some wheels are placed on the river beneath, to water, at pleasure, those plantations that have a lower situation.

The magnificence of the new country, which opens on you as you descend, surpasses description. It is a garden a mile long and broad, which lies quite flat at the foot of tall mountains and steep rocks, and is as neatly laid out as possible. By this way, about 1 o'clock on the 10th of September, I reached Verona, where I first write this, finish, and put together the first part of my diary, and indulge in the pleasing hope of seeing the amphitheatre in the evening.

Concerning the weather of these days I have to make the following statement:—The night from the 9th to the 10th was alternately clear and cloudy, the moon had always a halo round it. Towards 5 o'clock in the morning all the sky was overcast with gray, not heavy clouds, which vanished with the advance of day. The more I descended the finer was the weather. As at Botzen the great mass of the mountains took a northerly situation, the air displayed quite another quality. From the different grounds in the landscape, which were separated from each other in the most picturesque manner, by a tint more or less blue, it might be seen, that the atmosphere was full of vapors equally distributed, which it was able to sustain, and which, therefore, neither fell in the shape of dew, nor were collected in the form of clouds. As I descended further I could plainly observe, that all the exhalations from the Botzen valley, and all the streaks of cloud which ascended from the more southern mountains, moved towards the higher northern regions, which they did not cover, but veiled with a kind of yellow fog. In the remotest distance, over the mountains, I could observe what is called a "water-gull." To the south of Botzen they have had the finest weather all the summer, only a little *water* (they say *aqua* to denote a light rain), from time to time, and then a return of sunshine. Yesterday a few drops occasionally fell, and the sun throughout continued shining. They have not had so good a year for a long while; everything turns out well; the bad weather they have sent to us.

I mention but slightly the mountains and the species of stone, since Ferber's travels to Italy, and Hacquet's journey along the Alps, give sufficient information respecting this district. A quarter of a league from the Brenner, there is a marble quarry, which I passed at twilight. It may, nay, must lie upon mica-slate as on the other side. This I found near Colman, just as it dawned; lower down there was an appearance of porphyry. The rocks were so magnificent, and the heaps were so conveniently broken up along the highway, that a "Voigt" cabinet might have been made and packed up at once. Without any trouble of that kind I can take a piece, if it is only to accustom my eyes and my curiosity to a small quantity. A little below Colman, I found some porphyry, which splits into regular plates, and between Brandrol and Neumark some of a similar kind, in which, however, the laminæ separated in pillars. Ferber considered them to be volcanic productions, but that was fourteen years ago, when all the world had its head on fire. Even Hacquet ridicules the notion.

From Brenner to Verona.

Of the people I can say but little, and that is not very favorable. On my descent from the Brenner, I discovered, as soon as day came, a decided change of form, and was particularly displeased by the pale brownish complexion of the women. Their features indicated wretchedness, the children looked equally miserable;—the men somewhat better. I imagine that the cause of this sickly condition may be found in the frequent consumption of Indian corn and buckwheat. Both the former, which they also call "Yellow Blende," and the latter, which is called "Black Blende," is ground, made into a thick pap with water, and thus eaten. The Germans on this side, pull out the dough, and fry it in butter. The Italian Tyrolese, on the contrary, eat it just as it is, often with scrapings of cheese, and do not taste meat throughout the year. This necessarily glues up and stops the alimentary channels, especially with the women and children, and their cachectic complexion is an indication of the malady. They also eat fruit and green beans, which they boil down in water, and mix with oil and garlic. I asked if there were no rich peasants. "Yes, indeed," was the reply. "Don't they indulge themselves at all? don't they eat anything better?" "No, they are used to it." "What do they do with their money then? how do they lay it out?" "Oh, they have their ladies, who relieve them of that." This is the sum and substance of a conversation with mine host's daughter at Botzen.

I also learned from her, that the vine-tillers were the worst off, although they appeared to be the most opulent, for they were in the hands of commercial towns-people, who advanced them enough to support life in the bad seasons, and in winter took their wine at a low price. However, it is the same thing everywhere.

My opinion concerning the food is confirmed by the fact, that the women who inhabit the towns appear better and better. They have pretty plump girlish faces, the body is somewhat too short in proportion to the stoutness, and the size of the head, but sometimes the countenances have a most agreable expression. The men we already know through the wandering Tyrolese. In the country their appearance is less fresh than that of the women, perhaps because the latter have more bodily labour, and are more in motion, while the former sit at home as traders and workmen. By the Garda Lake I found the people very brown, without the slightest tinge of red in their cheeks; however they did not look unhealthy, but quite fresh and comfortable. Probably the burning sunbeams, to which they are exposed at the foot of their mountains, are the cause of their complexion.

FROM VERONA TO VENICE.

Verona, Sept. 16th.

Well then, the amphitheatre is the first important monument of the old times that I have seen—and how well it is preserved! When I entered, and still more when I walked round the edge of it at the top, it seemed strange to me, that I saw something great, and yet, properly speaking, saw nothing. Besides I do not like to see it empty, I should like to see it full of people, just as, in modern times, it was filled up in honour of Joseph I. and Pius VI. The Emperor, although his eye was accustomed to human masses, must have been astonished. But it was only in the earliest times, that it produced its full effect, when the people was more a people than it is now. For, properly speaking, such an amphitheatre is constructed to give the people an imposing view of itself,—to cajole itself.

When anything worth seeing occurs on the level ground, and any one runs to the spot, the hindermost try by every means to raise themselves above the foremost; they get upon benches, roll casks, bring up vehicles, lay planks in every direction, occupy the neighbouring heights, and a crater is formed in no time.

If the spectacle occur frequently on the same spot, light scaffoldings are built for those who are able to pay, and the rest of the multitude must get on as it can. Here the problem of the architect is to satisfy this general want. By means of his art he prepares such a crater, making it as simple as possible, that the people itself may constitute the decoration. When the populace saw itself so assembled, it must have been astonished at the sight, for whereas it was only accustomed to see itself running about in confusion, or to find itself crowded together without particular rule or order, so must this many-headed, many-minded, wandering animal now see itself combined into a noble body, made into a definite unity, bound and secured into a mass, and animated as one form by one mind. The simplicity of the oval is most pleasingly obvious to every eye, and every head serves as a measure to show the vastness of the whole. Now we see it empty, we have no standard, and do not know whether it is large or small.

Verona.

The Veronese deserve commendation for the high preservation in which this edifice is kept. It is built of a reddish marble, which has been affected by the atmosphere, and hence the steps which have been eaten, are continually restored, and look almost all new. An inscription makes mention of one Hieronymus Maurigenus, and of the incredible industry, which he has expended on this monument. Of the outer wall only a piece remains, and I doubt whether it was ever quite finished. The lower arches, which adjoin the large square, called "Il Bra," are let out to workmen, and the reanimation of these arcades produces a cheerful appearance.

Verona, Sept. 16.

The most beautiful gate, which, however, always remains closed, is called "Porta stupa," or "del Pallio." As a gate, and considering the great distance from which it is first seen, it is not well conceived, and it is not till we come near it, that we recognise the beauty of the structure.

All sorts of reasons are given to account for its being closed. I have, however, a conjecture of my own. It was manifestly the intention of the artist to cause a new *Corso* to be laid out from this gate, for the situation, or the present street, is completely wrong. On the left side there is nothing but barracks; and the line at right angles from the middle of the gate leads to a convent of nuns, which must certainly have come down. This was presently perceived, and besides the rich and higher classes might not have liked to settle in the remote quarter. The artist perhaps died, and therefore the door was closed, and so an end was put to the affair.

Verona, Sept. 16.

The portico of the theatre, consisting of six large Ionic columns, looks handsome enough. So much the more puny is the appearance of the Marchese di Maffei's bust, which as large as life, and in a great wig, stands over the door, and in front of a painted niche, which is supported by two Corinthian columns. The position is honorable, but to be in some degree proportionate to the magnitude and solidity of the columns, the bust should have been colossal. But now placed as it is on a corbel, it has a mean appearance, and is by no means in harmony with the whole.

The gallery, which incloses the fore-court, is also small, and the channelled Doric dwarfs have a mean appearance by the side of the smooth Ionic giants. But we pardon this discrepancy on account of the fine institution, which has been founded among the columns. Here is kept a number of antiquities, which have mostly been dug up in and about Verona. Something, they say, has even been found in the Amphitheatre. There are Etruscan, Greek, and Roman specimens, down to the latest times, and some even of more modern date. The bas-reliefs are inserted in the walls, and provided with the numbers, which Maffei gave them, when he described them in his work: "*Verona illustrata.*" There are altars, fragments of columns, and other relics of the sort; an admirable tripod of white marble, upon which there are genii occupied with the attributes of the gods. Raphael has imitated and improved this kind of thing in the scrolls of the Farnesina.

The wind which blows from the graves of the ancients, comes fragrantly over hills of roses. The tombs give touching evidences of a genuine feeling, and always bring life back to us. Here is a man, by the side of his wife, who peeps out of a niche, as if it were a window. Here are father and mother, with their son between them, eyeing each other as naturally as possible. Here a couple are grasping each other's hands. Here a father, resting on his couch, seems to be amused by his family. The immediate proximity of these stones was to me highly touching. They belong to a later school of art, but are simple, natural, and generally pleasing. Here a man in armour is on his knees in expectation of a joyful resurrection. With more or less of talent the artist has produced the mere simple presence of the persons, and has thus given a permanent continuation to their existence. They do not fold their hands, they do not look towards heaven, but they are here below just what they were and just what they are. They stand together, take interest in each other, love one another, and this is charmingly expressed on the stone, though with a certain want of technical skill. A marble pillar, very richly adorned, gave me more new ideas.

Verona.

Laudable as this institution is, we can plainly perceive that the noble spirit of preservation, by which it was founded, is no longer continued. The valuable tripod will soon be ruined, placed as it is in the open air, and exposed to the weather towards the west. This treasure might easily be preserved in a wooden case.

The palace of the Proveditore, which is begun, might have afforded a fine specimen of architecture, if it had been finished. Generally speaking, the *nobili* build a great deal, but unfortunately every one builds on the site of his former residence, and often, therefore, in narrow lanes. Thus, for instance, a magnificent façade to a seminary is now building in an alley of tire remotest suburb.

<hr>

While, with a guide, whom I had accidentally picked up, I passed before the great solemn gate of a singular building, he asked me good-humouredly, whether I should not like to step into the court for a while. It was the palace of justice, and the court, on account of the height of the building, looked only like an enormous wall. Here, he told me, all the criminals and suspicious persons are confined. I looked around, and saw that round all the stories there were open passages' fitted with iron balustrades, which passed by numerous doors. The prisoner, as he stepped out of his dungeon to be led to trial, stood in the open air, and was exposed to the gaze of all passers, and because there were several trial-rooms, the chains were rattling, now over this, now over that passage, in every story. It was a hateful sight, and I do not deny that the good humour, with which I had dispatched my "Birds," might here have come into a strait.

<hr>

I walked at sunset upon the margin of the crater-like amphitheatre, and enjoyed the most splendid prospect over the town and the surrounding country. I was quite alone, and multitudes of people were passing below me on the hard stones of the Bra; men of all ranks, and women of the middle-ranks were walking. The latter in their black outer garments look, in this bird's-eye view, like so many mummies.

The *Zendale* and the *Veste*, which serves this class in the place of an entire wardrobe, is a costume completely fitted for a people that does not care much for cleanliness, and yet always likes to appear in public, sometimes at church, sometimes on the promenade. The *Veste* is a gown of black taffeta, which is thrown over other gowns. If the lady has a clean white one beneath, she contrives to lift up the black one on one side. This is fastened on so, as to cut the waist, and to cover the lappets of a corset, which may be of any colour. The *Zendale* is a large hood with long ears; the hood itself is kept high above the head by a wire-frame, while the ears are fastened round the body like a scarf, so that the ends fall down behind.

<hr>

Verona, Sept. 16.

When I again left the Arena to-day, I came to a modern public spectacle, about a thousand paces from the spot. Four noble Veronese were playing ball against four people of Vicenza. This pastime is carried on among the Veronese themselves all the year round, about two hours before night. On this occasion there was a far larger concourse of people than usual, on account of the foreign adversaries. The spectators seem to have amounted to four or five thousand. I did not see women of any rank.

When, a little while ago, I spoke of the necessities of the multitude in such a case, I described the natural accidental amphitheatre as arising just in the manner, in which I saw the people raised one over another on this occasion. Even at a distance I could hear the lively clapping of hands, which accompanied every important stroke. The game is played as follows: Two boards, slightly inclined, are placed at a convenient distance from each other. He who strikes off the ball stands at the higher end, his right hand is armed with a broad wooden ring, set with spikes. While another of his party throws the ball to him, he runs down to meet it, and thus increases the force of the blow with which he strikes it. The adversaries try to beat it back, and thus it goes backwards and forwards till, at last, it remains on the ground. The most beautiful attitudes, worthy of being imitated in marble, are thus produced. As there are none but well-grown active young people, in a short, close, white dress, the parties are only distinguished by a yellow mark. Particularly beautiful is the attitude into which the man on the eminence falls, when he runs down the inclined plain, and raises his arm to strike the ball;—it approaches that of the Borghesian gladiator.

It seemed strange to me that they carry on this exercise by an old lime-wall, without the slightest convenience for spectators; why is it not done in the amphitheatre, where there would be such ample room?

Verona, September 17.

What I have seen of pictures I will but briefly touch upon, and add some remarks. I do not make this extraordinary tour for the sake of deceiving myself, but to become acquainted with myself by means of these objects. I therefore honestly confess that of the painter's art—of his manipulation, I understand but little. My attention, and observation, can only be directed to the practical part, to the subject, and the general treatment of it.

Verona.

S. Georgio is a gallery of good pictures, all altar-pieces, and all remarkable, if not of equal value. But what subjects were the hapless artists obliged to paint? And for whom? Perhaps a shower of manna thirty feet long, and twenty feet high, with the miracle of the loaves as a companion. What could be made of these subjects? Hungry men falling on little grains, and a countless multitude of others, to whom bread is handed. The artists have racked their invention in order to get something striking out of such wretched subjects. And yet, stimulated by the urgency of the case, genius has produced some beautiful things. An artist, who had to paint S. Ursula with the eleven thousand virgins, has got over the difficulty cleverly enough. The saint stands in the foreground, as if she had conquered the country. She is very noble, like an Amazonia's virgin, and without any enticing charms; on the other hand, her troop is shown descending from the ships, and moving in procession at a diminishing distance. The Assumption of the Virgin, by Titian, in the dome, has become much blackened, and it is a thought worthy of praise that, at the moment of her apotheosis, she looks not towards heaven, but towards her friends below.

In the Gherardini Gallery I found some very fine things by Orbitto, and for the first time became acquainted with this meritorious artist. At a distance we only hear of the first artists, and then we are often contented with names only; but when we draw nearer to this starry sky, and the luminaries of the second and third magnitude also begin to twinkle, each one coming forward and occupying his proper place in the whole constellation, then the world becomes wide, and art becomes rich. I must here commend the conception of one of the pictures. Sampson has gone to sleep in the lap of Dalilah, and she has softly stretched her hand over him to reach a pair of scissors, which lies near the lamp on the table. The execution is admirable. In the Canopa Palace I observed a Danäe.

The Bevilagua Palace contains the most valuable things. A picture by Tintoretto, which is called a "Paradise," but which, in fact, represents the Coronation of the Virgin Mary as Queen of Heaven, in the presence of all the patriarchs, prophets, apostles, saints, angels, &c., affords an opportunity for displaying all the riches of the most felicitous genius. To admire and enjoy all that care of manipulation, that spirit and variety of expression, it is necessary to possess the picture, and to have it before one all one's life. The painter's work is carried on ad infinitum,; even the farthest angels' heads, which are vanishing in the halo, preserve something of character. The largest figures may be about a foot high; Mary, and the Christ who is crowning her, about four inches. Eve is, however, the finest woman in the picture; a little voluptuous, as from time immemorial.

A couple of portraits by Paul Veronese have only increased my veneration for that artist. The collection of antiquities is very fine; there is a son of Niobe extended in death, which is highly valuable; and the busts, including an Augustus with the civic crown, a Caligula, and others, are mostly of great interest, notwithstanding the restoration of the noses.

It lies in my nature to admire, willingly and joyfully, all that is great and beautiful, and the cultivation of this talent, day after day, hour after hour, by the inspection of such beautiful objects, produces the happiest feelings.

Verona.

In a land, where we enjoy the days but take especial delight in the evenings, the time of nightfall is highly important. For now work ceases; those who have gone out walking turn back; the father wishes to have his daughter home again; the day has an end. What the day is we Cimmerians hardly know. In our eternal mist and fog it is the same thing to us, whether it be day or night, for how much time can we really pass and enjoy in the open air? Now, when night sets in, the day, which consisted of a morning and an evening, is decidedly past, four and twenty hours are gone, the bells ring, the rosary is taken in hand, and the maid, entering the chamber with the lighted lamp, says, "felicissima notte." This epoch varies with every season, and a man who lives here in actual life cannot go wrong, because all the enjoyments of his existence are regulated not by the nominal hour, but by the time of day. If the people were forced to use a German clock they would be perplexed, for their own is intimately connected with their nature. About an hour and a half, or an hour before midnight, the nobility begin to ride out. They proceed to the Piazza della Bra, along the long, broad street to the Porta Nuova out at the gate, and along the city, and when night sets in, they all return home. Sometimes they go to the churches to say their Ave Maria della sera: sometimes they keep on the Bra, where the cavaliers step up to the coaches and converse for a while with the ladies. The foot passengers remain till a late hour of night, but I have never stopped till the last. To-day just enough rain had fallen to lay the dust, and the spectacle was most cheerful and animated.

That I may accommodate myself the better to the custom of the country I have devised a plan for mastering more easily the Italian method of reckoning the hours. The accompanying diagram may give an idea of it. The inner circle denotes our four and twenty hours, from midnight to midnight, divided into twice twelve, as we reckon, and as our clocks indicate. The middle circle shows how the clocks strike at the present season, namely, as much as twelve twice in the twenty-four hours, but in such a way that it strikes one, when it strikes eight with us, and so on till the number twelve is complete. At eight o'clock in the morning according to our clock it again strikes one, and so on. Finally the outer circle shows how the four and twenty hours are reckoned in actual life. For example, I hear seven o'clock striking in the night, and know that midnight is at five o'clock; I therefore deduct the latter number from the former, and thus have two hours after midnight. If I hear seven o'clock strike in the day-time, and know that noon is at five, I proceed in the same way, and thus have two in the afternoon. But if I wish to express the hour according to the fashion of this country, I must know that noon is seventeen o'clock; I add the two, and get nineteen o'clock. When this method is heard and thought of for the first time, it seems extremely confused and difficult to manage, but we soon grow accustomed to it and find the occupation amusing. The people themselves take delight in this perpetual calculation, just as children are pleased with easily surmounted difficulties. Indeed they always have their fingers in the air, make any calculation in their heads, and like to occupy themselves with figures. Besides to the inhabitant of the country the matter is so much the easier, as he really does not trouble himself about noon and midnight, and does not, like the foreign resident, compare two clocks with each other. They only count from the evening the hours, as they strike, and in the day-time they add the number to the varying number of noon, with which they are acquainted. The rest is explained by the remarks appended to the diagram:—

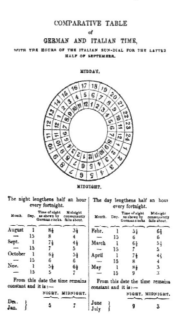

COMPARATIVE TABLE
of
GERMAN AND ITALIAN TIME,
WITH THE HOURS OF THE ITALIAN SUN-DIAL FOR THE LATTER HALF OF SEPTEMBER.

MIDDAY.

MIDNIGHT.

The night lengthens half an hour every fortnight.			The day lengthens half an hour every fortnight.		
Month.	Day.	Time of night as shewn by German clocks. / Midnight consequently falls about.	Month.	Day.	Time of night as shewn by German clocks. / Midnight consequently falls about.
August	1	8¼ 3¼	Febr.	1	3¼ 6¼
—	15	8 4	—	15	6 6
Sept.	1	7¼ 4¼	March	1	6¼ 5¼
—	15	7 5	—	15	7 5
October	1	6¼ 5¼	April	1	7¼ 4¼
—	15	6 6	—	15	8 4
Nov.	1	5¼ 6¼	May	1	8¼ 3
—	15	5 7	—	15	9 3
From this date the time remains constant and it is:—			From this date the time remains constant and it is:—		
		NIGHT. MIDNIGHT.			NIGHT. MIDNIGHT.
Dec. Jan. }		5 7	June July }		9 3

Verona, Sept. 17.

The people here jostle one another actively enough; the narrow streets, where shops and workmen's stalls are thickly crowded together, have a particularly cheerful look. There is no such thing as a door in front of the shop or workroom; the whole breadth of the house is open, and one may see all that passes in the interior. Half-way out into the path, the tailors are sewing; and the cobblers are pulling and rapping; indeed the work-stalls make a part of the street. In the evening, when the lights are burning, the appearance is most lively.

The squares are very full on market days; there are fruit and vegetables without number, and garlic and onions to the heart's desire. Then again throughout the day there is a ceaseless screaming, bantering, singing, squalling, huzzaing, and laughing. The mildness of the air, and the cheapness of the food, make subsistence easy. Everything possible is done in the open air.

At night singing and all sorts of noises begin. The ballad of "*Marlbrook*" is heard in every street;—then comes a dulcimer, then a violin. They try to imitate all the birds with a pipe. The strangest sounds are heard on every side. A mild climate can give this exquisite enjoyment of mere existence, even to poverty, and the very shadow of the people seems respectable.

The want of cleanliness and convenience, which so much strikes us in the houses, arises from the following cause:—the inhabitants are always out of doors, and in their light-heartedness think of nothing. With the people all goes right, even the middle-class man just lives on from day to day, while the rich and genteel shut themselves up in their dwellings, which are not so habitable as in the north. Society is found in the open streets. Fore-courts and colonnades are all soiled with filth, for things are done in the most *natural* manner. The people always feel their way before them. The rich man may be rich, and build his palaces; and the *nobile* may rule, but if he makes a colonnade or a fore-court, the people will make use of it for their own occasions, and have no more urgent wish than to get rid as soon as possible, of that which they have taken as often as possible. If a person cannot bear this, he must not play the great gentleman, that is to say, he must act as if a part of his dwelling belonged to the public. He may shut his door, and all will be right. But in open buildings the people are not to be debarred of their privileges, and this, throughout Italy, is a nuisance to the foreigner.

To-day I remarked in several streets of the town, the customs and manners of the middle-classes especially, who appear very numerous and busy. They swing their arms as they walk. Persons of a high rank, who on certain occasions wear a sword, swing only one arm, being accustomed to hold the left arm still.

Although the people are careless enough with respect to their own wants and occupations, they have a keen eye for everything foreign. Thus in the very first days, I observed that every one took notice of my boots, because here they are too expensive an article of dress to wear even in winter. Now I wear shoes and stockings nobody looks at me. Particularly I noticed this morning, when all were running about with flowers, vegetables, garlic, and other market-stuff, that a twig of cypress, which I carried in my hand, did not escape them. Some green cones hung upon it, and I held in the same hand some blooming caper-twigs. Everybody, large and small, watched me closely, and seemed to entertain some whimsical thought.

Verona-Vicenza.

I brought these twigs from the Giusti garden, which is finely situated, and in which there are monstrous cypresses, all pointed up like spikes into the air. The Taxus, which in northern gardening we find cut to a sharp point, is probably an imitation of this splendid natural product. A tree, the branches of which, the oldest as well as the youngest, are striving to reach heaven,— a tree which will last its three hundred years, is well worthy of veneration. Judging from the time when this garden was laid out, these trees have already attained that advanced age.

Vicenza, Sept. 19.

The way from Verona hither is very pleasant: we go north-eastwards along the mountains, always keeping to the left the foremost mountains, which consist of sand, lime, clay, and marl; the hills which they form, are dotted with villages, castles, and houses. To the right extends the broad plain, along which the road goes. The straight broad path, which is in good preservation, goes through a fertile field; we look into deep avenues of trees, up which the vines are trained to a considerable height, and then drop down, like pendant branches. Here we can get an admirable idea of festoons! The grapes are ripe, and are heavy on the tendrils, which hang down long and trembling. The road is filled with people of every class and occupation, and I was particularly pleased by some carts, with low solid wheels, which, with teams of fine oxen, carry the large vats, in which the grapes from the vineyards are put and pressed. The drivers rode in them when they were empty, and the whole was like a triumphal procession of Bacchanals. Between the ranks of vines the ground is used for all sorts of grain, especially Indian corn and millet (*Sörgel*).

As one goes towards Vicenza, the hills again rise from north to south and enclose the plain; they are, it is said, volcanic. Vicenza lies at their foot, or if you will, in a bosom which they form.

Though I have been here only a few hours, I have already run through the town, and seen the Olympian theatre, and the buildings of Palladio. A very pretty little book is published here, for the convenience of foreigners, with copper-plates and some letter-press, that shows knowledge of art. When once one stands in the presence of these works, one immediately perceives their great value, for they are calculated to fill the eye with their actual greatness and massiveness, and to satisfy the mind by the beautiful harmony of their dimensions, not only in abstract sketches, but with all the prominences and distances of perspective. Therefore I say of Palladio: he was a man really and intrinsically great, whose greatness was outwardly manifested. The chief difficulty with which this man, like all modern architects, had to struggle, was the suitable application of the orders of columns to buildings for domestic or public use; for there is always a contradiction in the combination of columns and walls. But with what success has he not worked them up together! What an imposing effect has the aspect of his edifices: at the sight of them one almost forgets that he is attempting to reconcile us to a violation of the rules of his art. There is, indeed, something divine about his designs, which may be exactly compared to the creations of the great poet, who, out of truth and falsehood elaborates something between both, and charms us with its borrowed existence.

Vicenza.

The Olympic theatre is a theatre of the ancients, realized on a small scale, and indescribably beautiful. However, compared with our theatres, it reminds me of a genteel, rich, well-bred child, contrasted with a shrewd man of the world, who, though he is neither so rich, nor so genteel, and well-bred, knows better how to employ his resources.

If we contemplate, on the spot, the noble buildings which Palladio has erected, and see how they are disfigured by the mean filthy necessities of the people, how the plans of most of them exceeded the means of those who undertook them, and how little these precious monuments of one lofty mind are adapted to all else around, the thought occurs, that it is just the same with everything else; for we receive but little thanks from men, when we would elevate their internal aspirations, give them a great idea of themselves, and make them feel the grandeur of a really noble existence. But when one cajoles them, tells them tales, and helping them on from day to day, makes them worse, then one is just the man they like; and hence it is that modern times take delight in so many absurdities. I do not say this to lower my friends, I only say that they are so, and that people must not be astonished to find everything just as it is.

How the Basilica of Palladio looks by the side of an old castellated kind of a building, dotted all over with windows of different sizes (whose removal, tower and all, the artist evidently contemplated),—it is impossible to describe—and besides I must now, by a strange effort, compress my own feelings, for, I too, alas! find here side by side both what I seek and what I fly from.

Sept. 20.

Yesterday we had the opera, which lasted till midnight, and I was glad to get some rest. The *three Sultanesses* and the *Rape of the Seraglio* have afforded several tatters, out of which the piece has been patched up, with very little skill. The music is agreeable to the ear, but is probably by an amateur; for not a single thought struck me as being new. The *ballets*, on the other hand, were charming. The principle pair of dancers executed an *Allemande* to perfection.

The theatre is new, pleasant, beautiful, modestly magnificent, uniform throughout, just as it ought to be in a provincial town. Every box has hangings of the same color, and the one belonging to the *Capitan Grande*, is only distinguished from the rest, by the fact that the hangings are somewhat longer.

The *prima donna*, who is a great favorite of the whole people, is tremendously applauded, on her entrance, and the "gods" are quite obstreperous with their delight, when she does anything remarkably well, which very often happens. Her manners are natural, she has a pretty figure, a fine voice, a pleasing countenance, and, above all, a really modest demeanour, while there might be more grace in the arms. However, I am not what I was, I feel that I am spoiled, I am spoiled for a "god."

Sept. 21.

To-day I visited Dr. Tura. Five years ago he passionately devoted himself to the study of plants, formed a *herbarium* of the Italian flora, and laid out a botanical garden under the superintendence of the former bishop. However, all that has come to an end. Medical practice drove away natural history, the *herbarium* is eaten by worms, the bishop is dead, and the botanic garden is again *rationally* planted with cabbages and garlic.

Dr. Tura is a very refined and good man. He told me his history with frankness, purity of mind, and modesty, and altogether spoke in a very definite and affable manner. At the same time he did not like to open his cabinets, which perhaps were in no very presentable condition. Our conversation soon came to a stand-still.

Sept. 21. *Evening.*

I called upon the old architect Scamozzi, who has published an edition of *Palladio's buildings*, and is a diligent artist, passionately devoted to his art. He gave me some directions, being delighted with my sympathy. Among Palladio's buildings there is one, for which I always had an especial predilection, and which is said to have been his own residence When it is seen close, there is far more in it than appears in a picture. I should have liked to draw it, and to illuminate it with colors, to show the material and the age. It must not, however, be imagined that the architect has built himself a palace. The house is the most modest in the world, with only two windows, separated from each other by a broad space, which would admit a third. If it were imitated in a picture, which should exhibit the neighbouring houses at the same time, the spectator would be pleased to observe how it has been let in between them. Canaletto was the man who should have painted it.

Vicenza.

To-day I visited the splendid building which stands on a pleasant elevation about half a league from the town, and is called the "Rotonda." It is a quadrangular building, enclosing a circular hall, lighted from the top. On all the four sides, you ascend a broad flight of steps, and always come to a vestibule, which is formed of six Corinthian columns. Probably the luxury of architecture was never carried to so high a point. The space occupied by the steps and vestibules is much larger than that occupied by the house itself; for every one of the sides is as grand and pleasing as the front of a temple. With respect to the inside it may be called habitable, but not comfortable. The hall is of the finest proportions, and so are the chambers; but they would hardly suffice for the actual wants of any genteel family in a summer-residence. On the other hand it presents a most beautiful appearance, as it is viewed on every side throughout the district. The variety which is produced by the principal mass, as, together with the projecting columns, it is gradually brought before the eyes of the spectator who walks round it, is very great; and the purpose of the owner, who wished to leave a large trust-estate, and at the same time a visible monument of his wealth, is completely obtained. And while the building appears in all its magnificence, when viewed from any spot in the district, it also forms the point of view for a most agreeable prospect. You may see the Bachiglione flowing along, and taking vessels down from Verona to the Brenta, while you overlook the extensive possessions which the Marquis Capra wished to preserve undivided in his family. The inscriptions on the four gable-ends, which together constitute one whole, are worthy to be noted down:

> Marcus Capra Gabrielis filius
> Qui ædes has Arctissimo
> primogenituræ gradui subjecit
> Una cum omnibus
> Censibus agrisvallibus et collibus
> Citra viam magnam
> Memorise perpetuæ mandans hæc
> Dum sustinet ac abstinet.

The conclusion in particular is strange enough. A man who has at command so much wealth and such a capacious will, still feels that he must *bear* and *forbear*. This can be learned at a less expense.

Sept. 22.

This evening I was at a meeting held by the academy of the "Olympians." It is mere play-work, but good in its way, and seems to keep up a little spice and life among the people. There is the great hall by Palladio's theatre, handsomely lighted up; the *Capitan* and a portion of the nobility are present, besides a public composed of educated persons, and several of the clergy; the whole assembly amounting to about five hundred.

The question proposed by the president for to-day's sitting was this: "Which has been most serviceable to the fine arts, invention or imitation?" This was a happy notion, for if the alternatives which are involved in the question are kept duly apart, one may go on debating for centuries. The academicians have gallantly availed themselves of the occasion, and have produced all sorts of things in prose and verse,—some very good.

Then there is the liveliest public. The audience cry *bravo*, and clap their hands and laugh. What a thing it is to stand thus before one's nation, and amuse them in person! We must set down our best productions in black and white; every one squats down with them in a corner, and scribbles at them as he can.

It may be imagined that even on this occasion Palladio would be continually appealed to, whether the discourse was in favour of invention or imitation. At the end, which is always the right place for a joke, one of the speakers hit on a happy thought, and said that the others had already taken Palladio away from him, so that he, for his part, would praise Franceschini, the great silk-manufacturer. He then began to show the advantages which this enterprising man, and through him the city of Vicenza, had derived from imitating the Lyonnese and Florentine stuffs, and thence came to the conclusion that imitation stands far above invention. This was done with so much humour, that uninterrupted laughter was excited. Generally those who spoke in favor of imitation obtained the most applause, for they said nothing but what was adapted to the thoughts and capacities of the multitude. Once the public, by a violent clapping of hands, gave its hearty approval to a most clumsy sophism, when it had not felt many good—nay, excellent things, that had been said in honour of invention. I am very glad I have witnessed this scene, for it is highly gratifying to see Palladio, after the lapse of so long a time, still honoured by his fellow-citizens, as their polar-star and model.

Sept. 22.

This morning I was at Tiene, which lies north towards the mountains, where a new building has been erected after an old plan, of which there may be a little to say. Thus do they here honour everything that belongs to the good period, and have sense enough to raise a new building on a plan which they have inherited. The *château* is excellently situated in a large plain, having behind it the calcareous Alps, without any mountains intervening. A stream of living water flows along the level causeway from each side of the building, towards those who approach it, and waters the broad fields of rice through which one passes.

I have now seen but two Italian cities, and for the first time, and have spoken with but few persons, and yet I know my Italians pretty well. They are like courtiers, who consider themselves the first people in the world, and who, on the strength of certain advantages, which cannot be denied them, can indulge with impunity in so comfortable a thought. The Italians appear to me a right good people. Only one must see the children and the common people as I see them now, and can see them, while I am always open to them,—nay, always lay myself open to them. What figures and faces there are!

It is especially to be commended in the Vicentians, that with them one enjoys the privileges of a large city. Whatever a person does, they do not stare at him, but if he addresses them, they are conversable and pleasant, especially the women, who please me much. I do not mean to find fault with the Veronese women; they are well made and have a decided pupil, but they are, for the most part, pale, and the *Zendal* is to their disadvantage, because one looks for something charming under the beautiful costume. I have found here some very pretty creatures, especially some with black locks, who inspire me with peculiar interest. There are also fairer beauties who, however, do not please me so well.

Padua, Sept. 26. Evening.

In four hours I have this day come here from Vicenza, crammed luggage and all into a little one-seated chaise, called a "*Sediola.*" Generally the journey is performed with ease in three hours and a half, but as I wished to pass the delightful day-time in the open air, I was glad that the *Vetturino* fell short of his duty. The route goes constantly southwards over the most fertile plains, and between hedges and trees, without further prospect, until at last the beautiful mountains, extending from the east towards the south, are seen on the right hand. The abundance of the festoons of plants and fruit, which hang over walls and hedges, and down the trees, is indescribable. The roofs are loaded with gourds, and the strangest sort of cucumbers are hanging from poles and trellises.

From the observatory I could take the clearest survey possible of the fine situation of the town. Towards the north are the Tyrolese mountains, covered with snow, and half hidden by clouds, and joined by the Vicentian mountains on the north-west. Then towards the west are the nearer mountains of Este, the shapes and recesses of which are plainly to be seen. Towards the south-east is a verdant sea of plants, without a trace of elevation, tree after tree, bush after bush, plantation after plantation, while houses, villas, and churches, dazzling with whiteness, peer out from among the green. Against the horizon I plainly saw the tower of St. Mark's at Venice, with other smaller towers.

Padua, Sept. 27.

> Padua.

I have at last obtained the works of Palladio, not indeed the original edition, which I saw at Vicenza, where the cuts are in wood, but a fac-simile in copper, published at the expense of an excellent man, named Smith, who was formerly the English consul at Venice. We must give the English this credit, that they have long known how to prize what is good, and have a magnificent way of diffusing it.

On the occasion of this purchase I entered a book-shop, which in Italy presents quite a peculiar appearance. Around it are arranged the books, all stitched, and during the whole day good society may be found in the shop, which is a lounge for all the secular clergy, nobility, and artists who are in any way connected with literature. One asks for a book, opens it, and amuses himself as one can. Thus I found a knot of half a dozen all of whom became attentive to me, when I asked for the works of Palladio. While the master of the shop looked for the book, they commended it, and gave me information respecting the original and the copy; they were well acquainted with the work itself and with the merits of the author. Taking me for an architect they praised me for having recourse to this master in preference to all the rest, saying that he was of more practical utility than Vitruvius himself, since he had thoroughly studied the ancients and antiquity, and had sought to adapt the latter to the wants of our own times. I conversed for a long time with these friendly men, learned something about the remarkable objects in the city, and took my leave.

Where men have built churches to saints, a place may sometimes be found in them, where monuments to intellectual men may be set up. The bust of Cardinal Bembo stands between Ionic columns. It is a handsome face, strongly drawn in, if I may use the expression, and with a copious beard. The inscription runs thus: "Petri Bembi Card. imaginem Hier. Guerinus Ismeni f. in publico ponendam curavit ut cujus ingenii monumenta æterna sint, ejus corporis quoque memoria ne a posteritate desideretur."

With all its dignity the University gave me the horrors, as a building. I am glad that I had nothing to learn in it. One cannot imagine such a narrow compass for a school, even though, as the student of a German university, one may have suffered a great deal on the benches of the Auditorium. The anatomical theatre is a perfect model of the art of pressing students together. The audience are piled one above another in a tall pointed funnel. They look down upon the narrow space where the table stands, and, as no daylight falls upon it, the Professor must demonstrate by lamplight. The botanic garden is much more pretty and cheerful. Several plants can remain in the ground during the winter, if they are set near the walls, or at no great distance from them. At the end of October the whole is built over, and the process of heating is carried on for the few remaining months. It is pleasant and instructive to walk through a vegetation that is strange to us. With ordinary plants, as well as with other objects that have been long familiar to us, we at last do not think at all, and what is looking without thinking?

Amidst this variety which comes upon me quite new, the idea that all forms of plants may, perhaps, be developed from a single form, becomes more lively than ever. On this principle alone it would be possible to define orders and classes, which, it seems to me, has hitherto been done in a very arbitrary manner. At this point I stand fast in my botanical philosophy, and I do not see how I am to extricate myself. The depth and breadth of this business seem to me quite equal.

The great square, called *Prato della Valle*, is a very wide space, where the chief fair is held in June. The wooden booths in the middle of it do not produce the most favourable appearance, but the inhabitants assure me that there will soon be a *fièra* of stone here, like that at Verona. One has hopes of this already, from the manner in which the *Prato* is surrounded, and which affords a very beautiful and imposing view.

A huge oval is surrounded with statues, all representing celebrated men, who have taught or studied at the University. Any native or foreigner is allowed to erect a statue of a certain size to any countryman or kinsman, as soon as the merit of the person and his academical residence at Padua are proved.

Padua.

A moat filled with water goes round the oval. On the four bridges which lead up to it stand colossal figures of Popes and Doges; the other statues, which are smaller, have been set up by corporations, private individuals, or foreigners. The King of Sweden caused a figure of Gustavus Adolphus to be erected, because it is said he once heard a lecture in Padua. The Archduke Leopold revived the memory of Petrarch and Galileo. The statues are in a good, modern style, a few of them rather affected, some very natural, and all in the costume of their rank and dignity. The inscriptions deserve commendation. There is nothing in them absurd or paltry.

At any university the thought would have been a happy one (and here it is particularly so), because it is very delightful to see a whole line of departed worthies thus called back again. It will perhaps form a very beautiful *Prato*, when the wooden *Fièra* shall be removed, and one built of stone, according to the aforesaid plan.

In the consistory of a fraternity dedicated to S. Anthony, there are some pictures of an early date, which remind one of the old German paintings, and also some by Titian, in which may be remarked the great progress which no one has made on the other side of the Alps. Immediately afterwards I saw works by some of the most modern painters. These artists, as they could not hope to succeed in the lofty and the serious, have been very happy in hitting the humorous. The decollation of John by Piazetta is, in this sense, a capital picture, if one can once allow the master's manner. John is kneeling, with his hands before him, and his right knee on a stone, looking towards heaven. One of the soldiers, who is binding him, is bending round on one side, and looking into his face, as if he was wondering at his patient resignation. Higher up stands another, who is to deal the fatal blow. He does not, however, hold the sword, but makes a motion with his hands, like one who is practising the stroke beforehand. A third is drawing the sword out of the scabbard. The thought is happy, if not grand, and the composition is striking and produces the best effect.

In the church of the *Eremitani* I have seen pictures by Mantegna, one of the older painters, at which I am astonished. What a sharp, strict actuality is exhibited in these pictures! It is from this actuality, thoroughly true, not apparent, merely and falsely effective, and appealing solely to the imagination, but solid, pure, bright, elaborated, conscientious, delicate, and circumscribed—an actuality which had about it something severe, credulous, and laborious; it is from this, I say, that the later painters proceeded (as I remarked in the pictures of Titian), in order that by the liveliness of their own genius, the energy of their nature illumined at the same time by the mind of the predecessors, and exalted by their force, they might rise higher and higher, and elevated above the earth, produce forms that were heavenly indeed, but still true. Thus was art developed after the barbarous period.

The hall of audience in the town-house, properly designated by the augmentative "Salone," is such a huge inclosure that one cannot conceive it, much less recall it to one's immediate memory. It is three hundred feet long, one hundred feet broad, and one hundred feet high, measured up to the roof, which covers it quite in. So accustomed are these people to live in the open air, that the architects look out for a market-place to over-arch. And there is no question that this huge vaulted space produces quite a peculiar effect. It is an inclosed infinity, which has more analogy to man's habits and feelings than the starry heavens. The latter takes us out of ourselves, the former insensibility brings us back to ourselves.

For the same reason I also like to stay in the Church of S. Justina. This church, which is eighty-five feet long, and high and broad in proportion, is built in a grand and simple style. This evening I seated myself in a corner, and indulged in quiet contemplation. Then I felt myself truly alone, for no one in the world, even if he had thought of me for the moment, would have looked for me here.

Now everything ought to be packed up again, for to-morrow morning I set off by water, upon the Brenta. It rained to-day, but now it has cleared up, and I hope I shall be able to see the lagunes and the Bride of the Sea by beautiful daylight, and to greet my friends from her bosom.

VENICE

Now it stood written on my page in the Book of Fate, that on the evening of the 28th of September, by 5 o'clock, German time, I should see Venice for the first time, as I passed from the Brenta into the lagunes, and that, soon afterwards, I should actually enter: and visit this strange island-city, this heaven-like republic. So now, Heaven be praised, Venice is no longer to me a bare and a hollow name, which has so long tormented me,—*me*, the mental enemy of mere verbal sounds.

As the first of the gondoliers came up to the ship (they come in order to convey more quickly to Venice those passengers who are in a hurry), I recollected an old plaything, of which, perhaps, I had not thought for twenty years. My father had a beautiful model of a gondola which he had brought with him [*from Italy*]; he set a great value upon it, and it was considered a great treat, when I was allowed to play with it. The first beaks of tinned iron-plate, the black gondola-gratings, all greeted me like old acquaintances, and I experienced again dear emotions of my childhood which had been long unknown.

I am well lodged at the sign of the *Queen of England*, not far from the square of S. Mark, which is, indeed, the chief advantage of the snot. My windows look upon a narrow canal between lofty houses, a bridge of one arch is immediately below me, and directly opposite is a narrow, bustling alley. Thus am I lodged, and here I shall remain until I have made up my packet for Germany, and until I am satiated with the sight of the city. I can now really enjoy the solitude for which I have longed so ardently, for nowhere does a man feel himself more solitary than in a crowd, where he must push his way unknown to every one. Perhaps in Venice there is only one person who knows me, and he will not come in contact with me all at once.

Venice, September 28, 1786.

A few words on my journey hither from Padua. The passage on the Brenta, in the public vessel, and in good company, is highly agreeable. The banks are ornamented with gardens and villas, little hamlets come down to the water's edge, and the animated highroad may be seen here and there. As the descent of the river is by means of locks, there is often a little pause, which may be employed in looking about the country, and in tasting the fruits, which are offered in great abundance. You then enter your vessel again, and move on through a world, which is itself in motion, and which is full of life and fertility.

To so many changing forms and images a phenomenon was added, which, although derived from Germany, was quite in its place here—I mean two pilgrims, the first whom I have seen closely. They have a right to travel gratis in this public conveyance; but because the rest of the passengers dislike coming into contact with them, they do not sit in the covered part, but in the after-part beside the steersman. They were stared at as a phenomenon even at the present day, and as in former times many vagabonds had made use of this cloak, they were but lightly esteemed. When I learned that they were Germans, and could speak no language but their own, I joined them, and found that they came from the Paderborn territory. Both of them were men of more than fifty years of age, and of a dark, but good-humoured physiognomy. They had first visited the sepulchre of the "Three Kings" at Cologne, had then travelled through Germany, and were now together on their way back to Borne and Upper Italy, whence one intended to set out for Westphalia, and the other to pay a visit of adoration to St. James of Compostella.

Their dress was the well-known costume of pilgrims, but they looked much better with this tucked up robe, than the pilgrims in long taffeta garments, we are accustomed to exhibit at our masquerades. The long cape, the round hat, the staff and cockle (the latter used as the most innocent drinking-vessel)—all had its signification, and its immediate use, while a tin-case held their passports. Most remarkable of all were their small, red morocco pocket-books, in which they kept all the little implements that might be wanted for any simple necessity. They took them out on finding that something wanted mending in their garments.

- -

The passage to Venice.

- -

The steersman, highly pleased to find an interpreter, made me ask them several questions, and thus I learned a great deal about their views, and especially about their expedition. They made bitter complaints against their brethren in the faith, and even against the clergy, both secular and monastic. Piety, they said, must be a very scarce commodity, since no one would believe in theirs, but they were treated as vagrants in almost every Catholic country, although they produced the route which had been clerically prescribed, and the passports given by the bishop. On the other hand, they described, with a great deal of emotion, how well they had been received by protestants, and made special mention of a country clergyman in Suabia, and still more of his wife, who had prevailed on her somewhat unwilling husband to give them an abundant repast, of which they stood in great need. On taking leave, the good couple had given them a "convention's dollar,"[3] which they found very serviceable, as soon as they entered the Catholic territory. Upon this, one of them said, with all the elevation of which he was capable: "We include this lady every day in our prayers, and implore God that he will open her eyes, as he has opened her heart towards us, and take her, although late, into the bosom of the Catholic Church. And thus we hope that we shall meet her in Paradise hereafter."

As I sat upon the little gang-way which led to the deck, I explained as much as was necessary and useful to the steers-man, and to some other persons who had crowded from the cabin into this narrow space. The pilgrims received some paltry donations, for the Italian is not fond of giving. Upon this they drew out some little consecrated tickets, on which might be seen the representation of the three sainted kings, with some prayers addressed to them. The worthy men entreated me to distribute these tickets among the little party, and explain how invaluable they were. In this I succeeded perfectly, for when the two men appeared to be greatly embarrassed as to how they should find the convent devoted to pilgrims in so large a place as Venice, the steersman was touched, and promised that, when they landed, he would give a boy a trifle to lead them to that distant spot. He added to me in confidence, that they would find but little welcome. "The institution," he said, "was founded to admit I don't know how many pilgrims, but now it has become greatly contracted, and the revenues are otherwise employed."

During this conversation we had gone down the beautiful Brenta, leaving behind us many a noble garden, and many a noble palace, and casting a rapid glance at the populous and thriving hamlets, which lay along the banks. Several gondolas wound about the ship as soon as we had entered the lagunes. A Lombard, well acquainted with Venice, asked me to accompany him, that we might enter all the quicker, and escape the nuisance of the custom-house. Those who endeavoured to hold us back, he contrived to put off with a little drink-money, and so, in a cheerful sunset, we floated to the place of our destination.

[3] A "convention's dollar" is a dollar coined in consequence of an agreement made between several of the German states, in the year 1750, when the Viennese standard was adopted.—Trans.

Sept. 29 (Michaelmas-Day). Evening.

So much has already been told and printed about Venice, that I shall not be circumstantial in my description, but shall only say how it struck me. Now, in this instance again, that which makes the chief impression upon me, is the people,—a great mass, who live an involuntary existence determined by the changing circumstances of the moment.

It was for no idle fancy that this race fled to these islands; it was no mere whim which impelled those who followed to combine with them; necessity taught them to look for security in a highly disadvantageous situation, that afterwards became most advantageous, enduing them with talent, when the whole northern world was immersed in gloom. Their increase and their wealth were a necessary consequence. New dwellings arose close against dwellings, rocks took the place of sand and marsh, houses sought the sky, being forced like trees inclosed in a narrow compass, to seek in height what was denied them in breadth. Being niggards of every inch of ground, as having been from the very first compressed into a narrow compass, they allowed no more room for the streets than was just necessary to separate a row of houses from the one opposite, and to afford the citizens a narrow passage. Moreover, water supplied the place of street, square, and promenade. The Venetian was forced to become a new creature; and thus Venice can only be compared with itself. The large canal, winding like a serpent, yields to no street in the world, and nothing can be put by the side of the space in front of St. Mark's square—I mean that great mirror of water, which is encompassed by Venice Proper, in the form of a crescent. Across the watery surface you see to the left the island of St. Georgio Maggiore, to the right a little, further off the Guidecca and its canal, and still more distant the *Dogana* (Custom-house) and the entrance into the *Canal Grande*, where right before us two immense marble temples are glittering in the sunshine. All the views and prospects have been so often engraved, that my friends will have no difficulty in forming a clear idea of them.

Venice.

After dinner I hastened to fix my first impression of the whole, and without a guide, and merely observing the cardinal points, threw myself into the labyrinth of the city, which though everywhere intersected by larger or smaller canals, is again connected by bridges. The narrow and crowded appearance of the whole cannot be conceived by one who has not seen it. In most cases one can quite or nearly measure the breadth of the street, by stretching out one's arms, and in the narrowest, a person would scrape his elbows if he walked with his arms a-kimbo. Some streets, indeed, are wider, and here and there is a little square, but comparatively all may be called narrow.

I easily found the grand canal, and the principal bridge—the Rialto, which consists of a single arch of white marble. Looking down from this, one has a fine prospect,—the canal full of ships, which bring every necessary from the continent, and put in chiefly at this place to unload, while between them is a swarm of gondolas. To-day, especially, being Michaelmas, the view was wonderfully animated; but to give some notion of it, I must go back a little.

The two principal parts of Venice, which are divided by the grand canal, are connected by no other bridge than the Rialto, but several means of communication are provided, and the river is crossed in open boats at certain fixed points. To-day a very pretty effect was produced, by the number of well-dressed ladies, who, their features concealed beneath large black veils, were being ferried over in large parties at a time, in order to go to the church of the Archangel, whose festival was being solemnised. I left the bridge and went to one of the points of landing, to see the parties as they left the boats. I discovered some very fine forms and faces among them.

After I had become tired of this amusement. I seated myself in a gondola, and, quitting the narrow streets with the intention of witnessing a spectacle of an opposite description, went along the northern part of the grand canal, into the lagunes, and then entered the canal della Guidecca, going as far as the square of St. Mark. Now was I also one of the birds of the Adriatic sea, as every Venetian feels himself to be, whilst reclining in his gondola. I then thought with due honour of my good father, who knew of nothing better than to talk about the things I now witnessed. And will it not be so with me likewise? All that surrounds me is dignified—a grand venerable work of combined human energies, a noble monument, not of a ruler, but of a people. And if their lagunes are gradually filling up, if unwholesome vapours are floating over the marsh, if their trade is declining and their power has sunk, still the great place and the essential character will not for a moment, be less venerable to the observer. Venice succumbs to time, like everything that has a phenomenal existence.

Sept. 30.

Towards evening I again rambled, without a guide, into the remotest quarters of the city. The bridges here are all provided with stairs, that gondolas, and even larger vessels, may pass conveniently under the arches. I sought to find my way in and out of this labyrinth, without asking anybody, and, on this occasion also, only guiding myself by the points of the compass. One disentangles one's self at last, but it is a wonderful complication, and my manner of obtaining a sensible impression of it, is the best. I have now been to the remotest points of the city, and observed the conduct, mode of life, manners, and character of the inhabitants; and in every quarter they are different. Gracious Heaven!—What a poor good sort of animal man is, after all!

Most of the smaller houses stand immediately on the canals, but there are here and there quays of stone, beautifully paved, along which one may take a pleasant walk between the water, and the churches, and palaces. Particularly cheerful and agreeable is the long stone quay on the northern side, from which the islands are visible, especially Murano, which is a Venice on a small scale. The intervening lagunes are all alive with little gondolas.

Sept. 30. *Evening.*

To-day I have enlarged my notions of Venice by procuring a plan of it. When I had studied it for some time, I ascended the tower of St. Mark, where an unique spectacle is presented to the eye. It was noon, and the sun was so bright that I could see places near and distant without a glass. The tide covered the lagunes, and when I turned my eyes towards what is called the *Lido* (this is a narrow strip of earth, which bounds the lagunes), I saw the sea for the first time with some sails upon it. In the lagunes themselves some gallies and frigates are lying, destined to join the Chevalier Emo, who is making war on the Algerines, but detained by unfavorable winds. The mountains of Padua and Vicenza, and the mountain-chain of Tyrol, beautifully bound the picture between the north and west.

October 1.

I went out and surveyed the city from many points of view, and as it was Sunday, I was struck by the great want of cleanliness in the streets, which forced me to make some reflections. There seems to be a sort of policy in this matter, for the people scrape the sweepings into the corners, and I see large ships going backwards and forwards, which at several points He to, and take off the accumulation. They belong to the people of the surrounding islands, who are in want of manure. But, however, there is neither consistency nor strictness in this method, and the want of cleanliness in the city is the more unpardonable, as in it, as much provision has been made for cleaning it, as in any Dutch town.

All the streets are paved—even those in the remotest quarters, with bricks at least, which are laid down lengthwise, with the edges slightly canting: the middle of the street where necessary is raised a little, while channels are formed on each side to receive the water, and convey it into covered drains. There are other architectural arrangements in the original well-considered plan, which prove the intention of the excellent architects to make Venice the most cleanly, as well as the most singular of cities. As I walked along I could not refrain from sketching a body of regulations on the subject, anticipating in thought some superintendent of police, who might act in earnest. Thus one always feels an inclination to sweep one's neighbour's door.

Oct. 2, 1786.

Before all things I hastened to the *Carità*. I had found in Palladio's works that he had planned a monastic building here, in which he intended to represent a private residence of the rich and hospitable ancients. The plan, which was excellently drawn, both as a whole and in detail, gave me infinite delight, and I hoped to find a marvel. Alas! scarcely a tenth part of the edifice is finished. However, even this part is worthy of that heavenly genius. There is a completeness in the plan, and an accuracy in the execution, which I had never before witnessed. One ought to pass whole years in the contemplation of such a work. It seems to me that I have seen nothing grander, nothing more perfect, and I fancy that I am not mistaken. Only imagine the admirable artist, born with an inner feeling for the grand and the pleasing, now, for the first time, forming himself by the ancients, with incredible labour, that he may be the means of reviving them. He finds an opportunity to carry out a favorite thought in building a convent, which is destined as a dwelling for so many monks, and a shelter for so many strangers, in the form of an antique private residence.

The church was already standing and led to an atrium of Corinthian columns. Here one feels delighted, and forgets all priestcraft. At one end, the sacristy, at another, a chapter-room is found, while there is the finest winding stair-case in the world, with a wide well, and the stone-steps built into the wall, and so laid, that one supports another. One is never tired of going up and down this stair-case, and we may judge of its success, from the fact that Palladio himself declares that he has succeeded. The fore-court leads to the large inner-court. Unfortunately, nothing is finished of the building which was to surround this, except the left side. Here there are three rows of columns, one over the other; on the ground-floor are the halls, on the first story is an archway in front of the cells, and the upper story consists of a plain wall with windows. However, this description should be illustrated by a reference to the sketches. I will just add a word about the execution.

Only the capitals and bases of the columns, and the key-stones of the arches, are of hewn stone; all the rest is—I will not say of brick, but-of burned clay. This description of tile I never saw before. The frieze and cornice are of the same material, as well as the parts of the arch. All is but half burnt, and lastly the building is put together with a very little lime. As it stands it looks as if it had been produced at one cast. If the whole had been finished, and it had been properly rubbed up and coloured, it would have been a charming sight.

However, as so often happens with buildings of a modern time, the plan was too large. The artist had pre-supposed not only that the existing convent would be pulled down, but also that the adjoining houses would be bought, and here money and inclination probably began to fail. Kind Destiny, thou who hast formed and perpetuated so much stupidity, why didst thou not allow this work to be completed!

Oct. 3.

The church *Il Redentore* is a large and beautiful work by Palladio, with a façade even more worthy of praise than that of S. Giorgio. These works, which have often been engraved, must be placed before you, to elucidate what is said. I will only add a few words.

Palladio was thoroughly imbued with the antique mode of existence, and felt the narrow, petty spirit of his own age, like a great man who will not give way to it, but strives to mould all that it leaves him, as far as possible, into accordance with his own ideas. From a slight perusal of his book I conclude that he was displeased with the continued practice of building Christian churches after the form of the ancient Basilica, and, therefore, sought to make his own sacred edifices approximate to the form of the antique temple. Hence arose certain discrepancies, which, as it seemed to me, are happily avoided in *Il Redentore*, but are rather obvious in the S. Giorgio. Volckmann says something about it, but does not hit the nail on the head.

The interior of *Il Redentore* is likewise admirable. Everything, including even the designs of the altars, is by Palladio. Unfortunately, the niches, which should have been filled with statues, are glaring with wooden figures, flat, carved, and painted.

October 3.

In honour of S. Francis, S. Peter's capuchins have splendidly adorned a side altar. There was nothing to be seen of stone but the Corinthian capitals; all the rest seemed to be covered with tasteful but splendid embroidery, in the arabesque style, and the effect was as pretty as could be desired. I particularly admired the broad tendrils and foliage, embroidered in gold. Going nearer, I discovered an ingenious deception. All that I had taken for gold was, in fact, straw pressed flat, and glued upon paper, according to some beautiful outlines, while the ground was painted with lively colours. This is done with such variety and tact, that the design, which was probably worked in the convent itself, with a material that was worth nothing, must have cost several thousand dollars, if the material had been genuine. It might on occasion be advantageously imitated.

On one of the quays, and in front of the water I have often remarked a little fellow telling stories in the Venetian dialect, to a greater or less concourse of auditors. Unfortunately I cannot understand a word, but I observe that no one laughs, though the audience, who are composed of the lowest class, occasionally smile. There is nothing striking or ridiculous in the man's appearance, but, on the contrary, something very sedate, with such admirable variety and precision in his gestures, that they evince art and reflection.

October 3.

With my plan in my hand I endeavored to find my way through the strangest labyrinth to the church of the *Mendicanti*. Here is the conservatorium, which stands in the highest repute at the present day. The ladies performed an oratorio behind the grating, the church was filled with hearers, the music was very beautiful, and the voices were magnificent. An alto sung the part of King Saul, the chief personage in the poem. Of such a voice I had no notion whatever; some passages of the music were excessively beautiful, and the words, which were Latin, most laughably Italianized in some places, were perfectly adapted for singing. Music here has a wide field.

Venice.

The performance would have been a source of great enjoyment, if the accursed *Maestro di Capella* had not beaten time with a roll of music against the grating, as conspicuously as if he had to do with school-boys, whom he was instructing. As the girls had repeated the piece often enough, his noise was quite unnecessary, and destroyed all impression, as much as he would, who, in order to make a beautiful statue intelligible to us, should stick scarlet patches on the joints. The foreign sound destroys all harmony. Now this man is a musician, and yet he seems not to be sensible of this; or, more properly speaking, he chooses to let his presence be known by an impropriety, when it would have been much better to allow his value to be perceived by the perfection of the execution. I know that this is the fault of the French, but I did not give the Italians credit for it, and yet the public seems accustomed to it. This is not the first time that that which spoils enjoyment, has been supposed to belong directly to it.

October 3.

Yesterday evening I went to the Opera at the S. Moses (for the theatres take their name from the church to which they lie nearest); nothing very delightful! In the plan, the music, and the singers, that energy was wanting, which alone can elevate opera to the highest point. One could not say of any part that it was bad, but the two female actresses alone took pains, not so much to act well, but to set themselves off and to please. That is something, after all. These two actresses have beautiful figures, and good voices, and are nice, lively, compact, little bodies. Among the men, on the other hand, there is no trace of national power, or even of pleasure, in working on the imaginations of their audience. Neither is there among them any voice of decided brilliancy.

The ballet, which was wretchedly conceived, was condemned as a whole, but some excellent dancers and *danseuses*, the latter of whom considered it their duty to make the spectators acquainted with all their person charms, were heartily applauded.

October 5.

To-day, however, I saw another comedy, which gave me more pleasure. In the ducal palace I heard the public discussion of a law case. It was important, and, happily for me, was brought forward in the holidays. One of the advocates had all the qualifications for an exaggerated *buffo*. His figure was short and fat, but supple; in profile his features were monstrously prominent. He had a stentorian voice, and a vehemence as if everything that he said came in earnest from the very bottom of his heart. I call this a comedy, because, probably, everything had been already prepared when the public exhibition took place. The judges knew what they had to say, and the parties what they had to expect. However, this plan pleases me infinitely more than our hobbling law affairs. I will endeavor to give some notion of the particulars, and of the neat, natural, and unostentatious manner in which everything takes place.

In a spacious hall of the palace the judges were sitting on one side, in a half circle. Opposite to them, in a tribune which could hold several persons, were the advocates for both parties; and upon a bench immediately in front of them, the plantiff, and defendant in person. The advocate for the plaintiff had descended from the tribune, since there was to be no controversy at this day's sitting. All the documents, on both sides, were to be read, although they were already printed.

A lean clerk, in a black scanty gown, and with a thick bundle in his hand, prepared to perform the office of a reader. The hall was completely crammed with persons who came to see and to hear. The point of law itself, and the persons whom it concerned, must have appeared highly important to the Venetians.

Trust-estates are so decidedly secured in Venice, that a property once stamped with this character, preserves it for ever, though it may have been divested ages ago by appropriations or other circumstances, and though it may have passed through ever so many hands. When the matter comes into dispute the descendants of the first family recover their right, and the property must be delivered up.

Venice.

On this occasion the discussion was highly important, for the action was brought against the doge himself, or rather against his wife, who veiled by her *zendal*, or little hood, sat only at a little distance from the plaintiff. She was a lady of a certain age, of noble stature, and with well-formed features, in which there was something of an earnest, not to say fretful character. The Venetians make it a great boast that the princess in her own palace, is obliged to appear before them and the tribunal.

When the clerk began to read, I for the first time clearly discerned the business of a little man who sat on a low stool behind a small table opposite the judges, and near the advocates. More especially I learned the use of an hour-glass, which was placed before him. As long as the clerk reads, time is not heeded, but the advocate is only allowed a certain time, if he speaks in the course of the reading. The clerk reads, and the hour-glass lies in a horizontal position, with the little man's hand upon it. As soon as the advocate opens his mouth, the glass is raised, and sinks again, as soon as he is silent. It is the great duty of the advocate to make remarks on what is read, to introduce cursory observations in order to excite and challenge attention. This puts the little Saturn in a state of the greatest perplexity. He is obliged every moment to change the horizontal and vertical position of the glass, and finds himself in the situation of the evil spirits in the puppet-show, who by the quickly varying "Berliche, Berloche" of the mischievous *Hanswurst*[4], are puzzled whether they are to come or to go.

Whoever has heard documents read over in a law-court, can imagine the reading on this occasion,—quick and monotonous, but plain and articulate enough. The ingenious advocate contrives to interrupt the tedium by jests, and the public shows its delight in his jokes by immoderate laughter. I must mention one, the most striking of those I could understand. The reader was just reciting the document, by which, one, who was considered to have been illegally possessed of it, had disposed of the property in question. The advocate bade him lead more slowly, and when he plainly uttered the words: "I give and bequeath," the orator flew violently at the clerk and cried: "What will you give? What will you bequeath? you poor starved-out devil, nothing in the world belongs to you?" "However,"—he continued, as he seemed to collect himself—"the illustrious owner was in the same predicament. He wished to give, he wished to bequeath that which belonged to him no more than to you." A burst of inextinguishable laughter followed this sally, but the hour-glass at once resumed its horizontal position. The reader went mumbling on, and made a saucy face at the advocate; but all these jokes are prepared beforehand.

[4] An allusion to the comic scene, in the puppet-play of Faust, from which Göethe took the subject of his poem. One of the two magic words (Berliche, Berloche) summons the devils, the other drives them away, and the Hanswurst (or buffoon), in a mock-incantation scene, perplexes the fiends, by uttering one word after the other, as rapidly as possible.—Trans.

Oct. 4.

I was yesterday at the play, in the theatre of S. Luke, and was highly pleased. I saw a piece acted *extempore* in masks, with a great deal of nature, energy, and vigour. The actors are not, indeed, all equal; the pantaloon is excellent, and one of the actresses, who is stout and well-built, speaks admirably, and deports herself cleverly, though she is no extraordinary actress. The subject of the piece is extravagant, and resembled that which is treated by us under the name of *Der Verschlag* (the partition). With inexhaustible variety it amused us for more than three hours. But even here the people is the base upon which everything rests, the spectators are themselves actors, and the multitude is melted into one whole with the stage. All day long the buyer and the seller, the beggar, the sailor, the female gossip, the advocate and his opponent, are living and acting in the square and on the bench, in the gondolas and in the palaces, and make it their business to talk and to asseverate, to cry and to offer for sale, to sing and to play, to curse and to brawl. In the evening they go into the theatre, and see and hear the life of the day artificially put together, prettily set off, interwoven with a story, removed from reality by the masks, and brought near to it by manners. In all this they take a childish delight and again shout and clap, and make a noise. From day to night,—nay, from midnight to midnight, it is always the same.

I have not often seen more natural acting than that by these masks. It is such acting as can only be sustained by a remarkably happy talent and long practice.

While I am writing this, they are making a tremendous noise on the canal under my window, though it is past midnight. Whether for good or for evil, they are always doing something.

October 4.

I have now heard public orators; viz., three fellows in the square and on the stone-bench, each telling tales after his fashion, two advocates, two preachers, and the actors, among whom I must especially commend the pantaloon. All these have something in common, both because they belong to one and the same nation, which, as it always lives in public, always adopts an impassioned manner of speaking, and because they imitate each other. There is besides a marked language of gesticulations, with which they accompany the expressions of their intentions, views, and feelings.

Venice.

This day was the festival of S. Francis, and I was in his church Alle Vigne. The loud voice of the capuchin was accompanied by the cries of the salesmen in front of the church, as by an antiphone. I stood at the church-door between the two, and the effect was singular enough.

Oct. 5.

This morning I was in the arsenal, which I found interesting enough, though I know nothing of maritime affairs, and visited the lower school there. It has an appearance like that of an old family, which still bustles about, although its best time of blossom and fruit has passed. By paying attention to the handicraftsmen, I have seen much that is remarkable, and have been on board an eighty-four gun ship, the hull of which is just completed.

Six months ago a thing of the sort was burned down to the water's edge, off the Riva dei Schiavoni. The powder-room was not very full, and when it blew up, it did no great damage. The windows of the neighbouring houses were destroyed.

I have seen worked the finest oak from Istria, and have made my observations in return upon this valuable tree. That knowledge of the natural things used by man as materials, and employed for his wants, which I have acquired with so much difficulty, has been incalculably serviceable in explaining to me the proceedings of artists and artisans. The knowledge of mountains and of the stone taken out of them has been to me a great advance in art.

Oct. 5.

To give a notion of the Bucentaur in one word, I should say that it is a state-galley. The older one, of which we still have drawings, justified this appellation still more than the present one, which, by its splendour makes us forget its original.

I am always returning to my old opinions. When a genuine subject is given to an artist, his productions will be something genuine also. Here the artist was commissioned to form a galley, worthy to carry the heads of the Republic, on the highest festivals in honour of its ancient rule on the sea; and the problem has been admirably solved. The vessel is all ornament; we ought to say, it is overladen with ornament; it is altogether one piece of gilt carving, for no other use, but that of a pageant to exhibit to the people its leaders in right noble style. We know well enough that a people, who likes to deck out its boats, is no less pleased to see their rulers bravely adorned. This state-galley is a good index to show what the Venetians were, and what they considered themselves.

Oct. 5. *Night.*

I came home laughing from a tragedy, and must at once make the jest secure upon paper. The piece was not bad, the author had brought together all the tragic *matadors,* and the actors played well. Most of the situations were well known, but some were new and highly felicitous. There are two fathers, who hate each other, sons and daughters of these severed families, who respectively are passionately in love with each other, and one couple is even privately married. Wild and cruel work goes on, and at last nothing remains to render the young people happy, but to make the two fathers kill each other, upon which the curtain falls amid the liveliest applause. Now the applause becomes more vehement, now "fuora" was called out, and this lasted until the two principal couples vouchsafed to crawl forward from behind the curtain, make their bow, and retire at the opposite side.

Venice.

The public was not yet satisfied, but went on clapping and crying: "i morti!" till the two dead men also come forward and made their bow, when some voices cried "bravi i morti!" The applause detained them for a long time, till at last they were allowed to depart. The effect is infinitely more droll to the eye-and-ear-witness, who, like me, has ringing in his ears the "bravo! bravi!" which the Italians have incessantly in their mouths, and then suddenly hears the dead also called forward with this word of honour.

We of the north can say "good night" at any hour, when we take leave after dark, but the Italian says: "Felicissima notte" only once, and that is when the candles are brought into a room. Day and night are thus divided, and something quite different is meant. So impossible is it to translate the idioms of any language! From the highest to the lowest word all has reference to the peculiarities of the natives, in character, opinions, or circumstances.

Oct. 6.

The tragedy yesterday taught me a great deal. In the first place, I have heard how the Italians treat and declaim their Eleven-syllable iambics, and in the next place, I have understood the tact of Gozzi in combining masks with his tragic personages. This is the proper sort of play for this people, which likes to be moved in a rough fashion. It has no tender, heart-felt sympathy for the unfortunate personage, but is only pleased when the hero speaks well. The Italians attach a great deal of importance to the speaking, and then they like to laugh, or to hear something silly.

Their interest in the drama is like that in a real event. When the tyrant gave his son a sword and required him to kill his own wife, who was standing opposite, the people began loudly to express their disapprobation of this demand, and there was a great risk that the piece would have been interrupted. They insisted that the old man should take his sword back, in which case all the subsequent situations in the drama would have been completely spoiled. At last, the distressed son plucked up courage, advanced to the proscenium, and humbly entreated that the audience would have patience for a moment, assuring them that all would turn out to their entire satisfaction. But even judging from an artistical point of view, this situation was, under the circumstances, silly and unnatural, and I commended the people for their feeling.

I can now better understand the long speeches and the frequent dissertations, *pro* and *con*, in the Greek tragedy. The Athenians liked still more to hear speaking, and were still better judges of it, than the Italians. They learned something from the courts of law, where they spent the whole day.

Oct. 6.

In those works of Palladio, which are completed, I have found much to blame, together with much that is highly valuable. While I was thinking it over in my mind how far I was right or wrong in setting my judgment in opposition to that of so extraordinary a man, I felt as if he stood by and said, "I did so and so against my will, but, nevertheless, I did it, because in this manner alone was it possible for me, under the given circumstances, to approximate to my highest idea." The more I think the matter over, it seems to me, that Palladio, while contemplating the height and width of an already existing church, or of an old house to which he was to attach facades, only considered: "How will you give the greatest form to these dimensions? Some part of the detail must from the necessity of the case, be put out of its place or spoiled, and something unseemly is sure to arise here and there. Be that as it may, the whole will have a grand style, and you will be pleased with your work."

And thus he carried out the great image which he had within his soul, just to the point where it was not quite suitable, and where he was obliged in the detail to mutilate or to overcrowd it.

On the other hand, the wing of the Carità cannot be too highly prized, for here the artist's hands were free, and he could follow the bent of his own mind without constraint. If the convent were finished there would, perhaps, be no work of architecture more perfect throughout the present world.

Venice.

How he thought and how he worked becomes more and more clear to me, the more I read his works, and reflect how he treated the ancients; for he says few words, but they are all important. The fourth book, which illustrates the antique temples, is a good introduction to a judicious examination of ancient remains.

Oct. 6.

Yesterday evening I saw the *Electra* of Crebillon—that is to say, a translation—at the theatre S. Crisostomo. I cannot say, how absurd the piece appeared to me, and how terribly it tired me out.

The actors are generally good, and know how to put off the public with single passages.

Orestes alone has three narratives, poetically set off, in one scene. Electra, a pretty little woman of the middle size and stature, with almost French vivacity, and with a good deportment, delivered the verses beautifully, only she acted the part madly from beginning to end, which, alas! it requires. However, I have again learned something. The Italian Iambic, which is invariably of eleven syllables, is very inconvenient for declamation, because the last syllable is always short, and causes an elevation of the voice against the will of the declaimer.

Oct. 6.

This morning I was present at high mass, which annually on this day the Doge must attend, in the church of St. Justina, to commemorate an old victory over the Turks. When the gilded barks, which carry the princes and a portion of the nobility approach the little square, when the boatmen, in their rare liveries, are plying their red-painted oars, when on the shore the clergy and the religious fraternities are standing, pushing, moving about, and waiting with their lighted torches fixed upon poles and portable silver chandeliers; then, when the gangways covered with carpet are placed from the vessels to the shore, and first the full violet dresses of the Savii, next the ample red robes of the Senators are unfolded upon the pavement, and lastly when the old Doge adorned with his golden Phrygian cap, in his long golden *talar* and his ermine cloak, steps out of the vessel—when all this, I say, takes place in a little square before the portal of a church, one feels as if one were looking at an old worked tapestry, exceedingly well designed and coloured. To me, northern fugitive as I am, this ceremony gave a great deal of pleasure. With us, who parade nothing but short coats in our processions of pomp, and who conceive nothing greater than one performed with shouldered arms, such an affair might be out of place. But these trains, these peaceful celebrations are all in keeping here.

The Doge is a well-grown and well-shaped man, who, perhaps, suffers from ill health, but, nevertheless, for dignity's sake, bears himself upright under his heavy robe. In other respects he looks like the grandpapa of the whole race, and is kind and affable. His dress is very becoming, the little cap, which he wears under the large one, does not offend the eye, resting as it does upon the whitest and finest hair in the world.

About fifty *nobili*, with long dark-red trains, were with him. For the most part they were handsome men, and there was not a single uncouth figure among them. Several of them were tall with large heads, so that the white curly wigs were very becoming to them. Their features are prominent; the flesh of their faces is soft and white, without looking flabby and disagreeable. On the contrary, there is an appearance of talent without exertion, repose, self-confidence, easiness of existence, and a certain joyousness-pervades the whole.

When all had taken their places in the church, and mass began, the fraternities entered by the chief door, and went out at the side door to the right, after they had received holy water in couples, and made their obeisance to the high altar, to the Doge, and the nobility.

Oct. 6.

This evening I bespoke the celebrated *song* of the mariners, who chaunt Tasso and Ariosto to melodies of their own. This must actually be ordered, as it is not to be beard as a thing, of course, but rather belongs to the half forgotten traditions of former times. I entered a gondola by moon-light, with one singer before and the other behind me. They sing their song taking up the verses alternately. The melody, which we know through Rousseau, is of a middle kind, between choral and recitative, maintaining throughout the same cadence, with out any fixed time. The modulation is also uniform, only varying with a sort of declamation both tone and measure, according to the subject of the verse. But the spirit—the life of it, is as follows:—

Without inquiring into the construction of the melody, suffice it to say that it is admirably suited to that easy class of people, who, always humming something or other to themselves, adapt such tunes to any little poem they know by heart.

Venice.

Sitting on the shore of an island, on the bank of a canal, or on the side of a boat, a gondolier will sing away with a loud penetrating voice—the multitude admire force above everything—anxious only to be heard as far as possible. Over the silent mirror it travels far. Another in the distance, who is acquainted with the melody and knows the words, takes it up and answers with the next verse, and then the first replies, so that the one is as it were the echo of the other. The song continues through whole nights and is kept up without fatigue. The further the singers are from each other, the more touching sounds the strain. The best place for the listener is halfway between the two.

In order to let me hear it, they landed on the bank of the Guidecca, and took up different positions by the canal. I walked backwards and forwards between them, so as to leave the one whose turn it was to sing, and to join the one who had just left off. Then it was that the effect of the strain first opened upon me. As a voice from the distance it sounds in the highest degree strange—as a lament without sadness: it has an incredible effect and is moving even to tears. I ascribed this to my own state of mind, but my old boatsman said: "è singolare, como quel canto intenerisce, e molto piu quando è piu ben cantato." He wished that I could hear the women of the Lido, especially those of Malamocco, and Pelestrina. These also, he told me, chanted Tasso and Ariosto to the same or similar melodies. He went on: "in the evening, while their husbands are on the sea fishing, they are accustomed to sit on the beach, and with shrill-penetrating voice to make these strains resound, until they catch from the distance the voices of their partners, and in this way they keep up a communication with them." Is not that beautiful? and yet, it is very possible that one who heard them close by, would take little pleasure in such tones which have to vie with the waves of the sea. Human, however, and true becomes the song in this way: thus is life given to the melody, on whose dead elements we should otherwise have been sadly puzzled. It is the song of one solitary, singing at a distance, in the hope that another of kindred feelings and sentiments may hear and answer.

Venice, Oct. 8, 1786.

I paid a visit to the palace Pisani Moretta, for the sake of a charming picture by *Paul Veronese.* The females of the family of Darius are represented kneeling before Alexander and Hephæstion; his mother, who is in the foreground, mistakes Hephæstion for the king;—turning away from her he points to Alexander. A strange story is told about this painting; the artist had been well received and for a long time honorably entertained in the palace; in return he secretly painted the picture and left it behind him as a present, rolled up under his bed. Certainly it well deserves to have had a singular origin, for it gives an idea of all the peculiar merits of this master.

The great art with which he manages by a skilful distribution of light and shade, and by an equally clever contrast of the local colors, to produce a most delightful harmony without throwing any sameness of tone over the whole picture, is here most strikingly visible. For the picture is in excellent preservation, and stands before us almost with the freshness of yesterday.—Indeed, whenever a painting of this order has suffered from neglect, our enjoyment of it is marred on the spot, even before we are conscious what the cause may be.

Whoever feels disposed to quarrel with the artist on the score of costume has only to say he ought to have painted a scene of the sixteenth century; and the matter is at an end. The gradation in the expression from the mother through the wife to the daughters, is in the highest degree true and happy. The youngest princess, who kneels behind all the rest, is a beautiful girl, and has a very pretty, but somewhat independent and haughty countenance. Her position does not at all seem to please her.

October 8, 1786.

My old gift of seeing the world with the eyes of that artist, whose pictures have most recently made an impression on me, has occasioned me some peculiar reflections. It is evident that the eye forms itself by the objects, which, from youth up, it is accustomed to look upon, and so the Venetian artist must see all things in a clearer and brighter light than other men. We, whose eye when out of doors, falls on a dingy soil, which, when not muddy, is dusty,—and which, always colourless, gives a sombre hue to the reflected rays, or at home spend our lives in close, narrow rooms, can never attain to such a cheerful view of nature.

Venice.

As I floated down the lagunes in the full sunshine, and observed how the figures of the gondoliers in their motley costume, and as they rowed, lightly moving above the sides of the gondola, stood out from the bright green surface and against the blue sky, I caught the best and freshest type possible of the Venetian school. The sunshine brought out the local colours with dazzling brilliancy, and the shades even were so luminous, that, comparatively, they in their turn might serve as lights. And the same may be said of the reflection from the sea-green water. All was painted "chiaro nell chiaro," so that foamy waves and lightning flashes were necessary to give it a grand finish (*um die Tüpfchen auf sie zu setzen*).

Titian and Paul have this brilliancy in the highest degree, and whenever we do not find it in any of their works, the piece is either damaged or has been touched up.

The cupola and vaulting of St. Mark's, with its side-walls,—are covered with paintings—a mass of richly colored figures on a golden ground; all in mosaic work: some of them very good, others but poor, according to the masters who furnished the cartoons.

Circumstances here have strangely impressed on my mind how everything depends on the first invention, and that this constitutes the right standard—the true genius—since with little square-pieces of glass (and here not in the soberest manner), it is possible to imitate the good as well as the bad. The art which furnished to the ancients their pavements, and to the Christians the vaulted ceilings of their churches, fritters itself away in our days on snuff-box lids and bracelets-clasps. The present times are worse even than one thinks.

Venice, October 8, 1786.

In the Farsetti palace there is a valuable collection of casts from the best antiques. I pass over all such as I had seen before at Mannheim or elsewhere, and mention only new acquaintances. A Cleopatra in intense repose, with the asp coiled round her arm, and sinking into the sleep of death;—a Niobe shrouding with her robe her youngest daughter from the arrows of Apollo;—some gladiators;—a winged genius, resting in his flight;—some philosophers, both in sitting and standing postures.

They are works from which, for thousands of years to come, the world may receive delight and instruction, without ever being able to equal with their thanks the merits of the artists.

Many speaking busts transported me to the old glorious times. Only I felt, alas, how backward I am in these studies; however, I will go on with them—at least I know the way. Palladio has opened the road for me to this and every other art and life. That sounds probably somewhat strange, and yet not so paradoxical as when Jacob Böhme says that, by seeing a pewter platter by a ray from Jupiter, he was enlightened as to the whole universe. There is also in this collection a fragment of the entablature of the temple of Antoninus and Faustina in Rome.

The bold front of this noble piece of architecture reminded me of the capitol of the Pantheon at Mannheim. It is, indeed, something very different from our queer saints, piled up one above the other on little consoles after the gothic style of decoration,—something different from our tobacco-pipe-like shafts,—our little steeple-crowned towers, and foliated terminals,—from all taste for these—I am now, thank God, set free for ever!

I will further mention a few works of statuary, which, as I passed along these last few days, I have observed with astonishment and instruction: before the gate of the arsenal two huge lions of white marble,-the one is half recumbent, raising himself up on his fore-feet,—the other is lying down: noble emblems of the variety of life. They are of such huge proportions, that all around appears little, and man himself would become as nought, did not sublime objects elevate him. They are of the best times of Greece, and were brought here from the Piraeus in the better days of the Republic.

Venice.

From Athens, too, in all probability, came two bas-reliefs which have been introduced in the church of St. Justina, the conqueress of the Turks. Unfortunately they are in some degree hidden by the church seats. The sacristan called my attention to them on account of the tradition that Titian, modelled from them the beautiful angel in his picture of the martyrdom of St. Peter. The relievos represent genii who are decking themselves out with, the attributes of the gods,—so beautiful in truth, as to transcend all idea or conception.

Next I contemplated with quite peculiar feelings the naked colossal statue of Marcus Agrippa, in the court of a palace; a dolphin which is twisting itself by his side, points out the naval hero. How does such a heroic representation make the mere man equal to the gods!

I took a close view of the horses of S. Mark's. Looking up at them from below, it is easy to see that they are spotted: in places they exhibit a beautiful yellow-metallic lustre, in others a coppery green has run over them. Viewing them more closely, one sees distinctly that once they were gilt all over, and long streaks are still to be seen over them, as the barbarians did not attempt to file off the gold, but tried to cut it off. That, too, is well: thus the shape at least has been preserved.

A glorious team of horses,—I should like to hear the opinion of a good judge of horse-flesh. What seemed strange to me was, that closely viewed, they appear heavy, while from the piazza below they look as light as deer.

October 8, 1786.

Yesterday I set out early with my tutelary genius for the "Lido," the tongue of land which shuts in the lagunes, and divides them from the sea. We landed and walked straight across the isthmus. I heard a loud hollow murmur,—it was the sea! I soon saw it: it crested high against the shore, as it retired,—it was about noon, and time of ebb. I have then at last seen the sea with my own eyes, and followed it on its beautiful bed, just as it quitted it. I wished the children had been there to gather the shells; child-like I myself picked up plenty of them; however, I attempted to make them useful; I tried to dry in them some of the fluid of the cuttle fish, which here dart away from you in shoals.

On the "Lido," not far from the sea, is the burial place of Englishmen, and a little further on, of the Jews: both alike are refused the privilege of resting in consecrated ground. I found here the tomb of Smith, the noble English consul, and of his first wife. It is to him that I owe my first copy of Palladio; I thanked him for it here in his unconsecrated grave. And not only unconsecrated, but half buried is the tomb. The "Lido" is at best but a sand-bank (*daune*): The sand is carried from it backwards and forwards by the wind, and thrown up in heaps is encroaching on every side. In a short time the monument, which is tolerably high, will no longer be visible.

But the sea—it is a grand *sight!* I will try and get a sail upon it some day in a fishing-boat: the gondolas never venture out so far.

Oct. 8, 1786.

On the sea-coast I found also several plants, whose characters similar to others I already knew, enabled me to recognize pretty well their properties. They are all alike, fat and strong-full of sap and clammy,—and it is evident that the old salt of the sandy soil, but still more the saline atmosphere, gives them these properties. Like aquatic plants they abound in sap, and are fleshy and tough, like mountainous ones; those whose leaves shew a tendency to put forth prickles, after the manner of thistles, have them extremely sharp and strong. I found a bush with leaves of this kind. It looked very much like our harmless coltsfoot, only here it is armed with sharp weapons,—the leaves like leather, as also are the seed-vessels, and the stalk very thick and succulent. I bring with me seeds and specimens of the leaves. (*Eryngium maritimum.*)

The fish-market, with its numberless marine productions, afforded me much amusement. I often go there to contemplate the poor captive inhabitants of the sea.

Venice, Oct. 9, 1786.

A delicious day from morning to night! I have been towards Chiozza, as far as Pelestrina, where are the great structures, called *Murazzi*, which the Republic has caused to be raised against the sea. They are of hewn stone, and properly are intended to protect from the fury of the wild element the tongue of land called the Lido, which separates the lagoons from the sea.

> Venice.

The lagunes are the work of old nature. First of all, the land and tide, the ebb and flow, working against one another, and then the gradual sinking of the primal waters, were, together, the causes why, at the upper end of the Adriatic, we find a pretty extensive range of marshes, which, covered by the flood-tide, are partly left bare by the ebb. Art took possession of the highest spots, and thus arose Venice, formed out of a groupe of a hundred isles, and surrounded by hundreds more. Moreover, at an incredible expense of money and labour, deep canals have been dug through the marshes, in order that at the time of high water, ships of war might pass to the chief points. What human industry and wit contrived and executed of old, skill and industry must now keep up. The Lido, a long narrow strip of land, separates the lagunes from the sea, which can enter only at two points—at the castle and at the opposite end near Chiozza. The tide flows in usually twice a-day, and with the ebb again carries out the waters twice, and always by the same channel and in the same direction. The flood covers the lower parts of the morass, but leaves the higher, if not dry, yet visible.

The case would be quite altered were the sea to make new ways for itself, to attack the tongue of land and flow in and out wherever it chose. Not to mention that the little villages on the Lido, Pelestrina, viz., S. Peter's and others would be overwhelmed, the canals of communication would be choked up, and while the water involved all in ruin, the Lido would be changed into an island, and the islands which now lie behind it be converted into necks and tongues of land. To guard against this it was necessary to protect the Lido as far as possible, lest the furious element should capriciously attack and overthrow what man had already taken possession of, and with a certain end and purpose given shape and use to.

In extraordinary cases when the sea rises above measure, it is especially necessary to prevent it entering at more than two points. Accordingly the rest of the sluice-gates being shut, with all its violence it is unable to enter, and in a few hours submits to the law of the ebb, and its fury lessens.

Otherwise Venice has nothing to fear; the extreme slowness with which the sea-line retires, assures to her thousands of years yet, and by prudently deepening the canals from time to time, they will easily maintain their possessions against the inroads of the water.

I could only wish that they kept their streets a little cleaner—a duty which is as necessary as it is easy of performance, and which in fact becomes of great consequence in the course of centuries. Even now in the principal thoroughfares it is forbidden to throw anything into the canals: the sweepings even of the streets may not be cast into them. No measures, however, are taken to prevent the rain, which here falls in sudden and violent torrents, from carrying off the dirt which is collected in piles at the corner of every street, and washing it into the lagunes—nay, what is still worse, into the gutters for carrying off the water, which consequently are often so completely stopped up, that the principal squares are in danger of being under water. Even in the smaller piazza of S. Mark's, I have seen the gullies which are well laid down there, as well as in the greater square, choked up and full of water.

When a rainy day comes, the filth is intolerable; every one is cursing and scolding. In ascending and descending the bridges one soils one's mantle and great coat (*Tabarro*), which is here worn all the year long, and as one goes along in shoes and silk stockings, one gets splashed, and then scolds, for it is not common mud, but mud that adheres and stains that one is here splashed with. The weather soon becomes fine again, and then no one thinks of cleaning the streets. How true is the saying: the public is ever complaining that is ill served, and never knows how to set about getting better served. Here if the sovereign-people wished it, it might be done forthwith.

Venice, Oct. 9, 1786.

Yesterday evening I ascended the tower of S. Mark's: as I had lately seen from its top the lagunes in their glory at flood time, I wished also to see them at low water; for in order to have a correct idea of the place, it is necessary to take in both views. It looks rather strange to see land all around one, where a little before the eye fell upon a mirror of waters. The islands are no longer islands—merely higher and house-crowned spots in one large morass of a gray-greenish colour, and intersected by beautiful canals. The marshy parts are overgrown with aquatic plants, a circumstance which must tend in time to raise their level, although the ebb and flow are continually shaking and tossing them and leave no rest to the vegetation.

I now turn with my narrative once more to the sea.—I there saw yesterday the haunts of the sea-snails, the limpets, and the crab, and was highly delighted with the sight. What a precious glorious object is a living thing!— how wonderfully adapted to its state of existence, how true, how *real* (*seyend*). What great advantages do I not derive now from my former studies of nature, and how delighted am I with the opportunity of continuing them! But as the present is a matter that admits of being communicated to my friends, I will not seek to excite their sympathy merely by exclamations.

The stone-works which have been built against the inroads of the sea consist first of all of several steep steps; then comes a slightly inclined plane, then again they rise a step, which is once more succeeded by a gently ascending surface, and last of all comes a perpendicular wall with an overhanging coping—over these steps—over these planes the raging sea rises until in extraordinary cases it even dashes over the highest wall with its projecting head.

The sea is followed by its inhabitants;—little periwinkles good to eat, monovalve limpets, and whatever else has the power of motion, especially by the pungar-crabs. But scarcely have these little creatures taken possession of the smooth walls, ere the sea retires again, swelling and cresting as it came. At first the crowd knows not where they are, and keep hoping that the briny flood will soon return to them—but it still keeps away; the sun comes out and quickly dries them up, and now begins the retreat. It is on these occasions that the pungars seek their prey. Nothing more wonderful or comical can be seen than the manœuvres of these little creatures, with their round bodies and two long claws (for the other spider-feet are scarcely worth noticing). On these stilted fore-legs, as it were, they stride along watching the limpets, and as soon as one moves itself under its shell on the rock, a pungar comes up and inserting the point of his claw in the tiny interstice between the shell and the rock turns it over, and so manages to swallow the oyster. The limpets, on the other hand, proceed cautiously on their way, and by suction fasten themselves firmly to the rocky surface as soon as they are aware of the proximity of their foe. In such cases the pungar deports himself amusingly enough; round and round the pulpy animal who keeps himself safe beneath his roof will he go with singular politeness; but not succeeding with all his coaxing and being unable to overcome its powerful muscle, he leaves in despair this intended victim, and hastens after another who may be wandering less cautiously on his way.

I never saw a crab succeed in his designs, although I have watched for hours the retreat of the little troop as they crawled down the two planes and the intermediate steps.

Venice, Oct. 10, 1786.

At last I am able to say that I have seen a comedy; Yesterday at the theatre of St. Luke, was performed "*Le Baruffe-Chiozotte*," which I should interpret the Frays and Feuds of Chiozza. The "*dramatis personæ*," are principally seafaring people, inhabitants of Chiozza, with their wives, sisters, and daughters. The usual noisy demonstrations of such sort of people in their good or ill luck—their dealings one with another, their vehemence, but goodness of heart, common-place remarks and unaffected manners, their naïve wit and humour—all this was excellently imitated. The piece, moreover, is Goldoni's, and as I had been only the day before in the place itself, and as the tones and manners of the sailors and people of the sea-port still echoed in my ears and floated before my eyes, it delighted me very much, and although I did not understand a single allusion, I was, nevertheless, on the whole, able to follow it pretty well. I will now give you the plan of the piece:—it opens with the females of Chiozza sitting, as usual, on the strand before their cabins, spinning, mending nets, sewing, or making lace; a youth passes by and notices one of them with a more friendly greeting than the rest. Immediately the joking begins—and observes no bounds; becoming tarter and tarter, and growing ill-tempered it soon bursts out into reproaches; abuse vies with abuse; in the midst of all one dame more vehement than the rest, bounces out with the truth; and now an endless din of scolding, railing, and screaming; there is no lack of more decided outrage, and at last the peace-officers are compelled to interfere.

Venice

The second act opens with the Court of Justice. In the absence of the *Podestà* (who as a noble could not lawfully be brought upon the stage) the *Actuarius* presides. He orders the women to be brought before him one by one. This gives rise to an interesting scene. It happens that this official personage is himself enamoured of the first of the combatants who is brought before him. Only too happy to have an opportunity of speaking with her alone, instead of hearing what she has to say on the matter in question, he makes her a declaration of love. In the midst of it a second woman, who is herself in love with the actuary, in a fit of jealousy rushes in, and with her the suspicious lover of the first damsel—who is followed by all the rest, and now the same demon of confusion riots in the court as a little before, had set at loggerheads the people of the harbour. In the third act the fun gets more and more boisterous, and the whole ends with a hasty and poor denouement. The happiest thought, however, of the whole piece, is a character who is thus drawn,—an old sailor who from the hardships he has been exposed to from his childhood, trembles and falters in all his limbs, and even in his very organs of speech, is brought on the scene to serve as a foil to this restless, screaming, and jabbering crew. Before he can utter a word, he has to make a long preparation by a slow twitching of his lips, and an assistant motion of his hands and arms; at last he blurts out what his thoughts are on the matter in dispute. But as he can only manage to do this in very short sentences, he acquires thereby a sort of laconic gravity, so that all he utters sounds like an adage or maxim; and in this way a happy contrast is afforded to the wild and passionate exclamations of the other personages.

But even as it was, I never witnessed anything like the noisy delight the people evinced at seeing themselves and their mates represented with such truth of nature. It was one continued laugh and tumultuous shout of exultation from beginning to end. I must, however, confess that the piece was extremely well acted by the players. According to the cast of their several parts, they had adopted among them the different tones of voice which usually prevail among the inhabitants of the place. The first actress was the universal favorite, more so even than she had recently been in an heroic dress and a scene of passion. The female players generally, but especially this one, in the most pleasing manner possible imitated the twang, the manners, and other peculiarities of the people they represented. Great praise is due to the author, who out of nothing has here created the most amusing *divertissement*. However, he never could have done it with any other people than his own merry and lighthearted countrymen. The farce is written throughout with a practised hand.

Of Sacchi's company, for whom Gozzi wrote (but which by-the-by is now broken up), I saw *Smeraldina*, a short plump figure, full of life, tact, and good humour. With her I saw *Brighella*—a slight well-made man and an excellent actor, especially in pantomime. These masks which we scarcely know except in the form of mummings, and which to our minds possess neither life nor meaning, succeed here only too well as the creation of the national taste. Here the most distinguished characters, persons of every age and condition, think nothing of dressing themselves out in the strangest costumes, and as for the greater part of the year they are accustomed to wander about in masks, they feel no surprise at seeing the black visors on the stage also.

Venice, October 11, 1786.

Since solitude, in the midst of a great crowd of human beings, is after all not possible, I have taken up with an old Frenchman, who knows nothing of Italian, and suspects that he is cheated on all hands and taken advantage of, and who, with plenty of letters of recommendation, nevertheless, does not make his way with the good people here. A man of rank, and living in good style, but one whose mind cannot go beyond himself and his own immediate circle—he is perhaps full fifty, and has at home a boy seven years old, of whom he is always anxious to get news. He is travelling through Italy for pleasure, but rapidly—in order to be able to say that he has seen it, but is willing to learn whatever is possible as he hurries along. I have shewn him some civilities, and have given him information about many matters. While I was speaking to him about Venice, he asked me how long I had been here, and when he heard that this was my first visit, and that I had only been here fourteen days, he replied: "*Il paraît que vous n'avez pas perdu votre temps.*" This is the first "testimonium" of my good behaviour that I can furnish you. This is the eighth day since he arrived here, and he leaves us to-morrow. It was highly delicious to me, to meet in a strange land with such a regular Versailles'-man. He is now about to quit me! It caused me some surprise to think that any one could ever travel in this temper without a thought for anything beyond himself, and yet he is in his way a polished, sensible, and well conducted person.

Venice, Oct. 12, 1786.

Venice.

Yesterday at S. Luke's a new piece was acted:—*L'Inglicismo in Italia* (the English in Italy). As there are many Englishmen living in Italy, it is not unnatural that their ways and habits should excite notice, and I expected to learn from this piece what the Italians thought of their rich and welcome visitors. But it was a total failure. There were, of course, (as is always the case here,) some clever scenes between buffoons, but the rest was cast altogether in too grave and heavy a mould, and yet nob a trace of the English good sense: plenty of the ordinary Italian commonplaces of morality, and those, too, upon the very commonest of topics.

And it did not take: indeed, it was on the very point of being hissed off the stage. The actors felt themselves out of their element—not on the strand of Chiozza. As this was the last piece that I saw here, my enthusiasm for these national representations did not seem likely to be increased by this piece of folly.

As I have at last gone through my journal and entered some occasional remarks from my tablets, my proceedings are now enrolled and left to the sentence of my friends. There is, I am conscious, very much in these leaves which I might qualify, enlarge upon, and improve. Let, however, what is written, stand as the memorial of first impressions, which, if not always correct, will nevertheless be ever dear and precious to me. Oh that I could but transmit to my friends a breath merely of this light existence! Verily to the Italian, "ultramontane" is a very vague idea; and to me even—"beyond the Alps," rises very obscurely before my mind, although from out of their mists friendly forms are beckoning to me. It is the climate only that seduces me to prefer awhile these lands to those; for birth and habit forge strong fetters. Here, however, I could not live, nor indeed in any place where I had nothing to occupy my mind; but at present novelty furnishes me here with endless occupation. Architecture rises, like an ancient spirit from the tombs, and bids me study its laws just as people do the rules of a dead language, not in order to practise or to take a living joy in them, but only in order to enable myself in the quiet depths of my own mind to do honor to her existence in bygone ages, and her for ever departed glory. As Palladio everywhere refers one to Vitruvius, I have bought an edition of the latter by Galiani; but this folio suffers in my portmanteau as much as my brain does in the study of it. Palladio by his words and works, by his method and way, both of thinking and of executing, has brought Vitruvius home to me and interpreted him far better than the Italian translator ever can. Vitruvius himself is no easy reading; his book is obscurely written, and requires a critical study. Notwithstanding I have read it through cursorily, and it has left on my mind many a glorious impression. To express my meaning better: I read it like a breviary: more out of devotion, than for instruction. Already the days begin to draw in and allow more time for reading and writing.

God be praised! whatever from my youth up appeared to me of worth, is beginning once more to be dear to me. How happy do I feel that I can again venture to approach the ancient authors. For now, I may dare tell it— and confess at once my disease and my folly. For many a long year I could not bear to look at a Latin author, or to cast my eye upon anything that might serve to awaken in my mind the thoughts of Italy. If by accident I did so, I suffered the most horrible tortures of mind. It was a frequent joke of Herder's at my expense, that I had learned all my Latin from Spinoza, for he had noticed that this was the only Latin work I ever read; but he was not aware how carefully I was obliged to keep myself from the ancients— how even these abstruse generalities were but cursorily read by me, and even then not without pain. At last matters came to that pitch that even the perusal of Wieland's translation of the Satires made me utterly wretched;

scarcely had I read two of them, before I was compelled to lay the book aside.

Venice.

Had I not made the resolve, which I am now carrying into effect, I should have been altogether lost—to such a degree of intensity had the desire grown to see these objects with my own eyes. Historical acquaintance with them did me no good;—the things stood only a hand's-breadth away from me; but still they were separated from me by an impenetrable wall. And, in fact, at the present moment, I somehow feel as if this were not the first time that I had seen these things, but as if I were paying a second visit to them. Although I have been but a short time in Venice, I have adapted myself pretty well to the ways of the place, and feel confident that I shall carry away with me, though a very incomplete, yet, nevertheless, clear and true idea of it.

Venice, Oct. 14, 1786. *2 o'clock, morning.*

In the last moments of my stay here: for I am to start almost immediately with the packet-boat for Ferrara. I quit Venice without reluctance; for to stay here longer with any satisfaction and profit to myself, I must take other steps which would carry me beyond my present plan. Besides everybody is now leaving this city and making for the beautiful gardens and seats on the Terra-Firma; I, however, go away well-loaded, and shall carry along with me its rich, rare, and unique image.

FROM FERRARA TO ROME.

Oct. 16, 1786.
Early and on board the packet.

My travelling companions, male and female alike, are all still fast asleep in their berths. For my part I have passed the two nights on deck, wrapped up in my cloak. It was only towards morning that I felt it at all cold. I am now actually in latitude forty-five, and yet go on repeating my old song: I would gladly leave all to the inhabitants of the land, if only, after the fashion of Dido, I could enclose enough of the heavens to surround our dwellings with. It would then be quite another state of existence. The voyage in this glorious weather has been most delightful, the views and prospects simple but agreeable. The Po, with its fertilizing stream, flows here through wide plains; nothing, however, is to be seen but its banks covered with trees or bushes;—you catch no distant view. On this river, as on the Adige, are silly water-works, which are as rude and ill-constructed as those on the Saal.

Ferrara, Oct. 16, 1786.
At night.

Although I only arrived here early this morning (by 7 o'clock, German time), I am thinking of setting off again to-morrow morning. For the first time since I left home, a feeling of dissatisfaction has fallen upon me in this great and beautiful, but flat and depopulated city. These streets, now so desolate, were, however, once kept in animation by a brilliant court. Here dwelt Ariosto discontented, and Tasso unhappy, and so, we fancy, we gain edification by visiting such scenes. Ariosto's monument contains much marble—ill arranged; for Tasso's prison, they shew you a wood-house or coalhouse where, most assuredly, he never was kept. Moreover, the people pretend to know scarcely anything you may ask about. But at last for "something to drink" they manage to remember. All this brings to my mind Luther's ink-spots, which the housekeeper freshens up from time to time. Most travellers, however, are little better than our "*Handwerksburschen*" or stolling journeymen, and content themselves with such palpable signs. For my part I became quite sulky, and took little interest even in a beautiful institute and academy, which a cardinal, a native of Ferrara, founded and endowed; however, some ancient monuments, in the Ducal Palace, served to revive me a little; and I was put in perfect good humor by a beautiful conception of a painter, John the Baptist before Herod and Herodias. The prophet, in his well-known dress of the wilderness, is pointing indignantly at Herodias. Quite unmoved, she looks at the prince, who is sitting by her side, while the latter regards the prophet with a calm but cunning look; a white middle-sized greyhound stands before the king, while from beneath the robe of Herodias, a small Italian one is peeping—both giving tongue at the prophet. To my mind, this is a most happy thought.

Cento, Oct. 17, 1786.

> Ferrara-Cento

In a better temper than yesterday, I write you to-day from Guercino's native city. It, however, is quite a different place: an hospitable well-built little town, of nearly 5000 inhabitants, flourishing, full of life, cleanly, and situated in a well cultivated plain, which stretches farther than the eye can reach. According to my usual custom, I ascended the tower. A sea of poplars, between which, and near at hand, one caught glimpses of little country-houses, each surrounded by its fields. A rich soil and a beautiful climate. It was an autumn evening, such as we seldom have to thank even summer for. The sky, which had been veiled all day, has cleared up, the clouds rolling off north and south towards the mountains, and I hope for a bright day to-morrow.

Here I first saw the Apennines, which I am approaching. The winter in this region lasts only through December and January: April is rainy—for the rest of the year beautiful weather, according to the nature of the season. Incessant rain is unknown. September here, to tell you the truth, was finer and warmer than August with you. The Apennines in the south have received a warm greeting from me, for I have now had enough of the plain. To-morrow I shall be writing at the foot of them.

Guercino loved his native town: indeed, the Italians almost universally cherish and maintain this sort of local patriotism, and it is to this beautiful feeling that Italy owes so many of its valuable institutions and its multitude of local sanctuaries. Under the management of this master, an academy of painting was formed here. He left behind him many paintings, which his townsmen are still very proud of, and which, indeed, fully justify their pride.

Guercino is here a sacred name, and that, too, in the mouths of children as well as of the old.

Most charmed was I with his picture, representing the risen Lord, appearing to his mother. Kneeling before Him, she looks upon Him with indescribable affection. Her left hand is touching His body just under the accursed wound which mars the whole picture. His hand lies upon her neck; and in order the better to gaze upon her, his body is slightly bent back. This gives to His figure a somewhat strange, not to say forced appearance. And yet for all that it is infinitely beautiful. The calm and sad look, with which He contemplates her, is unique and seems to convey the impression that before His noble soul there still floats a remembrance of His own sufferings and of hers, which the resurrection had not at once dispelled.

Strange has engraved the picture. I wish that my friends could see even his copy of it.

After it a Madonna won my admiration. The child wants the breast; she modestly shrinks from exposing her bosom. Natural, noble, exquisite, and beautiful.

Further, a Mary, who is guiding the arm of the infant Christ, standing before her with His face towards the people, in order that with uplifted fingers He may bestow His blessings upon them. Judged by the spirit of the Roman Catholic legends, this must be pronounced a very happy idea. It has been often repeated.

Guercino is an intrinsically bold, masculine, sensible painter, without roughness. On the contrary, his pieces possess a certain tender moral grace, a reposeful freedom and grandeur, but with all that, a certain mannerism, so that when the eye once has grown accustomed to it, it is impossible to mistake a piece of his hand. The lightness, cleanness, and finish of his touch are perfectly astonishing. For his draperies he is particularly fond of a beautiful brownish-red blend of colours. These harmonize very well with the blue which he loves to combine with them.

Bologna.

The subjects of the other paintings are more or less unhappily chosen. The good artist has strained all his powers, but his invention and execution alike are thrown away and wasted. However, I derived both entertainment and profit from the view of this cycle of art, although such a hasty and rapid glance as I could alone bestow upon them, affords but little, either of gratification or instruction.

Bologna, Oct. 18, 1786.
Night.

Yesterday I started very early—before daybreak—from Cento, and arrived here in pretty good time. A brisk and well-educated cicerone having learned that I did not intend to make a long stay here, hurried me through all the streets, and into so many palaces and churches that I had scarcely time to set down in my note-book the names of them, and I hardly know if hereafter, when I shall look again at these scrawls, I shall be able to call to mind all the particulars. I will now mention, however, a couple or so of objects which stand out bright and clear enough as they afforded me a real gratification at the time.

First of all the Cecilia of Raphael! It was exactly what I had been told of it; but now I saw it with my own eyes. He has invariably accomplished that which others wished in vain to accomplish, and I would at present say no more of it than that it is by him. Five saints, side by side, not one of them has anything in common with us; however their existence, stands so perfectly real that one would wish for the picture to last through eternity, even though for himself he could be content to be annihilated. But in order to understand Raphael aright, and to form a just appreciation of him, and not to praise him as a god or as Melchisedec "without descent" or pedigree, it is necessary to study his masters and his predecessors. These, too, had a standing on the firm soil of truth; diligently, not to say anxiously, they had laid the foundation, and vied with each other in raising, step by step, the pyramid aloft, until, at last, profiting by all their labors, and enlightened by a heavenly genius, Raphael set the last stone on the summit, above which, or even at which, no one else can ever stand.

Our interest in the history of art becomes peculiarly lively when we consider the works of the old masters. *Francesco Francia* is a very respectable artist. Pietro Perugino, so bold a man that one might almost call him a noble German fellow. Oh that fate had carried Albert Dürer further into Italy. In Munich I saw a couple of pieces by him of incredible grandeur. The poor man, how did he mistake his own worth in Venice, and make an agreement with the priests, on which he lost weeks and months! See him in his journey through the Netherlands exchanging his noble works of art for parrots, and in order to save his "douceur," drawing the portraits of the domestics, who bring him—a plate of fruit. To me the history of such a poor fool of an artist is infinitely touching.

Towards evening I got out of this ancient, venerable, and learned city, and extricated myself from its crowds, who, protected from the sun and weather by the arched bowers which are to be seen in almost every street, walk about, gape about, or buy, and sell, and transact whatever business they may have. I ascended the tower and enjoyed the pure air. The view is glorious! To the north we see the hills of Padua; beyond them the Swiss, Tyrolese, and Friulian Alps; in short, the whole northern chain, which, at the time, was enveloped in mist. Westward there stretched a boundless horizon, above which the towers of Modena alone stood out. Towards the east a similar plain reaching to the shores of the Adriatic, whose waters might be discerned in the setting sun. Towards the south, the first hills of the Apennines, which, like the Vicentine Hills, are planted up to their summits, or covered with churches, palaces, and summer-houses. The sky was perfectly clear, not a cloud to be seen, only on the horizon a kind of haze. The keeper of the tower assured me that for six years this mist had never left the distance. Otherwise, by the help of a telescope, you might easily discern the hills of Vicenza, with their houses and chapels, but now very rarely, even on the brightest days. And this mist lay chiefly on the Northern Chain, and makes our beloved Fatherland a regular Cimmeria. In proof of the salubrity of the situation and pure atmosphere of the city, he called my notice to the fact, that the roofs of the houses looked quite fresh, and that not a single tile was attacked by damp or moss. It must be confessed that the tiles look quite clean, and beautiful enough, but the good quality of the brick-earth may have something to do with this; at least we know that, in ancient times, excellent tiles were made in these parts.

Bologna.

The leaning tower has a frightful look, and yet it is most probable that it was built so by design. The following seems to me the explanation of this absurdity. In the disturbed times of the city every large edifice was a fortress, and every powerful family had its tower. By and bye the possession of such a building became a mark of splendour and distinction, and as, at last, a perpendicular tower was a common and every-day tiling, an oblique one was built. Both architect and owner have obtained their object; the multitude of slender, upright towers are just looked at, and all hurry to see the leaning one. Afterwards I ascended it. The bricks are all arranged horizontally. With clamps and good cement one may build any mad whim.

Bologna, Oct. 19, 1786.

I have spent this day to the best advantage I could in visiting and revisiting; but it is with art as with the world: the more we study it the larger we find it. In this heaven new stars are constantly appearing which I cannot count, and which sadly puzzle me; the Carracci, a Guido, a Domenichino, who shone forth in a later and happier period of art, but truly to enjoy whom requires both knowledge and judgment which I do not possess, and which cannot be acquired in a hurry. A great obstacle to our taking a pure delight in their pictures, and to an immediate understanding of their merits, is the absurd subjects of most of them. To admire or to be charmed with them one must be a madman.

It is as though the sons of God had wedded with the daughters of men, and out of such an union many a monster had sprung into existence. No sooner are you attracted by the *gusto* of a Guido and his pencil, by which nothing but the most excellent objects the eye sees are worthy to be painted, but you, at once, withdraw your eyes from a subject so abominably stupid that the world has no term of contempt sufficient to express its meanness; and so it is throughout. It is ever anatomy—an execution—a flaying scene-always some suffering, never an action of the hero-never an interest in the scene before you-always something for the fancy—some excitement accruing from without. Nothing but deeds of horror or convulsive sufferings, malefactors or fanatics, along side of whom the artist, in order to save his art, invariably slips in a naked boy or a pretty damsel as a spectator, in every case treating his spiritual heroes as little better than lay-figures (*gliedermanner*), on which to hang some beautiful mantle with its folds. In all there is nothing that suggests a human notion! Scarcely one subject in ten that ever ought to have been painted, and that one the painter has chosen to view from any but the right point of view.

Guido's great picture in the Church of the Mendicants is all that painting can do, but, at the same time, all that absurdity could task an artist with. It is a votive piece. I can well believe that the whole consistory praised it, and also devised it. The two angels, who were fit to console a Psyche in her misery, must here ....

The S. Proclus is a beautiful figure, but the others—bishops and popes! Below are heavenly children playing with attributes. The painter, who had no choice left him, laboured to help himself as best he could. He exerted himself merely to show that he was not the barbarian. Two naked figures by Guido; a St. John in the Wilderness; a Sebastian, how exquisitely painted, and what do they say? the one is gaping and the other wriggling.

Were I to contemplate history in my present ill humor, I should say, Faith revived art, but Superstition immediately made itself master of it, and ground it to the dust.

After dinner, seeming somewhat of a milder temper and less arrogantly disposed than in the morning, I entered the following remarks in my note-book. In the palace of the Tanari there is a famous picture by Guido, the Virgin suckling the infant Saviour—of a size rather larger than life—the head as if a god had painted it,—indescribable is the expression with which she gazes upon the sucking infant. To me it seems a calm, profound resignation, as if she were nourishing not the child of her joy and love, but a supposititious, heavenly changeling; and goes on suckling it because now she cannot do otherwise, although, in deep humility, she wonders how she ever came to do it. The rest of the canvass is filled up with a mass of drapery which connoisseurs highly prize. For my part I know not what to make of it. The colours, too, are somewhat dim; the room and the day were none of the brightest.

Notwithstanding the confusion in which I find myself I yet feel that experience, knowledge, and taste, already come to my aid in these mazes. Thus I was greatly won by a "Circumcision" by Guercino, for I have begun to know and to understand the man. I can now pardon the intolerable subject and delight in the masterly execution. Let him paint whatever can be thought of, everything will be praiseworthy and as highly finished as if it were enamel.

Bologna.

And thus it happened with me as with Balaam the over-ruled prophet, who blessed where he thought to curse; and I fear this would be the case still oftener were I to stay here much longer.

And then, again, if one happens to meet with a picture after Raphael, or what may with at least some probability be ascribed to him, one is soon perfectly cured and in good temper again. I fell in yesterday with a S. Agatha, a rare picture, though not throughout in good keeping. The artist has given to her the mien of a young maiden full of health and self-possession, but yet without rusticity or coldness. I have stamped on my mind both her form and look, and shall mentally read before her my "Iphigenia," and shall not allow my heroine to express a sentiment which the saint herself might not give utterance to.

And now when I think again of this sweet burden which I carry with me throughout my wanderings, I cannot conceal the fact that, besides the great objects of nature and art, which I have yet to work my way through, a wonderful train of poetical images keeps rising before me and unsettling me. From Cento to this place I have been wishing to continue my labors on the Iphigenia, but what has happened? inspiration has brought before my mind the plan of an "Iphigenia at Delphi," and I must work it out. I will here set down the argument as briefly as possible.

Electra, confidently hoping that Orestes will bring to Delphi the image of the Taurian Diana, makes her appearance in the Temple of Apollo, and as a final sin-offering dedicates to the god, the axe which has perpetrated so many horrors in the house of Pelops. Unhappily she is, at this moment, joined by a Greek, who recounts to her how, having accompanied Pylades and Orestes to Tauris, he there saw the two friends led to execution, but had himself luckily made his escape. At this news the passionate Electra is unable to restrain herself, and knows not whether to vent her rage against the gods or against men.

In the mean time Iphigenia, Orestes, and Pylades have arrived at Delphi. The heavenly calmness of Iphigenia contrasts remarkably with the earthly vehemence of Electra, as the two sisters meet without knowing each other. The fugitive Greek gains sight of Iphigenia, and recognizing in her the priestess, who was to have sacrificed the two friends, makes it known to Electra. The latter snatching the axe from the altar, is on the point of killing Iphigenia, when a happy incident averts this last fearful calamity from the two sisters. This situation, if only I can succeed in working it out well, will probably furnish a scene unequalled for grandeur or pathos by any that has yet been produced on the stage. But where is man to get time and hands for such a work, even if the spirit be willing.

As I feel myself at present somewhat oppressed with such a flood of thoughts of the good and desirable, I cannot help reminding my friends of a dream which I had about a year ago, and which appeared to me to be highly significant. I dreamt forsooth, that I had been sailing about in a little boat and had landed on a fertile and richly cultivated island, of which I had a consciousness that it bred the most beautiful pheasants in the world. I bargained, I thought, with the people of the island for some of these birds, and they killed and brought them to me in great numbers. They were pheasants indeed, but as in dreams all things are generally changed and modified, they seemed to have long, richly coloured tails, like the loveliest birds of Paradise, and with eyes like those of the peacock. Bringing them to me by scores, they arranged them in the boat so skilfully with the heads inwards, the long variegated feathers of the tail hanging outwards, as to form in the bright sunshine the most glorious pile conceivable, and so large as scarcely to leave room enough in the bow and the stern for the rower and the steersman. As with this load the boat made its way through the tranquil waters, I named to myself the friends among whom I should like to distribute those variegated treasures. At last, arriving in a spacious harbour, I was almost lost among great and many masted vessels, as I mounted deck after deck in order to discover a place where I might safely run my little boat ashore.

Such dreamy visions have a charm, inasmuch, as springing from our mental state, they possess more or less of analogy with the rest of our lives and fortunes.

But now I have also been to the famed scientific building, called the Institution or "Gli Studj." The edifice is large, and the inner court especially has a very imposing appearance, although not of the best style of architecture. In the staircases and corridors there was no want of stuccoes and frescoes: they are all appropriate and suitable, and the numerous objects of beauty, which, well worth seeing, are here collected together, justly command our admiration. For all that, however, a German, accustomed to a more liberal course of study than is here pursued, will not be altogether content with it.

Here again a former thought occurred to me, and I could not but reflect on the pertinacity which in spite of time, which changes all things, man shows in adhering to the old shapes of his public buildings, even long after they have been applied to new purposes. Our churches still retain the form of the Basilica, although probably the plan of the temple would better suit our worship. In Italy the courts of justice are as spacious and lofty as the means of a community are able to make them. One can almost fancy oneself to be in the open air, where once justice used to be administered. And do we not build our great theatres with their offices under a roof exactly similar to those of the first theatrical booths of a fair, which were hurriedly put together of planks? The vast multitude of those in whom, about the time of the Reformation, a thirst for knowledge was awakened, obliged the scholars at our universities to take shelter as they could in the burghers houses, and it was very long before any colleges for pupils (*Waisenhäuser*), were built, thereby facilitating for the poor youths the acquirement of the necessary education for the world.

I have spent the whole of this bright and beautiful day under the open heaven: scarcely do I ever come near a mountain, but my interest in rocks and stones again revives. I feel as did Antæus of old, who found himself endued with new strength, as often as he was brought into fresh contact with his mother earth. I rode towards Palermo, where is found the so-called Bolognese sulphate of Barytes, out of which are made the little cakes which, being calcined, shine in the dark, if previously they have been exposed to the light, and which the people here call shortly and expressively "fosfori."

On the road, after leaving behind me a hilly track of argillaceous sandstone, I came upon whole rocks of selenite, quite visible on the surface. Near a brickkiln a cascade precipitates its waters, into which many smaller ones also empty themselves. At first sight the traveller might suppose he saw before him a loamy hill, which had been worn away by the rain; on a closer examination I discovered its true nature to be as follows:—the solid rock of which this part of the line of hills consists is schistous, bituminous clay of very fine strata, and alternating with gypsum. The schistous stone is so intimately blended with pyrites that, exposed to the air and moisture, it wholly changes its nature. It swells, the strata gradually disappear, and there is formed a kind of potter's clay, crumbling, shelly, and glittering on the surface like stone-coal. It is only by examining large pieces of both (I myself broke several, and observed the forms of both), that it is possible to convince oneself of the transition and change. At the same time we observed the shelly strata studded with white points, and occasionally also variegated with yellow particles. In this way, by degrees, the whole surface crumbles away, and the hill looks like a mass of weather-worn pyrites on a large scale. Among the lamina some are harder, of a green and red color. Pyrites I very often found disseminated in the rock.

I now passed along the channels which the last violent gullies of rain had worn in the crumbling rock, and to my great delight found many specimens of the desired barytes, mostly of an imperfect egg-shape, peeping out in several places of the friable stone, some tolerably pure, and some slightly mingled with the clay in which they were imbedded. That they have not been carried hither by external agency any one may convince himself at the first glance; whether they were contemporaneous with the schistous clay, or whether they first arose from the swelling and dissolving of the latter, is matter calling for further inquiry. Of the specimens I found, the larger and smaller approximated to an imperfect egg-shape; the smallest might be said to verge upon irregular crystalline forms. The heaviest of the pieces I brought away weighed seventeen loth (8 1/2 oz.) Loose in the same clay, I also found perfect crystals of gypsum. Mineralogists will be able to point out further peculiarities in the specimens I bring with me. And I was now again loaded with stones! I have packed up at least half a quarter of a hundred-weight.

Oct. 20, 1786, *in the night.*

Bologna-Legano.

How much should I have still to say, were I to attempt to confess to you all that in this beautiful day has passed through my mind. But my wishes are more powerful than my thoughts. I feel myself hurried irresistibly forward; it is only with an effort that I can collect myself sufficiently to attend to what is before me. And it seems as if heaven heard my secret prayer. Word has just been brought me that there is a vetturino going straight to Rome, and so the day after to-morrow I shall set out direct for that city; I must, therefore, to-day and to-morrow, look after my affairs, make all my little arrangements, and despatch my many commissions.

---

*Legano on the Apennines,*br /> *Oct.* 21, 1786.

Whether I have to-day left Bologna, or whether I have been driven out of it, I cannot say. Enough that I eagerly availed myself of an earlier opportunity of quitting it. And so here I am at a wretched inn, in company with an officer of the Pope's army, who is going to Perugia, where he was born. In order to say something as I seated myself by his side in the two-wheeled carriage, I paid him the compliment of remarking, that as a German accustomed to associate with soldiers, I found it very agreeable to have to travel with an officer of the Pope. "Pray do not," he replied, "be offended at what I am about to answer—it is all very well for you to be fond of the military profession, for, in Germany, as I have heard, everything is military; but with regard to myself, although our service is light enough, so that in Bologna, where I am in garrison, I can do just as I like, still I heartily wish I were rid of this jacket, and had the disposal of my father's little property. But I am a younger son and so must be content."

Oct. 22, 1786. Evening.

Here, at Ciredo, which also is a little paltry place on the Apennines, I feel myself quite happy, knowing that I am advancing towards the gratification of my dearest wishes. To-day we were joined by a riding party—a gentleman and a lady—an Englishman and a soi-disant sister. Their horses are beautiful, but they ride unattended by any servants, and the gentleman, as it appears, acts the part both of groom and valet de chambre. Everywhere they find something to complain of—to listen to them is like reading a few pages out of Archenholz's book.

To me the Apennines are a most remarkable portion of the world. The great plains of the basin of the Po are followed by a hilly tract which rises out of the bottom, in order, after running between the two seas, to form the southern extremity of the Continent. If the hills had been not quite so steep and high above the level of the sea, and had not their directions crossed and recrossed each other as they do, the ebb and flow of the tides in primeval times might have exercised a greater and wider influence on them, and might have washed over and formed extensive plains, in which case this would have been one of the most beautiful regions of this glorious clime—somewhat higher than the rest of it. As it is, however, it is a strong net of mountain ridges, interlacing each other in all directions—one often is puzzled to know whither the waters will find their vent. If the valleys were better filled up, and the bottoms flatter and more irrigated, the land might be compared to Bohemia, only that the mountains have in every respect a different character. However, it must not for one moment be thought of as a mountainous waste, but as a highly cultivated though hilly district. The chestnut grows very fine here; the wheat excellent, and that of this year's sowing, is already of a beautiful green. Along the roads are planted evergreen oaks with their small leaves, but around the churches and chapels the slim cypress.

Perugia, October, 25, 1786. Evening.

For two evenings I have not written. The inns on the road were so wretchedly bad that it was quite useless to think of bringing out a sheet of paper. Moreover, I begin to be a little puzzled to find anything, for since quitting Venice the travelling bag has got more and more into confusion.

Early in the morning (at 23 o'clock, or about 10 of our reckoning) we left the region of the Apennines and saw Florence in an extensive valley, which is highly cultivated and sprinkled over with villas and houses without end.

I ran rapidly over the city, the cathedral, the baptistery. Here again a perfectly new and unknown world opened upon me, on which, however, I will not further dwell. The gardens of the Botoli are most delightfully situated. I hastened out of them as fast as I had entered them.

In the city we see the proof of the prosperity of the generations who built it; the conviction is at once forced upon us that they must have enjoyed a long succession of wise rulers. But above all one is struck with the beauty and grandeur which distinguish all the public works, and roads, and bridges in Tuscany. Everything here is at once substantial and clean; use and profit not less than elegance are alike kept in view, everywhere we discern traces of the care which is taken to v preserve them. The cities of the Papal States on the contrary only seem to stand, because the earth is unwilling to swallow them up.

The sort of country that I lately remarked, the region of the Apennines, might have been, is what Tuscany really is. As it lies so much lower the ancient sea was able to do its duty properly, and has thrown up here deep beds of excellent mark. It is a light yellow hue and easily worked. They plough deep, retaining, however, most exactly the ancient manner. Their ploughs have no wheels, and the share is not moveable. Bowed down behind his oxen the peasant pushes it down into the earth, and turns up the soil. They plough over a field as many as five times, and use but little dung, which they scatter with the hands. After this they sow the corn. Then they plough together two of the smaller ridges into one, and so form deep trenches of such a nature that the rain-water easily runs off the lands into them. When the corn is grown up on the ridges, they can also pass along these trenches in order to weed it. This way of tilling is a very sensible one, wherever there is a fear of over-moisture; but why it is practised on these rich, open plains I cannot understand. This remark I just made at Arezzo, where a glorious plain expands itself. It is impossible to find cleaner fields anywhere, not even a lump of earth is to be seen; all is as fine as if it had been sifted. Wheat thrives here most luxuriantly, and the soil seems to possess all the qualities required by its nature. Every second year beans are planted for the horses, who in this country get no oats. Lupins are also much cultivated, which at this season are beautifully green, being ripe in March. The flax, too, is up; it stands the winter, and is rendered more durable by frost.

The olive-trees are strange plants. They look very much like willows; like them also they lose the heart of the wood and the bark splits. But still they have a greater appearance of durability; and one sees from the wood, of which the grain is extremely fine, that it is a slow grower. The foliage, too, resembles that of the willow, only the leaves on the branches are thinner. All the hills around Florence are covered with olive-trees and vines, between which grain is sown, so that every spot of ground may be made profitable. Near Arezzo and farther on, the fields are left more free. I observed that they take little care to eradicate the ivy which is so injurious to the olive and the vine, although it would be so easy to destroy it. There is not a meadow to be seen. It is said that the Indian corn exhausts the soil; since it has been introduced, agriculture has suffered in its other crops. I can well believe it with their scanty manuring.

Yesterday I took leave of my Captain, with a promise of visiting him at Bologna on my return. He is a true representative of the majority of his countrymen. Here, however, I would record a peculiarity which personally distinguished him. As I often sat quiet and lost in thought he once exclaimed *"Che pensa? non deve mai pensar l'uomo, pensando s'invecchia;"* which being interpreted is as much as to say, "What are you thinking about; a man ought never to think; thinking makes one old." And now for another apophthegm of his; *"Non deve fermarsi l'uomo in una sola cosa, perche allora divien matto; bisogna aver mille cose, una confusione nella testa;"* in plain English, "A man ought not to rivet his thoughts exclusively on any one thing, otherwise he is sure to go mad; he ought to have in his head a thousand things, a regular medley."

A papal soldier's ideas of protestants.

Certainly the good man could not know that the very thing that made me so thoughtful was my having my head mazed by a regular confusion of things, old and new. The following anecdote will serve to elucidate still more clearly the mental character of an Italian of this class. Having soon discovered that I was a Protestant, he observed, after some circumlocution, that he hoped I would allow him to ask me a few questions, for he had heard such strange things about us Protestants that he wished to know for a certainty what to think of us. "May you," he said, "live with a pretty girl without being married to her? do your priests allow you to do that? To this I replied, that our priests are prudent folk who take no notice of such trifles. No doubt if we were to consult them upon such a matter they would not permit it." "Are you not then obliged to ask them?" He exclaimed; "Happy fellows! as they do not confess you, they do not of course find it out." Hereupon he gave vent, in many reproaches to his discontent with his own priests, uttering at the same time loud praises of our liberty. "But," he continued, "as regards confession; how stands it with you? We are told that all men, even if they are not Christians, must confess; but that inasmuch as many, from their obduracy, are debarred from the right way, they nevertheless make confession to an old tree; which indeed is impious and ridiculous enough, but yet serves to show that, at least, they recognize the necessity of confession." Upon this I explained to him our Lutheran notions of confession, and our practice concerning it. All this appeared to him very easy; for he expressed an opinion that it was almost the same as confessing to a tree. After a brief hesitation, he begged of me very gravely to inform him correctly on another point. He had, forsooth, heard from the mouth of his own confessor, (who, he said, was a truthful man,) that we Protestants are at liberty to marry our own sisters, which assuredly is a "chose un peu forte." As I denied this fact, and attempted to give him a more favourable opinion of our doctrine, he made no special remark on the latter, which evidently appeared to him a very ordinary and every-day sort of a thing; but turned aside my remarks by a new question. "We have been assured," he observed, "that Frederick the Great, who has won so many victories, even over the faithful, and filled the world with his glory—that he whom every one takes to be a heretic is really a Catholic, and has received a dispensation from the Pope to keep the fact secret. For while, as is well known, he never enters any of your churches, he diligently attends the true worship in a subterranean chapel, though with a broken heart, because he dare not openly avow the holy religion, since were he to do so, his Prussians, who are a British people and furious heretics, would no doubt murder him on the instant;—and to risk that would do no good to the cause. On these grounds the Holy Father has given him permission to worship in secret, in return for which he quietly does as much as possible to propagate and to favour the true and only saving faith." I allowed all this to pass, merely observing, as it was so great a secret no one could be a witness to its truth. The rest of our conversation was nearly of the same cast, so that I could not but admire the wise priests who sought to parry, and to distort whatever was likely to enlighten or vary the dark outline of their traditional dogmas.

I left Perugia on a glorious morning, and felt the happiness of being once more alone. The site of the city is beautiful, and the view of the lake in the highest degree refreshing. These scenes are deeply impressed on my memory. At first the road went downwards, then it entered a cheerful valley, enclosed on both sides by distant hills, till at last Assisi lay before us.

Here, as I had learned from Palladio and Volckmann, a noble temple of Minerva, built in the time of Augustus, was still standing in perfect repair. At *Madonna del Angelo*, therefore, I quitted my *vetturino*, leaving him to proceed by himself to Foligno, and set off in the face of a strong wind for Assisi, for I longed for a foot journey through a country so solitary for me.

I left on my left the vast mass of churches, piled Babel-wise one over another, in one of which rest the remains of the holy S. Francis of Assisi,— with aversion, for I thought to myself, that the people who assembled in them were mostly of the same stamp with my captain and travelling companion. Having asked of a good-looking youth the way to the *della Minerva*, he accompanied me to the top of the town, for it lies on the side of a hill. At last we reached what is properly the old town, and behold before my eyes stood the noble edifice, the first complete memorial of antiquity that I had ever seen. A modest temple, as befitting so small a town, and yet so perfect, so well conceived, that anywhere it would be an ornament. Moreover, in these matters, how grand were the ancients in the choice of their sites. The temple stands about half way up the mountain, where two hills meet on the level place, which is to this day called the Piazza. This itself slightly rises, and is intersected by the meeting of four roads, which make a somewhat dilated S. Andrew's Cross. In all probability the houses which are now opposite the temple, and block up the view from it, did not stand there in ancient times. If they were removed, we should have a south prospect over a rich and fertile country, and at the same time the temple of Minerva would be visible from all sides. The line of the roads is, in all probability, very ancient since they follow the shape and inclination of the hill, The temple does not stand in the centre of the flat, but its site is so arranged that the traveller approaching from Rome, catches a fine fore-shortened view of it. To give an idea of it, it is necessary to draw not only the building itself but also its happily-chosen site.

Looking at the façade, I could not sufficiently admire the genius-like identity of design which the architects have here, as elsewhere, maintained. The order is Corinthian, the inter-columnar spaces being somewhat above two modules. The bases of the columns and the plinths seem to rest on pedestale, but it is only an appearance. The socle is cut through in five places, and at each of these, five steps ascend between the columns, and bring you to a level, on which properly the columns rest, and from which also you enter the temple. The bold idea of cutting through the socle was happily hazarded; for, as the temple is situated on a hill, the flight of steps must otherwise have been earned up to such a height as would have inconveniently narrowed the area of the temple. As it is, however, it is impossible to determine how many steps there originally were; for, with the exception of a very few, they are all choked up with dirt or paved over. Most reluctantly did I tear myself from the sight, and determined to call the attention of architects to this noble edifice, in order that an accurate draught of it may be furnished. For what a sorry thing tradition is, I here again find occasion to remark. Palladio, whom I trust in every matter, gives indeed a sketch of this temple, but certainly he never can have seen it himself, for he gives it real pedestals above the area, by which means the columns appear disproportionately high, and the result is a sort of unsightly Palmyrene monstrosity, whereas, in fact, its look is so full of repose and beauty as to satisfy both the eye and the mind. The impression which the sight of this edifice left upon me is not to be expressed, and will bring forth imperishable fruits. It was a beautiful evening, and I now turned to descend the mountain. As I was proceeding along the Roman road, calm and composed, suddenly I heard behind me some rough voices in dispute; I fancied that it was only the Sbirri, whom I had previously noticed in the town. I, therefore, went on without care, but still with my ears listening to what they might be saying behind me. I soon became aware that I was the object of their remarks. Four men of this body (two of whom were armed with guns,) passed me in the rudest way possible, muttering to each other, and turning back, after a few steps, suddenly surrounded me. They demanded my name, and what I was doing there. I said that I was a stranger, and had travelled on foot to Assisi, while my vetturino had gone on to Foligno. It appeared to them very improbable, that any one should pay for a carriage and yet travel by foot. They asked me if I had been visiting the "Gran Convento." I answered "no;" but assured them that I knew the building of old, but being an architect, my chief object this time was simply to gain a sight of the Maria della Minerva, which they must be aware was an architectural model. This they could not contradict, but seemed to take it very ill that I had not paid a visit to the Saint, and avowed their suspicion that my business in fact was to smuggle contraband goods. I pointed out to them how ridiculous it was that a man who walked openly through the streets alone, and without packs and with empty pockets, should be taken for a contrabandist.

Assisi—an adventure.

However, upon this I offered to return to the town with them, and to go before the Podestà, and by showing my papers prove to him that I was an honest traveller. Upon this they muttered together for a while, and then expressed their opinion that it was unnecessary, and, as I behaved throughout with coolness and gravity, they at last left me, and turned towards the town. I looked after them. As these rude churls moved on in the foreground, behind them the beautiful temple of Minerva once more caught my eye, to soothe and console me with its sight. I turned then to the left to look at the heavy cathedral of S. Francisco, and was about to continue my way, when one of the unarmed Sbirri, separating himself from the rest, came up to me in a quiet and friendly manner. Saluting me, he said, Signior Stranger, you ought at least to give me something to drink your health, for I assure you, that from the very first I took you to be an honourable man, and loudly maintained this opinion in opposition to my comrades. They, however, are hot-headed and over-hasty fellows, and have no knowledge of the world. You yourself must have observed, that I was the first to allow the force of, and to assent to, your remarks. I praised him on this score, and urged him to protect all honourable strangers, who might henceforward come to Assisi for the sake either of religion or of art, and especially all architects, who might wish to do honour to the town, by measuring, and sketching the temple of Minerva, since a correct drawing or engraving of it had never yet been taken. If he were to accompany them, they would, I assured him, give him substantial proofs of their gratitude, and with these words I poured some silver into his hand, which, as exceeding his expectation, delighted him above measure. He begged me to pay a second visit to the town, remarking that I ought not on any account to miss the festival of the Saint, on which. I might with the greatest safety delight and amuse myself. In-deed if, being a good-looking fellow, I should wish to be introduced to the fair sex, he assured me that the prettiest and most respectable ladies would willingly receive me or any stranger, upon his recommendation. He took his leave, promising to remember me at vespers before the tomb of the Saint, and to offer up a prayer for my safety throughout my travels. Upon this we parted, and most delighted was I to be again alone with nature and myself. The road to Foligno was one of the most beautiful and agreeable walks that I ever took. For four full hours I walked along the side of a mountain, having on my left a richly cultivated valley.

It is but sorry travelling with a *vetturino*, it is always best to follow at one's ease on foot. In this way had I travelled from Ferrara to this place. As regards the arts and mechanical invention, on which however the ease and comforts of life mainly depend, Italy, so highly favoured by nature, is very far behind all other countries. The carriage of the vetturino, which is still called sedia, or seat, certainly took its origin from the ancient litters drawn by mules, in which females and aged persons, or the highest dignitaries, used to be carried about. Instead of the hinder mule, on whose yoke the shafts used to rest, two wheels have been placed beneath the carriage, and no further improvement has been thought of. In this way one is still jolted along, just as they were centuries ago; it is the same with their houses and everything else.

If one wishes to see realised the poetic idea of men in primeval times, spending most of their lives beneath the open heaven, and only occasionally, when compelled by necessity, retiring for shelter into the caves, one must visit the houses hereabouts, especially those in the rural districts, which are quite in the style and fashion of caves. Such an incredible absence of care do the Italians evince, in order not to grow old by thinking. With unheard of frivolity, they neglect to make any preparation for the long nights of winter, and in consequence, for a considerable portion of the year, suffer like dogs. Here, in Foligno, in the midst of a perfectly Homeric household, the whole family being gathered together in a large hall, round a fire on the hearth, with plenty of running backwards and forwards and of scolding and shouting, while supper is going on at a long table like that in the picture of the Wedding Feast at Cana, I seize an opportunity of writing this, as one of the family has ordered an inkstand to be brought me,—a luxury which, judging from other circumstances, I did not look for. These pages, however, tell too plainly of the cold and of the inconvenience of my writing table.

In fact I am now made only too sensible of the rashness of travelling in this country without a servant, and without providing oneself well with every necessary. What with the ever-changing currency, the *vetturini*, the extortion, the wretched inns, one who, like myself, is travelling alone, for the first time in this country, hoping to find uninterrupted pleasure, will be sure to find himself miserably disappointed every day. However, I wished to see the country at any cost, and even if I must be dragged to Rome on Ixion's wheel, I shall not complain.

Terni, Oct. 27, 1786.
Evening.

Again sitting in a "cave," which only a year before suffered from an earthquake. The little town lies in the midst of a rich country, (for taking a circuit round the city I explored it with pleasure,) at the beginning of a beautiful plain which lies between two ridges of lime-stone hills. Terni, like Bologna, is situated at the foot of the mountain range.

Terni.

Almost ever since the papal officer left me I have had a priest for my companion. The latter appears better contented with his profession than the soldier, and is ready to enlighten me, whom he very soon saw to be an heretic, by answering any question I might put to him concerning the ritual and other matters of his church. By thus mixing continually with new characters I thoroughly obtain my object. It is absolutely necessary to hear the people talking together, if you would form a true and lively image of the whole country. The Italians are in the strangest manner possible rivals and adversaries of each other; everyone is strongly enthusiastic in the praise of his own town and state; they cannot bear with one another, and even in the same city the different ranks nourish perpetual feuds, and all this with a profoundly vivacious and most obvious passionateness, so that while they expose one another's pretensions, they keep up an amusing comedy all day long; and yet they come to an understanding again together, and seem quite aware how impossible it is for a stranger to enter into their ways and thoughts.

I ascended to Spoleto and went along the aqueduct, which serves also for a bridge from one mountain to another. The ten brick arches which span the valley, have quietly stood there through centuries, and the water still flows into Spoleto, and reaches its remotest quarters. This is the third great work of the ancients that I have seen, and still the same grandeur of conception. A second nature made to work for social objects,—such was their architecture; and so arose the amphitheatre, the temple, and the aqueduct. Now at last I can understand the justice of my hatred for all arbitrary caprices, as, for instance, the winter casts on white stone—a nothing about nothing—a monstrous piece of confectionary ornament—and so also with a thousand other things. But all that is now dead; for whatever does not possess a true intrinsic vitality cannot live long, and can neither be nor ever become great.

What entertainment and instruction have I not had cause to be thankful for during these eight last weeks, but in fact it has also cost me some trouble. I kept my eyes continually open, and strove to stamp deep on my mind the images of all I saw; that was all-judge of them I could not, even if it had been in my power.

San Crocefisso, a singular chapel on the road side, did not look, to my mind, like the remains of a temple which had once stood on the same site; it was evident that columns, pillars, and pediments had been found, and incongruously put together, not stupidly but madly. It does not admit of description; however, there is somewhere or other an engraving of it.

And so it may seem strange to some that we should go on troubling ourselves to acquire an idea of antiquity, although we have nothing before us but ruins, out of which we must first painfully reconstruct the very thing we wish to form an idea of.

With what is called "*classical ground*" the case stands rather different. Here, if only we do not go to work fancifully, but take the ground really as it is, then we shall have the decisive arena which moulded more or less the greatest of events. Accordingly I have hitherto actively employed my geological and agricultural eye to the suppressing of fancy and sensibility, in order to gain for myself an unbiassed and distinct notion of the locality. By such means history fixes itself on our minds with a marvellous vividness, and the effect is utterly inconceivable by another. It is something of this sort that makes me feel so very great a desire to read *Tacitus* in Rome.

I must not, however, forget the weather. As I descended the Apennines from Bologna the clouds gradually retired towards the north, afterwards they changed their course and moved towards Lake Trasimene. Here they continued to hang, though perhaps they may have moved a little farther southward. Instead, therefore, of the great plain of the Po, sending as it does, during the summer, all its clouds to the Tyrolese mountains, it now sends a part of them towards the Apennines,—from thence perhaps comes the rainy season.

They are now beginning to gather the olives. It is done here with the hand, in other places they are beat down with sticks. If winter comes on before all are gathered, the rest are allowed to remain on the trees till spring. Yesterday I noticed, in a very strong soil, the largest and oldest trees I have ever yet seen.

The favour of the Muses, like that of the dæmons, is not always shown us in a suitable moment. Yesterday I felt inspired to undertake a work which at present would be ill-timed. Approaching nearer and nearer to the centre of Romanism, surrounded by Roman Catholics, boxed up with a priest in a sedan, and striving anxiously to observe and to study without prejudice true nature and noble art, I have arrived at a vivid conviction that all traces of original Christianity are extinct here. Indeed, while I tried to bring it before my mind in its purity, as we see it recorded in the Acts of the Apostles, I could not help shuddering to think of the shapeless, not to say grotesque, mass of Heathenism which heavily overlies its benign beginnings. Accordingly the "Wandering Jew" again occurred to me as having been a witness of all this wonderful development and envelopment, and as having lived to experience so strange a state of things, that Christ himself, when He shall come a second time to gather in His harvest, will be in danger of being crucified a second time. The Legend, "*Venio iterum crucifigi*" was to serve me as the material of this catastrophe.

Dreams of this kind floated before me; for out of impatience to get onwards, I used to sleep in my clothes; and I know of nothing more beautiful than to wake before dawn, and between sleeping and waking, to seat oneself in one's car, and travel on to meet the day.

Città Castellano, October 28, 1786.

I will not fail you this last evening. It is not yet eight o'clock, and all are already in bed; so I can for a good "last time" think over what is gone by, and revel in the anticipation of what is so shortly to come. This has been throughout a bright and glorious day; the morning very cold, the day clear and warm, the evening somewhat windy, but very beautiful.

It was very late when we set off from Terni, and we reached Narni before day, and so I did not see the bridge. Valleys and lowlands;—now near, now distant prospects;—a rich country, but all of limestone, and not a trace of any other formation.

Otricoli lies on an alluvial gravel-hill, thrown up by one of the ancient inundations; it is built of lava brought from the other side of the river.

As soon as one is over the bridge one finds oneself in a volcanic region, either of real lava, or of the native rock, changed by the heat and by fusion. You ascend a mountain, which you might set down at once for gray lava. It contains many white crystals of the shape of garnets. The causeway from the heights to the Città Castellana is likewise composed of this stone, now worn extremely smooth. The city is built on a bed of volcanic tufa, in which I thought I could discover ashes, pumice-stone, and pieces of lava. The view from the castle is extremely beautiful. Soracte stands out and alone in the prospect most picturesquely. It is probably a limestone mountain of the same formation as the Apennines. The volcanic region is far lower than the Apennines, and it is only the streams tearing through it, that have formed out of it hills and rocks, which, with their overhanging ledges, and other marked features of the landscape, furnish most glorious objects for the painter.

To-morrow evening and I shall be in Rome. Even yet I can scarcely believe it possible; and if this wish is fulfilled, what shall I wish for afterwards? I know not, except it be that I may safely stand in my little pheasant-loaded canoe, and may find all my friends well, happy, and unchanged.

ROME.

Rome, November 1, 1786.

At last I can speak out, and greet my friends with good humour. May they pardon my secrecy, and what has been, as it were, a subterranean journey hither. For scarcely to myself did I venture to say whither I was hurrying— even on the road I often had my fears, and it was only as I passed under the Porta del Popolo that I felt certain of reaching Rome.

And now let me also say that a thousand times—aye, at all times, do I think of you, in the neighbourhood of these objects which I never believed I should visit alone. It was only when I saw every one bound body and soul to the north, and all longing for those countries utterly extinct among them;

that I resolved to undertake the long solitary journey, and to seek that centre towards which I was attracted by an irresistible impulse. Indeed for the few last years it had become with me a kind of disease, which could only be cured by the sight and presence of the absent object. Now, at length I may venture to confess the truth: it reached at last such a height, that I durst not look at a Latin book, or even an engraving of Italian scenery. The craving to see this country was over ripe. Now, it is satisfied; friends and country have once more become right dear to me, and the return to them is a wished for object—nay, the more ardently desired, the more firmly I feel convinced that I bring with me too many treasures for personal enjoyment or private use, but such as through life may serve others, as weft as myself, for edification and guidance.

Rome, November 1, 1786.

Well, at last I am arrived in this great capital of the world. If fifteen years ago I could have seen it in good company, with a well informed guide, I should have thought myself very fortunate. But as it was to be that I should thus see it alone, and with my own eyes, it is well that this joy has fallen to my lot so late in life.

Over the mountains of the Tyrol I have as good as flown. Verona, Vicenza, Padua, and Venice I have carefully looked at; hastily glanced at Ferrara, Cento, Bologna, and scarcely seen Florence at all. My anxiety to reach Rome was so great, and it so grew with me every moment, that to think of stopping anywhere was quite out of the question; even in Florence, I only stayed three hours. Now I am here at my ease, and as it would seem, shall be tranquillized for my whole life; for we may almost say that a new life begins when a man once sees with his own eyes all that before he has but partially heard or read of. All the dreams of my youth I now behold realized before me; the subjects of the first engravings I ever remember seeing (several views of Borne were hung up in an ante-room of my father's house) stand bodily before my sight, and all that I had long been acquainted with through paintings or drawings, engravings, or wood-cuts, plaister-casts, and cork models are here collectively presented to my eye. Wherever I go I find some old acquaintance in this new world; it is all just as I had thought it, and yet all is new; and just the same might I remark of my own observations and my own ideas. I have not gained any new thoughts, but the older ones have become so defined, so vivid, and so coherent, that they may almost pass for new ones.

When Pygmalion's Elisa, which he had shaped entirely in accordance with his wishes, and had given to it as much of truth and nature as an artist can, moved at last towards him, and said, "I am!"—how different was the living form from the chiselled stone.

In a moral sense, too, how salutary is it for me to live awhile among a wholly sensual people, of whom so much has been said and written, and of whom every stranger judges according to the standard he brings with him. I can excuse every one who blames and reproaches them; they stand too far apart from us, and for a stranger to associate with them is difficult and expensive.

Rome, November 3, 1786.

Rome—Festival of all souls.

One of the chief motives which I had for hurrying to Rome was the Festival of All Saints; for I thought within myself, if Rome pays so much honour to a single saint, what will she not show to them all? But I was under a mistake. The Roman Church has never been very fond of celebrating with remarkable pomp any common festival; and so she leaves every order to celebrate in silence the especial memory of its own patron,— for the name Festival, and the day especially set apart to each saint is properly the occasion when each receives his highest commemoration.

Yesterday, however, which was the Festival of All Souls, things went better with me. This commemoration is kept by the Pope in his private chapel on the Quirinal. I hastened with Tischbein to the Monte Cavallo. The piazza before the palace has something altogether singular—so irregular is it, and yet so grand and so beautiful! I now cast eyes upon the Colossuses! neither eye nor mind was large enough to take them in. Ascending a broad flight of steps, we followed the crowd through a splendid and spacious hall. In this ante-chamber, directly opposite to the chapel, and in sight of the numerous apartments, one feels somewhat strange to find oneself beneath the same roof with the Vicar of Christ.

The office had begun; Pope and Cardinals were already in the church. The holy father, of a highly handsome and dignified form, the cardinals of different ages and figures; I was seized with a strange longing desire that the head of the Church might open his golden mouth, and speaking with rapture of the ineffable bliss of the happy soul, set us all too in a rapture. But as I only saw him moving backwards and forwards before the altar, and turning himself now to this side and now to that, and only muttering to himself, and conducting himself just like a common parish priest, then the original sin of Protestantism revived within me, and the well-known and

- 153 -

ordinary mass for the dead had no charms for me. For most assuredly Christ Himself—He who in his youthful days, and even as a child excited men's winder by His oral exposition of Scripture, did never thus teach and work in silence; but as we learn from the Gospels, He was ever ready to utter His wise and spiritual words. What, I asked myself, would He say, where He to come in among us, and see His image on earth thus mumbling, and sailing backwards and forwards? The "*Venio iterum crucifigi*" again crossed my mind, and I nudged my companion to come out into the freer air of the vaulted and painted hall.

Here we found a crowd of persons attentively observing the rich paintings; for the Festival of All Souls is also the holiday of all the artists in Rome. Not only the chapel, but the whole palace also, with all its rooms, is for many hours on this day open and free to every one, no fees being required, and the visitors not being liable to be hurried on by the chamberlain.

The paintings on the walls engaged my attention, and I now formed a new acquaintance with some excellent artists, whose very names had hitherto been almost unknown to me,—for instance, I now for the first time learned to appreciate and to love the cheerful *Carlo Maratti*.

But chiefly welcome to me were the masterpieces of the artists, of whose style and manner I already had some impression. I saw with amazement the wonderful Petronilla of *Guercino*, which was formerly in St. Peter's, where a mosaic copy now stands in the place of the original. The body of the Saint is lifted out of the grave, and the same person, just reanimated, is being received into the heights of heaven by a celestial youth. Whatever may be alleged against this double action, the picture is invaluable.

Still more struck was I with a picture of Titian's: it throws into the shade all I have hitherto seen. Whether my eye is more practised, or whether it is really the most excellent, I cannot determine. An immense mass-robe, stiff with embroidery and gold-embossed figures, envelops the dignified frame of a bishop. With a massive pastoral star in his left hand, he is gazing with a look of rapture towards heaven, while he holds in his right a book out of which he seems to have imbibed the divine enthusiasm with which he is inspired. Behind him a beautiful maiden, holding a palm branch in her hand, and, full of affectionate sympathy, is looking over his shoulder into the open book. A grave old man on the right stands quite close to the book, but appears to pay no attention to it; the key in his hand, suggests the possibility of his familiar acquaintance with its contents. Over against this group a naked, well-made youth, wounded with an arrow, and in chains, is looking straight before him with a slight expression of resignation in his countenance. In the intermediate space stand two monks, bearing a cross and lilies, and devoutly looking up to heaven. Then in the clear upper space is a semi-circular wall, which encloses them all; above moves a Madonna in highest glory, sympathising with all that passes below. The young sprightly child on her bosom, with a radiant countenance, is holding out a crown, and seems indeed on the point of casting it down. On both sides angels are floating by, who hold in their hands crowns in abundance. High above all the figures, and even the triple-rayed aureola, soars the celestial dove, as at once the centre and finish of the whole group.

Rome—Titian—Guido.

We said to ourselves, "Some ancient holy legend must have furnished the subject of this picture, in order that these various and ill-assorted personages should have been brought together so artistically and so significantly. We ask not, however, why and wherefore,—we take it all for granted, and only wonder at the inestimable piece of art. Less unintelligible, but still mysterious, is a fresco of Guido's in this chapel. A virgin, in childish beauty, loveliness, and innocence, is seated, and quietly sewing: two angels stand by her side, waiting to do her service at the slightest bidding. Youthful innocence and industry,—the beautiful picture seems to tell us,— are guarded and honoured by the heavenly beings. No legend is wanting here; no story needed to furnish an explanation."

Now, however, to cool a little my artistic enthusiasm, a merry incident occurred. I observed that several of the German artists, who came up to Tischbein as an old acquaintance, after staring at me, went their ways again. At last one, who had most recently been observing my person, came up to me again, and said, "We have had a good joke; the report that you were in Rome had spread among us, and the attention of us artists was called to the one unknown stranger. Now, there was one of our body who used for a long time to assert that he had met you—nay, he asseverated he had lived on very friendly terms with you,—a fact which we were not so ready to believe. However, we have just called upon him to look at you, and solve our doubts. He at once stoutly denied that it was you, and said that in the stranger there was not a trace of your person or mien." So, then, at least our *incognito* is for the moment secure, and will afford us something hereafter to laugh at.

I now mixed at my ease with the troop of artists, and asked them who were the painters of several pictures whose style of art was unknown to me. At last I was particularly struck by a picture representing St. George killing the dragon, and setting free the virgin; no one could tell me whose it was. Upon this a little modest man, who up to this time had not opened his mouth, came forward and told me it was Pordenone's, the Venetian painter; and that it was one of the best of his paintings, and displayed all his merits.

I was now well able to account for my liking for it: the picture pleased me, because I possessed some knowledge of the Venetian school, and was better able to appreciate the excellencies of its best masters.

The artist, my informant, was Heinrich Meyer, a Swiss, who for some years had been studying at Rome with a friend of the name of Rolla, and who had taken excellent drawings in Spain of antique busts, and was well read in the history of art.

Rome, November 7, 1786.

I have now been here seven days, and by degrees have formed in my mind a general idea of the city. We go diligently backwards and forwards. While I am thus making myself acquainted with the plan of old and new Rome, viewing the ruins and the buildings, visiting this and that villa, the grandest and most remarkable objects are slowly and leisurely contemplated. I do but keep my eyes open and see, and then go and come again, for it is only in Rome one can duly prepare oneself for Rome.

It must, in truth, be confessed, that it is a sad and melancholy business to prick and track out ancient Rome in new Rome; however, it must be done, and we may hope at least for an incalculable gratification. We meet with traces both of majesty and of ruin, which alike surpass all conception; what the barbarians spared, the builders of new Rome made havoc of.

Rome—Its present aspect.

When one thus beholds an object two thousand years old and more, but so manifoldly and thoroughly altered by the changes of time, but, sees nevertheless, the same soil, the same mountains, and often indeed the same walls and columns, one becomes, as it were, a contemporary of the great counsels of Fortune, and thus it becomes difficult for the observer to trace from the beginning Rome following Rome, and not only new Rome succeeding to the old, but also the several epochs of both old and new in succession. I endeavour, first of all, to grope my way alone through the obscurer parts, for this is the only plan by which one can hope fully and completely to perfect by the excellent introductory works which have been written from the fifteenth century to the present day. The first artists and scholars have occupied their whole lives with these objects.

And this vastness has a strangely tranquillizing effect upon you in Rome, while you pass from place to place, in order to visit the most remarkable objects. In other places one has to search for what is important; here one is oppressed, and borne down with numberless phenomena. Wherever one goes and casts a look around, the eye is at once struck with some landscape,—forms of every kind and style; palaces and ruins, gardens and statuary, distant views of villas, cottages and stables, triumphal arches and columns, often crowding so close together, that they might all be sketched on a single sheet of paper. He ought to have a hundred hands to write, for what can a single pen do here; and, besides, by the evening one is quite weary and exhausted with the day's seeing and admiring.

Rome, November 7, 1786.

Pardon me, my friends, if for the future you find me rather chary of my words. On one's travels one usually rakes together all that we meet on one's way; every day brings something new, and one then hastens to think upon and to judge of it. Here, however, we come into a very great school indeed, where every day says so much, that we cannot venture to say anything of the day itself. Indeed, people would do well if, tarrying here for years together, they observed awhile a Pythagorean silence.

Nov. 1786.

I am quite well. The weather, as the Romans say, is *brutto*. The south wind, the scirocco, is blowing, and brings with it every day more or less of rain; for my part, I do not find the weather disagreeable; such as it is, it is warmer than the rainy days of summer are with us.

Rome, November 7, 1786.

The more I become acquainted with Tischbein's talents, as well as his principles and views of art, the higher I appreciate and value them. He has laid before me his drawings and sketches; they have great merit, and are full of high promise. His visit to Bodmer led him to fix his thoughts on the infancy of the human race, when man found himself standing on the earth, and had to solve the problem, how he must best fulfil his destiny as the Lord of Creation.

As a suggestive introduction to a series of illustrations of this subject, he has attempted symbolically to vindicate the high antiquity of the world. Mountains overgrown with noble forests,—ravines worn out by watercourses,—burnt out volcanoes still faintly smoking. In the foreground the mighty stock of a patriarchal oak still remains in the ground, on whose half-bared roots a deer is trying the strength of his horns,—a conception as fine as it is beautifully executed.

In another most remarkable piece he has painted man yoking the horse, and by his superior skill, if not strength, bringing all the other creatures of the earth, the air, and the water under his dominion. The composition is of an extraordinary beauty; when finished in oils it cannot fail of producing a great effect. A drawing of it must, at any cost, be secured for Weimar. When this is finished, he purposes to paint an assembly of old men, aged and experienced in council,—in which he intends to introduce the portraits of living personages. At present, however, he is sketching away with the greatest enthusiasm on a battle-piece. Two bodies of cavalry are fighting with equal courage and resolution; between them yawns an awful chasm, which but few horses would attempt to clear. The arts of defensive warfare are useless here. A wild resolve, a bold attack, a successful leap, or else to be hurled in the abyss below! This picture will afford him an opportunity to display, in a very striking manner, the knowledge winch he possesses of horses, and of their make and movements.

Now it is Tischbein's wish to have these sketches, and a series of others to follow, or to be intercalated between them, connected together by a poem, which may serve to explain the drawings, and, by giving them a definite context, may lend to them both a body and a charm.

The idea is beautiful, only the artist and the poet must be many years together, in order to carry out and to execute such a work.

Rome, November 7, 1786.

Rome—Raffaele.

The "*Loggie*" of Raffaele, and the great pictures of the "School of Athens," &c., I have now seen for the first and only time; so that for me to judge of them at present is like a man having to make out and to judge of Homer from some half-obliterated and much-injured manuscript. The gratification of the first impression is incomplete; it is only when they have been carefully studied and examined, one by one, that the enjoyment becomes perfect. The best preserved are the paintings on the ceilings of the *Loggie*. They are as fresh as if painted yesterday The subjects are symbolical. Very few, however, are by Raffaele's own hand, but they are excellently executed, after his designs and under his eye.

Rome, November 7, 1786.

Many a time, in years past, did I entertain the strange whim, as ardently to wish that I might one day be taken to Italy by some well-educated man,— by some Englishman, well learned in art and in history; and now it has all been brought about much better than I could have anticipated. Tischbein has long lived here; he is a sincere friend to me, and during his stay here always cherished the wish of being able one day to show Rome to me. Our intimacy is old by letter though new by presence. Where could I meet with a worthier guide? And if my time is limited, I will at least learn and enjoy as much as possible; and yet, notwithstanding, I clearly foresee, that when I leave Rome I shall wish that I was coming to it.

Rome, November 8, 1786.

My strange, and perhaps whimsical, incognito proves useful to me in many ways that I never should have thought of. As every one thinks himself in duty bound to ignore who I am, and consequently never ventures to speak to me of myself and my works, they have no alternative left them but to speak of themselves, or of the matters in which they are most interested, and in this way I become circumstantially informed of the occupations of each, and of everything remarkable that is either taken in hand or produced. Hofrath Reiffenstein good-naturedly humours this whim of mine; as, however, for special reasons, he could not bear the name which I had assumed, he immediately made a Baron of me, and I am now called the "*Baron gegen Rondanini über*" (the Baron who lives opposite to the Palace Rondanini). This designation is sufficiently precise, especially as the Italians are accustomed to speak of people either by their Christian names, or else by some nickname. Enough; I have gained my object; and I escape the dreadful annoyance of having to give to everybody an account of myself and my works.

Rome, November 9, 1786.

I frequently stand still a moment to survey, as it were, the heights I have already won. With much delight I look back to Venice, that grand creation that sprang out of the bosom of the sea, like Minerva out of the head of Jupiter. In Rome, the Rotunda, both by its exterior and interior, has moved me to offer a willing homage to its magnificence. In S. Peter's I learned to understand how art, no less than nature, annihilates the artificial measures and dimensions of man. And in the same way the Apollo Belvidere also has again drawn me out of reality. For as even the most correct engravings furnish no adequate idea of these buildings, so the case is the same with respect to the marble original of this statue, as compared with the plaister models of it, which, however, I formerly used to look upon as beautiful.

Rome, November 10, 1786.

Here I am now living with a calmness and tranquillity to which I have for a long while been a stranger. My practice to see and take all things as they are, my fidelity in letting the eye be my light, my perfect renunciation of all pretension, have again come to my aid, and make me calmly, but most intensely, happy. Every day has its fresh remarkable object,—every day its new grand unequalled paintings, and a whole which a man may long think of, and dream of, but which with all his power of imagination he can never reach.

Rome-The Grotto of Egeria, &c.

Yesterday I was at the Pyramid of Cestius, and in the evening on the Palatine, on the top of which are the ruins of the palace of the Cæsars, which stand there like walls of rock. Of all this, however, no idea can be conveyed! In truth, there is nothing little here; although, indeed, occasionally something to find fault with,—something more or less absurd in taste, and yet even this partakes of the universal grandeur of all around.

When, however, I return to myself, as every one so readily does on all occasions, I discover within a feeling which does not infinitely delight me— one, indeed, which I may even express. Whoever here looks around with earnestness, and has eyes to see, must become in a measure solid—he cannot but apprehend an idea of solidity with a vividness which is nowhere else possible.

The mind becomes, as it were, primed with capacity, with an earnestness without severity, and with a definiteness of character with joy. With me, at least, it seems as if I had never before so rightly estimated the things of the world as I do here; I rejoice when I think of the blessed effects of all this on the whole of my future being. And let me jumble together the things as I may, order will somehow come into them. I am not here to enjoy myself after my own fashion, but to busy myself with the great objects around, to learn, and to improve myself, ere I am forty years old.

Rome, Nov. 11, 1786.

Yesterday I visited the nymph Egeria, and then the Hippodrome of Caracalla, the ruined tombs along the Via Appia, and the tomb of Metella, which is the first to give one a true idea of what solid masonry really is. These men worked for eternity—all causes of decay were calculated, except the rage of the spoiler, which nothing can resist. Right heartily did I wish you had been there. The remains of the principal aqueduct are highly venerable. How beautiful and grand a design, to supply a whole people with water by so vast a structure! In the evening we came upon the Coliseum, when it was already twilight. When one looks at it, all else seems little; the edifice is so vast, that one cannot hold the image of it in one's soul—in memory we think it smaller, and then return to it again to find it every time greater than before.

Frascati, Nov. 15.

The company are all in bed, and I am writing with Indian ink which they use for drawing. We have had two beautiful days without rain, warm and genial sunshine, so that summer is scarcely missed. The country around is very pleasant; the village lies on the side of a hill, or rather of a mountain, and at every step the draughtsman comes upon the most glorious objects. The prospect is unbounded—Rome lies before you, and beyond it, on the right, is the sea, the mountains of Tivoli, and so on. In this delightful region country houses are built expressly for pleasure, and as the ancient Romans had here their villas, so for centuries past their rich and haughty successors have planted country residences on all the loveliest spots. For two days we have been wandering about here, and almost every step has brought us upon something new and attractive.

And yet it is hard to say whether the evenings have not passed still more agreeably than the days. As soon as our stately hostess has placed on the round table the bronzed lamp with its three wicks, and wished us *felicissime notte*, we all form a circle round it, and the views are produced which have been drawn and sketched during the day; their merits are discussed, opinions are taken whether the objects might or not have been taken more favourably, whether their true characters have been caught, and whether all requisitions of a like general nature, which may justly be looked for in a first sketch, have been fulfilled.

Hofrath Reiffenstein, by his judgment and authority, contrives to give order to, and to conduct these sittings. But the merit of this delightful arrangement is due to Philipp Hackert, who has a most excellent taste both in drawing and finishing views from nature. Artists and dilettanti, men and women, old and young—he would let no one rest, but stimulated every one to make the attempt at any rate according to their gifts and powers, and led the way with his own good example. The little society thus collected, and held together, Hofrath Reiffenstein has, after the departure of his friend, faithfully kept up, and we all feel a laudable desire to awake in every one an active participation. The peculiar turn and character of each member of the society is thus shown in a most agreeable way. For instance, Tischbein, as an historical painter, looks upon scenery with very different eyes from the landscape painter; he sees significant groups, and other graceful speaking objects, where another can see nothing, and so he happily contrives to catch up many a naive-trait of humanity,—it may be in children, peasants, mendicants, or other such beings of nature, or even in animals, which with a few characteristic touches, he skilfully manages to portray, and thereby contributes much new and agreeable matter for our discussions.

When conversation is exhausted, at Hackert's suggestion, perhaps, some one reads aloud Sulzer's Theory; for although from a high point of view it is impossible to rest contented with this work, nevertheless, as some one observed, it is so far satisfactory as it is calculated to exercise a favourable influence on minds less highly cultivated.

Rome, Nov. 17, 1786.

We are back again! During the night we have had an awful torrent of rain, with thunder and lightning; it is still raining, but withal very warm.

> Rome-Farnese Gallery, &c.

As regards myself, however, it is only with few words that I can indicate the happiness of this day. I have seen the frescoes of *Domenichino* in *Andrea della Valle*, and also the Farnese Gallery of Caraccio's. Too much, forsooth, for months-what, then, for a single day!

Rome, Nov. 18, 1786.

It is again beautiful, weather, a bright genial warm day. I saw in the *Farnesine* palace the story of Psyche, coloured copies of which have so long adorned my room, and then at S. Peter's, in Montorio, the Transfiguration by Raffaelle—all well known paintings—like friends which one has made in the distance by means of letters, and which for the first time one sees face to face. To live with them, however, is something quite different; every true relation and false relation becomes immediately evident.

Moreover, in every spot and corner glorious things are to be met with, of which less has been said, and which have not been scattered over the world by engravings and copies. Of these I shall bring away with me many a drawing from the hands of young but excellent artists.

Rome, Nov. 18, 1786.

The fact that I long maintained a correspondence with Tischbein, and was consequently on the best terms possible with him, and that even when I had no hope of ever visiting Italy, I had communicated to him my wishes, has made our meeting most profitable and delightful; he has been always thinking of me, even providing for my wants. With the varieties of stone, of which all the great edifices, whether old or new are built, he has made himself perfectly acquainted; he has thoroughly studied them, and his studies have been greatly helped by his artistic eye, and the artist's pleasure in sensible things. Just before my arrival here he sent off to Weimar a collection of specimens which he had selected for me, which will give me a friendly welcome on my return.

An ecclesiastic who is now residing in France, and had it in contemplation to write a work on the ancient marbles, received through the influence of the Propaganda some large pieces of marble from the Island of Paros. When they arrived here they were cut up for specimens, and twelve different pieces, from the finest to the coarsest grain, were reserved for me. Some were of the greatest purity, while others are more or less mingled with mica, the former being used for statuary, the latter for architecture. How much an accurate knowledge of the material employed in the arts must contribute to a right estimate of them, must be obvious to every one.

There are opportunities enough here for my collecting many more specimens. In our way to the ruins of Nero's palace, we passed through some artichoke grounds newly turned up, and we could not resist the temptation to cram our pockets full of the granite, porphyry, and marble slabs which lie here by thousands, and serve as unfailing witnesses to the ancient splendour of the walls which were once covered with them.

Rome, Nov. 18, 1786.

I must now speak of a wonderful problematical picture, which even in the midst of the many gems here, still makes a good show of its own.

Rome.

For many years there had been residing here a Frenchman well known as an admirer of the arts, and a collector; he had got hold of an antique drawing in chalk, no one knows how or whence. He had it retouched by Mengs, and kept it in his collection as a work of very great value.

Winckelmann somewhere speaks of it with enthusiasm. The Frenchman died, and left the picture to his hostess as an antique. Mengs, too, died, and declared on his death-bed that it was not an antique, but had been painted by himself. And now the whole world is divided in opinion, some maintaining that Mengs had one day, in joke, dashed it off with much facility; others asserting that Mengs could never do anything like it— indeed, that it is almost too beautiful for Raffaelle. I saw it yesterday, and must confess that I do not know anything more beautiful than the figure of Ganymede, especially the head and shoulders; the rest has been much renovated. However, the painting is in ill repute, and no one will relieve the poor landlady of her treasure.

Rome, Nov. 20, 1786.

As experience fully teaches us that there is a general pleasure in having poems, whatever may be their subject, illustrated with drawings and engravings—nay, that the painter himself usually selects a passage of some poet or other for the subject of his most elaborate paintings, Tischbein's idea is deserving of approbation, that poets and painters should work together from the very first, in order to secure a perfect unity. The difficulty would assuredly be greatly lessened, if it were applied to little pieces, such as that the whole design would easily admit of being taken in at once by the mind, and worked out consistently with the original plan.

Tischbein has suggested for such common labours some very delightful idyllic thoughts, and it is really singular, that those which he wishes to see worked out in this way are really such as neither poetry nor painting, alone, could ever adequately describe. During our walks together he has talked with me about them, in the hopes of gaining me over to his views, and getting me to enter upon the plan. The frontispiece for such a joint work is already designed; and did I not fear to enter upon any new tasks at present, I might perhaps be tempted.

Rome, Nov. 22, 1786.
The Feast of St. Cecilia.

The morning of this happy day I must endeavour to perpetuate by a few lines, and at least by description to impart to others what I have myself enjoyed. The weather has been beautiful and calm, quite a bright sky, and a warm sun. Accompanied by Tischbein, I set off for the Piazza of St. Peter's, where we went about first of all from one part to another; when it became too hot for that, walked up and down in the shade of the great obelisk, which is full wide enough for two abreast, and eating grapes which we purchased in the neighbourhood. Then we entered the Sistine Chapel, which we found bright and cheerful, and with a good light for the pictures. "The Last Judgment" divided our admiration with the paintings on the roof by Michael Angelo. I could only see and wonder. The mental confidence and boldness of the master, and his grandeur of conception, are beyond all expression. After we had looked at all of them over and over again, we left this sacred building, and went to St. Peter's, which received from the bright heavens the loveliest light possible, and every part of it was clearly lit up. As men willing to be pleased, we were delighted with its vastness and splendour, and did not allow an over nice or hypocritical taste to mar our pleasure. We suppressed every harsher judgment: we enjoyed the enjoyable.

Rome—St. Peter's.

Lastly we ascended the roof of the church, where one finds in little the plan of a well-built city. Houses and magazines, springs (in appearance at least), churches, and a great temple all in the air, and beautiful walks between. We mounted the dome, and saw glistening before us the regions of the Apennines, Soracte, and towards Tivoli the volcanic hills. Frascati, Castelgandolfo, and the plains, and beyond all the sea. Close at our feet lay the whole city of Rome in its length and breadth, with its mountain palaces, domes, &c. Not a breath of air was moving, and in the upper dome it was (as they say) like being in a hot-house. When we had looked enough at these things, we went down, and they opened for us the doors in the cornices of the dome, the tympanum, and the nave. There is a passage all round, and from above you can take a view of the whole church, and of its several parts. As we stood on the cornices of the tympanum, we saw beneath us the pope passing to his mid-day devotions. Nothing, therefore, was wanting to make our view of St. Peter's perfect. We at last descended to the area, and took in a neighbouring hotel a cheerful but frugal meal, and then set off for St. Cecilia's.

It would take many words to describe the decorations of this church, which was crammed full of people; not a stone of the edifice was to be seen. The pillars were covered with red velvet wound round with gold lace; the capitals were overlaid with embroidered velvet, so as to retain somewhat of the appearance of capitals, and all the cornices and pillars were in like manner covered with hangings. All the entablatures of the walls were also covered with life-like paintings, so that the whole church seemed to be laid out in mosaic. Around the church, and on the high altar more than two hundred wax tapers were burning. It looked like a wall of lights, and the whole nave was perfectly lit up. The aisles and side altars were equally adorned and illuminated. Right opposite the high altar, and under the organ, two scaffolds were erected, which also were covered with velvet, on one of which were placed the singers, and on the other the instruments, which kept up one unbroken strain of music. The church was crammed full.

I have heard an excellent kind of musical accompaniment, just as there are concerts of violins, or of other instruments, so here they had concerts of voices; so that one voice—the soprano for instance—predominates, and sings solo, while from time to time the chorus of other voices falls in, and accompanies it, always of course with the whole orchestra. It has a good effect. I must end, as we in fact ended the day. In the evening we come upon the Opera, where no less a piece than "I Litiganti" was being performed, but we had all the day enjoyed so much of excellence, that we passed by the door.

Rome, Nov. 23, 1786.

In order that it may not be the same with my dear incognito as with the ostrich, which thinks itself to be concealed when it has hid its head, so in certain cases I give it up, still maintaining, however, my old thesis. I had without hesitation paid a visit of compliment to the Prince von Lichtenstein, the brother of my much-esteemed friend the Countess Harrach, and occasionally dined with him, and I soon perceived that my good-nature in this instance was likely to lead me much further. They began to feel their way, and to talk to me of the Abbé *Monti,* and of his tragedy of Aristodemus, which is shortly to be brought out on the stage. The author, it was said, wished above all things to read it to me, and to hear my opinion of it, but I contrived, however, to let the matter drop, without positively refusing; at last, however, I met the poet and some of his friends at the prince's house, and the play was read aloud.

The hero is, as is well known, the King of Sparta, who by various scruples of conscience was driven to commit suicide. Prettily enough they contrived to intimate to me their hope that the author of Werther would not take it ill if he found some of the rare passages of his own work made use of in this drama. And so even before the walls of Sparta I can not escape from this unhappy youth.

The piece has a very simple and calm movement, the sentiments as well as the language are well suited to the subject,—full of energy, and yet of tenderness. The work is a proof of very fair talents.

I failed not, according to my fashion, (not, indeed, after the Italian fashion) to point out, and to dwell upon all the excellencies and merits of the piece, with which, indeed, all present were tolerably satisfied, though still with

Southern impatience they seemed to require something more. I even ventured to predict what effect it was to be hoped the piece would have from the public. I excused myself on account of my ignorance of the country, its way of thinking and tastes, but was candid enough to add, that I did not clearly see how the Romans, with their vitiated taste, who were accustomed to see as an interlude either a complete comedy of three acts, or an opera of two, or could not sit out a grand opera, without the intermezzo of wholly foreign ballets, could ever take delight in the calm, noble movement of a regular tragedy. Then, again, the subject of a suicide seemed to me to be altogether out of the pale of an Italian's ideas. That they stabbed men to death, I knew by daily report of such events; but that any one should deprive himself of his own precious existence, or even should hold it possible for another to do so; of that no trace or symptom had ever been brought under my notice.

Rome—Monti's Aristodemus.

However I allowed myself to be circumstantially enlightened as to all that might be urged in answer to my objections, and readily yielded to their plausible arguments. I also assured them I wished for nothing so much as to see the piece acted, and with a band of friends to welcome it with the most downright and loudest applause. This assurance was received in the most friendly manner possible, and I had this time at least no cause to be dissatisfied with my compliance—for indeed Prince Lichstenstein is politeness itself, and found opportunity for my seeing in his company many precious works of art, a sight of which is not easily obtained without special permission, and for which consequently high influence is indispensable. On the other hand, my good humour failed me, when the daughter of the Pretender expressed a wish to see the strange marmoset. I declined the honour, and once more completely shrouded myself beneath my disguise.

But still that is not altogether the right way, and I here feel most sensibly what I have often before observed in life, that the man who makes good his first wish, must be on the alert and active, must oppose himself to very much besides the selfish, the mean, and the bad. It is easy to see this, but is extremely difficult to act in the spirit of it.

Nov. 24, 1786.

Of the people I can say nothing more than that they are fine children of nature, who, amidst pomp and honours of all kinds, religion and the arts, are not one jot different from what they would be in caves and forests. What strikes the stranger most, and what to-day is making the whole city to talk, but only to *talk*, is the common occurrence of assassination. To-day the victim has been an excellent artist—Schwendemann, a Swiss, a medallionist. The particulars of his death greatly resemble those of Windischmann's. The assassin with whom he was struggling gave him twenty stabs, and as the watch came up, the villain stabbed himself. This is not generally the fashion here; the murderer usually makes for the nearest church, and once there, he is quite safe.

And now, in order to shade my picture a little, I might bring into it crimes and disorders, earthquakes and inundations of all kinds, but for an eruption of Vesuvius, which has just broke out, and has set almost all the visitors here in motion; and one must, indeed, possess a rare amount of self-control, not to be carried away by the crowd. Really this phenomenon of nature has in it something of a resemblance to the rattle-snake, for its attraction is irresistible. At this moment it almost seems as if all the treasures of art in Rome were annihilated; every stranger, without exception, has broken off the current of his contemplations, and is hurrying to Naples; I, however, shall stay, in the hope that the mountain will have a little eruption, expressly for my amusement.

Rome, Dec. 1, 1786.

Moritz is here, who has made himself famous by his "Anthony the Traveller" (*Anton Reiser,*) and his "Wanderings in England" (*Wanderungen nach England.*) He is a right down excellent man, and we have been greatly pleased with him.

Rome, Dec. 1, 1786.

Here in Rome, where one sees so many strangers, all of whom do not visit this capital of the world merely for the sake of the fine arts, but also for amusements of every kind, the people are prepared for everything. Accordingly, they have invented and attained great excellence in certain half arts which require for their pursuit little more than manual skill and pleasure in such handiwork, and which consequently attract the interest of ordinary visitors.

Among these is the art of painting in wax. Requiring little more than tolerable skill in water-colouring, it serves as an amusement to employ one's time in preparing and adapting the wax, and then in burning it, and in such like mechanical labours. Skilful artists give lessons in the art, and, under the pretext of showing their pupils how to perform their tasks, do the chief part of the work themselves, so that when at last the figure stands out in bright relief in the gilded frame, the fair disciple is ravished with the proof of her unconscious talent.

Another pretty occupation is, with a very fine clay, to take impressions of cameos cut in deep relief. This is also done in the case of medallions, both sides of which are thus copied at once. More tact, attention, and diligence is required, lastly, for preparation of the glass-paste for mock jewels. For all these things Hofrath Reiffenstein has the necessary workshops and laboratories either in his house, or close at hand.

Dec. 2, 1786.

I have accidentally found here Archenholtz's Italy. A work written on the spot, in so contracted and narrow-minded a spirit as this, is just as if one were to lay a book purposely on the coals, in order that it might be browned and blackened, and its leaves curled up and disfigured with smoke.

Rome—Archenholtz's Italy.

No doubt he has seen all that he writes about, but he possesses far too little of real knowledge to support his high pretensions and sneering tone; and whether he praises or blames, he is always in the wrong.

Dec. 2, 1786.

Such beautiful warm and quiet weather at the end of November, (which however is often broken by a day's rain,) is quite new to me. We spend the fine days in the open air, the bad in our room; everywhere there is something to learn and to do, something to be delighted with.

On the 28th we paid a second visit to the Sistine Chapel, and had the galleries opened, in order that we might obtain a nearer view of the ceiling. As the galleries are very narrow, it is only with great difficulty that one forces one's way up them, by means of the iron balustrades. There is an appearance of danger about it, on which account those who are liable to get dizzy had better not make the attempt; all the discomfort, however, is fully compensated by the sight of the great masterpiece of art. And at this moment I am so taken with Michael Angelo, that after him I have no taste even for nature herself, especially as I am unable to contemplate her with the same eye of genius that he did. Oh, that there were only some means of fixing such paintings in my soul! At any rate, I shall bring with me every engraving and drawing of his pictures or drawings after him that I can lay hold of.

Then we went to the *Loggie*, painted by Raffaelle, and scarcely dare I say that we could not endure to look at them. The eye had been so dilated and spoiled by those great forms, and the glorious finish of every part, that it was not able to follow the ingenious windings of the Arabesques; and the Scripture histories, however beautiful they were, did not stand examination after the former. And yet to see these works frequently one after another, and to compare them together at leisure, and without prejudice, must be a source of great pleasure,—for at first all sympathy is more or less exclusive.

From hence, under a sunshine, if anything rather too warm, we proceeded to the Villa Pamphili, whose beautiful gardens are much resorted to for amusement; and there we remained till evening. A large flat meadow, enclosed by long ever green oaks and lofty pines, was sown all over with daisies, which turned their heads to the sun. I now revived my botanical speculations, which I had indulged in the other day during a walk towards Monte Mario, to the Villa Melini, and the Villa Madama. It is very interesting to observe the working of a vigorous unceasing vegetation, which is here unbroken by any severe cold. Here there are no buds: one has actually to learn what a bud is. The strawberry-tree (*arbutus unedo*) is at this season, for the second time, in blossom, while its last fruits are just ripening. So also the orange-tree may seen in flower, and at the same time bearing partially and fully ripened fruit. (The latter trees, however, if they are not sheltered by standing between buildings, are, at this season, generally covered). As to the cypress, that most "venerable" of trees, when it is old and well grown, it affords matter enough for thought. As soon as possible I shall pay a visit to the Botanical Gardens, and hope to add there much to my experience. Generally, there is nothing to be compared with the new life which the sight of a new country affords to a thoughtful person. Although I am still the same being, I yet think I am changed to the very marrow.

For the present I conclude, and shall perhaps fill the next sheet with murders, disorders, earthquakes, and troubles, in order that at any rate my pictures may not be without their dark shades.

Rome, Dec. 3, 1786.

The weather lately has changed almost every six days. Two days quite glorious, then a doubtful one, and after it two or three rainy ones, and then again fine weather. I endeavour to put each day, according to its nature, to the best use.

And yet these glorious objects are even still like new acquaintances to me. One has not yet lived with them, nor got familiar with their peculiarities. Some of them attract us with irresistible power, so that for a time one feels indifferent, if not unjust, towards all others. Thus, for instance, the Pantheon, the Apollo Belvedere, some colossal heads, and very recently the Sistine Chapel, have by turns so won my whole heart, that I scarcely saw any thing besides them. But, in truth, can man, little as man always is, and accustomed to littleness, ever make himself equal to all that here surrounds him of the noble, the vast, and the refined? Even though he should in any degree adapt himself to it, then how vast is the multitude of objects that immediately press upon him from all sides, and meet him at every turn, of which each demands for itself the tribute of his whole attention. How is one to get out of the difficulty? No other way assuredly than by patiently allowing it to work, becoming industrious, and attending the while to all that others have accomplished for our benefit.

Winckelmann's History of Art, translated by Rea, (the new edition), is a very useful book, which I have just procured, and here on the spot find it to be highly profitable, as I have around me many kind friends, willing to explain and to comment upon it.

Roman antiquities also begin to have a charm for me. History, inscriptions, coins, (of which formerly I knew nothing,) all are pressing upon me. As it happened to me in the case of natural history, so goes it with me here also; for the history of the whole world attaches itself to this spot, and I reckon a new-birth day,—a true new birth from the day that I entered Rome.

December 5, 1786.

During the few weeks I have been here, I have already seen many strangers come and go, so that I have often wondered at the levity with which so many treat these precious monuments. God be thanked that hereafter none of those birds of passage will be able to impose upon me. When in the north they shall speak to me of Rome, none of them now will be able to excite my spleen, for I also have seen it, and know too, in some degree, where I have been.

December 8, 1786.

We have every now and then the finest days possible. The rain which falls from time to time has made the grass and garden stuffs quite verdant.

Evergreens too are to be seen here at different spots, so that one scarcely misses the fallen leaves of the forest trees. In the gardens you may see orange-trees full of fruit, left in the open ground and not under cover.

I had intended to give you a particular account of a very pleasant trip which we took to the sea, and of our fishing exploits, but in the evening poor Moritz, as he was riding home, broke his arm, his horse having slipped on the smooth Roman pavement. This marred all our pleasure, and has plunged our little domestic circle in sad affliction.

Dec. 15, 1786.

I am heartily delighted that you have taken my sudden disappearance just as I wished you should. Pray appease for me every one that may have taken offence at it. I never wished to give any one pain, and even now I cannot say anything to excuse myself. God keep me from ever afflicting my friends with the premises which led me to this conclusion.

Here I am gradually recovering from my "salto mortale," and studying rather than enjoying myself. Rome is a world, and one must spend years before one can become at all acquainted with it. How happy do I consider those travellers who can take a look at it and go their way!

Rome—Winckelmann's letters.

Yesterday many of Winckelmann's letters, which he wrote from Italy, fell into my hands. With what emotions did I not begin to read them. About this same season, some one and thirty years ago, he came hither a still poorer simpleton than myself, but then he had such thorough German enthusiasm for all that is sterling and genuine, either in antiquity or art. How bravely and diligently did he not work his way through all difficulties; and what good does it not do me,—the remembrance of such a man in such a place!

After the objects of Nature, who in all her parts is true to herself and consistent, nothing speaks so loudly as the remembrance of a good intelligent man,—that genuine art which is no less consistent and harmonious than herself. Here in Rome we feel this right well, where so many an arbitrary caprice has had its day, where so many a folly has immortalized itself by its power and its gold.

The following passage in Winckelmann's letters to Franconia particularly pleased me. "We must look at all the objects in Rome with a certain degree of phlegm, or else one will be taken for a Frenchman. In Rome, I believe, is the high school for all the world, and I also have been purified and tried in it."

This remark applies directly to my mode of visiting the different objects here; and most certain is it, that out of Rome no one can have an idea how one is schooled in Rome. One must, so to speak, be new born, and one looks back on one's earlier notions, as a man does on the little shoes, which fitted him when a child. The most ordinary man learns something here, at least he gains one uncommon idea, even though it never should pass into his whole being.

This letter will reach you in the new year. All good wishes for the beginning; before the end of it we shall see one another again, and that will be no little gratification. The one that is passing away has been the most important of my life. I may now die, or I may tarry a little longer yet; in either case it will be alike well. And now a word or two more for the little ones.

To the children you may either read or tell what follows. Here there are no signs of winter. The gardens are planted with evergreens; the sun shines bright and warm; snow is nowhere to be seen, except on the most distant hills towards the north. The citron trees, which are planted against the garden walls, are now, one after another, covered with reeds, but the oranges are allowed to stand quite open. A hundred of the very finest fruit may be seen hanging on a single tree, which is not, as with us, dwarfed, and planted in a bucket, but stands in the earth free and joyous, amidst a long line of brothers. The oranges are even now very good, but it is thought they will be still finer.

We were lately at the sea, and had a haul of fish, and drew to the light fishes, crabs, and rare univalves of the most wonderful shapes conceivable; also the fish which gives an electric shock to all who touch it.

Rome, Dec. 20, 1786.

And yet, after all, it is more trouble and care than enjoyment. The Regenerator, which is changing me within and without, continues to work. I certainly thought that I had something really to learn here; but that I should have to take so low a place in the school, that I must forget so much that I had learnt, or rather absolutely unlearn so much,—that I had never the least idea of. Now, however, that I am once convinced of its necessity, I have devoted myself to the task; and the more I am obliged to renounce my former self, the more delighted I am. I am like an architect who has begun to build a tower, but finds he has laid a bad foundation: he becomes aware of the fact betimes, and willingly goes to work to pull down all that he has raised above the earth; having done so, he proceeds to enlarge his ground plan, and now rejoices to anticipate the undoubted stability of his future building. Heaven grant that, on my return, the moral consequences may be discernible of all that this living in a wider world has effected within me. For, in sooth, the moral sense as well as the artistic is undergoing a great change.

Rome—Dr. Münter.

Dr. Münter is here on his return from his tour in Sicily—an energetic, vehement man. What objects he may have, I cannot tell. He will reach you in May, and has much to tell you. He has been two years travelling in Italy. He is disgusted with the Italians, who have not paid due respect to the weighty letters of recommendation which were to have opened to him many an archive, many a private library; so that he is far from having accomplished his object in coming here.

He has collected some beautiful coins, and possesses, he tells me, a manuscript which reduces numismatics to as precise a system of characteristics as the Linnæan system of botany. Herder, he says, knows still more about it: probably a transcript of it will be permitted. To do something of the kind is certainly possible, and, if well done, it will be truly valuable; and we must sooner or later enter seriously into this branch of learning.

Rome, Dec. 25, 1786.

I am now beginning to revisit the principal sights of Rome: in such second views, our first amazement generally dies away into more of sympathy and a purer perception of the true value of the objects. In order to form an idea of the highest achievements of the human mind, the soul must first attain to perfect freedom from prejudice and prepossession.

Marble is a rare material. It is on this account that the Apollo Belvedere in the original is so infinitely ravishing; for that sublime air of youthful freedom and vigour, of never-changing juvenescence, which breathes around the marble, at once vanishes in the best even of plaster casts.

In the Palace Rondanini, which is right opposite to our lodgings, there is a Medusa-mask, above the size of life, in which the attempt to portray a lofty and beautiful countenance in the numbing agony of death has been indescribably successful. I possess an excellent cast of it, but the charm of the marble remains not. The noble semi-transparency of the yellow stone-approaching almost to the hue of flesh—is vanished. Compared with it, the plaster of Paris has a chalky and dead look.

And yet how delightful it is to go to a modeller in gypsum, and to see the noble limbs of a statue come out one by one from the mould, and thereby to acquire wholly new ideas of their shapes. And then, again, by such means all that in Rome is scattered, is brought together, for the purpose of comparison; and this alone is of inestimable service. Accordingly, I could not resist the temptation to procure a cast of the colossal head of Jupiter. It stands right opposite to my bed, in a good light, in order that I may address my morning devotions towards it. With all its grandeur and dignity it has, however, given rise to one of the funniest interludes possible.

Our old hostess, when she comes to make my bed, is generally followed by her pet cat. Yesterday I was sitting in the great hall, and could hear the old woman pursue her avocation within. On a sudden, in great haste, and with an excitement quite unusual to her, she opens the door, and calls to me to come quickly and see a wonder. To my question what was the matter, she replied the cat was saying its prayers. Of the animal she had long observed, she told me, that it had as much sense as a Christian—but this was really a great wonder. I hastened to see it with my own eyes; and it was indeed strange enough. The bust stood on a high pedestal, and as there was a good length of the shoulders, the head stood rather high. Now the cat had sprung upon the table, and had placed her fore-feet on the breast of the god, and, stretching her body to its utmost length, just reached with her muzzle his sacred beard, which she was licking most ceremoniously; and neither by the exclamation of the hostess, nor my entrance into the room, was she at all disturbed. I left the good dame to her astonishment; and she afterwards accounted for puss's strange act of devotion, by supposing that this sharp-nosed cat had caught scent of the grease which had probably been transferred from the mould to the deep lines of the beard, and had there remained.

Dec. 29, 1786.

Of Tischbein I have much to say and to boast. In the first place, a thorough and original German, he has made himself entirely what he is. In the next place, I must make grateful mention of the friendly attentions he has shewn me throughout the time of his second stay in Rome. For he has had prepared for me a series of copies after the best masters, some in black chalk, others in sepia and water colours; which in Germany, when I shall be at a distance from the originals, will grow in value, and will serve to remind me of all that is rarest and best.

At the commencement of his career as an artist, when he set up as a portrait painter, Tischbein came in contact, especially in Munich, with distinguished personages, and in his intercourse with them his feeling of art has been strengthened and his views enlarged.

The second part of the "*Zerstrente Blatter*" (stray leaves) I have brought with me hither, and they are doubly welcome. What good influence this little book has had on me, even on the second perusal, Herder, for his reward, shall be circumstantially informed. Tischbein cannot conceive how anything so excellent could ever have been written by one who has never been in Italy.

Dec. 29, 1786.

In this world of artists one lives, as it were, in a mirrored chamber, where, without wishing it, one sees one's own image and those of others continually multiplied. Latterly I have often observed Tischbein attentively regarding me; and now it appears that he has long cherished the idea of painting my portrait. His design is already settled, and the canvass stretched. I am to be drawn of the size of life, enveloped in a white mantle, and sitting on a fallen obelisk, viewing the ruins of the Campagna di Roma, which are to fill up the background of the picture. It will form a beautiful piece, only it mil be rather too large for our northern habitations. I indeed may again crawl into them, but the portrait will never be able to enter their doors.

Dec. 29, 1786.

I cannot help observing the great efforts that are constantly being made to draw me from my retirement—how the poets either read or get their pieces read to me; and I should be blind did I not see that it depends only on myself whether I shall play a part or not. All this is amusing enough; for I have long since measured the lengths to which one may go in Rome. The many little coteries here at the feet of the mistress of the world strongly remind one occasionally of an ordinary country town.

In sooth, things here are much like what they are every where else; and what *could be done with me and through me* causes me ennui long before it is accomplished. Here you must take up with one party or another, and help them to carry on their feuds and cabals; and you must praise these artists and those dilettanti, disparage their rivals, and, above all, be pleased with every thing that the rich and great do. All these little meannesses, then, for the sake of which one is almost ready to leave the world itself,—must I here mix myself up with them, and that too when I have neither interest nor stake in them? No; I shall go no further than is merely necessary to know what is going on, and thus to learn, in private, to be more contented with my lot, and to procure for myself and others all the pleasure possible in the dear wide world. I wish to see Rome in its abiding and permanent features, and not as it passes and changes with every ten years. Had I time, I might wish to employ it better. Above all, one may study history here quite differently from what one can on any other spot. In other places one has, as it were, to read oneself into it from without; here one fancies that he reads from within outwards: all arranges itself around you, and seems to proceed from you. And this holds good not only of Roman history, but also of that of the whole world. From Rome I can accompany the conquerors on their march to the Weser or to the Euphrates; or, if I wish to be a sight-seer, I can wait in the Via Sacra for the triumphant generals, and in the meantime receive for my support the largesses of corn and money; and so take a very comfortable share in all the splendour.

Rome, Jan. 2, 1787.

Men may say what they will in favour of a written and oral communication; it is only in a very few cases indeed that it is at all adequate, for it never can convey the true character of any object soever—no, not even of a purely intellectual one. But if one has already enjoyed a sure and steady view of the object, then one may profitably hear or read about it, for then there exists a living impression around which all else may arrange itself in the mind; and then one can think and judge.

You have often laughed at me, and wished to drive me away from the peculiar taste I had for examining stones, plants, or animals, from certain theoretical points of view: now, however, I am directing my attention to architects, statuaries, and painters, and hope to find myself learning something even from them.

Without date.

After all this I must further speak to you of the state of indecision I am in with regard to my stay in Italy. In my last letter I wrote you that it was my purpose immediately after Easter to leave Rome, and return home. Until then I shall yet gather a few more shells from the shore of the great ocean, and so my most urgent needs will have been appeased. I am now cured of a violent passion and disease, and restored to the enjoyment of life, to the enjoyment of history, poetry, and of antiquities, and have treasures which it will take me many a long year to polish and to finish.

Rome—My plans for the future.

Recently, however, friendly voices have reached me to the effect that I ought not to be in a hurry, but to wait till I can return home with still richer gains. From the Duke, too, I have received a very kind and considerate letter, in which he excuses me from my duties for an indefinite period, and sets me quite at ease with respect to my absence. My mind therefore turns to the vast field which I must otherwise have left untrodden. For instance, in the case of coins and cameos, I have as yet been able to do nothing. I have indeed begun to read Winckelmann's History of Art, but have passed over Egypt; for, I feel once again, that I must look out before me; and I have done so with regard to Egyptian matters. The more we look, the more distant becomes the horizon of art; and he who would step surely, must step slowly.

I intend to stay here till the Carnival; and, in the first week of Lent shall set off for Naples, taking Tischbein with me, both because it will be a treat to him, and because, in his society, all my enjoyments are more than doubled. I purpose to return hither before Easter, for the sake of the solemnities of Passion week. But there Sicily lies—there below. A journey thither requires more preparation, and ought to be taken too in the autumn: it must not be merely a ride round it and across it, which is soon done, but from which one brings away with us in return for our fatigue and money nothing but a simple—*I have seen it*. The best way is to take up one's quarters, first of all, in Palermo, and afterwards in Catania; and then from those points to make fixed and profitable excursions, having previously, however, well studied *Riedesel* and others on the locality.

If, then, I spend the summer in Rome, I shall set to work to study, and to prepare myself for visiting Sicily. As I cannot well go there before November, and must stay there till over December, it will be the spring of 1788 before I can hope to get home again. Then, again, I have had before my mind a *medius terminus*. Giving up the idea of visiting Sicily, I have thought of spending a part of the summer at Rome, and then, after paying a second visit to Florence, getting home by the autumn.

But all these plans have been much perplexed by the news of the Duke's misfortune. Since the letters which informed me of this event I have had no rest, and would most like to set off at Easter, laden with the fragments of my conquests, and, passing quickly through Upper Italy, be in Weimar again by June.

I am too much alone here to decide; and I write you this long story of my whole position, that you may be good enough to summon a council of those who love me, and who, being on the spot, know the circumstances better than I do. Let them, therefore, determine the proper course for me to take, on the supposition of what, I assure you, is the fact, that I am myself more disposed to return than to stay. The strongest tie that holds me in Italy is Tischbein. I should never, even should it be my happy lot to return a second time to this beautiful land, learn so much in so short a time as I have now done in the society of this well-educated, highly refined, and most upright man who is devoted to me both body and soul. I cannot now tell you how thickly the scales are falling from off my eyes. He who travels by night, takes the dawn for day, and a murky day for brightness: what will he think, then, when he shall see the sun ascending the mid-heaven? For I have hitherto kept myself from all the world, which yet is yearning to catch me by degrees, and which I, for my part, was not unwilling to watch and observe with stealthy glances.

I have written to Fritz a joking account of my reception into the *Arcadia*; and indeed it is only a subject of joke, for the Institute is really sunk into miserable insignificance.

Next Monday week Monti's tragedy is to be acted. He is extremely anxious, and not without cause. He has a very troublesome public, which requires to be amused from moment to moment; and his piece has no brilliant passages in it. He has asked me to go with him to his box, and to stand by him as confessor in this critical moment. Another is ready to translate my "Iphigenia;" another—to do I know not what, in honour of me. They are all so divided into parties, and so bitter against each other. But my countrymen are so unanimous in my favour, that if I gave them any encouragement, and yielded to them in the very least, they would try a hundred follies with me, and end with crowning me on the Capitol, of which they have already seriously thought—so foolish is it to have a stranger and a Protestant to play the first part in a comedy. What connexion there is in all this, and how great a fool I was to think that it was all intended for my honour,—of all this we will talk together one day.

January 6, 1787.

I have just come from Moritz, whose arm is healed, and loosed from its bandages. It is well set, firm, and he can move it quite freely. What during these last forty days I have experienced and learned, as nurse, confessor, and private secretary to this patient, may prove of benefit to us hereafter. The most painful sufferings and the noblest enjoyments went side by side throughout this whole period.

To refresh me, I yesterday had set up in our sitting-room a cast of a colossal head of Juno, of which the original is in the Villa Ludovisi. This was my first love in Rome; and now I have gained the object of my wishes. No words can give the remotest idea of it. It is like one of Homer's songs.

I have, however, deserved the neighbourhood of such good society for the future, for I can now tell you that Iphigenia is at last finished—*i.e.* that it lies before me on the table in two tolerably concordant copies, of which one will very soon begin its pilgrimage towards yourself. Receive it with all indulgence, for, to speak the truth, what stands on the paper is not exactly what I intended; but still it will convey an idea of what was in my mind.

You complain occasionally of some obscure passages in my letters, which allude to the oppression, which I suffer in the midst of the most glorious objects in the world. With all this my fellow traveller, this Grecian princess, has had a great deal to do, for she has kept me close at work when I wished to be seeing sights.

I often think of our worthy friend, who had long determined upon a grand tour, which one might well term a voyage of discovery. After he had studied and economized several years, with a view to this object, he took it in his head to carry away with him the daughter of a noble house, thinking it was all one still.

With no less of caprice, I determined to take Iphigenia with me to Carlsbad. I will now briefly enumerate the places where I held special converse with her.

When I had left behind me the Brenner, I took her out of my large portmanteau, and placed her by my side. At the Lago di Garda, while the strong south wind drove the waves on the beach, and where I was at least as much alone as my heroine on the coast of Tauris, I drew the first outlines, which afterwards I filled up at Verona, Vicenza, and Padua; but above all, and most diligently at Venice. After this, however, the work came to a stand-still, for I hit upon a new design, viz., of writing an Iphigenia at Delphi, which I should have immediately carried into execution, but for the distractions of my young, and for a feeling of duty towards the older piece.

In Rome, however, I went on with it, and proceeded with tolerable steadiness. Every evening before I went to sleep I prepared myself for my morning's task, which was resumed immediately I awoke. My way of proceeding was quite simple. I calmly wrote down the piece, and tried the melody line by line, and period by period. What has been thus produced, you shall soon judge of. For my part, doing this work, I have learnt more than I have done. With the piece itself there shall follow some further remarks.

Jan. 6, 1787.

To speak again of church matters, I must tell you that on the night of Christmas-day we wandered about in troops, and visited all the churches where solemn services were being performed; one especially was visited, because of its organ and music. The latter was so arranged, that in its tones nothing belonging to pastoral music was wanting—neither the singing of the shepherds, nor the twittering of birds, nor the bleating of sheep.

Rome—Christmas-day.

On Christmas-day I saw the Pope and the whole consistory in S. Peter's, where he celebrated high mass partly before and partly from his throne. It is of its kind an unequalled sight, splendid and dignified enough, but I have grown so old in my Protestant Diogenism, that this pomp and splendour revolt more than they attract me. I, like my pious forefathers, am disposed to say to these spiritual conquerors of the world, "Hide not from me the sun of higher art and purer humanity."

Yesterday, which was the Feast of Epiphany, I saw and heard mass celebrated after the Greek rite. The ceremonies appeared to me more solemn, more severe, more suggestive, and yet more popular than the Latin.

But there, too, I also felt again that I am too old for anything, except for truth alone. Their ceremonies and operatic music, their gyrations and ballet-like movements—it all passes off from me like water from an oilskin cloak. A work of nature, however, like that of a Sunset seen from the Villa Madonna—a work of art, like my much honoured Juno, makes a deep and vivid impression on me.

And now I must ask you to congratulate me with regard to theatrical matters. Next week seven theatres will be opened. Anfossi himself is here, and will act "Alexander in India." A Cyrus also will be represented, and the "Taking of Troy" as a ballet. That assuredly must be something for the children!

Rome, Jan. 10, 1787.

Here, then, comes the "child of sorrows," for this surname is due to "Iphigenia" in more than one sense. On the occasion of my reading it out to our artists, I put a mark against several lines, some of which I have in my opinion improved, but others I have allowed to stand—perhaps Herder will cross a few of them with his pen.

The true cause of my having for many years preferred prose for my works, is the great uncertainty in which our prosody fluctuates, in consequence of which many of my judicious, learned friends and fellow artists have left many things to taste, a course, however, which was little favourable to the establishing of any certain standard.

I should never have attempted to translate "Iphigenia" into iambics, had not Moritz's prosody shone upon me like a star of light. My conversation with its author, especially during his confinement from his accident, has still more enlightened me on the subject, and I would recommend my friends to think favourably of it.

It is somewhat singular, that in our language we have but very few syllables which are decidedly long or short. With all the others, one proceeds as taste or caprice may dictate. Now Moritz, after much thought, has hit upon the idea that there is a certain order of rank among our syllables, and that the one which in sense is more emphatic is long as compared with the less significant, and makes the latter short, but on the other hand, it does in its turn become short, whenever it comes into the neighbourhood of another which possesses greater weight and emphasis than itself. Here, then, is at least a rule to go by: and even though it does not decide the whole matter, still it opens out a path by which one may hope to get a little further. I have often allowed myself to be influenced by these rules, and generally have found my ear agreeing with them.

As I formerly spoke of a public reading, I must quietly tell you how it passed off. These young men accustomed to those earlier vehement and impetuous pieces, expected something after the fashion of Berlichingen, and could not so well make out the calm movement of "Iphigenia," and yet the nobler and purer passages did not fail of effect, Tischbein, who also could hardly reconcile himself to this entire absence of passion, produced a pretty illustration or symbol of the work. He illustrated it by a sacrifice, of which the smoke, borne down by a light breeze, descends to the earth, while the freer flame strives to ascend on high. The drawing was very pretty and significant. I have the sketch still by me. And thus the work, which I thought to despatch in no time, has employed, hindered, occupied, and tortured me a full quarter of a year. This is not the first time that I have made an important task a mere by-work; but we will on that subject no longer indulge in fancies and disputes.

I inclose a beautiful cameo,—a lion with a gad-fly buzzing at his nose; this seems to have been a favourite subject with the ancients, for they have repeated it very often. I should like you from this time forward to seal your letters with it, in order that through this (little) trifle an echo of art may, as it were, reverberate from you to me.

Rome, Jan. 13, 1787.

How much have I to say each day, and how sadly am I prevented, either by amusement or occupation, from committing to paper a single sage remark! And then again, the fine days when it is better to be anywhere rather than in one's room, which, without stove or chimney, receive us only to sleep or to discomfort! Some of the incidents of the last week, however, must not be left unrecorded.

In the Palace Giustiniani there is a Minerva, which claims my undivided homage. Winckelmann scarcely mentions it, and, at any rate, not in the right place; and I feel myself quite unworthy to say anything about it. As we contemplated the image, and stood gazing at it a long time, the wife of the keeper of the collection said—This must have once been a holy image; and the English, who happen to be of this religion, are still accustomed to pay worship to it by kissing this hand of it, (which in truth was quite white, while the rest of the statue was brownish). She further told us, that a lady of *this* religion had been there not long before, and, throwing herself on her knees before the statue, had regularly offered prayer to it; and I, she said, as a Christian, could not help smiling at so strange an action, and was obliged to run out of the room, lest I should burst out into a loud laugh before her face. As I was unwilling to move from the statue, she asked me if my beloved was at all like the statue that it charmed me so much. The good dame knew of nothing besides devotion or love; but of the pure admiration for a glorious piece of man's handiwork,—of a mere sympathetic veneration for the creation of the human intellect, she could form no idea. We rejoiced in that noble Englishwoman, and went away with a longing to turn our steps back again, and I shall certainly soon go once more thither. If my friends wish for a more particular description, let them read what Winckelmann says of the high style of art among the Greeks; unfortunately, however, he does not adduce this Minerva as an illustration. But if I do not greatly err, it is, nevertheless, of this high and severe style, since it passes into the beautiful,—it is, as it were, a bud that opens,—and so a Minerva, whose character this idea of transition so well suits.

Now for a spectacle of a different kind. On the feast of the Three Kings, or the Commemoration of Christ's manifestation to the Gentiles, we paid a visit to the Propaganda. There, in the presence of three cardinals and a large audience, an essay was first of all delivered, which treated of the place in which the Virgin Mary received the three Magi,—in the stable,—or if not, where? Next, some Latin verses were read on similar subjects, and after this a series of about thirty scholars came forward, one by one, and read a little piece of poetry in their native tongues; Malabar, Epirotic, Turkish, Moldavian, Hellenic, Persian, Colchian, Hebrew, Arabic, Syrian, Coptic, Saracenic, Armenian, Erse, Madagassic, Icelandic, Bohemian, Greek, Isaurian, Æthiopic, &c. The poems seemed for the most part to be composed in the national syllabic measure, and to be delivered with the vernacular declamation, for most barbaric rhythms and tones occurred. Among them the Greek sounded like a star in the night. The auditory laughed most unmercifully at the strange sounds; and so this representation also became a farce.

And now (before concluding) a little anecdote, to show with what levity holy things are treated in Holy Home. The deceased cardinal, Albani, was once present at one of those festal meetings which. I have just been describing. One of the scholars, with his face turned towards the Cardinals, began in a strange pronunciation, *Gnaja! Gnaja!* so that it sounded something like *canaglia! canaglia!* The Cardinal turned to his brothers with a whisper, "He knows us at any rate."

January 13, 1787.

How much has Winckelmann done, and yet how much reason has he left us to wish that he had done still more. With the materials which he had collected he built quickly, in order to reach the roof. Were he still living, he would be the first to give us a re-cast of his great work. What further observations, what corrections would he not have made—to what good use would he not have put all that others, following his own principles, have observed and effected. And, besides, Cardinal Albani is dead, out of respect to whom he has written much; and, perhaps, concealed much.

January 15, 1787.

And so then, "Aristodemo" has at last been acted, and with good success too, and the greatest applause; as the Abbate Monti is related to the house of the Nepoté, and is highly esteemed among the higher orders: from these, therefore, all was to be hoped for. The boxes indeed were but sparing in their plaudits; as for the pit, it was won from the very first, by the beautiful language of the poet and the appropriate recitation of the actors, and it omitted no opportunity of testifying its approbation. The bench of the German artists distinguished itself not a little; and this time they were quite in place, though it is at all times a little overloud.

The author himself remained at home, full of anxiety for the success of the piece. From act to act favourable despatches arrived, which changed his fear into the greatest joy. Now there is no lack of repetitions of the representation, and all is on the best track. Thus, by the most opposite things, if only each has the merit it claims, the favour of the multitude, as well as of the connoisseur, may be won.

But the acting was in the highest degree meritorious, and the chief actor, who appears throughout the piece, spoke and acted cleverly,—one could almost fancy one of the ancient Cæsars was marching before us. They had very judiciously transferred to their stage dresses the costume which, in the statue, strikes the spectator as so dignified; and one saw at once that the actor had studied the antique.

January 18, 1787.

Rome is threatened with a great artistic loss. The King of Naples has ordered the Hercules Farnese to be brought to his palace. The news has made all the artists quite sad; however, on this occasion, we shall see something which was hidden from our forefathers.

The aforesaid statue, namely, from the head to the knee, with the lower part of the feet, together with the sockle on which it stood, were found within the Farnesian domain, but the legs from the knee to the ancle were wanting, and had been supplied by Giuglielmo Porta; on these it had stood since its discovery to the present day. In the mean time, however, the genuine old legs were found in the lands of the Borghesi, and were to be seen in their villa.

Recently, however, the Prince Borghese has achieved a, victory over himself, and has made a present of these costly relics to the King of Naples. The legs by Porta are being removed, and the genuine ones replaced; and every one is promising himself, however well contented he has been hitherto with the old, quite a new treat, and a more harmonious enjoyment.

Rome, January 18, 1787.

Yesterday, which was the festival of the Holy Abbot S. Antony, we had a merry day; the weather was the finest in the world; though there had been a hard frost during the night, the day was bright and warm.

One may remark, that all religions which enlarge their worship or their speculations must at last come to this, of making the brute creation in some degree partakers of spiritual favours. S. Anthony,—Abbot or Bishop,—is the patron Saint of all four-footed creatures; his festival is a kind of Saturnalian holiday for the otherwise oppressed beasts, and also for their keepers and drivers. All the gentry must on this day either remain at home, or else be content to travel on foot. And there are no lack of fearful stories, which tell how unbelieving masters, who forced their coachmen to drive them on this day, were punished by suffering great calamities.

Rome—Death of Frederick the Great.

The church of the Saint lies in so wide and open a district, that it might almost be called a desert. On this day, however, it is full of life and fun. Horses and mules, with their manes and tails prettily, not to say gorgeously, decked out with ribbons, are brought before the little chapel, (which stands at some distance from the church,) where a priest, armed with a brush, and not sparing of the holy water, which stands before him in buckets and tubs, goes on sprinkling the lively creatures, and often plays them a roguish trick, in order to make them start and frisk. Pious coachmen offer their wax-tapers, of larger or smaller size; the masters send alms and presents, in order that the valuable and useful animals may go safely through the coming year without hurt or accidents. The donkies and horned cattle, no less valuable and useful to their owners, have, likewise, their modest share in this blessing.

Afterwards we delighted ourselves with a long walk under a delicious sky, and surrounded by the most interesting objects, to which, however, we this time paid very little attention, but gave full scope and rein to joke and merriment.

Rome, January 19, 1787.

So then the great king, whose glory filled the world, whose deeds make him worthy even of the Papists' paradise, has departed this life, and gone to converse with heroes like himself in the realm of shades. How disposed does one feel to sit still when such an one is gone to his rest.

This has been a very good day. First of all we visited a part of the Capitol, which we had previously neglected; then we crossed the Tiber, and drank some Spanish wine on board a ship which had just come into port:—it was on this spot that Romulus and Remus are said to have been found. Thus keeping, as it were, a double or treble festival, we revelled in the inspiration of art, of a mild atmosphere, and of antiquarian reminiscences.

January 20, 1787.

What at first furnishes a hearty enjoyment, when we take it superficially only, often weighs on us afterwards most oppressively, when we see that without solid knowledge the true delight must be missed.

As regards anatomy, I am pretty well prepared, and I have, not without some labour, gained a tolerable knowledge of the human frame; for the continual examination of the ancient statues is continually stimulating one to a more perfect understanding of it. In our Medico Chirurgical Anatomy, little more is in view than an acquaintance with the several parts, and for this purpose the *sorriest picture of the muscles* may serve very well; but in Rome the most exquisite parts would not even be noticed, unless as helping to make a noble and beautiful form.

In the great Lazaretto of San Spirito there has been prepared for the use of the artists a very fine anatomical figure, displaying the whole muscular system. Its beauty is really amazing. It might pass for some flayed demigod,—even a Marsyas.

Thus, after the example of the ancients, men here study the human skeleton, not merely as an artistically arranged series of bones, but rather for the sake of the ligaments with which life and motion are carried on.

When now I tell you, that in the evening we also study perspective, it must be pretty plain to you that we are not idle. With all our studies, however, we are always hoping to do more than we ever accomplish.

Rome, January 22, 1787.

Of the artistic sense of Germans, and of their artistic life, of these one may well say,—One hears sounds, but they are not in unison. When now I bethink myself what glorious objects are in my neighbourhood, and how little I have profited by them, I am almost tempted to despair; but then again I console myself with my promised return, when I hope to be able to understand these master-pieces, around which now I go groping miserably in the dark.

But, in fact, even in Rome itself, there is but little provision made for one who earnestly wishes to study art as a whole. He must patch it up and put it together for himself out of endless but still gorgeously rich ruins. No doubt but few only of those who visit Rome, are purely and earnestly desirous to see and to learn things rightly and thoroughly. They all follow, more or less, their own fancies and conceits, and this is observed by all alike who attend upon the strangers. Every guide has his own object, every one has his own dealer to recommend, his own artist to favour; and why should he not? for does not the inexperienced at once prize, as most excellent, whatever may be presented to him as such?

Rome—The removal of Antiques.

It would have been a great benefit to the study of art—indeed a peculiarly rich museum might have been formed—if the government, (whose permission even at present must be obtained before any piece of antiquity can be removed from the city,) had on such occasions invariably insisted on casts being delivered to it of the objects removed. Besides, if any Pope had established such a rule, before long every one would have opposed all further removals; for in a few years people would have been frightened at the number and value of the treasures thus carried off, for which, even now, permission can only be obtained by secret influence.

January 22, 1787.

The representation of the "Aristodemo" has stimulated, in an especial degree, the patriotism of our German artists, which before was far from being asleep. They never omit an occasion to speak well of my "Iphigenia;" some passages have from time to time been again called for, and I have found myself at last compelled to a second reading of the whole. And thus also I have discovered many passages winch went off the tongue more smoothly than they look on the paper.

The favorable report of it has at last sounded even in the ears of Reiffenstein and Angelica, who entreated that I should produce my work once more for their gratification. I begged, however, for a brief respite, though I was obliged to describe to them, somewhat circumstantially, the plan and movement of the plot. The description won the approbation of these person ages more even than I could have hoped for; and Signor Zucchi also, of whom I least of all expected it, evinced a warm and liberal sympathy with the piece. The latter circumstance, however, is easily accounted for by the fact that the drama approximates very closely to the old and customary form of Greek, French, and Italian tragedy, which is most agreeable to every one whose taste has not been spoilt by the temerities of the English stage.

Rome, Jan. 25, 1787.

It becomes every day more difficult to fix the termination of my stay in Rome; just as one finds the sea continually deeper the further one sails on it, so it is also with the examination of this city.

It is impossible to understand the present without a knowledge of the past; and to compare the two, requires both time and leisure. The very site of the city carries us back to the time of its being founded. We see at once that no great people, under a wise leader, settled here from its wanderings, and with wise forecast laid the foundations of the seat of future empire. No powerful prince would ever have selected this spot as well suited for the habitation of a colony. No; herdsmen and vagabonds first prepared here a dwelling for themselves: a couple of adventurous youths laid the foundation of the palaces of the masters of the world on *the* hill at whose foot, amidst the marshes and the silt, they had defied the officers of law and justice. Moreover, the seven hills of Rome are not elevations above the land which lies beyond them, but merely above the Tiber and its ancient bed, which afterwards became the Campus Martius. If the coming spring is favourable to my making wider excursions in the neighbourhood, I shall be able to describe more fully the unfavourable site. Even now I feel the most heartfelt sympathy with the grief and lamentation of the women of Alba whey they saw their city destroyed, and were forced to leave its beautiful site, the choice of a wise prince and leader, to share the fogs of the Tiber, and to people the miserable Cœlian hill, from which their eyes still fell upon the paradise they had been drawn from.

I know as yet but little of the neighbourhood, but I am perfectly convinced that no city of the ancient world was worse situated than Rome: no wonder, then, if the Romans, as soon as they had swallowed up all the neighbouring states, went out of it, and, with their villas, returned to the noble sites of the cities they had destroyed, in order to live and to enjoy life.

Rome, Jan. 25, 1787.

It suggests a very pleasing contemplation to think how many people are living here in retirement, calmly occupied with their several tastes and pursuits. In the house of a clergyman, who, without any particular natural talent, has nevertheless devoted himself to the arts, we saw most interesting copies of some excellent paintings which he had imitated in miniature. His most successful attempt was after the Last Supper of Leonardo da Vinci. The moment of time is when the Lord, who is sitting familiarly at supper with his disciples, utters the awful words, "One of you shall betray me."

Hopes are entertained that he will allow an engraving to be taken either of this or of another copy, on which he is at present engaged. It will be indeed a rich present to give to the great public a faithful imitation of this gem of art.

Rome—Father Jacquier.

A few days since I visited, at the Trinità de' Monte, Father Jacquier, a Franciscan. He is a Frenchman by birth, and well known by his mathematical writings; and although far advanced in years, is still very agreeable and intelligent. He has been acquainted with all the most distinguished men of his day, and has even spent several months with Voltaire, who had a great liking for him.

I have also become acquainted with many more of such good, sterling men, of whom countless numbers are to be found here, whom, however, a sort of professional mistrust keeps estranged from each other. The book-trade furnishes no point of union, and literary novelties are seldom fruitful; and so it befits the solitary to seek out the hermits. For since the acting of "Aristodemo," in whose favour we made a very lively demonstration, I have been again much sought after. But it was quite clear I was not sought for my own sake; it was always with a view to strengthen a party—to use me as an instrument; and if I had been willing to come forward and declare my side, I also, as a phantom, should for a time have played a short part. But now, since they see that nothing is to be made of me, they let me pass; and so I go steadily on my own way.

Indeed, my existence has lately taken in some ballast, which gives it the necessary gravity. I do not now frighten myself with the spectres which used so often to play before my eyes. Be, therefore, of good heart. You will keep me above water, and draw me back again to you.

Rome, Jan. 28, 1787.

Two considerations which more or less affect every thing, and which one is compelled at every moment to give way to, I must not fail to set down, now that they have become quite clear to me.

First of all, then, the vast and yet merely fragmentary riches of this city, and each single object of art, is constantly suggesting the question, To what date does it owe its existence? Winckelmann urgently calls upon us to separate epochs, to distinguish the different styles which the several masters employed, and the way in which, in the course of time, they gradually perfected them, and at last corrupted them again. Of the necessity of so doing, every real friend of art is soon thoroughly convinced. We all acknowledge the justice and the importance of the requisition. But now, how to attain to this conviction? However clearly and correctly the notion itself may be conceived, yet without long preparatory labours there will always be a degree of vagueness and obscurity as to the particular application. A sure eye, strengthened by many years' exercise, is above all else necessary. Here hesitation or reserve are of no avail. Attention, however, is now directed to this point; and every one who is in any degree in earnest seems convinced that in this domain a sure judgment is impossible, unless it has been formed by historical study.

The second consideration refers exclusively to the arts of the Greeks, and endeavours to ascertain how those inimitable artists proceeded in their successful attempts to evolve from the human form their system of divine types, which is so perfect and complete, that neither any leading character nor any intermediate shade or transition is wanting. For my part, I cannot withhold the conjecture that they proceeded according to the same laws that Nature works by, and which I am endeavouring to discover. Only, there is in them something more besides, which it is impossible to express.

Rome, Feb. 2, 1787.

Rome—The Coliseum.

Of the beauty of a walk through Rome by moonlight it is impossible to form a conception, without having witnessed it. All single objects are swallowed up by the great masses of light and shade, and nothing but grand and general outlines present themselves to the eye. For three several days we have enjoyed to the full the brightest and most glorious of nights. Peculiarly beautiful at such a time is the Coliseum. At night it is always closed; a hermit dwells in a little shrine within its range, and beggars of all kinds nestle beneath its crumbling arches: the latter had lit a fire on the arena, and a gentle wind bore down the smoke to the ground, so that the lower portion of the ruins was quite hid by it, while above the vast walls stood out in deeper darkness before the eye. As we stopped at the gate to contemplate the scene through the iron gratings, the moon shone brightly in the heavens above. Presently the smoke found its way up the sides, and through every chink and opening, while the moon lit it up like a cloud. The sight was exceedingly glorious. In such a light one ought also to see the Pantheon, the Capitol, the Portico of St. Peter's, and the other grand streets and squares:—and thus sun and moon, like the human mind, have quite a different work to do here from elsewhere, where the vastest and yet the most elegant of masses present themselves to their rays.

Rome, Feb. 13, 1787.

I must mention a trifling fall of luck, even though it is but a little one. However, all luck, whether great or little, is of one kind, and always brings a joy with it. Near the Trinità de' Monte the ground has been lately dug up to form a foundation for the new Obelisk, and now the whole of this region is choked up with the ruins of the Gardens of Lucullus, which subsequently became the property of the Emperors. My perruquier was passing early one morning by the spot, and found in the pile of earth a flat piece of burnt clay, with some figures on it. Having washed it, he showed it to me. I eagerly secured the treasure. It is not quite a hand long, and seems to have been part of the stem of a great key. Two old men stand before an altar; they are of the most beautiful workmanship, and I am uncommonly delighted with my new acquisition. Were they on a cameo, one would greatly like to use it as a seal.

I have by me a collection also of many other objects, and none is worthless or unmeaning,—for that is impossible; here everything is instructive and significant. But my dearest treasure, however, is even that which I carry with me in my soul, and which, every growing, is capable of a still greater growth.

Rome, Feb. 15, 1787.

Before departing for Naples, I could not get off from another public reading of my "Iphigenia." Madam Angelica and Hofrath Reiffenstein were the auditory, and even Signor Zucchi had solicited to be present, because it was the wish of his spouse. While it was reading, however, he worked away at a great architectural plan—for he is very skilful in executing drawings of this kind, and especially the decorative parts. He went with Clerisseau to Dalmatia, and was the associate of all his labours, drawing the buildings and ruins for the plates, which the latter published. In this occupation he learned so much of perspective and effect, that in his old days he is able to amuse himself on paper in a very rational manner.

The tender soul of Angelica listened to the piece with incredible profoundness of sympathy. She promised me a drawing of one of the scenes, which I am to keep in remembrance of her. And now, just as I am about to quit Rome, I begin to feel myself tenderly attached to these kindhearted people. It is a source of mingled feelings of pleasure and regret to know that people are sorry to part with you.

Rome, Feb. 16, 1787.

The safe arrival of "Iphigenia" has been announced to me in a most cheering and agreeable way. On my way to the Opera, a letter from a well-known hand was brought to me,—this time doubly welcome; since it was sealed with the "Lion" a premonitory token of the safe arrival of my packet. I hurried into the Opera-house, and bustled to get a place among the strange faces beneath the great chandelier. At this moment I felt myself drawn so close to my friends, that I could almost have sprung forward to embrace them. From my heart I thank you even for having simply mentioned the arrival of the "Iphigenia," may your next be accompanied with a few kind words of approval.

Inclosed is the list of those among whom I wish the copies which I am to expect from Gösche to be distributed; for although it is with me a perfect matter of indifference how the public may receive these matters, still I hope by them to furnish slight gratification to my friends at least.

One undertakes too much. When I think on my last four volumes together, I become almost giddy—I am obliged to think of them separately, and then the fit passes off.

Rome—"Iphigenia"—"Tasso."

I should perhaps have done better had I kept my first resolution to send these things one by one into the world, and so undertake with fresh vigour and courage the new subjects which have most recently awakened my sympathy. Should I not, perhaps, do better were I to write the "Iphigenia at Delphi," instead of amusing myself with my fanciful sketches of "Tasso." However, I have bestowed upon the latter too much of my thoughts to give it up, and let it fall to the ground.

I am sitting in the ante-room near the chimney, and the warmth of a fire, for once well fed, gives me courage to commence a fresh sheet, for it is indeed a glorious thing to be able, with our newest thoughts, to reach into the distance, and by words to convey thither an idea of one's immediate state and circumstances. The weather is right glorious, the days are sensibly lengthening, the laurels and box are in blossom, as also are the almond-trees. Early this morning I was delighted with a strange sight; I saw in the distance tall, pole-like trees, covered over and over with the loveliest violet flowers. On a closer examination I found it was the plant known in our hothouses as the Judas-tree, and to botanists as the "*cercis siliquastrum.*" Its papilionaceous violet blossoms are produced directly from out of the stem. The stakes which I saw had been lopped last winter, and out of their bark well-shaped and deeply-tinted flowers were bursting by thousands. The daisies are also springing out of the ground as thick as ants; the crocus and the pheasant's eye are more rare, but even on this account more rich and ornamental.

What pleasures and what lessons will not the more southern land impart to me, and what new results will arise to me from them! With the things of nature it is as with those of art; much as is written about them, every one who sees them forms them into new combinations for himself.

When I think of Naples, and indeed of Sicily,—when I read their history, or look at views of them, it strikes me as singular that it should be even in these paradises of the world that the volcanic mountains manifest themselves so violently, for thousands of years alarming and confounding their inhabitants.

But I willingly drive out of my head the expectation of these much-prized scenes, in order that they may not lessen my enjoyment of the capital of the whole world before I leave it.

For the last fourteen days I have been moving about from morning to night; I am raking up everything I have not yet seen. I am also viewing for a second or even a third time all the most important objects, and they are all arranging themselves in tolerable order within my mind: for while the chief objects are taking their right places, there is space and room between them for many a less important one. My enthusiasm is purifying itself, and becoming more decided, and now at last my mind can rise to the height of the greatest and purest creations of art with calm admiration.

In my situation one is tempted to envy the artist who, by copies and imitations of some kind or other can, as it were, come near to those great conceptions, and can grasp them better than one who merely looks at and reflects upon them. In the end, however, every one feels he must do his best; and so I set all the sails of my intellect, in the hope of getting round this coast.

The stove is at present thoroughly warm, and piled up with excellent coals, which is seldom the case with us, as no one scarcely has time or inclination to attend to the fire two whole hours together; I will therefore avail myself of this agreeable temperature to rescue from my tablets a few notes which are almost obliterated.

On the 2nd of February we attended the ceremony of blessing the tapers in the Sistine chapel. I was in anything but a good humour, and shortly went off again with my friends; for I thought to myself those are the very candles which, for these three hundred years, have been dimming those noble paintings, and it is their smoke which, with priestly impudence, not merely hangs in clouds around the only sun of art, but from year to year obscures it more and more, and will at last envelop it in total darkness.

We therefore sought the free air, and after a long walk came upon S. Onofrio's, in a corner of which Tasso is buried. In the library of the monastery there is a bust of him, the face is of wax, and I please myself with fancying that it was taken after death: although the lines have lost some of their sharpness, and it is in some parts injured, still on the whole it serves better than any other I have yet seen to convey an idea of a talented, sensitive, and refined but reserved character.

So much for this time. I must now turn to glorious Volckmann's 2nd part, which contains Rome, and which I have not yet seen. Before I start for Naples, the harvest must be housed; good days are coming for binding the sheaves.

Rome, Feb. 17, 1787.

The weather is incredibly and inexpressibly beautiful; for the whole of February, with the exception of four rainy days, a pure bright sky, and the days towards noon almost too warm. One is tempted out into the open air, and if till lately one spent all one's time in the city among gods and heroes, the country has now all at once resumed its rights, and one can scarcely tear oneself from the surrounding scenes, lit up as they are with the most glorious days. Many a time does the remembrance come across me how our northern artists labour to gain a charm from thatched roofs and ruined towers—how they turn round and round every bush and bourne, and crumbling rock, in the hope of catching some picturesque effect; and I have been quite surprised at myself, when I find these things from habit still retaining a hold upon me. Be this as it may, however, within these last fourteen days I have plucked up a little courage, and, sketch-book in hand, have wandered up and down the hollows and heights of the neighbouring villas, and, without much consideration, have sketched off a few little objects characteristically southern, and Roman, and am now trying (if good luck will come to my aid) to give them the requisite lights and shades.

It is a singular fact, that it is easy enough to clearly see and to acknowledge what is good and the excellent, but that when one attempts to make them one's own, and to grasp them, somehow or other they slip away, as it were, from between one's fingers; and we apprehend them, not by the standard of the true and right, but in accordance with our previous habits of thought and tastes. It is only by constant practice that we can hope to improve; but where am I to find time and a collection of models? Still I do feel myself a little improved by the sincere and earnest efforts of the last fourteen days.

The artists are ready enough with their hints and instructions, for I am quick in apprehending them. But then the lesson so quickly learnt and understood, is not so easily put in practice. To apprehend quickly is, forsooth, the attribute of the mind, but correctly to execute that, requires the practice of a life.

And yet the amateur, however weak may be his efforts at imitation, need not be discouraged. The few lines which I scratch upon the paper often hastily, seldom correctly facilitate any conception of sensible objects; for one advances to an idea more surely and more steadily the more accurately and precisely he considers individual objects.

Only it will not do to measure oneself with artists; every one must go on in his own style. For Nature has made provision for all her children; the meanest is not hindered in its existence even by that of the most excellent. "A little man is still a man;" and with this remark, we will let the matter drop.

I have seen the sea twice-first the Adriatic, then the Mediterranean, but only just to look at it. In Naples we hope to become better acquainted with it. All within me seems suddenly to urge me on: why not sooner—why not at a less sacrifice? How many thousand things, many quite new and for the first time, should I not have had to communicate!

Rome, Feb. 17, 1787.
Evening, after the follies of the Carnival.

I am sorry to go away and leave Moritz alone; he is going on well, but when he is left to himself, he immediately shuts himself up and is lost to the world. I have therefore exhorted him to write to Herder: the letter is enclosed. I should wish for an answer, which may be serviceable and helpful to him. He is a strange good fellow; he would have been far more so, had he occasionally met with a friend, sensible and affectionate enough to enlighten him as to his true state. At present he could not form an acquaintance likely to be more blessed to him than Herder's, if permitted frequently to write to him. He is at this moment engaged on a very laudable antiquarian attempt, which well deserves to be encouraged: Friend Herder could scarcely bestow his cares better nor sow his good advice in a more grateful soil.

The great portrait of myself which Tischbein has taken in hand begins already to stand out from the canvass. The painter has employed a clever statuary to make him a little model in clay, which is elegantly draperied with the mantle; with this he is working away diligently, for it must, he says, be brought to a certain point before we set out for Naples, and it takes no little time merely to cover so large a field of canvass with colours.

Rome, Feb. 19, 1787.

The weather continues to be finer than words can express. This has been a day miserably wasted among fools. At nightfall I betook myself to the Villa Medici. A new moon has just shone upon us, and below the slender crescent I could with the naked eye discern almost the whole of the dark disc through the perspective. Over the earth hangs that haze of the day which the paintings of Claude have rendered so well known. In Nature, however, the phenomenon is perhaps nowhere so beautiful as it is here. Flowers are now springing out of the earth, and the trees putting forth blossoms which hitherto I have been unacquainted with; the almonds are in blossom, and between the dark-green oaks they make an appearance as beautiful as it is new to me. The sky is like a blight blue taffeta in the sunshine; what will it be in Naples? Almost everything here is already green. My botanical whims gain food and strength from all around; and I am on the way to discover new and beautiful relations by means of which Nature—that vast prodigy, which yet is nowhere visible—evolves the most manifold varieties out of the most simple.

Vesuvius is throwing out both ashes and stones; in the evening its summit appears to glow. May travailing Nature only favour us with a stream of lava. I can scarcely endure to wait till it shall be really my lot to witness such grand phenomena.

Rome, Feb. 21, 1787.
Ash Wednesday.

The folly is now at an end. The countless lights of yesterday evening were, however, a strange spectacle. One must have seen the Carnival in Rome to get entirely rid of the wish to see it again. Nothing can be written of it: as a subject of conversation it may be amusing enough. The most unpleasant feeling about it is, that real internal joy is wanting—there is a lack of money, which prevents them enjoying the morsel of pleasure, which otherwise they might still feel in it. The great are economical, and hold back; those of the middle ranks are without the means, and the populace without spring or elasticity. In the last days there was an incredible tumult, but no heartfelt joy. The sky, so infinitely fine and clear, looked down nobly and innocently upon the mummeries.

However, as imitation is out of the question, and cannot be thought of here, I send you, to amuse the children, some drawings of carnival masks, and some ancient Roman costumes, which are also coloured, as they may serve to supply a missing chapter in the "Orbis Pictus."

Rome, Feb. 21, 1787.

I snatch a few moments in the intervals of packing, to mention some particulars which I have hitherto omitted. To-morrow we set off for Naples. I am already delighting myself with the new scenery, which I promise myself will be inexpressibly beautiful; and hope in this paradise of nature, to win fresh freedom and pleasure for the study of ancient art, on my return to sober Rome.

Packing up is light work to me, since I can now *do* it with a merrier heart than I had some six months ago, when I had to tear myself from all that was most dear and precious to me. Yes, it is now a full half year since; and of the four months I have spent in Rome, not a moment has been lost. The boast may sound big; nevertheless, it does not say too much.

That "Iphigenia" has arrived, I know,—may, I learn at the foot of Vesuvius that it has met with a hearty welcome.

That Tischbein, who possesses as glorious an eye for nature as for art, is to accompany me on this journey, is to me the subject of great congratulation: still, as genuine Germans, we cannot throw aside all purposes and thoughts of work. We have bought the best of drawing-paper, and we intend to sketch away; although, in all probability, the multitude, the beauty, and the splendour of the objects, will choke our good intentions.

Rome—The "Tasso."

One conquest I have gained over myself. Of all my unfinished poetical works I shall take with me none but the "Tasso," of which I have the best hopes. If I could only know what you are now saying to "Iphigenia," your remarks might be some guide to me in my present labours; for the plan of "Tasso" is very similar; the subject still more confined, and in its several parts will be even still more elaborately finished. Still I cannot tell as yet what it will eventually prove. What already exists of it must be destroyed; it is, perhaps, somewhat tediously drawn out, and neither the characters nor the plot, nor the tone of it, are at all in harmony with my present views.

In making a clearance I have fallen upon some of your letters, and in reading them over I have just lighted upon a reproach, that in my letters I contradict myself. It may be so, but I was not aware of it; for as soon as I have written a letter I immediately send it off: I must, however, confess that nothing seems to me more likely, for I have lately been tossed about by mighty spirits, and therefore it is quite natural if at times I know not where I am standing.

A story is told of a skipper, who, overtaken at sea by a stormy night, determined to steer for port. His little boy, who in the dark was crouching by him, asked him, "What silly light is that which I see—at one time above us and at another below us?" His father promised to explain it to him some other day; and then he told him that it the beacon of the lighthouse, which, to the eye now raised, now depressed, by the wild waves, appeared accordingly sometimes above and sometimes below. I too am steering on a passion-tossed sea for the harbour, and if I can only manage to hold steadily in my eye the gleam of the beacon, however it may seem to change its place, I shall at last enjoy the wished for shore.

When one is on the eve of a departure, every earlier separation, and also that last one of all, and which is yet to be, comes involuntarily into one's thoughts; and so, on this occasion, the reflection enforces itself on my mind more strongly than ever, that man is always making far too great and too many preparations for life. For we, for instance—Tischbein and I, that is—must soon turn our backs upon many a precious and glorious object, and even upon our well-furnished museum. In it there are now standing three gems for comparison, side by side, and yet we part from them as though they were not.

NAPLES.

Velletri, Feb. 22, 1787.

We arrived here in good time. The day before yesterday the weather became gloomy; and our fine days were overcast: still some signs of the air seemed to promise that it would soon clear up again, and so indeed it turned out. The clouds gradually broke, here and there appeared the blue sky, and at last the sun shone full on our journey. We came through Albano, after having stopped before Genzano, at the entrance of a park, which the owner, Prince Chigi, in a very strange way holds, but does not keep up, on which account he will not allow any one to enter it. In it a true wilderness has been formed. Trees and shrubs, plants and weeds grow, wither, fall, and rot at pleasure. That is all right, and indeed could not be better. The expanse before the entrance, is inexpressibly fine. A high wall encloses the valley, a lattice-gate affords a view into it; then the hill ascends, upon which, above you, stands the castle.

But now I dare not attempt to go on with the description; and I can merely say, that at the very moment when from the summit we caught sight of the mountains of Sezza, the Pontine Marshes, the sea and its islands, a heavy passing shower was traversing the Marshes towards the sea, and the light and shade, constantly changing and moving, wonderfully enlivened and variegated the dreary plain. The effect was beautifully heightened by the sun's beams which lit up with various hues, the columns of smoke as they ascended from scattered and scarcely visible cottages.

Velletri—A trick upon travellers.

Velletri is agreeably situated on a volcanic hill, which, towards the north alone, is connected with other hills, and towards three points of the heavens commands a wide and uninterrupted prospect.

We here visited the Cabinet of the Cavaliere Borgia, who, favoured by his relationship with the Cardinal has managed, by means of the Propaganda, to collect some valuable antiquities and other curiosities. Ægyptian charms, idols cut out of the very hardest rock, some small figures in metal, of earlier or later dates, some pieces of statuary of burnt clay, with figures in low relief, which were dug up in the neighbourhood, and on the authority of which one is almost tempted to ascribe to the ancient indigenous population a style of their own in art.

Of other kinds of varieties there are numerous specimens in this museum. I noticed two Chinese black-painted boxes; on the sides of one there was delineated the whole management of the silk-worm, and on the other the cultivation of rice: both subjects were very nicely conceived, and worked out with the utmost minuteness. Both the boxes and their covers are eminently beautiful, and, as well as the book in the library of the Propaganda, which I have already praised, are well worth seeing.

It is certainly inexplicable that these treasures should be within so short a distance of Rome, and yet should not be more frequently visited; but perhaps the difficulty and inconvenience of getting to these regions, and the attraction of the magic circle of Rome, may serve to excuse the fact. As we arrived at the inn, some women, who were sitting before the doors of their houses, called out to us, and asked if we wished to buy any antiquities; and then, as we showed a pretty strong hankering after them, they brought out some old kettles, fire-tongs, and such like utensils, and were ready to die with laughing at having made fools of us. When we seemed a little put out, our guide assured us, to our comfort, that it was a customary joke, and that all strangers had to submit to it.

I am writing this in a very miserable auberge, and feel neither strength nor humour to make it any longer: therefore I must bid you a very good night.

Fondi, Feb. 23, 1787.

We were on the road very early,—by three in the morning. As the day broke we found ourselves on the Pontine Marshes, which have not by any means so ill an appearance as the common description in Rome would make out. Of course, by merely once passing over the marshes, it is not possible to judge of so great an undertaking as that of the intended draining of them, which necessarily requires time to test its merits; still it does appear to me, that the works which have commenced by the Pope's orders, will, to a great extent at least, attain the desired end. Conceive to yourself a wide valley, which, as it stretches from north to south, has but a very slight fall, but which towards the east and the mountains is extremely low, but rises again considerably towards the sea on the west. Punning in a straight line through the whole length of it, the ancient Via Appia has been restored. On the right of the latter the principal drain has been cut, and in it the water flows with a rapid fall. By means of it the tract of land to the right has been drained, and is now profitably cultivated. As far as the eye can see, it is either already brought into cultivation or evidently might be so, if farmers could be found to take it, with the exception of one spot, which lies extremely low.

The left side, which stretches towards the mountains, is more difficult to be managed. Here, however, cross-drains pass under the raised way into the chief drain; as, however, the surface sinks again towards the mountains, it is impossible by this means to carry off the water entirely. To meet this difficulty it is proposed, I was told, to cut another leading drain along the foot of the mountains. Large patches, especially towards Terracina, are thinly planted with willows and poplars.

The posting stations consist merely of long thatched sheds. Tischbein sketched one of them, and enjoyed for his reward a gratification which only he could enjoy. A white horse having broke loose had fled to the drained lands. Enjoying its liberty, it was galloping backwards and forwards on the brown turf like a flash of lightning; in truth it was a glorious sight, rendered significant by Tischbein's rapture.

At the point where the ancient village of Meza once stood, the Pope has caused to be built a large and fine building, which indicates the centre of the level. The sight of it increases one's hopes and confidence of the success of the whole undertaking. While thus we travelled on, we kept up a lively conversation together, not forgetting the warning, that on this journey one must not go to sleep; and, in fact, we were strongly enough reminded of the danger of the atmosphere, by the blue vapour which, even in this season of the year, hangs above the ground. On this account the more delightful, as it was the more longed for, was the rocky site of Terracina; and scarcely had we congratulated ourselves at the sight of it, than we caught a view of the sea beyond. Immediately afterwards the other side of the mountain city presented to our eye a vegetation quite new to us. The Indian figs were pushing their large fleshy leaves amidst the gray green of dwarf myrtles, the yellowish green of the pomegranate, and the pale green of the olive. As we passed along, we noticed both flowers and shrubs quite new to, us. On the meadows the narcissus and the adonis were in flower. For a long time the sea was on our right, while close to us on the left ran an unbroken range of limestone rocks. It is a continuation of the Apennines, which runs down from Tivoli and touches the sea, which it does not leave again till you reach the Campagna di Romana, where it is succeeded by the volcanic formations of Frescati, Alba, and Velletri, and lastly by the Pontine Marshes. Monte Circello, with the opposite promontory of Terracina, where the Pontine Marshes terminate, in all probability consists also of a system of chalk rocks.

We left the sea coast, and soon reached the charming plain of Fondi. Every one must admire this little spot of fertile and well cultivated land, enclosed with hills, which themselves are by no means wild. Oranges, in great numbers, are still hanging on the trees; the crops, all of wheat, are beautifully green; olives are growing in the fields, and the little city is in the bottom. A palm tree, which stood out a marked object in the scenery, received our greetings. So much for this evening. Pardon the scrawl. I must write without thinking, for writing sake. The objects are too numerous, my resting place too wretched, and yet my desire to commit something to paper too great. With nightfall we reached this place, and it is now time to go to rest.

S. Agata, Feb. 24, 1787.

Although in a wretchedly cold chamber, I must yet try and give you some account of a beautiful day. It was already nearly light when we drove out of Fondi, and we were forthwith greeted by the orange trees which hang over the walls on both sides of our road. The trees are loaded with such numbers as can only be imagined and not expressed. Towards the top the young leaf is yellowish, but below and in the middle, of sappy green. Mignon was quite right to long for them.

After this we travelled through clean and well-worked fields of wheat, planted at convenient distances with olive-trees. A soft breeze was moving, and brought to the light the silvery under-surface of the leaves, as the branches swayed gently and elegantly. It was a gray morning; a north wind promised soon to dispel all the clouds.

Then the road entered a valley between stony but well-dressed fields; the crops of the most beautiful green. At certain spots one saw some roomy places, paved, and surrounded with low walls; on these the corn, which is never carried home in sheaves, is thrashed out at once. The valley gradually narrows, and the road becomes mountainous, bare rocks of limestone standing on both sides of us. A violent storm followed us, with a fall of sleet, which thawed very slowly.

The walls, of an ancient style, built after the pattern of net-work, charmed us exceedingly. On the heights the soil is rocky, but nevertheless planted with olive-trees wherever there is the smallest patch of soil to receive them. Next we drove over a plain covered with olive-trees, and then through a small town. We here noticed altars, ancient tombstones, and fragments of every kind built up in the walls of the pleasure-houses in the gardens. Then the lower stories of ancient villas, once excellently built, but now filled up with earth, and overgrown with olives. At last we caught a sight of Vesuvius, with a cloud of smoke resting on its brow.

Molo di Gäeta greeted us again with the richest of orange-trees; we remained there some hours. The creek before the town, which the tide flows up to, affords one the finest of views. Following the line of coast, on the right, till the eye reaches at last the horn of the crescent, one sees at a moderate distance the fortress of Gäeta on the rocks. The left horn stretches out still further, presenting to the beholder first of all aline of mountains, then Vesuvius, and, beyond all, the islands. Ischia lies before you nearly in the centre.

On the shore here I found, for the first time in my life, a starfish, and an echinus thrown up by the sea; a beautiful green leaf, (*tethys foliacea*), smooth as the finest bath paper, and other remarkable rubble-stones, the most common being limestone, but occasionally also serpentine, jasper, quartz, granite, breccian pebbles, porphyry, marble of different kinds, and glass of a blue and green colour. The two last-mentioned specimens are scarcely productions of the neighbourhood. They are probably the debris of ancient buildings; and thus we have seen the waves before our eyes playing with the splendours of the ancient world. We tarried awhile, and pleased ourselves with meditating on the nature of man, whose hopes, whether in the civilized or savage state, are so soon disappointed.

Departing from Molo, a beautiful prospect still accompanies the traveller, even after his quitting the sea; the last glimpse of it was a lovely bay, of which we took a sketch. We now came upon a good fruit country, with hedges of aloes. We noticed an aqueduct which ran from the mountains over some nameless and orderless masses of ruins.

S. Agata.

Next comes the ferry over the Garigliano; after crossing it one passes through tolerably fruitful districts, till we reach the mountains. Nothing striking. At length, the first hill of lava. Here begins an extensive and glorious district of hill and vale, over which the snowy summits are towering in the distance. On the nearest eminence lies a long town, which strikes the eye with an agreeable effect. In the valley lies S. Agata, a considerable inn, where a cheerful fire was burning in a chimney arranged as a cabinet; however, our room is cold—no window, only shutters, which I am just hastening to close.

Naples, Feb. 25, 1787.

And here we are happily arrived at last, and with good omens enough. Of our day's journey thus much only. We left S. Agata with sunrise, a violent north-east wind blowing on our backs, which continued the whole day through. It was not till noon that it was master of the clouds. We suffered much from the cold.

Our road again lay among and over volcanic hills, among which I did not notice many limestone rocks. At last we reached the plains of Capua, and shortly afterwards Capua itself, where we halted at noon. In the afternoon a beautiful but flat region lay stretched before us; the road is broad, and runs through fields of green corn, so even that it looked like a carpet, and was at least a span high. Along the fields are planted rows of poplars, from which the branches are lopped to a great height, that the vines may run up them; this is the case all the way to Naples. The soil is excellent, light, loose, and well worked. The vine stocks are of extraordinary strength and height, and their shoots hang in festoons like nets from tree to tree.

Vesuvius was all the while on our left with a strong smoke, and I felt a quiet joy to think that at last I beheld with my own eyes this most, remarkable object. The sky became clearer and clearer, and at length the sun shone quite hot into our narrow rolling lodging. The atmosphere was perfectly clear and bright as we approached Naples, and we now found ourselves, in truth, in quite another world. The houses, with flat roofs, at once bespeak a different climate; inwardly, perhaps, they may not be very comfortable. Every one is in the streets, or sitting in the sun as long as it shines. The Neapolitan believes himself to be in possession of Paradise, and entertains a very melancholy opinion of our northern lands. *Sempre neve, caso di legno, gran ignoranza, ma danari assai.* Such is the picture they draw of our condition. Interpreted for the benefit of all our German folk, it means—Always snow, wooden houses, great ignorance, but money enough.

Naples at first sight leaves a free, cheerful, and lively impression; numberless beings are passing and repassing each other: the king is gone hunting, the queen *promising*; and so things could not be better.

Naples, Monday, Feb. 26, 1787.
"Alla Locanda del Sgr. Moriconi al Largo del Castello."

Under this address, no less cheerful than high-sounding, letters from all the four quarters of heaven will henceforth find us. Round the castle, which lies by the sea, there stretches a large open space, which, although surrounded on all sides with houses, is not called a square or piazza, but a largo, or expanse. Perhaps the name is derived from ancient times, when it was still an open and unenclosed country. Here, in a corner house on one side of the Largo, we have taken up our lodgings in a corner room, which commands a free and lively view of the ever moving surface. An iron balcony runs before several windows, and even round the corner. One would never leave it, if the sharp wind were not extremely cutting.

Naples—My lodgings.

The room is cheerfully decorated, especially the ceiling, whose arabasques of a hundred compartments bear witness to the proximity of Pompeii and Herculaneum. Now, all this is very well and very fine; but there is no fire-place, no chimney, and yet February exercises even here its rights. I expressed a wish for something to warm me. They brought in a tripod of sufficient height from the ground for one conveniently to hold one's hands over it; on it was placed a shallow brazier, full of extremely fine charcoal red-hot, but covered smoothly over with ashes. We now found it an advantage to be able to manage this process of domestic economy; we had learned that at Rome. With the ring of a key, from time to time, one cautiously draws away the ashes of the surface, so that a few of the embers may be exposed to the free air. Were you impatiently to stir up the glowing coals, you would no doubt experience for a few moments great warmth, but you would in a short time exhaust the fuel, and then you must pay a certain sum to have the brasier filled again.

I did not feel quite well, and could have wished for more of ease and comfort. A reed matting was all there was to protect one's feet from the stone floor; skins are not usual. I determined to put on a sailor's cloak which we had brought with us in fun, and it did me good service, especially when I tied it round my body with the rope of my box. I must have looked very comical, something between a sailor and a capuchin. When Tischbein came back from visiting some of his friends, and found me in this dress, he could not refrain from laughing.

Naples, Feb. 27, 1787.

Yesterday I kept quietly at home, in order to get rid of a slight bodily ailment. To-day has been a regular carouse, and the time passed rapidly while we visited the most glorious of objects. Let man talk, describe and paint as he may—to be here is more than all. The shore, the creeks, and the bay, Vesuvius, the city, the suburbs, the castles, the atmosphere! In the evening, too, we went into the Grotto of Posilippo, while the setting sun was shining into it from the other side. I can pardon all who lose their senses in Naples, and remember with emotion my father, who retained to the last an indelible impression of those objects which to-day I have cast eyes upon for the first time. Just as it is said, that people who have once seen a ghost, are never afterwards seen to smile, so in the opposite sense it may be said of him, that he never could become perfectly miserable, so long as he remembered Naples. According to my fashion, I am quite still and calm, and when anything happens too absurd, only make large-large eyes.

Naples, Feb. 28, 1787.

To-day we visited Philip Hackert, the famous landscape-painter, who enjoys the special confidence and peculiar favour of the king and the queen. A wing of the palace Franca Villa has been assigned to him, which, having furnished it with true artistic taste, he feels great satisfaction in inhabiting. He is a very precise and prudent personage, who, with untiring industry, manages, nevertheless, to enjoy life.

After that we took a sail, and saw all kinds of fish and wonderful shapes drawn out of the waves. The day was glorious; the *tramontane* (north winds) tolerable.

Naples, March 1, 1787.

Even in Rome my self-willed hermit-like humour was forced to assume a more social aspect than I altogether liked: no doubt it appears a strange beginning to go into the world in order to be alone. Accordingly I could not resist Prince von Waldeck, who most kindly invited me, and by his rank and influence has procured me the enjoyment of many privileges. We had scarcely reached Naples, where he has been residing a long while, when he sent us an invitation to pay a visit with him to Puzzuoli and the neighbourhood. I was thinking already of Vesuvius for to-day; but Tischbein has forced me to take this journey, which, agreeable enough of itself, promises from the fine weather, and the society of a perfect gentleman, and well-educated prince, very much both of pleasure and profit. We had also seen in Rome a beautiful lady, who with her husband, is inseparable from the Prince. She also is to be of the party; and we hope for a most delightful day.

Moreover, I was intimately known to this noble society, having met them previously. The Prince, upon our first acquaintance, had asked me what I was then busy with; and the plan of my "Iphigenia" was so fresh in my recollection, that I was able one evening to relate it to them circumstantially. They entered into it; still, still I fancied I could observe that something livelier and wilder was expected of me.

Evening.

It would be difficult to give an account of this day. How often has the cursory reading of a book, which irresistibly carries one with it, exercised the greatest influence on a man's whole life, and produced at once a decisive effect, which neither a second perusal nor earnest reflection can either strengthen or modify. This I experienced in the case of the "Sakuntala"; and do not great men affect us somewhat in the same way? A sail to Puzzuoli, little trips by land, cheerful walks through the most wonderful regions in the world! Beneath the purest sky the most treacherous soil; ruins of inconceivable opulence, oppressive, and saddening; boiling waters, clefts exhaling sulphur, rocks of slag defying vegetable life, bare forbidding tracts, and then at last on all sides the most luxuriant vegetation seizing every spot and cranny possible, running over every lifeless object, edging the lakes and brooks, and nourishing a glorious wood of oak on the brink of an ancient crater!

And thus one is driven backwards and forwards between nature and the history of nations; one wishes to meditate, and soon feels himself quite unfit for it. In the mean time, however, the living lives on merrily, with a joyousness which we too would share. Educated persons, belonging to the world and the world's ways, but warned by serious events, become, nevertheless, disposed for reflection. A boundless view of earth, sea, and sky,—and then called away to the side of a young and amiable lady, accustomed and delighted to receive homage.

Amidst all this giddy excitement, however, I failed not to make many notes. The future reduction of these will be greatly facilitated by the map we consulted on the spot, and by a hasty sketch of Tischbein's. To-day it is not possible for me to make the least addition to these.

March 2.

Thursday I ascended Vesuvius, although the weather was unsettled, and the summit of the mountain surrounded by clouds. I took a carriage as far as Resina, and then, on the back of a mule, began the ascent, having vineyards on both sides. Next, on foot, I crossed the lava of the year '71, on the surface of which a fine but compact moss was already growing; then upwards on the side of the lava. The hut of the hermit on the height, was on my left hand. After this we climbed the Ash-hill, which is wearisome walking; two-thirds of the summit were enveloped in clouds. At last we reached the ancient crater, now filled up, where we found recent lava, only two months and fourteen days old, and also a slight streak of only five days, which was, however, already cold. Passing over these, we next ascended a height which had been thrown up by volcanic action; it was smoking from all its points. As the smoke rolled away from us, I essayed to approach the crater; scarcely, however, had we taken fifty steps in the steam, when it became so dense that I could scarcely see my shoes. It was to no purpose that we held snuff continually before our nostrils. My guide had disappeared; and the footing on the lava lately thrown up was very unsteady. I therefore thought it right to turn round, and to reserve the sight for a finer day, and for less of smoke. However, I now know how difficult it is to breathe in such an atmosphere.

Naples—Vesuvius.

Otherwise, the mountain was quite still. There was no flame, no roaring, no stones thrown up—all which it usually does at most times. I reconnoitered it well, with the intention of regularly storming it as soon as the weather shall improve.

The specimens of lava that I found, were mostly of well-known kinds. I noticed, however, a phenomenon which appeared to me extremely strange, which I intend to examine again still more closely, and also to consult connoisseurs and collectors upon it. It is a stalactite incrustation of a part of the volcanic funnel, which has been thrown down, and now rears itself in the centre of the old choked-up crater. This mass of solid greyish stalactite appears to have been formed by the sublimation of the very finest volcanic evaporation, without the co-operation of either moisture or fusion. It will furnish occasion for further thinking.

To-day, the 3rd of March, the sky is covered with clouds, and a sirocco is blowing. For post-day, good weather.

A very strange medley of men, beautiful houses, and most singular fishes are here to be seen in abundance.

Of the situation of the city, and of its glories, which have been so often described and commended, not a word from me. "*Vede Napoli e poi muori,*" the cry here. "See Naples, and die."

Naples, March 5, 1787.

That no Neapolitan will allow the merits of his city to be questioned, that their poets should sing in extravagant hyperbole of the blessings of its site, are not matters to quarrel about, even though a pair of Vesuviuses stood in its neighbourhood. Here one can almost cast aside all remembrances, even of Rome. As compared with this free, open situation, the capital of the world, in the basin of the Tiber, looks like a cloister built on a bad site.

The sea, with its vessels, and their destinations, presents wholly new matters for reflection. The frigate for Palermo started yesterday, with a strong, direct, north wind. This time it certainly will not be more than six-and-thirty hours on the passage. With what longing did I not watch the full sails as the vessel passed between Capri and Cape Minerva, until at last it disappeared. Who could see one's beloved thus sailing away and survive? The sirocco (south wind) is now blowing; if the wind becomes stronger, the breakers over the Mole will be glorious.

To-day being Friday, is the grand promenade of the nobility, when every one displays his equipages, and especially his stud. It is almost impossible to see finer horses anywhere than in Naples. For the first time in my life I have felt an interest in these animals.

Naples, March 3, 1787.

Here you have a few leaves, as reporters of the entertainment I have met with in this place; also a corner of the cover of your letter, stained with smoke, in testimony of its having been with me on Vesuvius. You must not, however, fancy, either in your waking thoughts or in your dreams, that I am surrounded by perils; be assured that wherever I venture, there is no more danger than on the road to Belvedere. The earth is everywhere the Lord's; may be well said in reference to such objects. I never seek adventure out of a mere rage for singularity; but even because I am most cool, and can catch at a glance, the peculiarities of any object, I may well do and venture more than many others. The passage to Sicily is anything but dangerous. A few days ago, the frigate sailed for Palermo with a favorable breeze from the north, and, leaving Capri on the right, has, no doubt, accomplished the voyage in six-and-thirty hours. In all such expeditions, one finds the danger to be far less in reality than, at a distance, one is apt to imagine.

Of earthquakes, there is not at present a vestige in Lower Italy; in the upper provinces Rimini and its neighbourhood has lately suffered. Thus the earth has strange humours, and people talk of earthquakes here just as we do of wind and weather, and as in Thuringia they talk of conflagrations.

I am delighted to find that you are now familiar with the two editions of my "Iphigenia," but still more pleased should I he had you been more sensible of the difference between them. I know what I have done for it, and may well speak thereof, since I feel that I could make still further improvements. If it be a bliss to enjoy the good, it is still greater happiness to discern the better; for in art the best only is good enough.

Naples, March 5, 1787.

We spent the second Sunday of Lent in visiting church after church. As in Rome all is highly solemn; so here every horn is merry and cheerful. The Neapolitan school of painting, too, can only be understood in Naples. One is astonished to see the whole front of a church painted from top to bottom. Over the door of one, Christ is driving out of the temple the buyers and sellers, who, terribly frightened, are nimbly huddling up their wares, and hurrying down the steps on both sides. In another church, there is a room over the entrance, which is richly ornamented with frescoes representing the deprivation of Heliodorus.[5] Luca Giordano must indeed have painted rapidly, to fill such large areas in a lifetime. The pulpit, too, is here not always a mere cathedra, as it is in other places,—a place where one only may teach at a time; but a gallery. Along one of these I once saw a Capuchin walking backwards and forwards, and, now from one end, now from another, reproaching the people with their sins. What had he not to tell them!

But neither to be told nor to be described is the glory of a night of the full moon such as we have enjoyed here, wandering through the streets and squares and on the quay, with its long promenade, and then backwards and forwards on the beach; one felt really possessed with the feeling of the infinity of space. So to dream is really worth all trouble.

Naples, March 5, 1787.

Naples-Filangieri.

I made to-day the acquaintance of an excellent individual, v and I must briefly give you a general description of him. It is the Chevalier Filangieri, famous for his work on legislation. He belongs to those noble young men who wish to promote the happiness and the moderate liberty of mankind. In his bearing you recognise at once the soldier, the chevalier, and the man of the world; but this appearance is softened by an expression of tender moral sensibility, which is diffused over his whole countenance, and shines forth most agreeably in his character and conversation; he is, moreover, heartily attached to his sovereign and country, even though he cannot approve of all that goes on. He is also oppressed with a fear of Joseph II. The idea of a despot, even though it only floats as a phantom in the air, excites the apprehensions of every noble-minded man. He spoke to me without reserve, of what Naples had to fear from him; but in particular he was delighted to speak of Montesquieu, Beccaria, and of some of his own writings—all in the same spirit of the best will, and of a heart full of youthful enthusiasm to do good. And yet he may one day be classed with the Thirty. He has also made me acquainted with an old writer, from whose inexhaustible depths these new Italian friends of legislation derive intense encouragement and edification. He is called Giambattista Vico, and is preferred even to Montesquieu. After a hasty perusal of his book, which was lent to me as a sacred deposit, I laid it down, saying to myself, Here are sybilline anticipations of good and right, which once must, or ought to be, realised, drawn apparently from a serious contemplation both of the past and of the present. It is well when a nation possesses such a forefather: the Germans will one day receive a similar codex from *Hamann*.

[5] Heliodorus, Bishop of Trieca, in Thessaly, in the fourth century, author of the "Œthiopics, or, the Amours of Theagenes and Chariclea," was, it is said, deprived of his bishopric for writing this work.—A. W. M.

Naples, March 6, 1787.

Most reluctantly, yet, for the sake of good-fellowship, Tischbein accompanied me to-day to Vesuvius. To him—the artist of form, who concerns himself with none but the most beautiful of human and animal shapes, and one also whose taste and judgment lead to humanise even the formless rock and landscape,—such a frightful and shapeless conglomeration of matter, which, moreover, is continually preying on itself, and proclaiming war against every idea of the beautiful, must have appeared utterly abominable.

We started in two caleches, as we did not trust ourselves to drive through the crowd and whirl of the city. The drivers kept up an incessant shouting at the top of their voice whenever donkeys with their loads of wood or rubbish, or rolling caleches met us, or else warning the porters with their burdens, or other pedestrians, whether children or old people to get out of the way. All the while, however, they drove at a sharp trot, without the least stop or check.

As you get into the remoter suburbs and gardens, the road soon begins to show signs of a Plutonic action. For as we had not had rain for a long time, the naturally evergreen leaves were covered with a thick gray and ashy dust; so that the glorious blue sky, and the scorching sun which shone down upon us, were the only signs that we were still among the living.

Naples—Ascent to Vesuvius.

At the foot of the steep ascent, we were received by two guides, one old, the other young, but both active fellows. The first pulled me up the path, the other Tischbein,—pulled I say, for these guides are girded round the waist with a leathern belt, which the traveller takes hold of, and being drawn up by his guide, makes his way the easier with foot and staff. In this manner we reached the flat from which the cone rises: towards the north lay the ruins of the Somma.

A glance westwards over the country beneath us, removed, as well as a bath could, all feeling of exhaustion and fatigue, and we now went round the ever-smoking cone, as it threw out its stones and ashes. Wherever the space allowed of our viewing it at a sufficient distance, it appeared a grand and elevating spectacle. In the first place, a violent thundering toned forth from its deepest abyss, then stones of larger and smaller sizes were showered into the air by thousands, and enveloped by clouds of ashes. The greatest part fell again into the gorge; the rest of the fragments, receiving a lateral inclination, and falling on the outside of the crater, made a marvellous rumbling noise. First of all the larger masses plumped against the side, and rebounded with a dull heavy sound; then the smaller came rattling down; and last of all, drizzled a shower of ashes. All this took place at regular intervals, which by slowly counting, we were able to measure pretty accurately.

Between the *Somma*, however, and the cone the space is narrow enough; moreover, several stones fell around us, and made the circuit anything but agreeable. Tischbein now felt more disgusted than ever with Vesuvius, as the monster, not content with being hateful, showed an inclination to become mischievous also.

As, however, the presence of danger generally exercises on man a kind of attraction, and calls forth a spirit of opposition in the human breast to defy it, I bethought myself that, in the interval of the eruptions, it would be possible to climb up the cone to the crater, and to get back before it broke out again. I held a council on this point with our guides under one of the overhanging rocks of the Somma, where, encamped in safety, we refreshed ourselves with the provisions we had brought with us. The younger guide was willing to run the risk with me; we stuffed our hats full of linen and silk handkerchiefs, and, staff in hand, we prepared to start, I holding on to his girdle.

The little stones were yet rattling around us, and the ashes still drizzling, as the stalwart youth hurried forth with me across the hot glowing rubble. We soon stood on the brink of the vast chasm, the smoke of which, although a gentle air was bearing it away from us, unfortunately veiled the interior of the crater, which smoked all round from a thousand crannies. At intervals, however, we caught sight through the smoke of the cracked walls of the rock. The view was neither instructive nor delightful; but for the very reason that one saw nothing, one lingered in the hope of catching a glimpse of something more; and so we forgot our slow counting. We were standing on a narrow ridge of the vast abyss: of a sudden the thunder pealed aloud; we ducked our heads involuntarily, as if that would have rescued us from the precipitated masses. The smaller stones soon rattled, and without considering that we had again an interval of cessation before us, and only too much rejoiced to have outstood the danger, we rushed down and reached the foot of the hill, together with the drizzling ashes, which pretty thickly covered our heads and shoulders.

Tischbein was heartily glad to see me again. After a little scolding and a little refreshment, I was able to give my especial attention to the old and new lava. And here the elder of the guides was able to instruct me accurately in the signs by which the age of the several strata was indicated.

The older were already covered with ashes, and rendered quite smooth; the newer, especially those which had cooled slowly, presented a singular appearance. As, sliding along, they carried away with them the solid objects which lay on the surface, it necessarily happened that from time to time several would come into contact with each other, and these again being swept still further by the molten stream, and pushed one over the other, would eventually form a solid mass with wonderful jags and corners, still more strange even than the somewhat similarly formed piles of the icebergs. Among this fused and waste matter I found many great rocks, which, being struck with a hammer, present on the broken face a perfect resemblance to the primeval rock formation. The guides maintained that these were old lava from the lowest depths of the mountain, which are very often thrown up by the volcano.

Upon our return to Naples, we noticed some small houses of only one story, and of a remarkable appearance and singular build, without windows, and receiving all their light from the doors, which opened on the road. The inhabitants sit before them at the door from the morning to the night, when they at last retire to their holes.

The city, which in the evening is all of a tumult, though of a different kind from the day, extorted from me the wish that I might be able to stay here for some time, in order to sketch to the best of my powers the moving scene. It will not, however, be possible.

Naples, Wednesday, March 7, 1787.

Naples—An antique-A horse's head.

This week Tischbein has shown to me, and without reserve commented upon, the greater part of the artistic treasures of Naples. An excellent judge and drawer of animals, he had long before called my attention to a horse's head in brass in the Palace Columbrano: we went there to-day. This relic of art is placed in the court right opposite the gateway, in a niche over a well, and really excites one's astonishment. What must have been the effect of the whole head and body together? The perfect horse must have been far larger than those at S. Mark's: moreover, the head alone, when closely viewed, enables you distinctly to recognise and admire the character and spirit of the animal. The splendid frontal bones, the snorting nostrils, the pricked ears, the stiff mane,—a strong, excited, and spirited creature!

We turned round to notice a female statue which stands in a niche over the gateway. It has been already described by Winckelmann as an imitation of a dancing girl, with the remark, that such artistes represent to us in living movement, and under the greatest variety, that beauty of form which the masters of statuary exhibit in the (as it were) petrified nymphs and goddesses. It is very light and beautiful; the head, which had been broken off, has been skilfully set on again: otherwise it is nowise injured, and most assuredly deserves a better place.

Naples.

To-day I received your dear letter of the 16th February only, keep on writing. I have made arrangements for the forwarding of my letters, and I shall continue to do so, if I move further. Quite strange does it seem to me to read that my friends do not often see each other; and yet perhaps nothing is more common than for men not to meet who are living close together.

The weather here has become dull: a change is at hand. Spring is commencing, and we shall soon have some rainy days. The summit of Vesuvius has not been clear since I paid it a visit. These few last nights flames have been seen to issue from it; to-day it is keeping itself quiet, and therefore more violent eruptions are expected.

The storms of these last few days have shown to us a glorious sea; it is at such times that the waves may be studied in their worthiest style and shape. Nature, indeed, is the only book which presents important matter on all its pages. On the other hand, the theatres have ceased to furnish any amusement. During Lent nothing but operas, which differ in no respect from more profane ones but by the absence of ballets between the acts; in all other respects they are as gay as possible. In the theatre of S. Carlo they are representing the destruction of Jerusalem by Nebuchadnezzar: to me it is only a great raree-show; my taste is quite spoilt for such things.

To-day we were with the Prince von Waldeck at Capo di Monte, where there is a great collection of paintings, coins, &c. It is not well arranged, but the things themselves are above praise: we can now correct and confirm many traditional ideas. Those coins, gems, and vases which, like the stunted citron-trees, come to us in the north one by one, have quite a different look here in the mass, and, so to speak, in their own home and native soil. For where works of art are rare, their very rarity gives them a value; here we learn to treasure none but the intrinsically valuable.

Naples.

A very high price is at present given for Etruscan vases, and certainly beautiful and excellent pieces are to be found among them. Not a traveller but wishes to possess some specimen or other of them; one does not seem to value money here at the same rate as at home: I fear that I myself shall yet be tempted.

Naples, Friday, March 9, 1787.

This is the pleasant part of travelling, that even ordinary matters, by their novelty and unexpectedness, often acquire the appearance of an adventure. As I came back from Capo di Monte, I paid an evening visit to Filangieri, and saw sitting on the sofa, by the side of the mistress of the house, a lady whose external appearance seemed to agree but little with the familiarity and easy manner she indulged in. In a light, striped, silk gown of very ordinary texture, and a most singular cap, by way of head-dress, but of a pretty figure, she looked like some poor dressmaker who, taken up with the care of adorning the persons of others, had little time to bestow on her own external appearance; such people are so accustomed to expect their labours to be remunerated, that they seem to have no idea of working gratis for themselves. She did not allow her gossip to be at all checked by my arrival, but went on talking of a number of ridiculous adventures which had happened to her that day, or which had been occasioned by her own *brusquerie* and impetuosity.

The lady of the house wished to help me to get in a word or two, and spoke of the beautiful site of Capo di Monte, and of the treasures there. Upon this the lively lady sprang up with a good high jump from the sofa, and as she stood on her feet seemed still prettier than before. She took leave, and running to the door, said, as she passed me, "The Filangieri are coming one of these days to dine with me—I hope to see you also." She was gone before I could say yes. I now learnt that she was the Princess ————, a near relative to the master of the house.[6] The Filangieri were not rich, and lived in a becoming but moderate style; and such I presumed was the case with my little Princess, especially as such titles are anything but rare in Naples. I set down the name, and the day and hour, and left them, without any doubt but that I should be found at the right place in due time.

Naples, Sunday, March 11, 1787.

As my stay in Naples cannot be long, I take the most remote points first of all—the near throw themselves, as it were, in one's way. I have been with Tischbein to Pompeii, and on our road all those glorious prospects which were already well known to us from many a landscape drawing, lay right and left, dazzling us by their number and unbroken succession.

Pompeii amazes one by its narrowness and littleness; confined streets, but perfectly straight, and furnished on both sides with a foot pavement; little houses without windows, the rooms being lit only by the doors, which opened on the atrium and the galleries. Even the public edifices, the tomb at the gate, a temple, and also a villa in its neighbourhood, are like models and dolls' houses, rather than real buildings. The rooms, corridors, galleries and all, are painted with bright and cheerful colours, the wall surfaces uniform; in the middle some elaborate painting (most of these have been removed); on the borders and at the corners, light tasteful arabesques, terminating in the pretty figures of nymphs or children; while in others, from out of garlands of flowers, beasts, wild and tame, are issuing. Thus does the city, which first of all the hot shower of stones and ashes overwhelmed, and afterwards the excavators plundered, still bear witness, even in its present utterly desolate state, to a taste for painting and the arts common to the whole people, of which the most enthusiastic dilettante of the present day has neither idea nor feeling, and so misses not.

[6] Filangieri's sister.

When one considers the distance of this town from Vesuvius, it is clear that the volcanic matter which overwhelmed it could not have been carried hither either by any sudden impetus of the mountain, or by the wind. We must rather suppose that these stones and ashes had been floating for a time in the air, like clouds, until at last they fell upon the doomed city.

In order to form a clear and precise idea of this event, one has only to think of a mountain village buried in snow. The spaces between the houses, and indeed the crushed houses themselves, were filled up; however, it is not improbable that some of the mason-work may, at different points, have peeped above the surface, and in this way have excited the notice of those by whom the hill was broken up for vineyards and gardens. And, no doubt, many an owner, on digging up his own portion, must have made valuable gleanings. Several rooms were found quite empty, and in the corner of one a heap of ashes was observed, under which a quantity of household articles and works of art was concealed.

The strange, and in some degree unpleasant impression which this mummied city leaves on the mind, we got rid of, as, sitting in the arbour of a little inn close to the sea (where we dispatched a frugal meal), we revelled in the blue sky, the glaring ripple of the sea, and the bright sunshine; and cherished a hope that, when the vine-leaf should again cover the hill, we might all be able to pay it a second visit, and once more enjoy ourselves together on the same spot.

As we approached the city, we again came upon the little cottages, which now appeared to us perfectly to resemble those in Pompeii. We obtained permission to enter one, and found it extremely clean—neatly-platted rush-bottomed chairs, a buffet, covered all over with gilding, or painted with variegated flowers, and highly varnished. Thus, after so many centuries, and such numberless changes, this country instils into its inhabitants the same customs and habits of life, the same inclinations and tastes.

Naples, Monday, March 12, 1787.

To-day, according to my custom, I have gone slowly through the city, noting several points, for a future description of it, of which unfortunately I cannot communicate anything to-day. All tends to this one conclusion: that a highly-favored land, which furnishes in abundance the chief necessaries of existence, produces men also of a happy disposition, who, without trouble or anxiety, trust to to-morrow to bring them what to-day has been wanting, and consequently live on in a lighthearted careless sort of life. Momentary gratification, moderate enjoyments, a passing sorrow, and a cheerful resignation!

The morning has been cold and damp, with a little rain. In my walk I came upon a spot where the great slabs of the pavement appeared swept quite clean. To my great surprise I saw, on this smooth and even spot, a number of ragged boys squatting in a circle, and spreading out their hands over the ground, as if to warm them. At first I took it to be some game that they were playing; when, however, I noticed the perfect seriousness and composure of their countenances, with an expression on it of a gratified want, I therefore put my brains to the utmost stretch, but they refused to enlighten me as I desired. I was, therefore, obliged to ask what it could be that had, induced these little imps to take up this strange position, and had collected them in so regular a circle.

Upon this I was informed that a neighbouring smith had been heating the tire of a wheel, and that this is done in the following manner:—The iron tire is laid on the pavement, and around is as much oak chips as is considered sufficient to soften the iron to the required degree. The lighted wood burns away, the tire is riveted to the wheel, and the ashes carefully swept up. The little vagabonds take advantage of the heat communicated to the pavement, and do not leave the spot till they have drawn from it the last radiation of warmth. Similar instances of contentedness, and sharp-witted profiting by what otherwise would be wasted, occur here in great number. I notice in this people the most shrewd and active industry, not to make riches, but to live free from care.

Evening.

In order that I might not make any mistake yesterday, as to the house of my odd little princess, and might be there in time, I called a hackney carriage. It stopped before the grand entrance of a spacious palace. As I had no idea of coming to so splendid a dwelling, I repeated to him most distinctly the name; he assured me it was quite rights I soon found myself in a spacious court, still and lonesome, empty and clean, enclosed by the principal edifice and side buildings. The architecture was the well-known light Neapolitan style, as was also the colouring. Right before me was a grand porch, and a broad but not very high flight of steps. On both sides of it stood a line of servants, in splendid liveries, who, as I passed them, bowed very low. I thought myself the Sultan in Wieland's fairy tale, and after his example, took courage. Next I was received by the upper domestics, till at last the most courtly of them opened a door, and introduced me into a spacious apartment, which was as splendid, but also as empty of people as all before. In passing backwards and forwards I observed, in a side-room, a table laid out for about forty persons, with a splendour corresponding with all around. A secular priest now entered, and without asking who I was, or whence I came, approached me as if I were already known to him, and conversed on the most common-place topics.

Naples—A dinner party.

A pair of folding doors were now thrown open and immediately closed again, as a gentleman rather advanced in years entered. The priest immediately proceeded towards him, as I also did; we greeted him with a few words of courtesy, which he returned in a barking stuttering tone, so that I could scarcely make out a syllable of his Hottentot dialect. When he had taken his place by the stove, the priest moved away, and I accompanied him. A portly Benedictine entered, accompanied by a younger member of his order. He went to salute the host, and after being also barked at, retired to a window. The *regular* clergy, especially those whose dress is becoming, have great advantage in society; their costume is a mark of humility and renunciation of self, while, at the same time it lends to its wearers a decidedly dignified appearance. In their behaviour they may easily, without degrading themselves, appear submissive and complying; and then again, when they stand upon their own dignity, their self-respect sits well upon them, although in others it would not be so readily allowed to pass. This was the case with this person. When I asked him about Monte Cassino, he immediately gave me an invitation thither, and promised me the best of welcomes. In the meanwhile the room had become full of people; officers, people of the court, more regulars, and even some Capuchins, had arrived. Once more a set of folding-doors opened and shut; an aged lady, somewhat older than my host, had entered; and now the presence of what I took to be the lady of the house, made me feel perfectly confident that I was in a strange mansion, where I was wholly unknown to its owners. Dinner was now served, and I was keeping close to the side of my friends the monks, in order to slip with them into the paradise of the dining-room, when all at once I saw Filangieri, with his wife, enter and make his excuses for being so late. Shortly after this my little princess came into the room, and with nods, and winks, and bows to all as she passed, came straight to me.—"It is very good of you to keep your word," she exclaimed; "mind you sit by me,—you shall have the best bits,—wait a minute though; I must find out which is my proper place, then mind and take your place by me." Thus commanded, I followed the various windings she made; and at last we reached our seats, having the Benedictine right opposite and Filangieri on my other side. "The dishes are all good," she observed,—"all lenten fare, but choice: I'll point out to you the best. But now I must rally the priests,—the churls! I can't bear them; every day they are cutting a fresh slice off our estate. What we have, we should like to spend on ourselves and our friends." The soup was now handed round,—the Benedictine was sipping his very deliberately. "Pray don't put yourself out of your way,—the spoon is too small, I fear; I will bid them bring you a larger one. Your reverences are used to a good mouthful." The good father replied,—"In your house, lady, every thing is so excellent, and so well arranged, that much more distinguished guests than your humble servant would find everything to their heart's content."

Of the pasties the Benedictine took only one; she called out to him,—"Pray take half a dozen; pastry, your reverence surely knows, is easy of digestion." With good sense he took another pasty, thanking the princess for her attention, just as if he had not seen through her malicious raillery. And so, also, some solid paste-work furnished her with occasion for venting her spite; for, as the monk helped himself to a piece, a second rolled off the dish towards his plate,—"A third! your reverence; you seem anxious to lay a foundation"—"When such excellent materials are furnished to his hand, the architect's labours are easy," rejoined his reverence. Thus she went on continually, only pausing awhile to keep her promise of pointing out to me the best dishes.

Naples—A dinner party.

All this while I was conversing with my neighbour on the gravest topics. Absolutely, I never heard Filangieri utter an unmeaning sentence. In this respect, and indeed in many others, he resembles our worthy friend,

George Schlosser, with this difference, that the former, as a Neapolitan, and a man of the world, had a softer nature and an easier manner.

During the whole of this time my roguish neighbour allowed the clerical gentry not a moment's truce. Above all, the fish at this lenten meal, dished up in imitation of flesh of all kinds, furnished her with inexhaustible opportunities for all manner of irreverent and ill-natured observations; especially in justification and defence of a taste for flesh, she observed that people would have the form to give a relish, even when the essence was prohibited.

Many more such jokes were noticed by me at the time, but I am not in the humour to repeat them. Jokes of this kind, fresh spoken, and falling from beautiful lips, may be tolerable, not to say amusing, but set down in black and white, they lose all charm, for me at least. Then again, the boldly hazarded stroke of wit has this peculiarity, that at the moment it pleases us while it astonishes us by its boldness, but when told afterwards, it sounds offensive, and disgusts us.

The dessert was brought in, and I was afraid that the cross-fire would still be kept up, when suddenly my fair neighbour turned quite composedly to me and said,—"The priests may gulp their Syracusan wine in peace, for I cannot succeed in worrying a single one to death,—no, not even in spoiling their appetites. Now, let me have some rational talk with you; for what a heavy sort of thing must a conversation with Filangieri be! The good creature; he gives himself a great deal of trouble for nothing. I often say to him, if you make new laws, we must give ourselves fresh pains to find out how we can forthwith transgress them, just as we have already set at naught the old. Only look now, how beautiful Naples is! For these many years the people have lived free from care and contented, and if now and then some poor wretch is hanged, all the rest still pursue their own merry course." She then proposed that I should pay a visit to Sorrento, where she had a large estate; her steward would feast me with the best of fish, and the delicious *mungana*, (flesh of a sucking calf). The mountain air, and the unequalled prospect, would be sure to cure me of all philosophy,—then she would come herself, and not a trace should remain of all my wrinkles, which, by the bye, I had allowed to grow before their time, and together we would have a right merry time of it.

Naples, March 13, 1787.

To-day also I write you a few lines, in order that letter may provoke letter. Things go well with me—however, I see less than I ought. The place induces an indolent and easy sort of life; nevertheless, my idea of it is gradually becoming more and more complete.

On Sunday we were in Pompeii. Many a calamity has happened in the world, but never one that has caused so much entertainment to posterity as this one. I scarcely know of anything that is more interesting. The houses are small and close together, but within they are all most exquisitely painted. The gate of the city is remarkable, with the tombs close to it. The tomb of a priestess, a semicircular bench, with a stone back, on which was the inscription cut in large characters. Over the back you have a sight of the sea and the setting sun—a glorious spot, worthy of the beautiful idea.

We found there good and merry company from Naples; the men are perfectly natural and light-hearted. We took our dinner at the "Torre del' Annunziata," with our table placed close to the sea. The day was extremely fine. The view towards Castell a Mare and Sorrento, near and incomparable. My companions were quite rapturous in praise of their native place; some asserted that without a sight of the sea it was impossible to live. To me it is quite enough that I have its image in my soul, and so, when the time comes, may safely return to my mountain home.

Fortunately, there is here a very honest painter of landscapes, who imparts to his pieces the very impression of the rich and open country around. He has already executed some sketches for me.

Naples—Pompeii—Portici.

The Vesuvian productions I have now pretty well studied; things, however, assume a different signification when one sees them in connection. Properly, I ought to devote the rest of my life to observation: I should discover much that would enlarge man's knowledge. Pray tell Herder that my botanical discoveries are continually advancing; it is still the same principle, but it requires a whole life to work it out. Perhaps I am already in a situation to draw the leading lines of it.

I can now enjoy myself at the museum of Portici. Usually people make it the first object,—we mean to make it our last. As yet I do not know whether I shall be able to extend my tour; all things tend to drive me back to Rome at Easter. I shall let things take their course.

Angelica has undertaken to paint a scene out of my "Iphigenia." The thought is a very happy subject for a picture, and she will delineate it excellently. It is the moment when Orestes finds himself again in the presence of his sister and his friend. What the three characters are saying to each other she has indicated by the grouping, and given their words in the expressions of their countenances. From this description you may judge how keenly sensitive she is, and how quick she is to seize whatever is adapted to her nature. And it is really the turning point of the whole drama.

Fare you well, and love me! Here the people are all very good, even though they do not know what to make of me. Tischbein, on the other hand, pleases them far better. This evening he hastily painted some heads of the size of life, and about which they disported themselves as strangely as the New Zealanders at the sight of a ship of war. Of this an amusing anecdote.

Tischbein has a great knack of etching with a pen the shapes of gods and heroes, of the size of life, and even more. He uses very few lines, but cleverly puts in the shades with a broad pencil, so that the heads stand out roundly and nobly. The bystanders looked on with amazement, and were highly delighted. At last an itching seized their fingers to try and paint; they snatched the brushes and painted—one another's beards, daubing each other's faces. Was not this an original trait of human nature? And this was done in an elegant circle, in the house of one who was himself a clever draughtsman and painter! It is impossible to form an idea of this race without having seen it.

Caserta, Wednesday, March 14, 1787.

I am here on a visit to Hackert, in his highly agreeable apartments, which have been assigned him in the ancient castle. The new palace, somewhat huge and Escurial-like, of a quadrangular plan, with many courts, is royal enough. The site is uncommonly fine, on one of the most fertile plains in the world, and yet the gardens trench on the mountains. From these an aqueduct brings down an entire river, to supply water to the palace and the district; and the whole can, on occasion, be thrown on some artificially-arranged rocks, to form a most glorious cascade. The gardens are beautifully laid out, and suit well with a district which itself is thought a garden.

The castle is truly kingly. It appears to me, however, particularly gloomy; and no one of us could bring himself to think the vast and empty rooms comfortable. The King probably is of the same opinion, for he has caused a house to be built on the mountains, which, smaller and more proportioned to man's littleness, is intended for a hunting-box and country-seat.

Caserta, Thursday, March 15, 1787.

Hackert is lodged very comfortably in the old castle—it is quite roomy enough for all his guests. Constantly busy with drawing and painting, he nevertheless is very social, and easily draws men around him, as in the end he generally makes every one become his scholar; he has also quite won me by putting up patiently with my weaknesses, and insists, above all things, on distinctness of drawing, and marked and clear keeping. When he paints, he has three colours always ready; and as he works on and uses one after another, a picture is produced, one knows not how or whence. I wish the execution were as easy as it looks. With his usual blunt honesty he said to ———, "You have capacity, but you are unable to accomplish anything; stay with me a year and a half, and you shall be able to produce works which shall be a delight to yourself and to others." Is not this a text on which one might preach eternally to dilettanti:—We would like to see what sort of a pupil we can make of you.

Naples—Sulzer's theory of the fine arts.

The special confidence with which the queen honors him is evinced not merely by the fact that he gives lessons in practice to the princesses, but still more so by his being frequently summoned on an evening to talk with and instruct them on art and kindred subjects. He makes Sulzer's book the basis of such lectures, selecting the articles, as entertainment or conviction may be his object.

I was obliged to approve of this, and, in consequence, to laugh at myself. What a difference is there between him who wishes to investigate principles, and one whose highest object is to work on the world and to teach them for their mere private amusement. Sulzer's theory was always odious to me on account of the falseness of its fundamental maxim, but now I saw that the book contained much more than the multitude require. The varied information which is here communicated, the mode of thinking with which alone so active a mind as Sulzer's could be satisfied, must have been quite sufficient for the ordinary run of people.

Many happy and profitable hours have I spent with the picture-restorer Anders, who has been summoned hither from Rome, and resides in the Castle, and industriously pursues his work, in which the king takes a great interest. Of his skill in restoring old paintings, I dare not begin to speak, since it would be necessary to describe the whole process of this yet difficult craft,—and wherein consists the difficulty of the problem, and the merit of success.

Caserta, March 16, 1787.

Your dear letter of the 19th February reached me to-day, and I must forthwith dispatch a word or two in reply. How glad should I be to come to my senses again, by thinking of my friends!

Naples is a paradise: in it every one lives in a sort of intoxicated self-forgetfulness. It is even so with me; I scarcely know myself—I seem quite an altered man. Yesterday I said to myself: either you have always been mad, or you are so now.

I have paid a visit to the ruins of ancient Capua, and all that is connected with it.

In this country one first begins to have a true idea of what vegetation is, and why man tills the fields. The flax here is already near to blossoming, and the wheat a span and a-half high. Around Caserta the land is perfectly level, the fields worked as clean and as fine as the beds of a garden. All of them are planted with poplars, and from tree to tree the vine spreads; and yet, notwithstanding this shade, the soil below produces the finest and most abundant crops possible. What will they be when the spring shall come in power! Hitherto we have had very cold winds, and there has been snow on the mountains.

Within fourteen days I must decide whether to go to Sicily or not. Never before have I been so tossed backwards and forwards in coming to a resolution: every day something will occur to recommend the trip; the next morning—some circumstance will be against it. Two spirits are contending for me.

I say this in confidence, and for my female friends alone: speak not a word of it to my male friends. I am well aware that my "Iphigenia" has fared strangely. The public were so accustomed to the old form, expressions which it had adopted from frequent hearing and reading, were familiar to it; and now quite a different tone is sounding in its ears; and I clearly see that no one, in fact, thanks me for the endless pains I have been at. Such a work is never finished: it must, however, pass for such, as soon as the author has done his utmost, considering time and circumstances.

All this, however, will not be able to deter me from trying a similar operation with "Tasso." Perhaps it would be better to throw it into the fire; however, I shall adhere to my resolution, and since it must be what it is, I shall make a wonderful work of it. On this account, I am pleased to find that the printing of my works goes on so slowly; and then, again, it is well to be at a distance from the murmurs of the compositor. Strange enough that even in one's most independent actions, one expects, nay, requires a stimulus.

Caserta, March 16, 1787.

If in Rome one can readily set oneself to study, here one can do nothing but live. You forget yourself and the world; and to me it is a strange feeling to go about with people who think of nothing but enjoying themselves. Sir William Hamilton, who still resides here as ambassador from England, has at length, after his long love of art, and long study, discovered the most perfect of admirers of nature and art in a beautiful young woman. She lives with him: an English woman of about twenty years old. She is very handsome, and of a beautiful figure. The old knight has had made for her a Greek costume, which becomes her extremely. Dressed in this, and letting her hair loose, and taking a couple of shawls, she exhibits every possible variety of posture, expression, and look, so that at the last the spectator almost fancies it is a dream. One beholds here in perfection, in movement, in ravishing variety, all that the greatest of artists have rejoiced to be able to produce. Standing, kneeling, sitting, lying down, grave or sad, playful, exulting, repentant, wanton, menacing, anxious—all mental states follow rapidly one after another. With wonderful taste she suits the folding of her veil to each expression, and with the same handkerchief makes every kind of head-dress. The old knight holds the light for her, and enters into the exhibition with his whole soul. He thinks he can discern in her a resemblance to all the most famous antiques, all the beautiful profiles on the Sicilian coins—aye, of the Apollo Belvedere itself. This much at any rate is certain—the entertainment is unique. We spent two evenings on it with thorough enjoyment. To-day Tischbein is engaged in painting her.

What I have seen and inferred of the *personnel* of the Court requires to be further tested, before I set it down. To-day the king is gone hunting the wolves: they hope to kill at least five.

Naples, March 17, 1787.

When I would write words, images only start before my eyes,—the beautiful land, the free sea; the hazy islands, the roaring mountain;—powers to delineate all this fail me.

Here in this country one at last understands how it ever came into the head of man to till the ground—here where it produces everything, and where one may look for as many as from three to five crops in the year.

I have seen much, and reflected still more. The world opens itself to me more and more—all even that I have long known is at last becoming my own. How quick to know, but how slow to put in practice, is the human creature!

The only pity is, that I cannot at each moment communicate to others my observations. But, both as man and artist, one is here driven backwards and forwards by a hundred ideas of his own, while his services are put in requisition by hundreds of persons. His situation is peculiar and strange; he cannot freely sympathize with another's being, because he finds his own exertions so put to the stretch.

And after all, the world is nothing but a wheel; in its whole periphery it is every where similar, but, nevertheless, it appears to us so strange, because we ourselves are carried round with it.

What I always said has actually come to pass: in this land alone do I begin to understand and to unravel many a phenomenon of nature, and complication of opinion. I am gathering from every quarter, and shall bring back with me a great deal,—certainly much love of my own native land, and joy to live with a few dear friends.

With regard to my Sicilian tour, the gods still hold the scales in their hands: the index still wavers.

Who can the friend be who has thus mysteriously announced? Only, may I not neglect him in my pilgrimage and tour in the island!

The frigate from Palermo has returned: in eight days she sets sail again. Whether I shall sail with it, and be back at Rome by Passion Week, I have not as yet determined. Never in my life have I been so undecided: a trifle will turn the scale.

With men I get on rather better: for I feel that one must weigh them by avoirdupois weight, and not by the jeweller's scales; as, unfortunately, friends too often weigh one another in their hypochondriacal humours and in an over-exacting spirit.

Here men know nothing of one another; they scarcely observe that others are also going on their way, side by side with them. They run all day backwards and forwards in a Paradise, without looking around them; and if the neighbouring jaws of hell begin to open and to rage, they have recourse to S. Januarius.

To pass through such a countless multitude, with its restless excitement, is strange, but salutary. Here they are all crossing and recrossing one another, and yet every one finds his way and his object. In so great a crowd and bustle I feel myself perfectly calm and solitary; the more bustling the streets become, the more quietly I move.

Naples—Rousseau.

Often do I think of Rousseau and his hypochondriacal discontent; and I can thoroughly understand how so fine an organization may have been deranged. Did I not myself feel such sympathy with natural objects; and did I not see that, in the apparent perplexity, a hundred seemingly contrary observations admit of being reconciled, and arranged side by side, just as the geometer by a cross line tests many measurements, I should often think myself mad.

Naples, March 18, 1787.

We must not any longer put off our visit to Herculaneum, and the Museum of Portici, where the curiosities which have been dug out of it are collected and preserved. That ancient city, lying at the foot of Vesuvius, was entirely covered with lava, which subsequent eruptions successively raised so high, that the buildings are at present sixty feet below the surface. The city was discovered by some men coming upon a marble pavement, as they were digging a well. It is a great pity that the excavation was not executed systematically by German miners; for it is admitted that the work, which was carried on at random, and with the hope of plunder, has spoilt many a noble monument of ancient art. After descending sixty steps into a pit, by torch-light you gaze in admiration at the theatre which once stood beneath the open sky, and listen to the guide recounting all that was found there, and carried off.

We entered the museum well recommended, and were well received; nevertheless we were not allowed to take any drawings. Perhaps on this account we paid the more attention to what we saw, and the more vividly transported ourselves into those long-passed times, when all these things surrounded their living owners, and ministered to the use and enjoyment of life. The little houses and rooms of Pompeii now appeared to me at once more spacious and more confined—more confined, because I fancied them to myself crammed full of so many precious objects: more spacious, because these very objects could not have been furnished merely as necessaries, but, being decorated with the most graceful and ingenious devices of the imitative arts, while they delighted the taste, must also have enlarged the mind far beyond what the amplest house-room could ever have done.

One sees here, for instance, a nobly-shaped pail, mounted at the top with a highly-ornamented edge. When you examine it more closely, you find that this rim rises on two sides, and so furnishes convenient handles by which the vessel may be lifted. The lamps, according to the number of their wicks, are ornamented with masks and mountings, so that each burner illuminates a genuine figure of art. We also saw some high and gracefully slender stands of iron for holding lamps, the pendant burners being suspended with figures of all kinds, which display a wonderful fertility of invention; and as, in order to please and delight the eye, they sway and oscillate, the effect surpasses all description.

In the hope of being able to pay a second visit, we followed the usher from room to room, and snatched all the delight and instruction that was possible from a cursory view.

Naples, Monday, March 19, 1787.

Naples—Engagement with Kniep.

Within these last few days I have formed a new connexion. Tischbein for three or four weeks has faithfully lent me all the assistance in his power, and diligently explained to me the works both of nature and art. Yesterday, however, after being at the Museum of Portici, we had some conversation together, and we came to the conclusion that, considering his own artistic objects, he could not perform, with credit to himself, the works which, in the hope of some future appointment in Naples, he has undertaken for the Court and for several persons in the city, nor do justice to my views, wishes, and fancies. With sincere good wishes for my success, he has therefore recommended to me for my constant companion a young man whom, since I arrived here, I have often seen, not without feeling some inclination and liking for him. His name is Kniep, who, after a long stay at Rome, has come to Naples as the true field and element of the landscape-painter. Even in Rome I had heard him highly spoken of as a clever draughtsman—only his industry was not much commended. I have tolerably studied his character, and think the ground of this censure arises rather from a want of a decision, which certainly may be overcome, if we are long together A favourable beginning confirms me in this hope; and if he continues to go on thus, we shall continue good companions for some time.

Naples, March 19, 1787.

One needs only to walk along the streets, and keep one's eyes well open, and one is sure to see the most unequalled of scenes. At the Mole, one of the noisiest quarters of the city, I saw yesterday a Pulcinello, who on a temporary stage of planks was quarrelling with an ape, while from a balcony above a right pretty maiden was exposing her charms to every eye. Not far from the ape and his stage a quack doctor was recommending to the credulous crowd his nostrums for every evil. Such a scene painted by a Gerard Dow would not fail to charm contemporaries and posterity.

To-day, moreover, was the festival of S. Joseph. He is the patron of all Fritaruoli—that is, pastry-cooks, and understands baking in a very extensive sense. Because beneath the black and seething oil hot flames will, of course, rage,—therefore, every kind of torture by fire falls within his province. Accordingly, yesterday evening, being the eve of the Saint's day, the fronts of the houses were adorned with pictures, to the best of the inmates' skill, representing souls in Purgatory, or the Last Judgment, with plenty of fire and flame. Before the doors frying-pans were hissing on hastily-constructed hearths. One partner was working the dough, another shaped it into twists, and threw it into the boiling lard; a third stood by the frying-pan, holding a short skewer, with which he drew out the twists as soon as they were done, and shoved them off on another skewer to a fourth party, who offered them to the bystanders. The two last were generally young apprentices, and wore white curly wigs,—this head-dress being the Neapolitan symbol of an angel. Other figures besides completed the group; and these were busy in presenting wine to the busy cooks, or in drinking themselves, crying, and puffing the article all the while; the angels, too, and cooks were all clamouring. The people crowded to buy—for all pastry is sold cheap on this evening, and a part of the profits given to the poor.

Scenes of this kind may be witnessed without end. Thus fares it every day; always something new—some fresh absurdity. The variety of costume, too, that meets you in the streets; the multitude, too, of passages in the Toledo street alone!

Thus there is plenty of most original entertainment, if only one will live with the people; it is so natural, that one almost becomes natural oneself. For this is the original birth-place of Pulcinello, the true national mask— the Harlequin of Pergamo, and the Hanswurth of the Tyrol. This Pulcinello now is a thoroughly easy, sedate, somewhat indifferent, perhaps lazy, and yet humorous fellow. And so one meets everywhere with a "Kellner" and a "Hausknecht." With ours I had special fun yesterday, and yet there was nothing more than my sending him to fetch some paper and pens. A half misunderstanding, a little loitering, good humour and roguery, produced a most amusing scene, which might be very successfully brought out on any stage.

Naples, Tuesday, March 20, 1787.

The news that an eruption of lava had just commenced, which, taking the direction of Ottajano, was invisible at Naples, tempted me to visit Vesuvius for the third time. Scarcely had I jumped out of my cabriolet (zweirädrigen einpferdigen Fuhrwerk), at the foot of the mountain, when immediately appeared the two guides who had accompanied us on our previous ascent. I had no wish to do without either, but took one out of gratitude and custom, the other for reliance on his judgment,—and the two for the greater convenience. Having ascended the summit, the older guide remained with our cloaks and refreshment, while the younger followed me, and we boldly went straight towards a dense volume of smoke, which broke forth from the bottom of the funnel; then we quickly went downwards by the side of it, till at last, under the clear heaven, we distinctly saw the lava emitted from the rolling clouds of smoke.

We may hear an object spoken of a thousand times, but its peculiar features will never be caught till we see it with our own eyes. The stream of lava was small, not broader perhaps than ten feet, but the way in which it flowed down a gentle and tolerably smooth plain was remarkable. As it flowed along, it cooled both on the sides and on the surface, so that it formed a sort of canal, the bed of which was continually raised in consequence of the molten mass congealing oven beneath the fiery stream, which, with uniform action, precipitated right and left the scoria which were floating on its surface. In this way a regular dam was at length thrown up, in which the glowing stream flowed on as quietly as any mill-stream. We passed along the tolerably high dam, while the scoria rolled regularly off the sides at our feet. Some cracks in the canal afforded opportunity of looking at the living stream from below, and as it rushed onwards, we observed it from above.

A very bright sun made the glowing lava look dull; but a moderate steam rose from it into the pure air. I felt a great desire to go nearer to the point where it broke out from the mountain; there my guide averred, it at once formed vaults and roofs above itself, on which he had often stood. To see and experience this phenomenon, we again ascended the hill, in order to come from behind to this point. Fortunately at this moment the place was cleared by a pretty strong wind, but not entirely, for all round it the smoke eddied from a thousand crannies; and now at last we stood on the top of the solid roof, (which looked like a hardened mass of twisted dough), but which, however, projected so far outwards, that it was impossible to see the welling lava.

We ventured about twenty steps further, but the ground on which we stepped became hotter and hotter, while around us rolled an oppressive steam, which obscured and hid the sun; the guide, who was a few steps in advance of me, presently turned back, and seizing hold of me, hurried out of this Stygian exhalation.

After we had refreshed our eyes with the clear prospect, and washed our gums and throat with wine, we went round again to notice any other peculiarities which might characterise this peak of hell, thus rearing itself in the midst of a Paradise. I again observed attentively some chasms, in appearance like so many Vulcanic forges, which emitted no smoke, but continually shot out a steam of hot glowing air. They were all tapestried, as it were, with a kind of stalactite, which covered the funnel to the top, with its knobs and chintz-like variation of colours. In consequence of the irregularity of the forges, I found many specimens of this sublimation hanging within reach, so that, with our staves and a little contrivance, we were able to hack off a few, and to secure them. I saw in the shops of the dealers in lava similar specimens, labelled simply "Lava;" and I was delighted to have discovered that it was volcanic soot precipitated from the hot vapour, and distinctly exhibiting the sublimated mineral particles which it contained.

The most glorious of sunsets, a heavenly evening, refreshed me on my return; still I felt how all great contrasts confound the mind and senses. From the terrible to the beautiful—from the beautiful to the terrible; each destroys the other, and produces a feeling of indifference. Assuredly, the Neapolitan would be quite a different creature, did he not feel himself thus hemmed in between Elysium and Tartarus.

Naples, March 22, 1787.

Were I not impelled by the German spirit, and desire to learn and to do rather than to enjoy, I should tarry a little longer in this school of a light-hearted and happy life, and try to profit by it still more. Here it is enough for contentment, if a man has ever so little an income. The situation of the city, the mildness of the climate, can never be sufficiently extolled; but it is almost exclusively to these that the stranger is referred.

Naples-Sir William Hamilton.

No doubt, one who has abundance of time, tact, and means, might remain here for a long time, with profit to himself. Thus Sir William Hamilton has contrived highly to enjoy a long residence in this city, and now, in the evening of his life, is reaping the fruits of it. The rooms which he has had furnished in the English style, are most delightful, and the view from the corner room, perhaps, unique. Below you is the sea, with a view of Capri, Posilippo on the right, with the promenade of Villa Real between you and the grotto; on the left an ancient building belonging to the Jesuits, and beyond it the coast stretching from Sorrento to Cape Minerva. Another prospect equal to this is scarcely to be found in Europe,—at least, not in the centre of a great and populous city.

Hamilton is a person of universal taste, and after having wandered through the whole realm of creation, has found rest at last in a most beautiful wife, a masterpiece of the great artist—Nature.

And now after all this, and a hundred-fold more of enjoyment, the sirens from over the sea are beckoning me; and if the wind is favorable, I shall start at the same time with this letter,—it for the north, I for the south. The human mind will not be confined to any limits—I especially require breadth and extent in an eminent degree; however, I must content myself on this occasion with, a rapid survey, and must not think of a long fixed look. If by hearing and thinking, I can only attain to as much of any object as a finger's tip, I shall be able to make out the whole hand.

Singularly enough, within these few days, a friend has spoken to me of *Wilhelm Meister*, and urged me to continue it. In this climate, I don't think it possible; however, something of the air of this heaven may, perhaps, be imparted to the closing books. May my existence only unfold itself sufficiently to lengthen the stem, and to produce richer and finer flowers; certainly it were better for me never to have come here at all, than to go away unregenerated.

Naples, March 22, 1787.

Yesterday we saw a picture of Correggio's, which is for sale. It is not, indeed, in very good preservation; however, it still retains the happiest stamp possible of all the peculiar charms of this painter. It represents a Madonna, with the infant, hesitating between the breast and some pears which an angel is offering it; the subject, therefore, is the weaning of Christ. To me the idea appears extremely tender; the composition easy and natural, and happily and charmingly executed. It immediately reminded me of the Vow of S. Catherine, and, in my opinion, the painting is unquestionably from the hand of Correggio.

Naples, Friday, March 23, 1787.

The terms of my engagement with Kniep are now settled, and it has commenced in a right practical way. We went together to Pæstuin, where, and also on our journey thither and back, he showed the greatest industry with his pencil. He has taken some of the most glorious outlines possible. He seems to relish this moving but busy sort of life, which has called for a talent which he was scarcely conscious of. This comes of being resolute: but it is exactly here that his accurate and nice skill shows itself. He never stops to surround the paper on which he is about to draw with the usual rectangular lines; however, he seems to take as much pleasure in cutting points to his pencil, which is of the best English lead, as in drawing itself. Thus his outlines are just what one would wish them to be.

Naples—A sketching excursion.

Now we have come to the following arrangement:—From this day forward, we are to live and travel together; while he is to have nothing to trouble himself about but drawing, as he has done for the last few days.

All the sketches are to be mine; but in order to a further profit, after our return, from our connexion, he is to finish for a certain sum a number of them, which I am to select; and then, remuneration for the others is to be settled according to the dexterity he evinces in them, and the importance of the views taken, and other considerations. This arrangement has made me quite happy, and now at last I can give you an account of our journey.

Sitting in a light two-wheeled carriage, and driving in turn, with a rough good-natured boy behind, we rolled through the glorious country, which Kniep greeted with a true artistic eye. We now reached the mountain stream, which, running along a smooth artificial channel, skirts most delightful rocks and woods. At last, in the district of *Alla Cava*, Kniep could not contain himself, but set to work to fix on paper a splendid mountain, which right before us stood out boldly against the blue sky, and with a clever and characteristic touch drew the outlines of the summit, with the sides also, down to its very base. We both made merry with it, as the earnest of our contract.

A similar sketch was taken in the evening from the window, of a singularly lovely and rich country, which passes all my powers of description. Who would not have been disposed to study at such a spot, in those bright times, when a high school of art was flourishing? Very early in the morning we set off by an untrodden path, coming occasionally on marshy spots towards two beautifully shaped hills. We crossed brooks and pools, where the wild bulls, like hippopotamuses, were wallowing, and looking upon us with their wild red eyes.

The country grew flatter and more desolate; the scarcity of the buildings bespoke a sparing cultivation. At last, when we were doubting whether we were passing through rocks or ruins, some great oblong masses enabled us to distinguish the remains of temples and other monuments of a once splendid city. Kniep, who had already sketched on the way the two picturesque limestone hills, suddenly stopped to find a spot from which to seize and exhibit the peculiarity of this most unpicturesque region.

A countryman, whom I took for my guide, led me the meanwhile through the buildings. The first sight of them excited nothing but astonishment. I found myself in a perfectly strange world; for, as centuries pass from the severe to the pleasing, they form man's taste at the same time—indeed, create him after the same law. But now our eyes, and through them our whole inner being, has been used to, and decidedly prepossessed in favor of, a lighter style of architecture; so that these crowded masses of stumpy conical pillars appear heavy, not to say frightful. But I soon recollected myself, called to mind the history of art, thought of the times when the spirit of the age was in unison with this style of architecture, and realised the severe style of sculpture; and in less than an hour found myself reconciled to it,—nay, I went so far as to thank my genius for permitting me to see with my own eyes such well-preserved remains, since drawings give us no true idea of them; for, in architectural sketches, they seem more elegant, and in perspective views even more stumpy than they actually are. It is only by going round them, and passing through them, that you can impart to them their real character; you evoke for them, not to say infuse into them, the very feeling which the architect had in contemplation. And thus I spent the whole day, Kniep the while working away most diligently in taking very accurate sketches. How delighted was I to be exempt from that care, and yet to acquire such unfailing tokens for the aid of memory! Unfortunately, there was no accommodation for spending the night here. We returned to Sorrento, and started early next morning for Naples.

Vesuvius, seen from the back, is a rich country; poplars, with their colossal pyramids, on the road-side, in the foreground; these, too, formed an agreeable feature, which we halted a moment to take.

We now reached an eminence. The most extensive area in the world opened before us. Naples, in all its splendour: its mile-long line of houses on the flat shore of the bay, the promontories, tongues of land and walls of rock; then the islands, and, behind all, the sea,—the whole was a ravishing sight.

A most hideous singing, or rather exulting cry and howl of joy, from the boy behind, frightened and disturbed us. Somewhat angrily, I called out to him; he had never had any harsh words from us,—he had been a very good boy.

For a while he did not move; then he patted me lightly on the shoulder, and pushing between us both his right arm, with the fore-finger stretched out, exclaimed, "*Signor, perdonate! questa è la mia patria!*"—which, being interpreted, runs, "Forgive me, Sir, for that is my native land!" And so I was ravished a second time. Something like a tear stood in the eyes of the phlegmatic child of the north.

Naples, March 25, 1787.

Although I saw that Kniep was delighted to go with me to the festival of the Annunciation, still I could not fail to observe that there was a something he was sorry to part from. His candour could not let him long conceal from me the fact, that he had formed here a close and faithful attachment. It was a pretty tale to listen to, the story of their first meeting, and the description of the fair one's behaviour up to this time told in her favour; Kniep, moreover, insisted on my going and seeing for myself how pretty she really was. Accordingly, an opportunity was contrived, and so as to afford me the enjoyment of one of the most agreeable views over Naples. He took me to the flat roof of a house, which commanded a survey of the lower town, near the Mole, the bay, and the shore of Sorrento; all that lay beyond on the left, became fore-shortened in the strangest way possible, and which, except from this particular spot, was never witnessed. Naples is, every where, beautiful and glorious.

Naples—An apparition.

While we were admiring the country around, suddenly, (although expected), a very beautiful face presented itself above the roof—for the entrance to these flat roofs is generally an oblong opening in the roof, which can be covered, when not used, by a trap-door. While, then, the little angel appeared in full figure above the opening, it occurred to me that ancient painters usually represent the Annunciation by making the angel ascend by a similar trap-door. But the angel on this occasion was really of a very fine form, of a very pretty face, and a good natural carriage. It was a real joy to me, under the free heaven, and in presence of the finest prospect in the world, to see my new friend so happy. After her departure, he confessed to me that he had hitherto voluntarily endured poverty, as by that means he had enjoyed her love; and at the same time, had learned to appreciate her contented disposition: and now his better prospects, and improved condition, were chiefly prized, because they procured him the means of making her days more comfortable.

Naples, March 25, 1787.

After this pleasant little incident I walked on the shore, calm and happy. There a good insight into botanical matters opened on me. Tell Herder that I am very near finding the primal vegetable type; only I fear that no one will be able to trace in it the rest of the vegetable kingdom. My famous theory of the Cotyledons is so refined, that perhaps it is impossible to go further with it.

Naples, March 26, 1787.

To-morrow this letter will leave this for you. On Thursday, the 29th, I go to Palermo in the corvette, which formerly, in my ignorance of sea matters, I promoted to the rank of a frigate. The doubt whether I should go or remain made me unsettled even in the use of my stay here; now I have made up my mind, things go on better. For my mental state this journey is salutary—indeed necessary. I see Sicily pointing to Africa, and to Asia, and to the wonderful, whither so many rays of the world's history are directed: even to stand still is no trifle!

I have treated Naples quite in its own style. I have been anything but industrious. And yet I have seen a great deal, and formed a pretty general idea of the land, its inhabitants, and condition. On my return there is much that I shall have to go over again; indeed, only "go over," for by the 29th of June I must be in Rome again. As I have missed the Holy Week, I must not fail to be present at the festivities of St. Peter's Day. My Sicilian expedition must not altogether draw me off from my original plans.

The day before yesterday we had a violent storm, with thunder, lightning, and rain. Now it is again clear; a glorious Tramontane is blowing; if it lasts, we shall have a rapid passage.

Yesterday I went with my fellow-traveller to see the vessel, and to take our cabin. A sea voyage is utterly out of the pale of my ideas; this short trip, which will probably be a mere coasting one, will help my imagination, and enlarge my world. The captain is a young lively fellow; the ship trim and clean, built in America, and a good sailer.

Naples-Departure for Sicily.

Here every spot begins to look green; Sicily, they tell me, I shall find still more so. By the time you get this letter I shall be on my return, leaving Trinacria behind me. Such is man; he is always either anticipating or recalling; I have not yet been there; and yet I now am, in thought, back again with you! However, for the confusion of this letter I am not to blame. Every moment I am interrupted, and yet I would, if possible, fill this sheet to the very corner.

Just now I have had a visit from a Marchese Berio, a young man who appears to be well informed. He was anxious to make the acquaintance of the author of "Werther." Generally, indeed, the people here evince a great desire for, and delight in, learning and accomplishments. Only they are too happy to go the right way to acquire them. Had I more time, I would willingly devote it to observing the Neapolitans. These four weeks—what are they, compared with the endless variety of life?

Now, fare you well. On these travels I have learnt one thing at least—how to travel well; whether I am learning to live, I know not. The men who pretend to understand that art, are, in nature and manner, too widely different from me, for setting up any claim to such a talent.

Farewell, and love me as sincerely as I from my heart remember you.

Naples, March 28, 1787.

These few days have been entirely passed in packing and leave-taking; with making all necessary arrangements, and paying bills; looking for missing articles, and with preparations of all kinds. I set the time down as lost.

The Prince of Walbeck has, just at my departure, unsettled me again. For he has been talking of nothing less than that I should arrange, on my return, to go with him to Greece and Dalmatia. When one enters once into the world, and gives way to it, it is necessary to be very cautious, lest one should be carried away, not to say driven mad by it. I am utterly incapable of adding another syllable.

Naples, March 29, 1787.

For some days the weather has been very unsettled; to-day, (the appointed time for our sailing), it is again as fine as possible. A favourable north wind, a bright sunny sky, beneath which one wishes oneself in the wide world! Now I bid an affectionate farewell to all my friends in Weimar and Gotha. Your love accompanies me; for wherever I am I feel my need of you. Last night I dreamt I was again among old familiar faces. It seems as if I could not unload my boat of pheasants' feathers any where but among you. May it be well loaded.

SICILY.

At Sea, Thursday, March 29, 1787.

A fresh and favourable breeze from the north-east is not blowing this time, as it did at the last sailing of the packet. But, unfortunately, a direct head-wind comes from the opposite quarter, the south-west—and so we are experiencing to our cost how much the traveller by sea depends upon the caprice of the wind and weather. Out of all patience, we whiled away the morning either on the shore or in the coffee-house; at last, at noon we went on board, and the weather being extremely fine, we enjoyed the most glorious of views. The corvette lay at anchor near to the Mole. With an unclouded sun the atmosphere was hazy, giving to the rocky walls of Sorrento, which were in the shade, a tint of most beautiful blue. Naples, with its living multitudes, lay in the full sunshine, and glittered brilliantly with countless tints. It was not until sunset that the vessel began slowly to move from her moorings; then the wind which was contrary drove us over to Posilippo, and its promontory. All night long the ship went quietly on its way. She is a swift sailer, and was built in America, and is well fitted with, cabins and berths. The passengers cheerful, but not boisterous. Opera-singers and dancers, consigned to Palermo.

Friday, March 30, 1787.

By day-break we found ourselves between Ischia and Capri—perhaps not more than a mile from the latter. The sun rose from behind the mountains of Capri and Cape Minerva. Kniep diligently sketched the outlines of the coasts and the islands, and took several beautiful views. The slowness of the passage was favourable to his labours. We were making our way but slowly under a light side-wind. We lost sight of Vesuvius about four, just as we came in dew of Cape Minerva and Ischia. These, too, disappeared about evening. The sun set in the sea, attended with clouds, and a long streak of light, reaching for miles, all of a brilliant purple. This phenomenon was also sketched by Kniep. At last we lost sight altogether of the land, and the watery horizon surrounded us, the night being clear, with lovely moonlight.

The voyage to Sicily.

These beautiful sights, however, I could only enjoy for a few moments, for I was soon attacked with sea-sickness. I betook myself to my cabin, chose an horizontal position, and abstaining from all meat or drink, except white bread and red wine, soon found myself pretty comfortable again. Shut out from the external world, I let the internal have full sway; and, as a tedious voyage was to be anticipated, I immediately set myself a heavy task in order to while away the time profitably. Of all my papers I had only brought with me the first two acts of "Tasso," written in poetic prose. These two acts, as regards their plan and evolution, were nearly similar to the present ones, but, written full ten years ago, had a somewhat soft and misty tone, which soon disappeared, while, in accordance with my later notions, I made form more predominant, and introduced more of rhythm.

Saturday, March 31, 1787.

The sun rose this morning from the water quite clear. About seven we overtook a French vessel, which had left Naples two days before us, so much the better sailer was our vessel: still we had no prospect as yet of the end of our passage. We were somewhat cheered by the sight of Ustica, but, unfortunately, on our left, when we ought to have had it, like Capri, on our right. Towards noon the wind became directly contrary, and we did not make the least way. The sea began to get rough, and every one in the ship was sick.

I kept in my usual position, and the whole piece was thought over and over, and through and through again. The hours passed away, and I should not have noticed how they went, but for the roguish Kniep, on whose appetite the waves had no influence. When, from time to time, he brought me some wine and some bread, he took a mischievous delight in expatiating on the excellent dinner in the cabin, the cheerfulness and good nature of our young but clever captain, and on his regrets that I was unable to enjoy my share of it. So, likewise, the transition from joke and merriment to qualmishness and sickness, and the various ways in which the latter manifested themselves in the different passengers, afforded him rich materials for humorous description.

At four in the afternoon the captain altered the course of our vessel. The mainsails were again set, and we steered direct for Ustica, behind which, to our great joy, we discerned the mountains of Sicily. The wind improved, and we bore rapidly towards Sicily, and a few little islands appeared in view. The sunset was murky, the light of heaven being veiled beneath a mist. The wind was pretty fair for the whole of the evening; towards midnight the sea became very rough.

Sunday, April 1, 1787.

About 3 in the morning a violent storm. Half asleep and dreaming, I went on with the plan of my drama; in the mean time there was great commotion on deck; the sails were all taken in, and the vessel pitched on the top of the waves. As day broke the storm abated, and the sky cleared up. Now Ustica lay right on our left. They pointed out to me a large turtle swimming a great distance off; by my telescope I could easily discern it, as a living point. Towards noon we were clearly able to distinguish the coast of Sicily with its headlands and bays, but we had got very far to the leeward, and tacked on and off. Towards mid-day we came nearer to the shore. The weather being clear, and the sun shining bright, we saw quite distinctly the western coast from the promontory of Lilybæum to Cape Gallo.

A shoal of dolphins attended our ship on both bows, and continually shot a-head. It was amusing to watch them as they swam along, covered by the clear transparent waves at one time, and at another springing above the water, showing their fins and spine-ridged back, with their sides playing in the light from gold to green, and from green to gold.

The voyage to Sicily.

As the land was direct on our lee, the captain lay to in a bay behind Cape Gallo. Kniep failed not to seize the opportunity to sketch the many beautiful scenes somewhat in detail. Towards sunset the captain made again for the open sea, steering north-east, in order to make the heights of Palermo. I ventured several times on deck, but never intermitted for a moment my poetical labours; and thus I became pretty well master of the whole piece. With a cloudy sky, a bright but broken moonlight, the reflection on the sea was infinitely beautiful. Paintings, in order to heighten the effect, generally lead us to believe, that the reflection from the heavenly luminaries on the water has its greatest breadth nearest to the spectator, where it also possesses its greatest brilliancy. On this occasion, however, the reflection was broadest at the horizon, and, like a sharp pyramid, ended with sparkling waves close to the ship. During the night our captain again frequently changed the tack.

Monday, April 2, 1787.

This morning, about 8 o'clock, we found ourselves over against Palermo. The morning seemed to me highly delightful. During the days that I had been shut up in my cabin, I had got on pretty well with the plan of my drama. I felt quite well now, and was able to stay on deck, and observe attentively the Sicilian coast. Kniep went on sketching away, and by his accurate, but rapid pencil, many a sheet of paper was converted into highly valuable mementoes of our landing, which, however, we still had to wait for.

PALERMO.

Monday, April 2, 1787.

By 3 o'clock p.m., we at last, after much trouble and difficulty, got into harbour, where a most glorious view lay before us. Perfectly recovered from my sea-sickness, I enjoyed it highly. The town facing north, lay at the foot of a high hill, with the sun (at this time of day) shining above it. The sides of the buildings which looked towards us, lay in a deep shade, which, however, was clear, and lit up by the reflection from the water. On our right Monte Pellegrino, with its many elegant outlines, in full light; on the left the coast, with its bays, isthmuses, and headlands, stretching far away into the distance; and the most agreeable effect was produced by the fresh green of some fine trees, whose crowns, lit up from behind, swayed backwards and forwards before the dark buildings, like great masses of glow-worms. A brilliant haze gave a blueish tint to all the shades.

Instead of hurrying impatiently on shore, we remained on deck till we were actually forced to land; for where could we hope soon to find a position equal to this, or so favourable a point of view?

Through the singular gateway, which consists of two vast pillars, which are left unconnected above, in order that the tower-high car of S. Rosalia may be able to pass through, on her famous festival, we were driven into the city, and alighted, almost immediately, at a large hotel on our left. The host, an old, decent person, long accustomed to see strangers of every nation and tongue, conducted us into a large room, the balcony of which commanded a view of the sea, with the roadstead, where we recognised our ship, Monte Rosalia, and the beach, and were enabled to form an idea of our whereabouts. Highly satisfied with the position of our room, We did not for some time observe that, at the farther end of it, was an alcove, slightly raised, and concealed by curtains, in which was a most spacious bed, with a magnificent canopy and curtains of silk, in perfect keeping with the other stately, but old fashioned, furniture of our apartment. This display of splendour made me uneasy; so, as my custom was, I wished to make an agreement with my host. To this the old man replied that conditions were unnecessary, and he trusted I should have nothing to complain of in him. We were also at liberty to make use of the ante-room, which was next to our apartment, and cool, airy, and agreeable from its many balconies.

We amused ourselves with the endless variety of views, and endeavoured to sketch them one by one in pencil, or in colours, for here the eye fell upon a plentiful harvest for the artist.

Sicily—Palermo.

In the evening the lovely moonlight attracted us once more to the roadstead, and even after our return riveted us for some time on the balcony. The light was peculiar,—the repose and loveliness of the scene were extreme.

Palermo, Tuesday, April 3, 1787.

Our first business was to examine the city, which is easy enough to survey, but difficult to know; easy, because a street a mile long, from the lower to the upper gate, from the sea to the mountain, intersects it, and is itself again crossed, nearly in its middle, by another. Whatever lies on these two great lines is easily found; but in the inner streets a stranger soon loses himself, and without a guide will never extricate himself from their labyrinths.

Towards evening our attention was directed to the long line of carriages, (of the well-known build,) in which the principal persons of the neighbourhood were taking their evening drive from the city to the beach, for the sake of the fresh air, amusement, and perhaps also for intrigue.

It was full moon about two hours before midnight, and the evening was in consequence indescribably glorious. The northerly position of Palermo produces a very strange effect; as the city and shore come between the sun and the harbour, its reflection is never observed on the waves. On this account, though it was one of the very brightest of days yesterday, I found the sea of a deep blue colour, solemn, and oppressive; whereas, at Naples, after noon-day, it gets brighter and brighter, and glitters with more airy lightness, and to a greater distance.

Kniep has to-day left me to make my pilgrimages and observations by myself, in order that he might accurately sketch the outline of Monte Pellegrino, the most beautiful headland in the whole world.

Palermo, April 3, 1787.

Here again I must put a few things together, something in the way of an appendix, and with the carelessness of familiarity.

At sunset of the 29th of March we set sail for Naples, and at last, after a passage of four days and three hours, cast anchor in the harbour of Palermo. The little diary which I enclose, will give an account of ourselves and our fortunes. I never entered upon a journey so calmly as I did this, and never have I had a quieter time of it than during our passage, which a constant headwind has unusually prolonged, even though I passed the time chiefly on my bed, in a close little berth, to which I was obliged to keep during the first day, in consequence of a violent attack of sea-sickness. Now my thoughts pass over towards you; for if ever anything has exercised a decided influence on my mind, this voyage has certainly done so.

He who has never seen himself surrounded on all sides by the sea, can never possess an idea of the world, and of his own relation to it. As a landscape painter, this great simple line has given me entirely new ideas.

During our voyage we had, as the diary records, many changes, and, on a small scale, experienced all a sailor's fortunes. However, the safety and convenience of the packet-boat cannot be sufficiently commended. Our captain is a very brave and an extremely handsome man. My fellow-passengers consisted of a whole theatrical troop, well mannered, tolerable, and agreeable. My artist, who accompanies me, is a merry true-hearted fellow. In order to shorten the weary hours of the passage, he has explained to me all the mechanical part of *aquarell*, or painting in water colours,—an art which has been carried to a great height of perfection in Italy. He thoroughly understands the effect of particular colours in effecting certain tones, to produce which, without knowing the secret, one might go on mixing for ever. I had, it is true, learned a good deal of it in Rome, but never before so systematically. The artists must have studied and perfected the art in a country like Italy or this. No words can express the hazy brilliancy which hung around the coasts, as on a most beautiful noon we neared Palermo. He who has once seen it will never forget it. Now, at last, I can understand Claude Lorraine, and can cherish a hope that hereafter, in the north, I shall be able to produce, from my soul, at least a faint idea of these glorious abodes. Oh! that only all littleness had departed from it as entirely as the little charm of thatched roofs has vanished from among my ideas of what a drawing should be. We shall see what this "Queen of Islands" can do.

Sicily-Palermo.

No words can express the welcome—with its fresh green mulberry trees, evergreen oleanders, and hedges of citron, &c. In the open gardens you see large beds of ranunculuses and anemones. The air is mild, warm, and fragrant; the wind refreshing. The full moon, too, rose from behind a promontory, and shone upon the sea;—and this joyous scene after being tossed about four days and nights on the waves!

Forgive me if, with a stump of a pen and the Indian-ink my fellow-traveller uses for his sketches, I scribble down these remarks. I send them to you as a faint lisping murmur; since I am preparing for all that love me another record of these, my happy hours. What it is to be I say not; and when you will receive it, that also it is out of my power to tell.

Palermo, Tuesday, April 3.

This letter must, as far as possible, impart to you, my dearest friends, a high treat; it is intended to convey to you a description of an unrivalled bay, embracing a vast mass of waters. Beginning from the east, where a flattish headland runs far out into the sea, it is dotted with many rugged, beautifully-shaped, wood-crowned rocks, until it reaches the fishing-huts of the suburbs; then the town itself, whose foremost houses (and among them our own hotel) all look towards the harbour and to the great gate by which we entered.

Then it stretches westwards, and passing the usual landing-place, where vessels of smaller burden can lie to, comes next to what is properly the harbour, near the Mole, which is the station of all larger vessels; and then, at the western point, to protect the shipping, rises Monte Pellegrino, with its beautiful contour, after leaving between it and the mainland a lovely fertile valley, which at its other end again reaches the sea.

Kniep sketched away. I took, with my mind's eye, the plan of the country— (*ich schematisirte*)—with great delight; and now, glad to have reached home again, we feel neither strength nor energy to tell a long story, and to go into particulars. Our endeavours must, therefore, be reserved for a future occasion; and this sheet must serve to convince you of our inability adequately to seize these objects, or rather of our presumption in thinking to grasp and master them in so short a time.

———

Palermo, Wednesday April 4, 1787.

In the afternoon we paid a visit to the fertile and delightful valley at the foot of the Southern Mountains, running by Palermo, and through which the Oreto meanders. Here, too, is a call for the painter's eye, and a practised hand to convey an idea of it. Kniep, however, hastily seized an excellent point of view at a spot where the pent-up water was dashing down from a half-broken weir, and was shaded by a lovely group of trees, behind which an uninterrupted prospect opened up the valley, affording a view of several farm buildings.

Beautiful spring weather, and a budding luxuriance, diffused over the whole valley a refreshing feeling of peace, which our stupid guide marred by his ill-timed erudition, telling us that in former days, Hannibal had fought a battle here, and circumstantially detailing all the dreadful feats of war which had been perpetrated on the spot. In no friendly mood I reproved him for thus fatally calling up again such departed spectres. It was bad enough, I said, that from time to time the crops should be trodden down, if not by elephants, yet by men and horses. At any rate, it was not right to scare away the peaceful dreams of imagination by reviving such tumults and horrors.

The guide was greatly surprised that I could, on such a spot, despise classical reminiscences; and I, too, could not make him understand how greatly such a mingling of the past with the present displeased me.

Still more singular did our guide deem me, when at all the shallow places, of which many were left quite dry by the stream, I searched for pebbles, and carried off with me specimens of each sort. I again found it difficult to make him understand that there was no readier way of forming an idea of a mountainous district like that before us, than by examining the nature of the stones which are washed down by the streams, and that in so doing, the purpose was to acquire a right notion of those eternally classic heights of the ancient world.

———

Sicily-Palermo.

And, indeed, my gains from this stream were large enough: I carried away nearly forty specimens, which, however, may be comprised under a few classes. Most of these were of a species of rock, which, in one respect, might be regarded as a sort of jasper or hornblende; in another, looked like clay-slate. I found some pebbles rounded, others of a rhomboidal shape, others of irregular forms, and of various colours. Moreover, many varieties of the primeval limestone, not a few specimens of breccia, of which the substratum was lime, and holding jasper, or modifications of limestone. Rubbles of muschelkalk also were not wanting.

The horses here are fed on barley, chaff, (*hackerling*) and clover. In spring they give them the green barley, in order to refresh them—*per rinfrescar* is the phrase. As there are no meadows here, they have no hay. On the hill-sides there are some pasture-lands, and also in the corn-fields, as a third is always left fallow. They keep but few sheep, and these are of a breed from Barbary. On the whole they have more mules than horses, because the hot food suits the former better than the latter.

The plain on which Palermo lies, as well as the districts of Ai Colli, which lie without the city, and a part also of Baggaria, have for their basis the muschelkalk, of which the city is built. There are, for this purpose, extensive quarries of it in the neighbourhood. In one place, near Monte Pellegrino, they are more than fifty feet deep, The lower layers are of a whiter hue. In it are found many petrified corals and other shell-fish, but principally great scallops. The upper stratum is mixed with red marl, and contains but few, if any, fossils. Right above it lies the red marl, of which, however, the layer is not very stiff.

Monte Pellegrino, however, rises out of all this; it is a primary limestone, has many hollows and fissures, which, although very irregular, when closely observed are found to follow the order of the strata. The stone is close, and rings when struck.

Palermo, Thursday, April 5, 1787.

We have gone carefully through, the city. The style of architecture resembles for the most part that of Naples; but the public buildings, for instance the fountains, are still further removed from good taste. Here there is no artistic mind to regulate the public works; the edifices owe both their shape and existence to chance accidents. A fountain, which is the admiration of the whole island, would, perhaps, never have existed, had not Sicily furnished a beautiful variegated marble, and had not a sculptor, well practised in animal shapes happened to be in favour precisely at the time. It would be a difficult matter to describe this fountain. In a moderately-sized site stands a round piece of masonry, not quite a staff high (*Stock hoch*). The socle, the wall, and the cornice are of variegated marble. In the wall are several niches in a row, from which animals of all kinds in white marble, are looking with stretched-out necks. Horses, lions, camels, and elephants, are interchanged one with another; and one scarcely expects to find, within the circle of this menagerie, a fountain, to which, through four openings, marble steps lead you down to draw from the water, which flows in rich abundance.

The same nearly may be said of the churches, in which even the Jesuits' love of show and finery is surpassed—but not from design or plan, but by accident—just as artist after artist, whether sculptor or carver, gilder, lackerer, or worker in marble chose, without taste or rule, to display on each vacant spot his own abilities.

Amidst all this, however, one cannot fail to recognize a certain talent in imitating natural objects; for instance, the heads of the animals around the fountains are very well executed. By this means it is, in truth, that the admiration of the multitude is excited, whose artistic gratification consists chiefly in comparing the imitation with its living prototype.

Towards evening I made a merry acquaintance, as I entered the house of a small dealer in the Long Street, in order to purchase some trifles. As I stood before the window to look at the wares, a slight breeze arose, which eddying along the whole, street, at last distributed through all the windows and doors the immense cloud of dust which it had raised. "By all the saints," I cried, "whence comes till the dust of your town—is there no helping it? In its length and beauty, this street vies with any in the Corso in Rome. On both sides a fine pavement, which each stall and shop-holder keeps clean by interminable sweeping, but brushes everything into the middle of the street, which is, in consequence, so much the dirtier, and with every breath of wind sends back to you the filth which has just before been swept into the roadway. In Naples busy donkeys carry off day by day the rubbish to the gardens and farms. Why should you not here contrive and establish some similar regulation?"

Sicily—Palermo.

"Things with us are as they are," he replied; "we throw everything out of the house, and it rots before the door; you see here horse-dung and filth of all kinds—it lies there and dries, and returns to us again in the shape of dust. Against it we are taking precautions all day long. But look, our pretty little and ever-busy brooms, worn out at last, only go to increase the heap of filth before our doors."

And oddly enough it was actually so. They had nothing but very little besoms of palm-branches, which, slightly altered, might have been really useful; but as it was, they broke off easily, and the stumps were lying by thousands in the streets. To my repeated questioning, whether there was no board or regulations to prevent all this; he replied, "A story is current among the people that those whose duty it was to provide for the cleansing of our streets, being men of great power and influence, could not be compelled to disburse the money on its lawful objects; and besides that there was also the strange fact that certain parties feared that if the dirty straw and dung were swept away, every one would see how badly the pavement beneath was laid down." And so the dishonesty of a second body would be thereby exposed. "All this, however," he remarked, with a most humorous expression, "is merely the interpretation which the ill-disposed put upon it." For his part, he was of the opinion of those who maintained that the nobles preserved this soft litter for their carriages, in order that, when they take their drive for amusement in the evening, they might ride at ease over the elastic ground. And as the man was now in the humour, he joked away at many of the abuses of the police,—a consolatory proof to me that man has always humour enough to make merry with what he cannot help.

S. Rosalia, the patron saint of Palermo, is so universally known, from the description which Brydone has given of her festival, that it must assuredly be agreeable to my friends to read some account of the place and the spot where she is most particularly worshipped.

Monte Pellegrino, a vast mass of rocks, of which the breadth is greater than the height, lies on the north-west extremity of the Bay of Palermo. Its beautiful form admits not of being described by words; a most excellent view of it may be seen in the *Voyage Pittoresque de la Sicile*. It consists of a gray limestone of the earlier epoch. The rocks are quite barren, not a tree nor a bush will grow on them; even the more smooth and level portions are but barely covered with grasses or mosses.

In a cavern of this mountain, the bones of the saint were discovered, at the beginning of the last century, and brought to Palermo. The presence of them delivered the city from a pestilence, and ever since S. Rosalia has been the Patron Saint of the people. Chapels have been built in her honour, splendid festivals have been instituted.

The pious and devout frequently made pilgrimages to the mountain; and in consequence a road has been made to it, which, like an ancient aqueduct, rests on arches and columns, and ascends zigzag between the rocks.

The place of worship is far more suitable to the humility of the saint who retired thither, than are the splendid festivities which have been instituted in honour of her total renunciation of the world. And perhaps the whole of Christendom, which now, for eighteen hundred years, has based its riches, pomps, and festival amusements, on the memory of its first founders and most zealous confessors, cannot point out a holy spot which has been adorned and rendered venerable in so eminent and delightful a way.

When you have ascended the mountain, you proceed to the corner of a rock, over against which there rises a high wall of stone. On this the Church and the monastery are very finely situated.

The exterior of the church has nothing promising or inviting; you open its door without any high expectation, but on entering are ravished with wonder. You find yourself in a vast vestibule, which extends to the whole breadth of the church, and is open towards the nave. You see here the usual vessel of holy water and some confessionals. The nave is an open space, which on the right is bounded by the native rock, and on the left by the continuation of the vestibule. It is paved with flat stones on a slight inclination, in order that the rain water may run off. A small well stands nearly in the centre.

Palermo—S. Rosalia.

The cave itself has been transformed into the choir, without, however, any of its rough natural shape being altered. Descending a few steps, close upon them stands the choristers' desk with the choir books, and on each side are the seats of the choristers. The whole is lighted by the daylight, which is admitted from the court or nave. Deep within, in the dark recesses of the cave, stands the high-altar.

As already stated, no change has been made in the cave; only, as the rocks drop incessantly with water, it was necessary to keep the place dry. This has been effected by means of tin tubes, which are fastened to every projection of the rock, and are in various ways connected together. As they are broad above and come to a narrow edge below, and are painted of a dull green colour, they give to the rock an appearance of being overgrown with a species of cactus. The water is conducted into a clear reservoir, out of which it is taken by the faithful as a remedy and preventative for every kind of ill.

As I was narrowly observing all this, an ecclesiastic came up to me and asked whether I was a Genoese, and wished a mass or so to be said? I replied upon this that I had come to Palermo with a Genoese, who would to-morrow, as it was a festival, come up to the shrine; but, as one of us must always be at home, I had come up to day in order to look about me. Upon this he observed, I was at perfect liberty to look at everything at my leisure, and to perform my devotions. In particular he pointed out to me a little altar which stood on the left as especially holy, and then left me.

Through the openings of a large trellis work of lattice, lamps appeared burning before an altar. I knelt down close to the gratings and peeped through. Further in, however, another lattice of brass wire was drawn across, so that one looked as it were through gauze at the objects within. By the light of some dull lamps I caught sight of a lovely female form.

She lay seemingly in a state of ecstasy—the eyes half-closed, the head leaning carelessly on her right hand, which was adorned with many rings. I could not sufficiently discern her face, but it seemed to be peculiarly charming. Her robe was made of gilded metal, which imitated excellently a texture wrought with gold. The head and hands were of white marble. I cannot say that the whole was in the lofty style, still it was executed so naturally and so pleasingly that one almost fancied it must breathe and move. A little angel stands near her, and with a bunch of lilies in his hand appears to be fanning her.

In the meanwhile the clergy had come into the cave, taken their places, and began to chant the Vespers.

I took my seat right before the altar, and listened to them for a while; then I again approached the altar, knelt down and attempted to obtain a still more distinct view of the beautiful image. I resigned myself without reserve to the charming illusion of the statue and the locality.

The chant of the priests now resounded through the cave; the water was trickling into the reservoir near the altar; while the over-hanging rocks of the vestibule—the proper nave of the church—shut in the scene. There was a deep stillness in this waste spot, whose inhabitants seemed to be all dead-a singular neatness in a wild cave: the tinsel and tawdry pomp of the Roman Catholic ceremonial, especially as it is vividly decked out in Sicily, had here reverted to its original simplicity. The illusion produced by the statue of the fair sleeper—which had a charm even for the most practised eye:—enough, it was with the greatest difficulty that I tore myself from the spot, and it was late at night before I got back to Palermo.

Palermo, Saturday, April 7, 1787.

In the public gardens, which are close to the roadstead, I have passed some most delightful hours. It is the most wonderful place in the world. Regularly laid out by art, it still looks a fairy spot; planted but a short time ago, it yet transports you into ancient times. Green edgings surround beds of the choicest exotics; citron-espaliers arch over low-arboured walks; high walls of the oleander, decked with thousands of its red carnation-like blossoms, dazzle the eye. Trees wholly strange and unknown to me, as yet without leaf, and probably, therefore, natives of a still warmer climate, spread out their strange looking branches. A raised seat at the end of the level space gives you a survey of these curiously mixed rarities, and leads the eye at last to great basins in which gold and silver fish swim about with their pretty movements; now hiding themselves beneath moss-covered reeds; now darting in troops to catch the bit of bread which has tempted them from their hiding place. All the plants exhibit tints of green which I am not used to; yellower and bluer than are found with us. What however lent to every object the rarest of charms was a strong halo which hung around everything alike, and produced the following singular effect: objects which were only distant a few steps from others, were distinguished from them by a decided tint of light blue, so that at last the distinctive colours of the most remote were almost merged in it, or at least assumed to the eye a decidedly strong blue tint.

Sicily—Palermo.

The very singular effect which such a halo imparts to distinct objects, vessels, and headlands, is remarkable enough to an artistic eye; it assists it accurately to distinguish, and, indeed, to measure distances. It makes, too, a walk on the heights extremely charming. One sees Nature no more; nothing but pictures; just as if a painter of exquisite taste had arranged them in a gallery.

But these wonderful gardens have made a deep and lasting impression on my mind. The black waves on the northern horizon, as they broke on the irregular points of the bay—and even the smell of the sea-all seemed to recall to my imagination, as well as my memory, the happy island of the Phæacians. I hastened to purchase a *Homer*, and began to read this book with the highest delight, making an impromptu translation of it for the benefit of Kniep, who had well deserved by his diligent exertions this day some agreeable refreshment over a glass of wine.

Palermo, April 8, 1787.
(*Easter Day.*)

The morning rejoicings in the blissful Resurrection of the Lord commenced with break of day. Crackers, wild-fires, rockets, serpents, &c., were let off by wholesale in front of the churches, as the worshippers crowded in at the open doors. The chiming of bells, the pealing of organs, the chanting of processions, and of the choirs of priests who came to meet them, were enough to stun the ears of all who had not been used to such noisy worship.

The early mass was scarcely ended, when two well-dressed couriers of the Viceroy visited our hotel, with the double object of offering to all strangers his Highness's congratulations on the festival, and to exact a douceur in return. As I was specially honoured with an invitation to dinner, my gift was, of course, expected to be considerable.

After spending the morning in visiting the different churches, I proceeded to the Viceroy's palace, which is situated at the upper end of the city. As I arrived rather early, I found the grand saloon still empty; there was only a little lively man, who came up to me, and whom I soon discovered to be a Maltese.

When he had learnt that I was a German, he asked if I could give him any account of Erfurt, where he had spent a very pleasant time on a short visit.

As he asked me about the family of the Däckerödes, and about the Coadjutor von Dalberg, I was able to give some account of them, at which he seemed much delighted, and inquired after other people of Thuringia. With considerable interest he then inquired about Weimar. "And how," he asked, "is the person, who, full of youth and vivacity when I was there, was the life of society? I have forgotten his name, but he is the author of 'Werther.'"

After a little pause, as if for the sake of tasking my memory, I answered, "I am the person whom you are inquiring about." With the most visible signs of astonishment, he sprung back, exclaiming, "There must have been a great change then!" "O yes," I rejoined, "between Palermo and Weimar I have gone through many a change."

At this moment the Viceroy and suite entered the apartment. His carriage evinced that graceful freedom which became so distinguished a personage. He could not refrain from laughing at the Maltese, as he went on expressing his astonishment to see me here. At table I sat by the side of the Viceroy, who inquired into the objects of my journey, and assured me that he would give orders that everything in. Palermo should be open to my inspection, and that every possible facility should be given me during my tour through Sicily.

Sicily—Palermo.

Palermo, Monday, April 9, 1787.

This whole day has been taken up with the stupidities of the Prince Pallagonia, whose follies are thoroughly different from what one would form an idea of either by reading or hearing of them. For, with the slightest love of truth, he who wishes to furnish an account of the absurd, gets into a dilemma; he is anxious to give an idea of it, and so makes it something, whereas, in reality, it is a nothing which seeks to pass for something. And here I must premise another general reflection, viz., that neither the most tasteless, nor the most excellent production comes entirely and immediately from a single individual or a single age, but that with a little attention any one may trace its pedigree and descent.

The fountain already described in Palermo belongs to the forefathers of the Pallagonian follies, only that the latter, in their own soil and domain, develope themselves with the greatest freedom, and on the largest scale.

When in these parts a country seat is built, it is usually placed in the middle of a whole property, and therefore, in order to reach the princely mansion you have to pass through cultivated fields, kitchen gardens, and similar rural conveniences, for these southerns show far more of economy than we northmen, who often waste a good strip of rich land on a park, which, with its barren shrubs, can only charm the eye. But here it is the fashion to build two walls, between which you pass to the castle, without knowing in the least what is doing on your right and left. This passage begins generally with a grand portico, and sometimes with a vaulted hall, and ends with the mansion itself. But, in order that the eye may not be entirely without relief between these bye walls, they are generally arched over, and ornamented with scrolls, and also with pedestals, on which, here and there, a vase is placed. The flat surfaces are plastered, divided into compartments, and painted. The court is formed by a circle of one-storied cabins, in which work-people of all sorts reside, while the quadrangular castle towers over all.

This is the sort of building which is here traditionally adopted, and which probably was the old form, when the father of the present prince rebuilt the castle, not in the best, but still in tolerable taste. But the present possessor, without abandoning the general features of this style, gave free course to his humour and passion for the most ill-shaped and tasteless of erections. One would do him too much honour by giving him credit for even one spark of taste.

We entered, therefore, the great hall, which stands at the beginning of the property, and found ourselves in an octagonal loom, of a breadth altogether disproportioned to its height. Four vast giants with modern spatterdashes, which had just been *buttoned* on, support the cornice, on which, directly meeting the eye as you enter, is a representation of the Holy Trinity.

The passage to the castle is broader than usual, the wall being converted into one continuous high socle; from which basement the strangest groups possible reach to the top, while in the spaces between them several vases are placed. The ugliness of these unshapely figures, (the bungling work of the most ordinary mason,) is increased by their having been cut out of a very crumbly muscheltufa, although, perhaps, a better material would have made the badness of the form still more striking to the eye. I used the word "groups" a moment ago, but I have employed a false term, and most inappropriate one for anything here. For they are mere juxtapositions, determined by no thought, but by mere arbitrary caprice. In each case three form the ornament of a square pedestal, their bases being so arranged as to fill up the space by their various postures. The principal groups have generally two figures which occupy the chief face of the pedestal, and then two are yet wanting to fill up the back part of the pedestal; one of a moderate size generally represents a shepherd or shepherdess—a cavalier or a lady—a dancing ape or a hound. Still there is a vacant spot on the pedestal; this is generally held by a dwarf—as, indeed, in dull jokes, this sort of gentry usually play a conspicuous part.

That we may not omit any of the elements of Prince Pallagonia's folly, we give you the accompanying catalogue. Men: Beggars, male and female, Spanish men and women, Moors, Turks, hunchbacks, cripples of all sorts, strolling musicians, pulcinellos, soldiers in ancient uniforms, gods, goddesses, gentlemen in old French costumes, soldiers with cartouche boxes and gaiters, mythological personages (with most ridiculous companions, Achilles and Charon, for instance, with Punch). Animals (merely parts of them): Heads of horses on human bodies, misshapen apes, lots of dragons and serpents, all sorts of feet under figures of all kinds, double-headed monsters, and creatures with heads that do not belong to them. Vases: All sorts of monsters and scrolls, which below end in the hollows and bases of vases.

Palermo—Castle of Count Pallagonia.

Just let any one think of such figures furnished by wholesale, produced without thought or sense, and arranged without choice or purpose—only let him conceive to himself this socle, these pedestals and unshapely objects in an endless series, and he will be able to sympathize with the disagreeable feelings which must seize every one whose miserable fate condemns him to run the gauntlet of such absurdities.

We now approach the castle, and are received into a semi-circular fore-court. The chief wall before us, through which is the entrance-door, is in the castle style. Here we find an Egyptian figure, built into the wall, a fountain without water, a monument, vases stuck around in no sort of order, statues designedly laid on their noses. Next we came to the castle court, and found the usual round area, enclosed with little cottages, distorted into small semicircles, in order, forsooth, that there might be no want of variety.

The ground is, for the most part, overgrown with grass. Here, as in the neighbourhood of a church in ruins, are marble urns with strange scrolls and foliations, collected by his father; dwarfs and other abortions of the later epoch, for which, as yet fitting places have not been found; one even comes upon an arbour, propped up with ancient vases, and stone scrolls of various shapes.

The absurdities produced by such want of judgment and taste, however, are strikingly instanced by the fact, that the window sills in these cottages are, without exception, oblique, and lean to one side or the other, so as to offend and violate all sense of the level and perpendicular, which are so indispensable in the human mind, and form the foundation of all architectural propriety. And then, again, the edges of all the roofs are embellished with hydras and little busts, with choirs of monkeys playing music, and similar conceits. Dragons alternate with deities: an Atlas, who sustains not the mundane sphere, but an empty wine-barrel!

One hopes to escape from all this by entering the castle, which, having been built by the father, presents relatively a more rational appearance when viewed from the exterior. But in vain, for at no great distance from the door, one stumbles upon the laurel-crowned head of a Roman emperor on the body of a dwarf, who is sitting astride on a dolphin.

Now, in the castle itself, of which the exterior gives hope of, at least, a tolerable interior, the madness of the Prince begins again to rave. Many of the seats have lost their legs, so that no one can sit upon them; and if some appear to promise a resting-place, the Chamberlain warns you against them, as having sharp prickles beneath their satin-covered cushions. In all the corners are candelabras of porcelain china, which, on a nearer view, you discover to be cemented together out of different bowls, cups, saucers, &c., &c. Not a corner but some whim peeps out of it. Even the unequalled prospect over the promontory into the sea is spoiled by coloured glass, which, by its false lights, gives either a cold or a fiery tint to the neighbouring scenes. I must, also, mention a cabinet, which is inlaid with old gold frames, cut in pieces. All the hundred-fold carvings, all the endless varieties of ancient and modern, more or less dust-stained and time-injured, gilding, closely huddled together, cover all the walls, and give you the idea of a miniature lumber-room.

To describe the chapel alone, would require a volume. Here one finds the solution of the whole folly, which could never have reached such a pitch in any but a bigoted mind. How many monstrous creations of a false and misled devotion are here to be found, I must leave you to guess for yourself. However, I cannot refrain from mentioning the most outrageous: a carved crucifix is fastened flat to the roof, painted after nature, lackered, and gilded; into the navel of the figure, attached to the cross, a hook is screwed, and from the latter hangs a chain, which is fastened to the head of a man who, in a kneeling and praying posture, is suspended in the air, and, like all the other figures in the church, is painted and lackered. In all probability it is intended to serve as a type of the owner's unceasing devotion.

Moreover, the house is not finished internally. A saloon, built by the father, and intended to be decorated with rich and varied ornaments, but not tricked out in a false and offensive taste, is still incomplete: so that, it would seem, even the boundless madness of the possessor is at a stand still.

Kniep's artistic feeling was almost driven to desperation in this mad-house; and, for the first time in my life, I found him quite impatient. He hurried me away, when I wished to take a note of, and to perpetuate the memory of these monstrous absurdities, one by one. Good-naturedly enough, he at last took a sketch of one of these compositions, which did, at least, form a kind of group. It represents a woman with a horse's head, sitting on a stool, and playing at cards, with a cavalier, dressed, as to his lower extremities, in the old fashion, while his gray head is ornamented with a large wig and a crown. The statue reminded me of the arms of the house of Pallagonia,-a satyr, holding up a mirror *before* a woman with a horse's head, which, even after all the strange follies of its present head, seems to me highly singular.

Palermo, Tuesday, *April* 10, 1787.

To-day we took a drive up the mountains to Monreale,—along a glorious road, which was laid down by an abbot of this cloister, in the times of its opulence and wealth: broad, of easy ascent, trees here and there, springs, and dripping wells, decked out with ornaments and scrolls,—somewhat Pallagonian in style—but still, in spite of all that, refreshing to both man and beast.

The monastery of S. Martin, which lies on the height, is a respectable building. One bachelor alone, as we see in the case of Prince Pallagonia, has seldom produced any thing rational; but several together, on the other hand, have effected the greatest works, such as churches and monasteries. But perhaps these spiritual fraternities produced so much, simply because, beyond most fathers of a family, they could reckon with certainty on a numerous posterity.

The monks readily permitted us to view their collection of antiques and natural objects. They contained many excellent specimens of both. Our attention was particularly fixed by a medallion, with the *figure* of a young goddess, which must excite the rapture of every beholder. The good monks would willingly have given us a copy, but there was nothing within reach which would do to make a mould.

After they had exhibited to us all their treasures,—not without entering on an unfavorable comparison of their present with their former condition,— they led us into a small but pleasant saloon, from the balcony of which one enjoyed a lovely prospect. Here covers were laid for us alone, and we had a very excellent dinner to ourselves. When the dessert was served, the abbot and the senior monks entered, and took their seats. They remained nearly half an hour, during which time we had to answer many questions. We took a most friendly farewell of them; the younger brethren accompanied us once more to the rooms where the collections were kept, and at last to our carriage.

We drove home with very different feelings from what we did yesterday. To-day we had to regret a noble institution, which was falling with time; while, on the other hand, a most tasteless undertaking had a constant supply of wealth for its support.

The road to S. Martin ascends a hill of the earlier lime-stone formation. The rock is quarried and broken, and burnt into lime, which is very white. For burning the stone they make use of a long coarse sort of grass, which is dried in bundles. Here too it is that the calorex is produced. Even on the most precipitous heights lies a red clay of alluvial origin, which serve the purposes of our dam-earth,—the higher it lies the redder it is, and is but little blackened by vegetation. I saw, at a distance, a ravine, where it was red as cinnabar.

The monastery stands in the middle of the limestone hill, which is very rich in springs.

Palermo, Wednesday, April 11, 1787.

Having explored the two principal objects without the city, we betook ourselves to the palace, where a busy courier showed us the rooms, and their contents. To our great horror, the saloon in which the antiques are generally placed was in the greatest disorder, in consequence of the walls being under the process of decoration. The statues were removed from their usual places, covered with cloth, and protected by wooden frames; so that in spite of the good will of our guide, and some trouble on the part of the work-people, we could only gain a very imperfect idea of them. My attention was chiefly occupied with two rams, in bronze, which, notwithstanding the unfavorable circumstances, highly delighted our artistic taste. They are represented in a recumbent posture, with one foot stretched out before them, with the heads (in order to form a pair) turned on different sides. Powerful forms, belonging to the mythological family, and well worthy to carry Phrixus and Helle. The wool, not short and crisp, but long and flowing, with a slight wave, and shape most true to nature, and extremely elegant—they evidently belonged to the best period of Grecian art. They are said to have stood originally in the harbour of Syracuse.

Sicily—Palermo.

The courier now took us out of the city to the catacombs, which, laid out on a regular architectural plan, are anything but quarries converted into burial places. In a rock of Tufa, of tolerable hardness, the side of winch has been worked level and perpendicular, vaulted openings have been cut, and in these again are hewn several tiers of sarcophagi, one above the other—all of the natural material without masonry of any kind. The upper tiers are smaller, and in the spaces over the pillars are tombs for children.

Palermo, Thursday, April 12.

To day we have been shown Prince Torremuzza's cabinet of medals. I went there in a certain degree against my will. I am too little versed in these matters, and a mere curiosity-mongering traveller is thoroughly detested by all true connoisseurs and scholars. But as one must in every case make a beginning, I made myself easy on this head, and have derived both gratification and profit from my visit. What a satisfaction, even cursorily, to glance at the fact that the old world was thickly sown with cities; the very meanest of which has bequeathed to us in its precious coins, if not a complete series, yet at least some epochs, of its history of art. Out of these cabinets, there smiles upon us an eternal spring of the blossoms and flowers of art—of a busy life, ennobled with high tastes, and of much more besides. Out of these form-endowed pieces of metal the glory of the Sicilian cities, now obscured, still shines forth fresh before us.

Unfortunately, we in our youth had seen none but family coins, which say nothing, and the coins of the Cæsars, which repeat to satiety the same profile—portraits of rulers, who are to be regarded as any thing but models of humanity. How sadly had our youth been confined to a shapeless

Palestine, and to a shape perplexing Rome! Sicily and Nova Grecia give me hopes again of a fresh existence.

That on these subjects I should enter into general reflections, is a proof that as yet I do not understand much about them: yet that, with all the rest, will in degrees be improved.

Palermo, Thursday, April 12, 1787.

Yesterday evening, a wish of mine was gratified, and that in a very singular fashion. I was standing on the pavement of the principal street, joking at the window with the shop-keeper, I formerly mentioned, when suddenly, a courier, tall and well-dressed, came up to me, and quickly poked a silver salver before me, on which were several copper coins, and a few pieces of silver. As I could not make out what it all meant, I shook my head, and shrugged my shoulders, the usual token by which in this country you get rid of those whose address or question you either cannot, or do not wish, to understand.

"What does all this mean?" I asked of my friend the shop-keeper, who, with a very significant mien, and somewhat stealthily, pointed to a lank and haggard gentleman, who, elegantly dressed, was walking with great dignity and indifference, through the dung and dirt. Frizzled and powdered, with his hat under his arm, in a silken vest, with his sword by his side, and having a neat shoe ornamented with a jewelled buckle—the old man walked on calmly and sorrowfully. All eyes were directed towards him.

"It is the Prince Pallagonia," said the dealer, "who, from time to time, goes through the city collecting money to ransom the slaves in Barbary. It is true, he does not get much by his collection, but the object is kept in memory; and so it often happens that those who, in their life-time, were backward in giving, leave large legacies at their death. The prince has for many years been at the head of this society, and has done a great deal of good."

"Instead of wasting so much on the follies of his country house," I cried, "he might have spent the same large sum on this object. Then no prince in the world would have accomplished more."

To this the shopkeeper rejoined: "But is not that the way with us all? We are ready enough to pay for our own follies. Our virtues for their support must look to the purses of others."

Palermo, April 13, 1787.

Count Borck has very diligently worked before us in the mineralogy of Sicily, and whoever of the same mind visits the island after him, must willingly acknowledge his obligations to him. I feel it a pleasure, no less than a duty, to celebrate the memory of my predecessor. And what am I more than a forerunner of others yet to be, both in my travels and life.

However, the industry of the Count seems to me to have been greater than his knowledge. He appears to have gone to work with a certain reserve, which is altogether opposed to that stern earnestness with which grand objects should be treated.

Sicily—Palermo.

Nevertheless, his essay in quarto, which is exclusively devoted to the mineralogy of Sicily, has been of great use to me; and, prepared by it, I was able to profit by my visit to the Quarries which formerly, when it was the custom to case the churches and altars with marble and agate, were more busily worked, though even now they are not idle. I purchased at them specimens of the hard and soft stones: for it is thus that they usually designate the marble and agate, chiefly because a difference of price mainly depends on this difference of quality. But, besides these, they have still another for a material which is the produce of the fire of their kilns. In these, after each burning, they find a sort of glassy flux, which in colour varies from the lightest to the darkest, and even blackest blue. These lumps are, like other stones, cut into thin lamina, and then pierced according to the height of their colour and their purity, and are successfully employed in the place of lapis lazuli, in the decoration of churches, altars, and sepulchral monuments.

A complete collection, such as I wished, is not to be had at present; it is to be sent after me to Naples. The agates are of the greatest beauty; especially such as are variegated with irregular pieces of yellow or red jasper, and with white, and as it were frozen quartz, which produce the most beautiful effect.

A very accurate imitation of these agates, produced by lake colouring on the back of thin plates of glass, is the only rational thing that I observed the other day among the Pallagonian follies. Such imitations are far better for decorations than the real agate, since the latter are only found in very small pieces, whereas the size of the former depends on nothing but the size of the artist's plate. This contrivance of art well deserves to be imitated.

Palermo, April 13, 1787.

Italy without Sicily leaves no image on the soul: here is the key to all.

Of the climate, it is impossible to say enough. It is now rainy weather, but not uninterruptedly wet: yesterday it thundered and lightened, and to day all is intensely green. The flax has in places already put forth joints—in others it is boiling. Looking down from the hills, one fancies one sees in the plain below little ponds; so beautifully blue-green are the flax fields here and there. Living objects without number surround you. And my companion is an excellent fellow, the true *Hoffegut* (Hopeful) and I honestly sustain the part of the *True friend.* He has already made some beautiful sketches, and will take still more before we go. What a prospect—to return home some day, happy, and with all these treasures!

Of the meat and drink here, in the country, I have said nothing as yet; however, it is by no means an indifferent matter. The garden stuffs are excellent, especially the lettuce; which is particularly tender, with a milky taste: it makes one understand at once why the ancients termed it *lactuca.* The oil and wine of all kinds very good; and it might be still better if more care were bestowed on its preparation:—Fish of the very best and tenderest. We have had, too, very good beef, though generally people do not praise it.

Now, after dinner, to the window!—to the streets! A malefactor has just been pardoned—an event which takes place every year in honour of the festival of Easter. The brethren of some order or other led him to the foot of a gallows, which had been erected for sake of the ceremony: then the criminal at the foot of the ladder offers up a prayer or two; and having kissed the scaffold, is led away again. He was a good-looking fellow of the middle age, in a white coat, white hat, and all else white. He carried his hat in his hand; at different points they attached variegated ribbons to him, so that at last he was quite in tune to go to any masquerade in the character of a shepherd.

Palermo, April 13 *and* 14, 1787.

So then, before my departure, I was to meet with a strange adventure, of which I must forthwith give you a circumstantial account.

> Sicily—Palermo.

The whole time of my residence here, I have heard scarcely any topic of conversation at the ordinary, but Cagliostro, his origin and adventures. The people of Palermo are all unanimous in asserting that a certain Joseph Balsamo was born in their city, and having rendered himself infamous by many disgraceful acts, was banished. But whether this person is identical with the Count Cagliostro, was a point on which opinions were divided. Some who knew Balsamo personally asserted they recognized his features in the engraving, which is well known in Germany, and which has also travelled as far as Palermo.

In one of these conversations, one of the guests referred to the trouble which a Palermitan lawyer had taken in examining this matter. He seems to have been commissioned by the French Ministry to trace the origin of an individual, who, in the face of France, and, indeed, of the whole world, had had the temerity to utter the silliest of idle tales in the midst of a legal process which involved the most important interests and the reputation of the highest personages.

This lawyer, it was asserted, had prepared the pedigree of Giuseppe Balsamo, together with an explanatory memoir and documentary proofs. It has been forwarded to France, where in all probability public use will be made of it.

As I expressed a wish to form the acquaintance of this lawyer, of whom besides people spoke very highly, the person who had recounted these facts offered to mention me to him and to introduce me.

After a few days we paid him a visit, and found him busily engaged with his clients. When he had dismissed them and we had taken a luncheon, he produced a manuscript which contained a transcript of Cagliostro's pedigree, and the rough draught of the memoir which had been sent to France.

He laid the genealogy before me, and gave me the necessary explanations, of which I shall here give you as much as is necessary to facilitate the understanding of the whole business.

Giuseppe Balsamo's great-grandfather on his mother's side was Matteo Martello. The maiden name of his great-grand-mother is unknown. The issue of this marriage was two daughters; Maria, who married Giuseppe Bracconerie, and the grandmother of Giuseppe Balsamo—and Vincenza, married to Giuseppe Cagliostro, who was born in a little village called La Noava, about eight miles from Messina. (I must note here that there are at this moment living at Messina two bellfounders of this name.) This great aunt was subsequently godmother of Giuseppe Balsamo, who was named after his great uncle, and at last in foreign countries assumed also the surname of this relation.

The Bracconerie had three children,—Felicitá, Mattéo, and Antonia.

Felicitá was married to Piedro Balsamo, who was the son of Antonia Balsamo, ribbon dealer in Palermo, and probably of Jewish descent. Piedro Balsamo, the father of the notorious Giuseppe, became bankrupt, and died in his five-and-fortieth year. His widow, who is still living, had born him, besides the above-named Giuseppe Giovanna—Giuseppe Maria, who married Giovanna Battista Capitummino, who begot three children of her body, and died.

The memoir, which was read to us by its obliging author, and was at my request lent to me for a few days, was founded on baptismal and marriage certificates and other instruments which he had with great diligence collected. It contains pretty nearly (as I conclude from a comparison with a summary which I then made) all the circumstances which have lately been made better known to the world by the acts of the legal process at Borne, viz., that Giuseppe Balsamo was born at Palermo, in the beginning of June, 1743, and that at his baptism he was received back from the priest's arms by Vincenza Cagliostro (whose maiden name was Martello); that in his youth he took the habit of an order of the Brothers of Mercy, which paid particular attention to the sick; that he soon showed great talent and skill for medicine, but that for his disorderly practices he was expelled the order, and thereupon set up in Palermo as a dealer in magic, and treasure finder.

Palermo—Count Cagliostro.

His great dexterity in imitating every kind of handwriting was not allowed by him to lie idle. He falsified or rather forged altogether an ancient document, by which the possession of some lands was brought into litigation. He was soon an object of suspicion, and cast into prison; but made his escape, and was cited to appear under penalty of outlawry. He passed through Calabria towards Rome, where he married the daughter of a belt-maker. From Rome he came back to Naples, under the name of the Marchese Pellegrini. He even ventured to pay a visit to Palermo, was recognized, and taken prisoner, and made his escape in a manner that well deserves being circumstantially detailed.

One of the principal nobles of Sicily, who possessed very large property, and held several important posts at the Neapolitan court, had a son, who to a frame of unusual strength and an uncontrollable temper united all the wanton excesses which the rich and great, without education, can think themselves privileged to indulge in.

Donna Lorenza had managed to attract him, and on him the pretended Marchese Pellegrini relied for impunity. The Prince avowed openly his patronage of this couple of new comers, and set no bounds to his rage when Giuseppe Balsamo, at the instance of the party whom he had injured, was a second time cast into prison. He had recourse to various means to obtain his liberation; and, when these were unsuccessful, in the very ante-room of the President's court, he threatened the advocate of the opposite party with the most dreadful consequences if he did not consent to the release of Balsamo. As the opposing advocate refused his consent, he rushed upon him, struck him, knocked him down and kicked him, and was only with difficulty restrained from further violence when the judge, hearing the noise, rushed in and commanded peace.

The latter, a weak and cringing character, had not the courage to punish the wrong-doer; the opposite party, advocate and all, were men of little minds; and so Balsamo was set at liberty, without, however, any record of his liberation being found among the proceedings—neither by whose orders or in what manner it was effected.

Shortly after this he left Palermo, and traveled in different countries; of which travels, however, the author of the memoir had been only able to collect very imperfect information.

The memoir ended with an acute argument to prove the identity of Balsamo and Cagliostro,—a position which was at this time more difficult to prove than at present, now that the whole history of this individual has been made public.

Had I not been led to form a conjecture that a public use would have been made in France of this essay, and that on my return I should find it already in print, I doubt not but I should have been permitted to take a transcript of it, and to give my friends and the public an early account of many interesting circumstances.

However, we have received the fullest account, (and even more particulars than this memoir contains,) from a quarter which usually is the source of nothing but errors. Who would have believed that Rome would ever have done so much for the enlightening of the world, and for the utter exposure of an impostor, as she has done by publishing the summary of the proceedings in this case? For although this work ought and might be much more interesting, it is nevertheless an excellent document in the hands of every rational mind, who cannot but feel deep regret to see the deceived, and those who were not more deceived than deceivers, going on for years admiring this man and his mummeries; feeling themselves by fellowship with him raised above the common mass, and from the heights of their credulous vanity pitying if not despising the sound common sense of mankind in general.

Who was not willingly silent all the while? And even now, at last, when the whole affair is ended and placed beyond dispute, it is only with difficulty that I can bring myself, in order to complete the official account, to communicate some particulars which have here become known to me.

When I found in the genealogy so many persons (especially his mother and sisters) mentioned as still living, I expressed to the author of the memoir a wish to see them, and to form the acquaintance of the other relatives of so notorious an individual. He remarked that it would be difficult to bring it about, since these persons, poor but respectable, and living very retired, were not accustomed to receive visitors, and that their natural suspicion would be roused by any attempt of the kind. However, he was ready to send to me his copying clerk, who had access to the family, and by whose means he had procured the information and documents out of which the pedigree had been compiled.

Palermo—Count Cagliostro.

The next day his amanuensis made his appearance, and expressed several scruples upon the matter. "I have, hitherto," he said, "carefully avoided coming within sight of these persons. For, in order to get into my hands the certificates of baptism and marriage, so as to be able to take legally authenticated copies of them, I was obliged to have recourse to a little trick. I took occasion to speak of some little family property that was somehow or other unclaimed; made it appear probable to them that the young Capitummino was entitled to it; but I told them that first of all it was necessary to make out a pedigree, in order to see how far the youth could establish his claim: that, however, his success must eventually depend upon law proceedings, which I would willingly undertake on condition of receiving for my trouble a fair proportion of the amount recovered. The good people readily assented to everything. I got possession of the papers I wanted, took copies of them, and finished the pedigree; since then, however, I have cautiously kept out of their sight. A few weeks ago old Capitummino met me, and it was only by pleading the tardiness with which such matters usually proceed that I managed to excuse myself."

Thus spoke the copyist. As, however, I stuck to my purpose, after some consideration he consented to take me to their house, and suggested that it would be best for me to give myself out to be an Englishman, who had brought to the family tidings of Cagliostro, who, immediately after his release from the Bastille, had proceeded to London.

At the appointed hour—about two o'clock in the afternoon—we set out on our expedition. The house was situated in the corner of a narrow lane, not far from the great street, "Il Casaro." We ascended a few wretched steps, and entered at once upon the kitchen. A woman of the middle size, strong and broad, without being fat, was busy washing up the cooking utensils. She was neatly and cleanly clad, and as we entered, turned up the corner of her apron, in order to conceal from us its dirty front. She seemed glad to see my guide, and exclaimed, "Do you bring us good news, Signor Giovanni? Have you obtained a decree?"

He replied, "No! I have not as yet been able to do anything in our matter. However, here is a foreigner who brings you a greeting from your brother, and who can give you an account of his present state and abode."

The greeting that I was to bring did not exactly stand in our bond. However, the introduction was now made. "You know my brother?" she asked me. "All Europe knows him," I replied, "and I am sure you will be glad to hear that he is at present safe and well; for assuredly you must have been in great anxiety about him." "Walk in," she said, "I will follow you immediately;" and so, with the copying-clerk, I entered the sitting-room.

It was spacious and lofty, and would pass with us for a saloon. It seemed, however, to form the whole dwelling of the family. A single window lighted the large walls, which were once coloured, and around which figures of the Saints—taken in black—hung in gilt frames. Two large beds, without curtains, stood against one wall, while a brown press, which had the shape of an escritoire, was placed against the opposite one. Old chairs, with rush bottoms, the backs of which seemed once to have been gilded, stood on each side of it; while the bricks of the floors were in many places sunk deep below the level. In other respects, everything was clean and tidy, and we made our way towards the family, who were gathered around the only large window at the other end of the room.

While my guide was explaining to the old widow Balsamo, who sat in the corner, the cause of our visit, and in consequence of the deafness of the good old woman, had frequently to repeat his words, I had time to observe the room and the rest of its occupants. A young girl, of about sixteen years of age, well grown, whose features, however, the small-pox had robbed of all expression, was standing at the window; by her side a young man, whose unpleasant countenance, sadly disfigured by the small-pox, also struck me. In an arm-chair, opposite the window, sat, or rather reclined, a sick and sadly deformed person, who seemed to be afflicted with a sort of torpor.

When my guide had made himself understood, they compelled us to sit down. The old woman put some questions to me, which I required to have interpreted before I could answer them, as I was not very familiar with the Sicilian dialect.

I was pleased with the examination, which, during this conversation, I made of the old woman. She was of middle size, but of a good figure; over her regular features an expression of calmness was diffused, which people usually enjoy who are deprived of hearing; the tone of her voice was soft and agreeable.

I answered her questions, and my answers had, in their turn, to be interpreted to her.

The slowness of such a dialogue gave me an opportunity of weighing my words. I told her that her son having been acquitted in France, was at present in London, where he had been well received. The joy which she expressed at this news was accompanied with exclamations of a heartfelt piety, and now, as she spoke louder and slower I could understand her better.

In the meanwhile her daughter had come in, and had seated herself by the side of my guide, who faithfully repeated to her what I had been saying. She had tied on a clean apron, and arranged her hair under a net. The more I looked at her, and compared her with her mother, the more surprised was I at the difference of their persons. A lively, healthy sensibility spoke in every feature of the daughter; she was, in all probability, about forty years old. With lovely blue eyes, she looked cautiously around, without, however, my being able to trace the least symptom of suspicion. As she sat, her figure seemed to promise greater height than it showed when she stood up; her posture bespoke determination; she sat with her body bent forwards, and her hands resting on her knees. Moreover, her full, rather than sharp profile, reminded me of the portraits of her brother, which I had seen in engravings. She asked me several questions about my travels: about my purpose in visiting Sicily, and would persuade herself that I should most assuredly come back again, and keep with them the Festival of S. Rosalie.

The grandmother having, in the mean time, put some questions to me, while I was busied in answering them, the daughter was speaking in a half whisper to my guide; so that my curiosity was stimulated to ask what they were talking about. Upon this he said, Donna Capitummino was just telling him that her brother owed her fourteen once. In order to facilitate his rapid departure from Palermo, she had redeemed some of his things which were in pawn; but since then she had not heard a word from him, nor received any money, nor help of any kind, although, as she had heard, he possessed great wealth, and kept a princely establishment. Would I not engage on my return, at the first favourable moment to remind him of this debt, and to get him to make them an allowance—nay, would I not take a letter to him, or at least frank one to him? I offered to do so. She asked me where I lived? and where she could send me the letter. I avoided giving her my address, and engaged to call myself for the letter on the evening of the next day.

She then recounted to me her pitiable situation: she was a widow, with three children: one girl was being educated in a nunnery, the other was here at home; and her son was gone to school. Besides these three children she had her mother on her hands, for whose support she must provide, and besides all this, out of Christian love she had taken into her house the unfortunate sick person-and thus augmented her miseries—all her industry scarcely sufficed to furnish herself and children with the very barest necessaries. She well knew that God would reward all such good works; still she could not help sighing beneath the heavy burthen she had so long borne.

The young people joined in the conversation, and the dialogue became livelier. While I was speaking to the others I heard the old woman ask her daughter if I belonged to their holy religion. I was able to observe that the daughter skilfully parried the question by assuring her mother (as well as I could make out her words) that the stranger appeared well disposed towards them; and that it was not proper to question any one all at once on this point.

When they heard that I was soon to depart from Palermo, they became still more urgent, and entreated me to come back again at all events; especially they praised the heavenly day of S. Rosalie's festival, the like of which was not to be seen or enjoyed in the world.

My guide, who for a long while had been wishing to get away, at last by his signs put an end to our talk, and I promised to come on the evening of the next day, and fetch the letter. My guide expressed his satisfaction that all had gone off so well, and we parted, well satisfied with each other.

You may imagine what impression this poor, pious, and well-disposed family made upon me. My curiosity was satisfied; but their natural and pleasing behaviour had excited my sympathy, and reflection only confirmed my good will in their favour.

Palermo—Count Cagliostro.

But then some anxiety soon arose in my mind about to-morrow. It was only natural that my visit, which at first had so charmed them, would, after my departure, be talked and thought over by them. From the pedigree I was aware that others of the family were still living. Nothing could be more natural than that they should call in their friends to consult them on all that they had been so astonished to hear from me the day before. I had gained my object, and now it only remained for me to contrive to bring this adventure to a favourable issue. I therefore, set off the next day, and arrived at their house just after their dinner. They were surprised to see me so early. The letter, they told me, was not yet ready; and some of their relatives wished to make my acquaintance, and they would be there towards evening.

I replied that I was to depart early in the morning; that I had yet some visits to make, and had also to pack up, and that I had determined to come earlier than I had promised rather than not come at all.

During this conversation the son entered, whom I had not seen the day before. In form and countenance he resembled his sister. He had brought with him the letter which I was to take. As usual in these parts, it had been written by one of the public notaries. The youth who was of a quiet, sad, and modest disposition, inquired about his uncle, asked about his riches and expenditure, and added, "How could he forget his family so long? It would be the greatest happiness to us," he continued, "if he would only come back and help us but he further asked, "How came he to tell you that he had relations in Palermo? It is said that he everywhere disowns us, and gives himself out to be of high birth." These questions, which my guide's want of foresight on our first visit had given rise to, I contrived to satisfy, by making it appear possible that, although his uncle might have many reasons for concealing his origin from the public, he would, nevertheless make no secret of it to his friends and familiar acquaintances.

His sister, who had stepped forward during this conversation, and who had taken courage from the presence of her brother, and probably, also, from the absence of yesterday's friend, began now to speak. Her manner was very pretty and lively. She earnestly begged me, when I wrote to her uncle, to commend her to him; and not less earnestly, also, to come back when I had finished my tour through the kingdom of Sicily, and to attend with them the festivities of S. Rosalie.

The mother joined her voice to that of her children. "Signor," she exclaimed, "although it does not in propriety become me, who have a grown-up daughter, to invite strange men to my house,—and one ought to guard not only against the danger itself, but even against evil tongues,—still you, I can assure you, will be heartily welcome, whenever you return to our city."

"Yes! yes!" cried the children, "we will guide the Signor throughout the festival; we will show him every thing; we will place him on the scaffolding from which you have the best view of the festivities. How delighted will he be with the great car, and especially with the splendid illuminations!"

In the mean while, the grandmother had read the letter over and over again. When she was told that I wished to take my leave, she stood up and delivered to me the folded paper. "Say to my son," she said, with a noble vivacity, not to say enthusiasm, "tell my son how happy the news you have brought me of him has made us. Say to my son, that I thus fold him to my heart," (here she stretched out her arms and again closed them over her bosom)—"that every day in prayer I supplicate God and our blessed Lady for him; that I give my blessing to him and to his wife, and that I have no wish but, before I die, to see him once again, with these eyes, which have shed so many tears on his account."

The peculiar elegance of the Italian favoured the choice and the noble arrangement of her words, which, moreover, were accompanied with those very lively gestures, by which this people usually give an incredible charm to everything they say. Not unmoved, I took my leave; they all held out their hands to me: the children even accompanied me to the door, and while I descended the steps, ran to the balcony of the window which opened from the kitchen into the street, called after me, nodded their adieus, and repeatedly cried out to me not to forget to come again and see them. They were still standing on the balcony, when I turned the corner.

I need not say that the interest I took in this family excited in me the liveliest desire to be useful to them, and to help them in their great need. Through me they were now a second time deceived, and hopes of assistance, which they had no previous expectation of, had been again raised, through the curiosity of a son of the north, only to be disappointed.

Palermo—Count Cagliostro.

My first intention was to pay them before my departure these fourteen once, which, at his departure, the fugitive was indebted to them, and by expressing a hope that he would repay me, to conceal from them the fact of its being a gift from myself. When, however, I got home, and cast up my accounts, and looked over my cash and bills, I found that, in a country where, from the want of communication, distance is infinitely magnified, I should perhaps place myself in a strait if I attempted to make amends for the dishonesty of a rogue, by an act of mere good nature.

The subsequent issue of this affair may as well be here introduced.

I set off from Palermo, and never came back to it; but notwithstanding the great distance of my Sicilian and Italian travels, my soul never lost the impression which the interview with this family had left upon it.

I returned to my native land, and the letter of the old widow, turning up among the many other papers, which had come with it from Naples by sea, gave me occasion to speak of this and other adventures.

Below is a translation of this letter, in which I have purposely allowed the peculiarities of the original to appear.

"MY DEAREST SON,

"On the 16th April, 1787, I received tidings of you through Mr. Wilton, and I cannot express to you how consoling it was to me; for ever since you removed from France, I have been unable to hear any tidings of you.

"My dear Son,—I entreat you not to forget me, for I am very poor, and deserted by all my relations but my daughter, and your sister Maria Giovanna, in whose house I am living. She cannot afford to supply all my wants, but she does what she can. She is a widow, with three children: one daughter is in the nunnery of S. Catherine, the other two children are at home with her.

"I repeat, my dear son, my entreaty. Send me just enough to provide for my necessities; for I have not even the necessary articles of clothing to discharge the duties of a Catholic, for my mantle and outer garments are perfectly in rags.

"If you send me anything, or even write me merely a letter, do not send it by post, but by sea; for Don Mattéo, my brother (Bracconeri), is the postmaster.

"My dear Son, I entreat you to provide me with a tari a-day, in order that your sister may, in some measure, be relieved of the burthen I am at present to her, and that I may not perish from want. Remember the divine command, and help a poor mother, who is reduced to the utmost extremity. I give you my blessing, and press to my heart both thee and Donna Lorenza, thy wife.

"Your sister embraces you from her heart, and her children kiss your hands.

"Your mother, who dearly loves you, and presses you to her heart.

"FELICE BALSAMO.

"*Palermo, April* 18, 1787."

Some worthy and exalted persons, before whom I laid this document, together with the whole story, shared my emotions, and enabled me to discharge my debt to this unhappy family, and to remit them a sum which they received towards the end of the year 1787. Of the effect it had, the following letter is evidence.

"*Palermo, December* 25, 1787.

"DEAR AND FAITHFUL BROTHER,

"DEAREST SON,

"The joy which we have had in hearing that you are in good health and circumstances, we cannot express by any writing. By sending them this little assistance, you have filled with the greatest joy and delight a mother and a sister who are abandoned by all, and have to provide for two daughters and a son: for, after that Mr. Jacob Joff, an English merchant had taken great pains to find out the Donna Giuseppe Maria Capitummino (by birth Balsamo), in consequence of my being commonly known, merely as Marana Capitummino, he found us at last in a little tenement, where we live on a corresponding scale. He informed us that you had ordered a sum of money to be paid us, and that he had a receipt, which I, your sister, must sign—which was accordingly done; for he immediately put the money in our hands, and the favorable rate of the exchange has brought us a little further gain.

"Now, think with what delight we must have received this sum, at a time when Christmas Day was just at hand, and we had no hope of being helped to spend it with its usual festivity.

"The Incarnate Saviour has moved your heart to send us this money, which has served not only to appease our hunger, but actually to clothe us, when we were in want of everything.

"It would give us the greatest gratification possible if you would gratify our wish to see you once more—especially mine, your mother, who never cease to bewail my separation from an only son, whom I would much wish to see again before I die.

"But if, owing to circumstances, this cannot be, still do not neglect to come to the aid of my misery, especially as you have discovered so excellent a channel of communication, and so honest and exact a merchant, who, when we knew nothing about it, and when he had the money entirely in his own power, has honestly sought us out and faithfully paid over to us the sum you remitted.

"With you that perhaps will not signify much. To us, however, every help is a treasure. Your sister has two grown up daughters, and her son also requires a little help. You know that she has nothing in the world; and what a good act will you not perform by sending her enough to furnish them all with a suitable outfit.

"May God preserve you in health! We invoke Him in gratitude, and pray that He may still continue the prosperity you have hitherto enjoyed, and that He may move your heart to keep us in remembrance. In His name I bless you and your wife, as a most affectionate mother— and I your sister, embrace you: and so does your nephew, Giuseppe (Bracconeri), who wrote this letter. We all pray for your prosperity, as do also my two sisters, Antonia and Theresa.

"We embrace you, and are,

"Your sister,	"Your mother,
who loves you,	who loves and blesses you,
Giuseppe-Maria,	who blesses you every hour,
Capitummino,	Felice Balsamo,
and Balsamo.	and Bracconeri."

The signatures to the letter are in their own handwriting. I had caused the money to be paid to them without sending any letter, or intimation whence it came; this makes their mistake the more natural, and their future hopes the more probable.

Now, that they have been informed of the arrest and imprisonment of their relative, I feel myself at liberty to explain matters to them, and to do something for their consolation. I have still a small sum for them in my hands, which I shall remit to them, and profit by the opportunity to explain the true state of the matter. Should any of my friends, should any of my rich and noble countrymen, be disposed to enlarge, by their contributions, the sum I have already in my hands, I would exhort them in that case to forward their land gifts to me before Michaelmas-day, in order to share the gratitude, and to be rewarded with the happiness of a deserving family, out of which has proceeded one of the most singular monsters that has appeared in this century.

I shall not fail to make known the further course of this story, and to give an account of the state in which my next remittance finds the family; and perhaps also I shall add some remarks which this matter induced me to make, but which, however, I withhold at present in order not to disturb my reader's first impressions.

Palermo, April 14, 1787.

Towards evening I paid a visit to my friend the shop-keeper, to ask him how he thought the festival was likely to pass off; for to-morrow there is to be a solemn procession through the city, and the Viceroy is to accompany the host on foot. The least wind will envelop both man and the sacred symbols in a thick cloud of dust.

With much humour he replied: In Palermo, the people look for nothing more confidently than for a miracle. Often before now on such occasions, a violent passing shower had fallen and cleansed the streets partially at least, so as to make a clean road for the procession. On this occasion a similar hope was entertained, and not without cause, for the sky was overcast, and promised rain during the night.

Palermo, Sunday, April 15, 1787.

And so it has actually turned out! During the night the most violent of showers have fallen. In the morning I set cut very early in order to be an eye-witness of the marvel. The stream of rain-water pent up between the two raised pavements had carried the lightest of the rubbish down the inclined street, either into the sea or into such of the sewers as were not stopped up, while the grosser and heavier dung was driven from spot to spot. In this a singular meandering line of cleanliness was marked out along the streets. On the morning hundreds and hundreds of men were to be seen with brooms and shovels, busily enlarging this clear space, and in order to connect it where it was interrupted by the mire; and throwing the still remaining impurities now to this side, now to that. By this means when the procession started, it found a clear serpentine walk prepared for it through the mud, and so both the long robed priests and the neat-booted nobles, with the Viceroy at their head, were able to proceed on their way unhindered and unsplashed.

I thought of the children of Israel passing through the waters by the dry path prepared for them by the hand of the Angel, and this remembrance served to ennoble what otherwise would have been a revolting sight—to see these devout and noble peers parading their devotions along an alley, flanked on each side by heaps of mud.

Palermo—Its streets.

On the pavement there was now, as always, clean walking; but in the more retired parts of the city whither we were this day carried in pursuance of our intention of visiting the quarters which we had hitherto neglected, it was almost impossible to get along, although even here the sweeping and piling of the filth was by no means neglected.

The festival gave occasion to our visiting the principal church of the city and observing its curiosities. Being once on the move, we took a round of all the other public edifices. We were much pleased with a Moorish building, which is in excellent preservation—not very large, but the rooms beautiful, broad, and well proportioned, and in excellent keeping with the whole pile. It is not perhaps suited for a northern climate, but in a southern land a most agreeable residence. Architects may perhaps some day furnish us with a plan and elevation of it.

We also saw in most unsuitable situations various remains of ancient marble statues, which, however, we had not patience to try to make out.

Palermo, April 16, 1787.

As we are obliged to anticipate our speedy departure from this paradise, I hoped to-day to spend a thorough holiday by sitting in the public gardens; and after studying the task I had set myself out of the Odyssey, taking a walk through the valley, and at the foot of the hill of S. Rosalie, thinking over again my sketch of Nausicaa, and there trying whether this subject is susceptible of a dramatic form. All this I have managed, if not with perfect success, yet certainly much to my satisfaction. I made out the plan, and could not abstain from sketching some portions of it which appeared to me most interesting, and tried to work them out.

Palermo, Tuesday, April 17, 1787.

It is a real misery to be pursued and hunted by many spirits! Yesterday I set out early for the public gardens, with a firm and calm resolve to realize some of my poetical dreams; but before I got within sight of them, another spectre got hold of me which has been following me these last few days. Many plants which hitherto I had been used to see only in pots and tubs, or under glass-frames, stand here fresh and joyous beneath the open heaven, and as they here completely fulfil their destination, their natures and characters became more plain and evident to me. In presence of so many new and renovated forms, my old fancy occurred again to me: Might I not discover the primordial plant among all these numerous specimens? Some such there must be! For, otherwise, how am I able at once to determine that this or that form is a plant unless they are all formed after one original type? I busied myself, therefore, with examining wherein the many varying shapes differed from each other. And in every case I found them all to be more similar than dissimilar, and attempted to apply my botanical terminology. That went on well enough; still I was not satisfied; I rather felt annoyed that it did not lead further. My pet poetical purpose was obstructed; the gardens of Antinous all vanished—a real garden of the world had taken their place. Why is it that we moderns have so little concentration of mind? Why is it that we are thus tempted to make requisitions which we can neither exact nor fulfil?

Alcamo, Wednesday, April 18, 1787.

At an early hour, we rode out of Palermo. Kniep and the Vetturino showed their skill in packing the carnage inside and out. We drove slowly along the excellent road, with which we had previously become acquainted during our visit to San Martino, and wondered a second time at the false taste displayed in the fountains on the way. At one of these our driver stopped to supply himself with water according to the temperate habits of this country. He had at starting, hung to the traces a small wine-cask, such as our market-women use, and it seemed to us to hold wine enough for several days. We were, therefore, not a little surprised when he made for one of the many conduit pipes, took out the plug of his cask, and let the water run into it. With true German amazement, we asked him what ever he was about? was not the cask full of wine? To all which, he replied with great nonchalance: he had left a third of it empty, and as no one in this country drank unmixed wine, it was better to mix it at once in a large quantity, as then the liquids combined better together, and besides you were not sure of finding water everywhere. During this conversation the cask was filled, and we had some talk together of this ancient and oriental wedding custom.

And now as we reached the heights beyond Mon Reale, we saw wonderfully beautiful districts, but tilled in traditional rather than in a true economical style. On the right, the eye reached the sea, where, between singular shaped head-lands, and beyond a shore here covered with, and there destitute of, trees, it caught a smooth and level horizon, perfectly calm, and forming a glorious contrast with the wild and rugged limestone rocks. Kniep did not fail to take miniature outlines of several of them.

Alcamo.

We are at present in Alcamo, a quiet and clean little town, whose well-conducted inn is highly to be commended as an excellent establishment, especially as it is most conveniently situated for visitors to the temple of Segeste, which lies out of the direct road in a very lonely situation.

Alcamo, Thursday, April 19, 1787.

Our agreeable dwelling in this quiet town, among the mountains, has so charmed us that we have determined to pass a whole day here. We may then, before anything else, speak of our adventures yesterday. In one of my earlier letters, I questioned the originality of Prince Pallagonia's bad taste. He has had forerunners and can adduce many a precedent. On the road towards Mon Reale stand two monstrosities, beside a fountain with some vases on a balustrade, so utterly repugnant to good taste that one would suppose they must have been placed there by the Prince himself.

After passing Mon Reale, we left behind us the beautiful road, and got into the rugged mountain country. Here some rocks appeared on the crown of the road, which, judging from their gravity and metallic incrustations, I took to be ironstone. Every level spot is cultivated, and is more or less prolific. The limestone in these parts had a reddish hue, and all the pulverized earth is of the same colour. This red argillaceous and calcareous earth extends over a great space; the subsoil is hard; no sand underneath; but it produces excellent wheat. We noticed old very strong, but stumpy, olive trees.

Under the shelter of an *airy* room, which has been built as an addition to the wretched inn, we refreshed ourselves with a temperate luncheon. Dogs eagerly gobbled up the skins of the sausages we threw away, but a beggar-boy drove them off. He was feasting with a wonderful appetite on the parings of the apples we were devouring, when he in his turn was driven away by an old beggar. Want of work is here felt everywhere. In a ragged toga the old beggar was glad to get a job as house-servant, or waiter. Thus I had formerly observed that whenever a landlord was asked for anything which he had not at the moment in the house, he would send a beggar to the shop for it.

However, we are pretty well provided against all such sorry attendance; for our Vetturino is an excellent fellow—he is ready as ostler, cicerone, guard, courier, cook, and everything.

On the higher hills you find every where the olive, the caruba, and the ash. Their system of farming is also spread over three years. Beans, corn, fallow; in which mode of culture the people say the dung does more marvels than all the Saints. The grape stock is kept down very low.

Alcamo is gloriously situated on a height, at a tolerable distance from a bay of the sea. The magnificence of the country quite enchanted us. Lofty rocks, with deep valleys at their feet, but withal wide open spaces, and great variety. Beyond Mon Beale you look upon a beautiful double valley, in the centre of which a hilly ridge again raises itself. The fruitful fields lie green and quiet, but on the broad roadway the wild bushes and shrubs are brilliant with flowers—the broom one mass of yellow, covered with its pupilionaceous blossoms, and not a single green leaf to be seen; the white-thorn cluster on cluster; the aloes are rising high and promising to flower; a rich tapestry of an amaranthine-red clover, of orchids and the little Alpine roses, hyacinths, with unopened bells, asphodels, and other wild flowers.

Sicily—Segeste.

The streams which descend from M. Segeste leave deposits, not only of limestone, but also of pebbles of horn-stone. They are very compact, dark blue, yellow, red, and brown, of various shades. I also found complete lodes of horn, or fire-stone, in the limestone rocks, edged with lime. Of such gravel one finds whole hills just before one gets to Alcamo.

Segeste, April 20, 1787.

The temple of Segeste was never finished; the ground around it was never even levelled; the space only being smoothed on which the peristyle was to stand. For, in several places, the steps are from nine to ten feet in the ground, and there is no hill near, from which the stone or mould could have fallen. Besides, the stones lie in their natural position, and no ruins are found near them.

The columns are all standing; two which had fallen, have very recently been raised again. How far the columns rested on a socle is hard to say; and without an engraving it is difficult to give an idea of their present state. At some points it would seem as if the pillars rested on the fourth step. In that ease to enter the temple you would have to go down a step. In other places, however, the uppermost step is cut through, and then it looks as if the columns had rested on bases; and then again these spaces have been filled up, and so we have once more the first case. An architect is necessary to determine this point.

The sides have twelve columns, not reckoning the corner ones; the back and front six, including them. The rollers on which the stones were moved along, still lie around you on the steps. They have been left in order to indicate that the temple was unfinished. But the strongest evidence of this fact is the floor. In some spots (along the sides) the pavement is laid flown, in the middle, however, the red limestone rock still projects higher than the level of the floor as partially laid; the flooring, therefore, cannot ever have been finished. There is also no trace of an inner temple. Still less can the temple have ever been overlaid with stucco; but that it was intended to do so, we may infer from the fact that the abaci of the capitals have projecting points probably for the purpose of holding the plaster. The whole is built of a limestone, very similar to the travertine; only it is now much fretted. The restoration which was carried on in 1781, has done much good to the building. The cutting of the stone, with which the parts have been reconnected, is simple, but beautiful. The large blocks standing by themselves, which are mentioned by Riedesel, I could not find; probably they were used for the restoration of the columns.

The site of the temple is singular; at the highest end of a broad and long valley, it stands on an isolated hill. Surrounded, however, on all sides by cliffs, it commands a very distant and extensive view of the land, but takes in only just a corner of the sea. The district reposes in a sort of melancholy fertility—every where well cultivated, but scarce a dwelling to be seen. Flowering thistles were swarming with countless butterflies, wild fennel stood here from eight to nine feet high, dry and withered of the last year's growth, but so rich and in such seeming order that one might almost take it to be an old nursery-ground. A shrill wind whistled through the columns as if through a wood, and screaming birds of prey hovered around the pediments.

The wearisomeness of winding through the insignificant ruins of a theatre took away from us all the pleasures we might otherwise have had in visiting the remains of the ancient city. At the foot of the temple, we found large pieces of the horn-stone. Indeed, the road to Alcamo is composed of vast quantities of pebbles of the same formation. From the road a portion of a gravelly earth passes into the soil, by which means it is rendered looser. In some fennel of this year's growth, I observed the difference of the lower and upper leaves; it is still the same organisation that develops multiplicity out of unity. They are most industrious weeders in these parts. Just as beaters go through a wood for game, so here they go through the fields weeding. I have actually seen some insects here. In Palermo, however, I saw nothing but worms, lizards, leeches, and snakes, though not more finely coloured than with us—indeed, they are mostly all gray.

Castel   *Vetrano,*
Saturday, April 21, 1787.

From Alcamo to Castel Vetrano you come on the limestone, after crossing some hills of gravel. Between precipitous and barren limestone mountains, lie wide undulating valleys, everywhere tilled, with scarcely a tree to be seen. The gravelly hills are full of large bolders, giving signs of ancient inundations of the sea. The soil is better mixed and lighter than any we have hitherto seen, in consequence of its containing some sand. Leaving Salemi about fifteen miles to our right, we came upon hills of gypsum, lying on the limestone. The soil appears, as we proceed, to be better and more richly compounded. In the distance you catch a peep of the Western sea. In the foreground the country is everywhere hilly. We found the fig-trees just budding, but what most excited our delight and wonder was endless masses of flowers, which had encroached on the broad road, and flourish in large variegated patches. Closely bordering on each other, the several sorts, nevertheless, keep themselves apart and recur at regular intervals. The most beautiful convolvuluses, hibiscuses, and mallows, various kinds of trefoil, here and there the garlic, and the galega-gestrauche. On horseback you may ride through this varied tapestry, by following the numberless and ever-crossing narrow paths which run through it. Here and there you see feeding fine red-brown cattle, very clean-limbed and with short horns of an extremely elegant form.

The mountains to the north-east stand all in a line. A single peak, Cuniglione, rises boldly from the midst of them. The gravelly hills have but few streams; very little rain seems to fall here; we did not find a single gully giving evidence of having ever overflowed.

In the night I met with a singular incident. Quite worn out, we had thrown ourselves on our beds in anything but a very elegant room. In the middle of the night I saw above me a most agreeable phenomenon—a star brighter, I think, than I ever saw one before. Just, however, as I began to take courage at a sight which was of good omen, my patron star suddenly disappeared, and left me in darkness again. At daybreak, I at last discovered the cause of the marvel: there was a hole in the roof, and at the moment of my vision one of the brightest stars must have been crossing my meridian. This purely natural phenomenon was, however, interpreted by us travellers as highly favourable.

Sciacca, April 22, 1787.

The road hither, which runs over nothing but gravelly hills, has been mineralogically uninteresting. The traveller here reaches the shore from which, at different points, bold limestone rocks rise suddenly. All the flat land is extremely fertile; barley and oats in the finest condition; the salsola-kali is here cultivated; the aloes since yesterday, and the day before, have shot forth their tall spikes. The same numerous varieties of the trefoil still attended us. At last we came on a little wood, thick with brushwood, the tall trees standing very wide apart;—the cork-tree at last!

Girgenti, April 23, 1787. Evening.

From Sciacca to this place is a hard day's ride. We examined the baths at the last named place. A hot stream burst from the rock with a strong smell of sulphur; the water had a strong saline flavour, but it was not at all thick. May not the sulphureous exhalation be formed at the moment of its breaking from the rock? A little higher is a spring, quite cool and without smell; right above is the monastery, where are the vapour baths; a thick mist rises above it into the pure air.

The shingles on the shore are nothing but limestone: the quartz and hornstone have wholly disappeared. I have examined all the little streams: the Calta Bellota, and the Maccasoli, carry down with them nothing but limestone; the Platani, a yellow marble and flint, the invariable companion of this nobler calcareous formation. A few pieces of lava excited my attention, but I saw nothing in this country that indicated the presence of volcanic action. I supposed, therefore, they must be fragments of millstones, or of pieces brought from a distance for some such use or other. Near Monte Allegro, the stone is all gypsum and selenite; whole rocks of these occurring before and between the limestone. The wonderful strata of Calta Bellota!

Girgenti, Tuesday, April 24, 1787.

Such a glorious spring view as we enjoyed at sunset to-day will most assuredly never meet our eyes again in one life-time. Modern Girgenti stands on the lofty site of the ancient fortifications, an extent sufficient for the present population. From our window we looked over the broad but gentle declivity, on which stood the ancient town, which is now entirely covered with gardens and vineyards, beneath whose verdure it would be long before one thought of looking for the quarters of an ancient city. However, towards the southern end of this green and flourishing spot the Temple of Concord rears itself, while on the east are a few remains of the Temple of Juno. Other ruins of some ancient buildings, which lying in a straight line with those already spoken of, are scarcely noticed by the eye from above, while it hurries over them southwards to the shore, or ranges over the level country, which reaches at least seven miles from the sea-mark. To-day we were obliged to deny ourselves the pleasure of a stroll among the trees and the wild rockets and over this region, so green, so flourishing, and so full of promise for the husbandman, because our guide, (a good-natured little parish priest,) begged us before all things to devote this day to the town.

Sicily-Girgenti.

He first showed us the well-built streets; then he took us to the higher points, from which the view, gaining both in extent and breadth, was still more glorious, and lastly, for an artistic treat, conducted us to the principal church. In it there is an ancient sarcophagus in good preservation. The fact of its being used for the altar has rescued from destruction the sculptures on it—Hippolytus attended by his hunting companions and horses, has just been stopped by Phædra's nurse, who wishes to deliver him a letter. As in this piece the principal object was to exhibit beautiful youthful forms, the old woman as a mere subordinate personage, is represented very little and almost dwarfish, in order not to disturb the intended effect. Of all the alto-relivoes I have ever seen, I do not, I think, remember one more glorious, and at the same time, so well preserved as this. Until I meet with a better it must pass with me as a specimen of the most graceful period of Grecian art.

We were carried back to still earlier periods of art by the examination of a costly vase of considerable size, and in excellent condition. Moreover, many relics of ancient architecture appeared worked up here and there in the walls of the modern church.

As there is no inn or hotel in this place, a kind and worthy family made room for us, and gave up for our accommodation an alcove belonging to a large room. A green curtain separated us and our baggage from the members of the family, who, in the more spacious apartment were employed in preparing macaroni, of the whitest and smallest kind. I sat down by the side of the pretty children, and caused the whole process to be explained to me, and was informed that it is prepared from the finest and hardest wheat, called *Grano forte*. That sort they also told me fetches the highest price, which, after being formed into long pipes, is twisted into coils, and by the tip of the fair artiste's fingers made to assume a serpentine shape. The preparation is chiefly by the hand; machines and moulds are very little used. They also prepared for us a dish of the most excellent macaroni, regretting, however, that at that moment they had not even a single dish of the very best kind, which could not be made out of Girgenti, nor indeed, out of their house. What they did dress for me appeared to me to be unequalled in whiteness and tenderness.

By leading us once more to the heights and to the most glorious points of view, our guide contrived to appease the restlessness which during the evening kept us constantly out of doors. As we took a survey of the whole neighbourhood, he pointed out all the remarkable objects which on the morrow we had proposed to examine more nearly.

Girgenti, Wednesday, April 25, 1787.

With sun rise we took our way towards the plain, while at every step the surrounding scenery assumed a still more picturesque appearance. With the consciousness that it was for our advantage, the little man led us, without stopping, right across the rich vegetation over a thousand little spots, each of which might have furnished the locale for an idyllic scene. To this variety of scene the unevenness of the country greatly contributed, which undulated as it passed over hidden ruins, which probably were very quickly covered with fertile soil, as the ancient buildings consisted of a light muscheltufa. At last we arrived at the eastern end of the city, where are the ruins of the Temple of Juno, of which, every year must have accelerated the decay, as the air and weather are constantly fretting the soft stone of which it is built. To-day we only devoted a cursory examination to it, but Kniep has already chosen the points from which to sketch it to-morrow. The temple stands on a rock which is now much worn by the weather. From this point the city walls stretched in a straight line eastwards, to a bed of limestone, that rises perpendicular from the level strand, which the sea has abandoned, after having shaped these rocks and long washed the foot of them. Hewn partly out of the native rock, and partly built of it were the walls of ancient Agrigentum, from behind which towered a line of temples. No wonder, then, if from the sea the lower, middle, and upper tows, presented together a most striking aspect.

The Temple of Concord has withstood so many centuries; its light style of architecture closely approximates it to our present standard of the beautiful and tasteful; so that as compared with that of Pæstum, it is, as it were, the shape of a god to that of a gigantic figure. I will not give utterance to my regrets that the recent praiseworthy design of restoring this monument should have been so tastelessly carried out, that the gaps and defects are actually filled up with a dazzling white gypsum. In consequence this monument of ancient art stands before the eye, in a certain sense, dilapidated and disfigured. How easy it would have been to give the gypsum the same tint as the weather-eaten stone of the rest of the building? In truth, when one looks at the muschelkalk of which the walls and columns are composed, and sees how easily it crumbles away, one's only surprise is that they have lasted so long. But the builders reckoning on a posterity of similar religion to themselves, had taken precautions against it. One observes on the pillars the remains of a fine plaster, which would at once please the eye and ensure durability.

Our next halt was at the ruins of the Temple of Jupiter. Like the bones of a gigantic skeleton, they are scattered over a large space, having several small cottages interspersed among them, and being intersected by hedgerows, while amidst them plants are growing of different sizes.

From this pile of ruins all the carved stone has disappeared, except an enormous triglyph, and a part of a round pilaster of corresponding proportions. I attempted to span it with out-stretched arms, but could not reach round it. Of the fluting of the column, however, some idea may be formed from the fact that, standing in it as in a niche, I just filled it up and touched it on both sides with my shoulders. Two-and-twenty men arranged in a circle would give nearly the periphery of such a column. We went away with the disagreeable feeling that there was nothing here to tempt the draughtsman.

On the other hand, the Temple of Hercules still showed some traces of its former symmetry. The pillars of the peristyles, which ran along the temple on its upper and lower side, lie parallel, as if they had all fallen together, and at once, from north to south—the one row lying up the hill, the other down it. The hill may have possibly been formed by the ruined cells or shrines. The columns, held together in all probability by the architrave, fell all at once being suddenly thrown down, perhaps by a violent wind, and lie in regular order, only broken into the pieces of which they were originally composed. Kniep was already, in imagination, preparing his pencil for an accurate sketch of this singular phenomenon.

The Temple of Æsculapius, lying beneath the shade of a most beautiful carob-tree, and closely built upon by some mean farm-buildings, presented, to our minds, a most agreeable aspect.

Next we went down to Theron's tomb, and were delighted with the actual sight of this monument, of which we had seen so many models, especially as it served for the foreground of a most rare prospect; for from west to east we looked on the line of rocks on which lay the fragments of the walls, while through the gaps of the latter, and over them, the remains of the temples were visible.

This view has, under Hackert's skilful hand, furnished a most delightful picture. Kniep too, will not omit to make a sketch of it.

Girgenti, April 26, 1787.

When I awoke, Kniep was all ready to start on his artistic journey, with a boy to show him the way, and to carry his portfolio. I enjoyed this most glorious morning at the window, with my secret and silent, but not dumb friend by my side. A devout reverence has hitherto kept me from mentioning the name of the Mentor whom, from time to time, I have looked up and listened to. It is the excellent Von Reidesel, whose little volume I carry about with me in my bosom, like a breviary or talisman. At all times I have had great pleasure in looking up to those whom I know to be possessed of what I am most wanting in myself. And this is exactly the case here. A steady purpose, a fixed object, direct and appropriate means, due preparation and store of knowledge, an intimate connexion with a masterly teacher—he studied under Winckelmann—all these advantages I am devoid of, as well as of all that follows from them. And yet I cannot feel angry with myself that I am obliged to gain by indirect arts and means, and to seize at once what my previous existence has refused to grant me gradually in the ordinary way. Oh that this worthy person could, at this moment, in the midst of his bustling world, be sensible of the gratitude with which a traveller in his footsteps celebrates his merits, in that beautiful but solitary spot, which had so many charms for him, as to induce the wish that he might end his days there.

Oblitusque *suorum* obliviscendus et illis.

With my guide, the little parson, I now retraced our yesterday's walk, observing the objects from several points, and every now and then taking a peep at my industrious friend.

My guide called my attention to a beautiful institution of the once flourishing city. In the rocks and masses of masonry, which stand for bulwarks of the ancient Agrigentum, are found graves, probably intended for the resting place of the brave and good. Where could they more fitly have been buried, for the sake of their own glory, or for perpetuating a vivid emulation of their great and good deeds!

In the space between the walls and the sea there are still standing the remains of an ancient temple, which are preserved as a Christian chapel. Here also are found round pilasters, worked up with, and beautifully united to the square blocks of the wall, so as to produce an agreeable effect to the eye. One fancies that one here discerns the very spot where the Doric style reached its perfection.

Many an insignificant monument of antiquity was cursorily glanced at; but more attention was paid to the modern way of keeping the corn under the earth in great vaulted chambers. Of the civil and ecclesiastical condition of the city, my guide gave me much information; but I heard of nothing that showed any signs of improvement. The conversation suited well with the ruins, which the elements are still preying upon.

The strata of the muschelkalk all incline towards the sea,—banks of rock strangely eaten away from beneath and behind, while the upper and front portions still remain, looking like pendant fringes.

Great hatred is here felt against the French, because they have made peace with the people of Barbary. They are even charged with betraying the Christians to the infidels.

From the sea there was an ancient gateway, which was cut through the solid rock. The foundation of the walls, which are still standing, rests as it were on steps in the rocks.

Our cicerone is Don Michaele Vella, antiquary, residing at the house of Signore Cerio, near S. Maria's.

In planting the marsh-beans they proceed in the following way:—Holes are made in the earth at a convenient distance from each other, and a handful of dung is thrown in. A shower is then waited for, after which they put in the seed. The people here burn the bean-haulms, and wash their linen with the ashes. They never make use of soap. The outer shells of almonds are likewise burnt and used instead of soda. They first of all wash the clothes with pure water, and then with the ley of these ashes.

The succession of their crops is, beans, wheat, and tumenia. By beans I mean the marsh-bean. Their wheat is wonderfully fine. Tumenia, of which the name is derived from bimenia or trimenia, is a glorious gift of Ceres. It is a species of spring wheat, which is matured within three months. It is sown at different times, from the first of January to June, so that for a certain period there is always a crop ripe. It requires neither much rain nor great warmth. At first it has a very delicate leaf, but in its growth it soon overtakes the wheat, and at last is very strong. Wheat is sown in October and November, and ripens in June. The barley sown in November is ripe by the first of June. Near the coast it ripens sooner, but on the mountains more slowly.

The flax is already ripe. The acanthus has unrolled its splendid leaves. The *Salsala fruticosa* is growing luxuriantly.

On the uncultivated hills grows a rich sainfoin. It is farmed out, and then carried into the town in small bundles. In the same way the oats which are weeded out of the wheat, are done up for sale.

For the sake of irrigation, they make very pretty divisions with edgings in the plots where they plant their cabbages.

The figs have put forth all their leaves, and the fruit is set. They are generally ripe by midsummer, when the tree sets its fruit again. The almond trees are well loaded; a sheltered carob-tree has produced numberless pods. The grapes for the Table are trained on arbours supported by high props. Melons set in March and ripen by June. Among the ruins of Jupiter's temple they thrive vigorously without a trace of moisture.

Our vetturino eats with, great zest raw artichokes and the turnip-cabbage. However, it is necessary to add that they are tenderer and more delicate than with us. When you walk through the fields the farmers allow you to take as many of the young beans, or other crops, as you like.

As my attention was caught by some hard black stones, which looked like lava, my antiquary observed that they were from Ætna; and that at the harbour, or rather landing-place, many similar ones were to be found.

Of birds there are not many kinds native here: quails are the most common. The birds of passage are, nightingales, larks, and swallows. The Rinnine— small black birds, which come from the Levant—hatch their young in Sicily, and then go further or retire. The Ridene come in December or January, and after alighting and resting awhile on Acragas, take their flight towards the mountains.

Of the vase in the cathedral one word more. The figures in relief on it are, a hero in full armour, seemingly a stranger, before an old man whom a crown and sceptre, point out to be a king. Behind the latter stands a female figure, with her head slightly inclined, and her hand under her chin—a posture indicating thoughtful attention. Right opposite to her, and behind the hero, is an old man who also wears a crown, and is speaking to a man armed with a spear, probably one of the body-guard of the former royal personage. This old man would appear to have introduced the hero, and to be saying to the guard, "Just let him speak to the king; he is a brave man."

Red seems to be the ground of the vase, the black to be laid on. It is only in the female's robe that red seems to be laid on the black.

Girgenti, Friday, April 27, 1787.

If Kniep is to finish all he proposes, he must sketch away incessantly. In the meantime I walk about with my little antiquary. We took a walk towards the sea, from which Agrigentum must, as the ancients asserted, have looked extremely well. Our view was turned to the billowy expanse, and my guide called my attention to a broad streak of clouds towards the south, which, like a ridge of hills, seemed to rest on the line of the horizon. "This," he said, "indicated the coast of Africa." About the same time another phenomenon struck me as singular. It was a rainbow in a light cloud, which, resting with one limb on Sicily, threw its arch high against the clear sky, and appeared to rest with the other on the sea. Beautifully tinted by the setting sun, and shewing but little movement, it was to the eye an object as rare as it was agreeable. This bow, I was assured, was exactly in the direction of Malta, and in all probability its other limb rested on that island. The phenomenon, I was told, was of common occurrence. It would be singular if the attractive force of these two islands should thus manifest itself even in the atmosphere.

This conversation excited again the question I had so often asked myself: whether I ought to give up all idea of visiting Malta. The difficulties and dangers, however, which had been already well considered, remained the same; and we, therefore, resolved to engage our vetturino to take us to Messina.

But, in the meantime, a strange and peculiar whim was to determine our future movements. For instance, in my travels through Sicily, I had, as yet seen but few districts rich in corn: moreover, the horizon had everywhere been confined by nearer or remoter lines of hills, so that the island appeared to be utterly devoid of level plains, and I found it impossible to conceive why Ceres had so highly favoured this island. As I sought for information on this point, I was answered that, in order to see this, I ought, instead of going to Syracuse, to travel across the island, in which case I should see corn-fields in abundance. We followed this temptation, of giving up Syracuse, especially as I was well aware that of this once glorious city scarcely anything but its splendid name remained. And, at any rate, it was easy to visit it from Catania.

Caltanisetta, Saturday, April 28, 1787.

At last, we are able to understand how Sicily gained the honourable title of the Granary of Italy. Shortly after leaving Girgenti, the fertile district commenced. It does not consist of a single great plain, but of the sides of mountains and hills, gently inclined towards each other, everywhere planted with wheat, or barley which present to the eye an unbroken mass of vegetation. Every spot of earth suited to these crops is so put to use and so jealously looked after, that not a tree is anywhere to be seen. Indeed, the little villages and farm-houses all lie on the ridges of the hills, where a row of limestone rocks, which often appear on the surface, renders the ground unfit for tillage. Here the females reside throughout the year, busily employed in spinning and weaving; but the males, while the work in the fields is going on, spend only Saturday and Sunday at home, staying away at their work during the other days, and spending their nights under temporary straw-sheds.

And so our wish was gratified—even to satiety; we almost wished for the winged car of Triptolemus to escape from the monotony of the scene.

Sicily—Caltanisetta.

After a long drive under the hot sun, through this wilderness of fertility, we were glad enough when, at last, we reached the well-situated and well-built Caltanisetta; where, however, we had again to look in vain for a tolerable inn. The mules are housed in fine vaulted stables; the grooms sleep on the heaps of clover which are intended for the animals' food; but the stranger has to look out for and to prepare his own lodging. If, by chance, he can hire a room, it has first of all to be swept out and cleaned. Stools or chairs, there are none: the only seats to be had are low little forms of hard wood: tables are not to be thought of.

If you wish to convert these forms into a bedstead, you must send to a joiner, and hire as many planks as you want. The large leathern bag, which Hackert lent me, was of good use now, and was, by way of anticipation, filled with chaff.

But, before all things, provisions must be made for your meals. On our road we had bought a fowl; our vetturino ran off to purchase some rice, salt, and spice. As, however, he had never been here before, he was for a long time in a perplexity for a place to cook our meal in, as in the post-house itself there was no possibility of doing it. At last, an old man of the town agreed for a fair recompense to provide us with a hearth together with fuel, and cooking and table utensils. While our dinner was cooking, he undertook to guide us round the town, and finally to the market-house, where the principal inhabitants, after the ancient fashion, met to talk together, and also to hear what we or other strangers might say.

We were obliged to talk to them of Frederick the Second, and their interest in this great king was such that we thought it advisable to keep back the fact of his death lest our being the bearers of such untoward news should render us unwelcome to our hosts.

Caltanisetta, Saturday, April 28, 1787.

Geology by way of an appendix! From Girgenti, the muschelkalk rocks; there also appeared a streak of whitish earth, which afterwards we accounted for: the older limestone formation again occurs, with gypsum lying immediately upon it. Broad flat vallies; cultivated almost up to the top of the hill-side, and often quite over it: the older limestone mixed with crumbled gypsum. After this appeal's a looser, yellowish, easily crumbling, limestone; in the arable fields you distinctly recognize its colour, which often passes into darker, indeed occasionally violet shades. About half-way the gypsum again recurs. On it you see, growing in many places, a beautiful violet, almost rosy red sedum, and on the limestone rocks a beautiful yellow moss.

This very crumbling limestone often shows itself; but most prominently in the neighbourhood of Caltanisetta, where it lies in strata, containing a few fossils; there its appearance is reddish, almost of a vermilion tint, with little of the violet hue, which we formerly observed near San Martino.

Pebbles of quartz I only observed at a spot about half-way on our journey, in a valley which, shut in on three sides, is open towards the east, and consequently also towards the sea.

On the left, the high mountain in the distance, near Camerata, was remarkable, as also was another looking like a propped up cone. For the greatest half of the way not a tree was to be seen. The crops looked glorious, though they were not so high as they were in the neighbourhood of Girgenti and near the coast; however, as clean as possible. In the fields of corn, which stretched further than the eye could reach, not a weed to be seen. At first we saw nothing but green fields, then some ploughed lands, and lastly, in the moister spots, little patches of wheat, close to Girgenti. We saw apples and pears everywhere else; on the heights, and in the vicinity of a few little villages, some fig-trees.

These thirty miles, together with all that I could distinguish, either on the right or left of us, was limestone of earlier or later formations, with gypsum here and there. It is to the crumbling and elaboration of these three together by the atmosphere that this district is indebted for its fertility. It must contain but very little sand, for it scarcely grates between the teeth. A conjecture of mine with regard to the river Achates must wait for the morrow to confirm or not.

Sicily—Castro Giovanni.

The valleys have a pretty form, and although they are not flat, still one does not observe any trace of rain gullies; merely a few brooks, scarcely noticeable, ripple along them for all of them flow direct to the sea. But little of the red clover is to be seen; the dwarf palm also disappears here, as well as all the other flowers and shrubs of the south-western side of the island. The thistles are permitted to take possession of nothing but the way-sides, every other spot is sacred to Ceres. Moreover, this region has a great similarity to the hilly and fertile parts of Germany—for instance, the tract between Erfurt and Gotha, especially when you look out for points of resemblance. Very many things must combine together in order to make Sicily one of the most fertile regions of the world.

On our whole tour, we have seen but few horses; ploughing is carried on with oxen; and a law exists which forbids the killing of cows and calves. Goats, asses, and mules, we met in abundance. The horses are mostly dapple grey, with black feet and manes; the stables are very splendid, with well-paved and vaulted stalls. For beans and flax the land is dressed with dung; the other crops are then grown after this early one has been gathered in. Green barley in the ear, done up in bundles, and red clover, in like fashion, art: offered for sale to the traveller as he goes along.

On the hill above Caltanisetta, I found a hard limestone with fossils: the larger shells lay lowermost, the smaller above them. In the pavement of this little town, we noticed a limestone with pectinites.

April 28, 1787.

Behind Caltanisetta, the hill subsided suddenly into many little valleys, all of which pour their streams into the river Salso. The soil here is reddish and very loamy; much of it unworked; what was in cultivation bore tolerably good crops, though inferior to what we had elsewhere seen.

Castro Giovanni, Sunday, April 29, 1787.

To-day we had to observe still greater fertility and want of population. Heavy rains had fallen, which made travelling anything but pleasant, as we had to pass through many streams, which were swollen and rapid. At the Salso, where one looks round in vain for a bridge, I was struck with a very singular arrangement for passing the ford. Strong powerful men were waiting at the river-side; of these two placed themselves on each side of a mule, and conducted him, rider, baggage and all, through the deep part of the river, till they reach a great bank of gravel in the middle; when the whole of the travellers have arrived at this spot, they are again conducted in the same manner through the second arm of the stream, while the fellows, by pushing and shoving, keep the animal in the right tract, and support him against the current.

On the water-side I observed bushes, which, however, do not spread far into the land. The Salso washes down rubbles of granite—a transition of the gneiss, and marble, both breccian and also of a single colour.

We now saw before us the isolated mountain ridge on which Castro Giovanni is situate, and which imparts to the country about it a grave and singular character. As we rode up the long road which traverses its side, we found that the rock consisted of muschelkalk; large calcined shells being huddled together in heaps. You do not see Castro Giovanni until you reach the very summit of the ridge, for it lies on the northern declivity of the mountain. The singular little town, with its tower, and the village of Caltaseibetta, at a little distance on the left, stand, as it were, solemnly gazing at each other. In the plains we saw the bean in full blossom; but who is there that could take pleasure in such a sight? The roads here were horrible, and the more so because they once were paved, and it rained incessantly. The ancient *Enna* received us most inhospitably,—a room with a paved floor, with shutters and no window, so that we must either sit in darkness or be again exposed to the beating rain, from which we had thought to escape by putting up here. Some relics of our travelling provisions were greedily devoured; and the night passed most miserably. We made a solemn vow never to direct our course again towards never so mythological a name.

Monday, April 30, 1787.

The road leading from Castro Giovanni was so rough and bad, that we were obliged to lead our horses down it. The sky before us was covered with thick and low clouds, while high above them a singular phenomenon was observable. It was striped white and grey, and seemed to be something corporeal; but how could aught corporeal get into the sky? Our guide enlightened us. This subject of our amazement was a side of Mount Ætna, which appeared through the opening clouds. Snow alternating with the crags formed the stripes—it was not, however, the highest peak that we saw.

Sicily—Castro Giovanni.

The precipitous rock on which the ancient Enna was situated lay behind us; and we drove through long, long, lonely valleys: there they lay, uncultivated and uninhabited, abandoned to the browsing cattle, which we observed were of a beautiful brown colour, not large, short-horned, clean-limbed, lank and lively as deer. These poor cattle had pasturage enough, but it was greatly encroached upon, and in some parts wholly taken possession of by the thistles. These plants have here the finest opportunities possible to disperse their seed and to propagate their kind; they take up an incredible space, which would make pasture land enough for two large estates. As they are not perennial, they might, if mowed down before flowering, be easily eradicated.

However, after having thus seriously meditated an agricultural campaign against the thistles, I must, to my shame, admit they are not altogether useless. At a lonely farm-house where we pulled up to bait, there were also stopping two Sicilian noblemen, who on account of some process were riding straight across the country to Palermo. With amazement we saw both these grave personages standing before a patch of these thistles, and with their pocket-knives cutting off the tops of the tall shoots. Then holding their prickly booty by the tips of their fingers, they pealed off the rind, and devoured the inner part with great satisfaction. In this way they occupied themselves a considerable time, while we were refreshing ourselves with wine (this time it was unmixed) and bread. The vetturino prepared for us some of this marrow of thistle stalks, and assured us that it was a wholesome, cooling food; it suited our taste, however, as little as the raw cabbage at Segeste.

On the Road, April 30, 1787.

Having reached the valley through which the rivulet of S. Pacio winds its way, we found the district consisting of a reddish, black, and crumbly limestone: many brooks, a very white soil, a beautiful valley, which the rivulet made extremely agreeable. The well compounded loamy soil is in some places twenty feet deep, and for the most part of similar quality throughout. The crops looked beautiful; but some of them were not very clean, and all of them very backward as compared with those on the southern side. Here there are the same little dwellings—and not a tree, as was the case immediately after leaving Castro Giovanni. On the banks of the river plenty of pasture land, but sadly confined by vast masses of thistles. In the gravel of the river we again found quartz, both simple and breccian.

Molimenti, quite a new village, wisely built in the centre of beautiful fields, and on the banks of the rivulet S. Paolo. The wheat in its neighbourhood was unrivalled: it will be ready to cut as early as by the 20th May. In the whole district I could not discover as yet a trace of volcanic influence: even the stream brings down no pebbles of that character. The soil is well mixed, heavy rather than light, and has on the whole a coffee-brown and slightly violet hue. All the hills on the left, which inclose the stream, are limestone, whose varieties I had no opportunity of observing. They, however, as they crumble under the influence of the weather, are evidently the causes of the great fertility that marks the district throughout.

Tuesday, May 1, 1787.

Through a valley which, although by nature it was throughout alike destined to fertility, was unequally cultivated, we rode along very moodily because among so many prominent and irregular shapes not one appeared to suit our artistic designs. Kniep had sketched a highly interesting outline, but because the foreground and intermediate space was thoroughly revolting, he had with a pleasant joke appended to it a foreground of Poussin's, which cost him nothing. However, they made together a very pretty picture. How many "picturesque tours" in all probability contain half truths of the like kind.

Our courier, with the view of soothing our grumbling humour, promised us a good inn for the evening. And in fact, he brought us to an hotel which had been built but a few years since on the road side, and being at a considerable distance from Catania, cannot but be right welcome to all travellers. For our part, finding ourselves, after twelve days of discomfort, in a tolerable apartment, we were right glad to be so much at our ease again. But we were surprised at an inscription pencilled on the wall in an English character. The following was its purport:—"Traveller, whoever you may be, be on your guard against the inn known in Catania by the sign of the Golden Lion; it is better to fall into the claws of all the Cyclops, Sirens, and Scylla together than to go there." Although we at once supposed that the good-meaning counsellor had no doubt by his mythological figures magnified the danger, we nevertheless determined to keep out of the reach of the "Golden Lion," which was thus proclaimed to us to be so savage a beast. When, therefore, our muleteer demanded of us where we would wish to put up in Catania, we answered anywhere but at the Golden Lion! Whereupon he ventured to recommend us to stop where he put up his beasts, only he said we should have to provide for ourselves just as we had hitherto done.

Towards Hybla Major pebbles of lava present themselves, which the stream brings down from the north. Over the ferry you find limestone, which contains all sorts of rubble, hornstone, lava, and calx; and then hardened volcanic ashes, covered over with calcareous tufa. The hills of mixed gravel continue till you come near to Catania, at and beyond which place you find the lava flux, from Ætna. You leave on the left what looks like a crater. (Just under Molimenti the peasants were pulling up the flax.) Nature loves a motly garb; and here you may see how she contrives gaily to deck out the dark bluish-gray lava of the mountains. A few seasons bring over it a moss of a high yellow colour, upon which a beautiful red sedum grows luxuriantly, and some other lovely violet flowers. The plantations of Cactus and the vine-rows bespeak a careful cultivation. Now immense streams of lava begin to hem us in. Motta is a beautiful and striking rock. The beans are like very high shrubs. The fields vary very much in their geological features; now very gravelly, now better mixed.

Sicily—Molimenti.

The vetturino, who probably had not for a long time seen the vegetation of the south-eastern side of the island, burst into loud exclamations about the beauty of the crops, and with self complaisant patriotism demanded of us, if we ever saw such in our own country? Here, however, every thing is sacrificed to them; you see few if any trees. But the sight that most pleased us was a young girl, of a splendid but slight form, who, evidently an old acquaintance, kept up with the mule of our vetturino, chatting the while, and spinning away with all the elegance possible.

Now yellow tints begin to predominate in the flowers. Towards Misterbianco the cactuses are again found in the hedges; but hedges entirely of this strangely grown plant become, as you approach Catania, more and more general, and are even still more beautiful.

Catania, May 2, 1787.

In our auberge we found ourselves, we must confess, most uncomfortable. The meal, such as our muleteer could alone furnish, was none of the best. A fowl stewed in rice would have been tolerable, but for an immoderate spice of saffron, which made it not more yellow than disagreeable. The most abominable of bad beds had almost driven me a second time to bring out Hackert's leathern bag, and we therefore next morning spoke on this subject to our obliging host. He expressed his regret that it was not in his power to provide better for us; "but," he said, "there is, above there, a house where strangers are well entertained, and have every reason to be satisfied."

Saying this, he pointed to a large corner house, of which the part that was turned towards us seemed to promise well. We immediately hurried over to it, and found a very testy personage, who declared himself to be a waiter, and who in the absence of the landlord showed us an excellent bedroom with a sitting-room adjoining, and assured us at the same time that we should be well attended to. Without delay we demanded, according to our practice, what was the charge for dinner, for wine, for luncheon, and other particulars. The answers were all fair; and we hastily had our trifles brought over to the house, and arranged them in the spacious and gilded buffets. For the first time since we left Palermo, Kniep found an opportunity to spread out his portfolio, and to arrange his drawings, as I did my notes. Then delighted with our fine room, we stept out on the balcony of the sitting-room to enjoy the view. When we got tired of looking at and extolling the prospect, we turned to enter our apartment, and commence our occupations, when, lo! over our head was a large golden lion, regarding us with a most threatening aspect. Quite serious we looked for a moment in one another's face, then smiled, and laughed outright. From this moment, however, we began to look around us to see whether we could discover any of these Homeric goblins.

Nothing of the kind was to be seen. On the contrary, we found in the sitting-room a pretty young woman, who was playing about with a child from two to three years old, who stood suddenly still on being hastily scolded by the vice-landlord:—"You must take yourself off!" he testily exclaimed; "you have no business here." "It is very hard," she rejoined, "that you drive me away; the child is scarcely to be pacified in the house when you are away, and the signori will allow me, at least while you are present, to keep the child quiet." The husband made no reply, but proceeded to drive her away; the child at the door cried most miserably, and at last we did most heartily wish that the pretty young madam had stayed.

Warned by the Englishman, it was no art to see through the comedy: we played the *Neulinge*, the *Unschuldige*—he, however, with his very loving paternal feelings, prevailed very well. The child in fact was evidently very fond of him—and probably the seeming mother had pinched him at the door to make him cry so.

And so, too, with the greatest innocence possible she came and stayed with him as the man went out to deliver for us a letter of introduction to the Domestic Chaplain of Prince Biscari. She played and toyed with the child till he came back bringing word from the Abbé that he would come himself and talk with us on the matter.

Catania, Thursday, May 3, 1787.

The Abbé, who yesterday evening came and paid his respects to us, appeared this morning in good time, and conducted us to the palace, which is of one story, and built on a tolerably high socle. First of all we visited the museum, where there is a large collection of marble and bronze figures, vases, and all sorts of such like antiques. Here we had once more an opportunity of enlarging our knowledge; and the trunk of a Jupiter, which I was already acquainted with through a cast in Tischbein's studio, particularly ravished me. It possesses merits far higher than I am able to estimate. An inmate of the house gave us all necessary historical information. After this we passed into a spacious and lofty saloon. The many chairs around and against the walls indicated that a numerous company was often assembled here. We seated ourselves in hope of a favourable reception. Soon afterwards two ladies entered and walked several times up and down the room. From time to time they spoke to each other. When they observed us, the Abbé rose, and I did the same, and we both bowed. I asked, Who are they? and I learned that the younger lady was daughter of the Prince, but the elder a noble lady of Catania. We resumed our seats, while they continued to walk up and down as people do in a market-place.

We were now conducted to the Prince, who (as I had been already given to understand) honoured me with a singular mark of his confidence in showing me his collection of coins, since, by such acts of kindness, both his father and himself had lost many a rare specimen; and so his general good nature, and wish to oblige, had been naturally much contracted. On this occasion I probably appeared a little better informed than formerly, for I had learned something from the examination of Prince Torremuzza's collection. I again contrived to enlarge my knowledge, being greatly helped by Winckelmann's never-failing clues, which safely led the way through all the different epochs of art. The Prince, who was well informed in all these matters, when he saw that he had before him not a connoisseur, but an attentive amateur, willingly informed me of every particular that I found it necessary to ask about.

After having given to these matters, considerable, but still far less time than they deserved, we were on the point of taking our leave, when the Prince conducted us to the Princess, his mother, in whose apartments the smaller works of art are to be seen.

We found a venerable, naturally noble lady, who received us with the words, "Pray look round my room, gentlemen; here you still see all that my dear departed husband collected and arranged for me. This I owe to the affection of my son, who not only allows me still to reside in his best room, but has even forbidden the least thing to be taken away or removed that his late father purchased for me, and chose a place for. Thus I enjoy a double pleasure; not only have I been able these many years to live in my usual ways and habits, but also I have, as formerly, the opportunity to see and form the acquaintance of those worthy strangers who come hither from widely distant places to examine our treasures."

Catania—The Prince Biscani's Palace.

She thereupon, with her own hands, opened for us the glass-case in which the works in amber were preserved. The Sicilian amber is distinguished from the northern, by its passing from the transparent and non-transparent,—from the wax and the honey-coloured,—through all possible shades of a deep yellow, to the most beautiful hyacinthian red. In the case there were urns, cups, and other things, and for executing which large pieces of a marvellous size must have been necessary; for such objects, and also for cut-shells, such as are executed at Trapani, and also for exquisitely manufactured articles in ivory, the Princess had an especial taste, and about some of them she had amusing stories to tell. The Prince called our attention to those of more solid value among them; and so several hours slipped away—not, however, without either amusement or edification.

In the course of our conversation, the Princess discovered that we were Germans: she therefore asked us after Riedesel, Bartels, and Münter, all of whom she knew, and whose several characters she seemed well able to appreciate, and to discriminate. We parted reluctantly from her, and she seemed also unwilling to bid us farewell. An insular life has in it something very peculiar to be thus excited and refreshed by none but passing sympathies.

From the palace the Abbé led us to the Benedictine Monastery, and took us to the cell of a brother of the order, whose reserved and melancholy expression (though he was not of more than the middle age) promised but little of cheerful conversation. He was, however, the skilful musician who alone could manage the enormous organ in the church of this monastery. As he rather guessed than waited to hear our request, so he complied with it in silence. We proceeded to the very spacious church, where, sitting down at the glorious instrument, he made its softest notes whisper through its remotest corners, or filled the whole of it with the crash of its loudest tones.

If you had not previously seen the organist, you would fancy that none but a giant could exercise such power; as, however, we were already acquainted with his personal appearance, we only wondered that the necessary exertion had not long since worn him out.

Catania, Friday, May 4, 1787.

Soon after dinner our Abbé arrived with a carriage, and proposed to show us a distant part of the city. Upon entering it we had a strange dispute about precedence. Having got up first, I had seated myself on the left-hand side. As he ascended, he begged of me to move, and to take the right-hand seat. I begged him not to stand on such ceremony. "Pardon me," he replied, "and let us sit as I propose; for if I take my place on your right, every one will believe that I am taking a ride with you; but if I sit on your left, it is thereby indicated that you are riding with me, that is, with him who has, in the Prince's name, to show you the city." Against this nothing could, of course, be objected, and it was settled accordingly.

We drove up the streets where the lava, which, in 1699, destroyed a great part of this city, remains visible to this day. The solid lava had been worked like any other rock,—streets had even been marked out on its surface, and partly built. I placed under the seat of the carriage an undoubted specimen of the molten rock, remembering that, just before my departure from Germany, the dispute had arisen about the volcanic origin of basalt. And I did so in many other places, in order to have several varieties.

However, if natives had not proved themselves the friends of their own land, had they not even laboured, either for the sake of profit or of science, to bring together whatever is remarkable in this neighbourhood, the traveller would have had to trouble himself long, and to little purpose. In Naples I had received much information from the dealer in lava, but still more instruction did I get here from the Chevalier Gioeni. In his rich and excellently arranged museum I learned more or less correctly to recognise the various phenomena of the lava of Ætna; the basalt at its foot, stones in a changed state—everything, in fact, was pointed out tome in the most friendly maimer possible. What I saw most to be wondered at, was some zeolites from the rugged rocks which rise out of the sea below Jaci.

As we inquired of the Chevalier which was the best course to take in order to ascend Ætna, he would not hear of so dangerous an attempt as trying to reach the summit, especially in the present season of the year. "Generally," he observed, begging my pardon, however, "the strangers who come here think far too lightly of the matter; we, however, who are neighbours of the mountain, are quite contented if, twice in our life, we hit on a very good opportunity to reach the summit. *Brydone*, who was the first by his description to kindle a desire to see this fiery peak, did not himself ascend it. Count Borch leaves his readers in uncertainty; but, in fact, even he ascended only to a certain height: and the same may be said of many others. At present the snow comes down far too low, and presents insuperable obstacles. If you would take my advice, you will ride very early some morning for Monte Rosso, and be contented with ascending this height. From it you will enjoy a splendid view of Ætna, and at the same time have an opportunity of observing the old lava, which, bursting out from that point in 1697, unhappily poured down upon the city. The view is glorious and distinct; it is best to listen to a description for all the rest."

Catania, Saturday, May 5, 1787.

Sicily—Catania.

Following this good counsel, we set out early on a mule; and, continually looking behind us on our way, reached at last the region of the lava, as yet unchanged by time. Jagged lumps and slabs stared us in the face, among which a chance road had been tracked out by the beasts. We halted on the first considerable eminence. Kniep sketched with wonderful precision, what lay before us. The masses of lava in the foreground, the double peak of Monte Rosso on the left, right before us the woods of Nicolosi, out of which rose the snow-capped and slightly smoking summit. We drew near to the Red Mountain. I ascended it. It is composed entirely of red volcanic rubbish, ashes, and stones, heaped together. It would have been very easy to go round the mouth of the crater, had not a violent and stormy east wind made my footing unsteady. When I wished to go a little way, I was obliged to take off my cloak, and then my hat was every moment in danger of being blown into the crater, and I after it. On this account I sat down in order to recover myself, and to take a view of the surrounding objects; but even this position did not help meat all. The wind came direct from the east, over the glorious land which, far and near, and reaching to the sea, lay below me. The outstretched strand, from Messina to Syracuse, with its bays and headlands, was before my eyes, either quite open, or else (though only in a few small points) covered with rocks. When I came down quite numbed, Kniep, under the shelter of the hill, had passed his time well, and with a few light lines on the paper had perpetuated the memory of what the wild storm had allowed me scarcely to see, and still less to fix permanently in my mind.

Returned once more to the jaws of the Golden Lion, we found the waiter, whom we had with difficulty prevented from accompanying us. He praised our prudence in giving up the thought of visiting the summit, but urgently recommended for the next day a walk by the sea to the rocks of Jaci—it was the most delightful pleasure-trip that could be made from Catania: but it would be well to take something to eat and drink with us, and also utensils for warming our viands. His wife offered herself to perform this duty. Moreover, he spoke of the jubilee there was when some Englishmen hired a boat with a band of music to accompany them—which made it more delightful than it was possible to form any idea of.

The rocks of Jaci had a strong attraction for me; I had a strong desire to knock off from them as fine zeolites as I had seen in Gioeni's possession. It was true we might reduce the scale of the affair, and decline the attendance of the wife; but the warning of the Englishman prevailed over every other consideration. We gave up all thoughts of zeolites, and prided ourselves not a little at this act of self-denial.

Catania, Sunday, May 6, 1787.

Our clerical companion has not failed us to-day. He conducted us to some remains of ancient architecture; in examining which, however, the visitor needs to bring with him no ordinary talent of restoration. We saw the remains of the great cisterns of a naumachy, and other similar ruins, which, however, have been filled up and depressed by the many successive destructions of the city by lava, earthquakes, and wars. It is only those who are most accurately acquainted with the architecture of the ancients that can now derive either pleasure or instruction from seeing them.

The kind Abbé engaged to make our excuses for not waiting again on the Prince, and we parted with lively expressions of mutual gratitude and good will.

Taormina, Monday, May 7, 1787.

Sicily—Taormina.

God be thanked that all that we have here seen this day has been already amply described—but still more, that Kniep has resolved to spend the whole of to-morrow in the open air, taking sketches. When you have ascended to the top of the wall of rocks, which rise precipitously at no great distance from the sea, you find two peaks, connected by a semi-circle. Whatever shape this may have had originally from Nature has been helped by the hand of man, which has formed out of it an amphitheatre for spectators. Walls and other buildings have furnished the necessary passages and rooms. Right across, at the foot of the semicircular range of seats, the scene was built, and by this means the two rocks were joined together, and a most enormous work of nature and art combined.

Now, sitting down at the spot where formerly sat the uppermost spectators, you confess at once that never did any audience, in any theatre, have before it such a spectacle as you there behold. On the right, and on high rocks at the side, castles tower in the air-farther on the city lies below you; and although its buildings are all of modern date, still similar ones, no doubt, stood of old on the same site. After this the eye falls on the whole of the long ridge of Ætna, then on the left it catches a view of the sea-shore, as far as Catania, and even Syracuse, and then the wide and extensive view is closed by the immense smoking volcano, but not horribly, for the atmosphere, with its softening effect, makes it look more distant, and milder than it really is.

If now you turn from this view towards the passage running at the back of the spectators, you have on the left the whole wall of the rocks between which and the sea runs the road to Messina. And then again you behold vast groups of rocky ridges in the sea itself, with the coast of Calabria in the far distance, which only a fixed and attentive gaze can distinguish from the clouds which rise rapidly from it.

We descended towards the theatre, and tarried awhile among its ruins, on which an accomplished architect would do well to employ, at least on paper, his talent of restoration. After this I attempted to make a way for myself through the gardens to the city. But I soon learnt by experience what an impenetrable bulwark is formed by a hedge of agaves planted close together. You can see through their interlacing leaves, and you think, therefore, it will be easy to force a way through them; but the prickles on their leaves are very sensible obstacles. If you step on these colossal leaves, in the hope that they will bear you, they break off suddenly; and so, instead of getting out, you fall into the arms of the next plant. When, however, at last we had wound our way out of the labyrinth, we found but little to enjoy in the city; though from the neighbouring country we felt it impossible to part before sunset. Infinitely beautiful was it to observe this region, of which every point had its interest, gradually enveloped in darkness.

Below Taormina: on the Sea-shore,
Tuesday, May 8, 1787.

Kniep, whom, by good luck, I brought with me hither, cannot be praised enough for relieving me of a burden which would have been intolerable to me, and which goes directly counter to my nature. He has gone to sketch in detail the objects which yesterday he took a general survey of. He will have to point his pencil many a time, and I know not when he will have finished, I shall have it in my power to see all these sights again. At first I wished to ascend the height with him; but then, again, I was tempted to remain here; I sought a corner like the bird about to build its nest. In a sorry and neglected peasant's garden I have seated myself, on the trunk of an orange-tree, and lost myself in reveries. Orange-branches, on which a traveller can sit, sounds rather strangely; but seems quite natural when one knows that the orange-tree, left to nature, sends out at a little distance from the root, twigs, which, in time, become decided branches.

And so, thinking over again the plan of the "Nausicaa," I formed the idea of a dramatic concentration of the "Odyssey." I think the scheme is not impracticable, only it will be indispensable to keep clearly in view the difference of the Drama and the Epopée.

Kniep has come down, quite happy and delighted, and has brought back with him two large sheets of drawing-paper, covered with the clearest outlines. Both will contribute to preserve in my mind a perpetual memory of these glorious days.

It must not be left unrecorded, that on this shore, and beneath the clearest sky, we looked around us, from a little, balcony, and saw roses, and heard the nightingales. These we are told sing here during at least six months of the twelve.

From Memory.

The activity of the clever artist who accompanies me, and my own more desultory and feeble efforts, having now assured me the possession of well-selected sketches of the country and its most remarkable points (which, either in outline, or if I like, in well-finished paintings, will be mine for ever), I have been able to resign myself more entirely to an impulse which has been daily growing in strength. I have felt an irresistible impulse to animate the glorious scenes by which I am surrounded—the sea, the island, the heavens, with appropriate poetical beings, and here, in and out of this locality, to finish a composition in a tone and spirit such as I have not yet produced. The clear sky; the smell of the sea, the halo which merges, as it were, into one the sky, the headlands, and the sea—all these afforded nourishment to my purpose; and whilst I wandered in those beautiful gardens, between blossoming hedges of oleander, and through arbours of fruit-bearing orange, and citron-trees, and between other trees and shrubs, which were unknown to me, I felt the strange influence in the most agreeable way possible.

Sicily—Sketch of Nausicaa, a tragedy.

Convinced that for me there could be no better commentary on the "Odyssey" than even this very neighbourhood, I purchased a copy, and read it, after my own fashion, with incredible interest. But I was also excited by it to produce something of my own, which, strange as it seemed at the first look, became dearer and dearer, and at last took entire possession of me. For I entertained the idea of treating the story of Nausicaa as the subject of a tragedy.

It is impossible for me even to say what I should have been able to make of it, but the plan I had quite settled in my mind. The leading idea was to paint in Nausicaa, an amiable and excellent maiden who, wooed by many suitors, but conscious of no preference, coldly rejected all advances, who, however, falling in love with a remarkable stranger, suddenly alters her own conduct, and by an over-hasty avowal of her affection compromises herself; and consequently gives rise to a truly tragic situation. This simple fable might, I thought, be rendered highly interesting by an abundance of subordinate motives, and especially by the naval and insular character of the locality, and of the personages where and among whom the scene was laid, and by the peculiar tone it would thence assume.

The first act began with the game at ball. The unexpected acquaintance is made; the scruple to lead him herself into the city is already the harbinger of her love.

The second act unfolds the characters of the household of Alcinous, and of the suitors, and ends with the arrival of Ulysses.

The third is devoted entirely to exhibiting the greatness and merits of the new comer, and I hoped to be able in the course of the dialogue, (which was to bring out the history of his adventures), to produce a truly artistic and agreeable effect by representing the various ways in which this story was received by his several hearers. During the narrative, the passions were to be heightened, and Nausicaa's lively sympathy with the stranger to be thrown out more and more by conflicting feelings.

In the fourth act, Ulysses, (off the scene,) gives convincing proofs of his valour; while the women remain, and give full scope to their likings, their hopes, and all other tender emotions. The high favour in which the stranger stands with all, makes it impossible for Nausicaa to restrain her own feelings, and so she becomes irreparably compromised with her own people. Ulysses, who, partly innocent, partly to blame, is the cause of all this, now announces his intention to depart; and nothing remains for the unhappy Nausicaa, but in the fifth act to seek for an end of existence.

In this composition, there was nothing which I was not able by experience to paint after nature. Even while travelling—even in peril—to excite favourable feelings which, although they did not end tragically, might yet prove painful enough, and perhaps dangerous, and would, at all events, leave deep wounds behind—even the supposed accidents of describing, in lively colours, for the entertainment of others, objects observed at a great distance from home, travelling adventures and chances of life—to be looked upon by the young as a demigod, but by the more sedate as a talker of rhodomontade, and to meet now with unexpected favour, and now with unexpected rebuffs—all this caused me to feel so great an attachment to this plan, that in thinking of it, I dreamed away all the time of my stay at Palermo, and, indeed, of all the rest of my Sicilian tour. It was this that made me care little for all the inconvenience and discomfort I met with; for, on this classic ground, a poetic vein had taken possession of me, causing all that I saw, experienced, or observed, to be taken and regarded in a joyous mood.

After my usual habit—whether a good or a bad one—I wrote down little or nothing of the piece; but worked in my mind the most of it, with all the minutest detail. And there, in my mind, pushed out of thought by many subsequent distractions, it has remained until tills moment, when, however, I can recollect nothing but a very faint idea of it.

* * *

May 8, 1787. On the road to Messina.

High limestone rocks on the left. They become more deeply coloured as you advance, and form many beautiful caves. Presently there commences a sort of rock which may be called clay slate, or sand-stone (greywacke). In the brooks you now meet pebbles of granite. The yellow apples of the solanum, the red flowers of the oleander, give beauty to the landscape. The little stream of Nisi brings down with it mica-pebbles, as do also all the streams we afterwards came to.

* * *

Wednesday, May 9, 1787.

Beaten by a stormy east wind, we rode between the raging sea on the right, and the wall of rocks, from the top of which we were yesterday looking down; but this day we have been continually at war with the water. We had to cross innumerable brooks, of which the largest bears the honourable title of a river. However, these streams, as well as the gravel which they bring down with them, were easier to buffet with than the sea, which was raging violently, and at many places dashed right over the road against the rocks, which threw back the thick spray on the travellers. It was a glorious sight, and its rarity to us made us quite ready to put up with all its inconvenience.

At the same time there was no lack of objects for the mineralogical observer. Enormous masses of limestone, undermined by the wind and the waves, fall from time to time; the softer particles are worn away by the continual motion of the waves, while the harder substances imbedded in them are left behind; and so the whole strand is strewed with variegated flints verging on the hornstone, of which I selected and carried off many a specimen.

* * *

Messina, Thursday, May 10, 1787.

Sicily-The road to Messina.

And so at last we arrived in Messina, where, as we knew of no lodging, we made up our minds to pass the first night at the quarters of our vetturino, and then look out in the morning for a more comfortable habitation. In consequence of i his resolution, our first entrance gave us the terrible idea of entering a ruined city. For, during a whole quarter of an hour as we rode along, we passed ruin after ruin, before we reached the auberge, which, being the only new building that has sprung up in this quarter, opens to you from its first story window a view of nothing but a rugged waste of ruins. Beyond the circle of the stable yard not a living being of any kind was to be seen. During the night the stillness was frightful. The doors would neither bolt nor even close; there was no more provision here for the entertainment of human guests than at any other of the similar posting stations. However, we slept away very comfortably on a mattress which our vetturino took away from beneath the very body of our host.

Friday, May 11, 1787.

To-day we parted from our worthy muleteer, and a good largesse rewarded him for his attentive services. We parted very amicably, after he had first procured us a servant, to take us at once to the best inn in the place, and afterwards to show us whatever was at all remarkable in Messina. Our first host, in order that his wish to get rid of us might be gratified as quickly as possible, helped to carry our boxes and other packages to a pleasant lodging nearer to the inhabited portion of the city—that is to say, beyond the city itself. The following description will give some idea of it. The terrible calamity which visited Messina and swept away twelve thousand of its inhabitants, did not leave behind it a single dwelling for the thirty thousand who survived. Most of the houses were entirely thrown down; the cracked and shaking walls of the others made them quite unsafe to live in. On the extensive meads, therefore, to the north of Messina, a city of planks was hastily erected, of which any one will quickly form an idea who has ever seen the Römerberg at Frankfort during the fair, or has passed through the market-place at Leipzig; for all the retail houses and the workshops are open towards the street, and the chief business is carried on in front of them. Therefore, there are but few of the larger houses even that are particularly well closed against publicity. Thus, then, have they been living for three years, and the habits engendered by such booth-like, hut-like, and, indeed, tent-like dwellings, has had a decided influence on the character of the occupants. The horror caused by this unparalleled event, the dread of its recurrence, impels them with light-hearted cheerfulness to enjoy to the utmost the passing moment. A dreadful expectation of a fresh calamity was excited on 21st April—only twenty days ago, that is—by an earthquake, which again sensibly shook the ground. We were shown a small church where a multitude of people were crowded together at the very moment, and perceived the trembling. Some persons who were present at the time do not appear even yet to have recovered from their fright.

In seeking out and visiting these spots we were accompanied by a friendly consul, who spontaneously put himself to much trouble on our account—a kindness to be gratefully acknowledged in this wilderness more than in any other place. At the same time, having learned that we were soon about to leave, he informed us that a French merchantman was on the point of sailing for Naples. The news was doubly welcome, as the flag of France is a protection against the pirates.

We made our kind cicerone aware of our desire to examine the inside of one of the larger (though still one storied) huts, and to see their plain and extemporized economy. Just at this moment we were joined by an agreeable person, who presently described himself to be a teacher of French. After finishing our walk, the consul made known to him our wish to look at one of these buildings, and requested him to take us home with him and show us his.

We entered the hut, of which the sides and roof consisted alike of planks. The impression it left on the eye was exactly that of one of the booths in a fair, where wild beasts or other curiosities are exhibited. The timber work of the walls and the roof was quite open. A green curtain divided off the front room, which was not covered with deals, but the natural floor was left just as in a tent. There were some chairs and a table; but no other article of domestic furniture. The space was lighted from above by the openings which had been accidentally left in the roofing. We stood talking together for some time, while I contemplated the green curtain and the roof within, which was visible over it, when all of a sudden from the other side of the curtain two lovely girls' heads, black-eyed, and black-haired, peeped over full of curiosity, but vanished again as soon as they saw they were perceived. However, upon being asked for by the consul, after the lapse of just so much time as was necessary to adorn themselves, they came forward, and with their well dressed and neat little bodies crept before the green tapestry. From their questions we clearly perceived that they looked upon us as fabulous beings from another world, in which most amiable delusion our answers must have gone far to confirm them. The consul gave a merry description of our singular appearance: the conversation was so very agreeable, that we found it hard to part with them. It was not until we had got out of the door that it occurred to us that we had never seen the inner room, and had forgotten all about the construction of the house, being entirely taken up with its fair inhabitants.

Messina, Saturday, May 12, 1787.

Among other things we were told by the consul, that although it was not indispensably necessary, still it would be as well to pay our respects to the governor, a strange old man, who, by his humours and prejudices, might as readily injure as benefit us: that besides it always told in his (the consul's) favour if he was the means of introducing distinguished personages to the governor; and besides, no stranger arriving here can tell whether some time or other he may not somehow or other require the assistance of this personage. So to please my friend, I went with him.

As we entered the ante-chamber, we heard in the inner room a most horrible hubbub; a footman, with a very punch-like expression of countenance, whispered in the consul's ear:—"An ill day—a dangerous moment!" However we entered, and found the governor, a very old man, sitting at a table near the window, with his back turned towards us. Large piles of old discoloured letters were lying before him, from which, with the greatest sedateness, he went on cutting out the unwritten portion of the paper—thus giving pretty strong proofs of his love of economy. During this peaceful occupation, however, he was fearfully rating and cursing away at a respectable looking personage, who, to judge from his costume, was probably connected with Malta, and who, with great coolness and precision of manner, was defending himself, for which, however, he was afforded but little opportunity. Though thus rated and scolded, he yet with great self-possession endeavoured by appealing to his passport and to his well-known connections in Naples, to remove a suspicion which the governor, as it would appear, had formed against him as coming backwards and forwards without any apparent business. All this, however, was of no use: the governor went on cutting his old letters, and carefully separating the clean paper, and scolding all the while.

Sicily—Messina.

Besides ourselves there were about twelve other persons in the room, spectators of the bull-baiting, standing hovering in a very wide circle, and apparently envying us our proximity to the door, as a desirable position should the passionate old man seize his crutch, and strike away right and left. During this scene our good consul's face had lengthened considerably; for my part, my courage was kept up by the grimaces of a footman, who, though just outside the door, was close to me, and who, as often as I turned round, made the drollest gestures possible to appease my alarm, by indicating that all this did not matter much.

And indeed the awful affair was quickly brought to an end. The old man suddenly closed it with observing that there was nothing to prevent him clapping the Maltese in prison, and letting him cool his heels in a cell—

however, he would pass it over this time; he might stay in Messina the few days he had spoken of—but after that he must pack off, and never show his face there again. Very coolly, and without the slightest change of countenance, the object of suspicion took his leave, gracefully saluting the assembly, and ourselves in particular, as he passed through the crowd to get to the door. As the governor turned round fiercely, intending to add yet another menace, he caught sight of us, and immediately recovering himself, nodded to the consul, upon which he stepped forward to introduce me.

The governor was a person of very great age; his head bent forwards on his chest, while from beneath his grey shaggy brows, black sunken eyes cast forth stealthy glances. Now, however, he was quite a different personage, from what we had seen a few moments before. He begged me to be seated; and still uninterruptedly pursuing his occupation, asked me many questions, which I duly answered, and concluded by inviting me to dine with him as long as I should remain here. The consul, satisfied as well as myself, nay, even more satisfied, since he knew better than I did the danger we had escaped, made haste to descend the stairs; and, for my part, I had no desire ever again to approach the lion's den.

Messina, Sunday, May 13, 1787.

Waking this morning, we found ourselves in a much pleasanter apartment, and with the sun shining brightly, but still in poor afflicted Messina. Singularly unpleasant is the view of the so-called Palazzata, a crescent-shaped row of real palaces, which for nearly a quarter of a league encloses and marks out the roadstead. All were built of stone, and four stories high; of several the whole front, up to the cornice of the roof, is still standing, while others have been thrown down as low as the first, or second, or third story. So that this once splendid line of buildings exhibits at present with its many chasms and perforations, a strangely revolting appearance: for the blue heaven may be seen through almost every window. The interior apartments in all are utterly destined and fallen.

One cause of this singular phenomenon is the fact that the splendid architectural edifices erected by the rich, tempted their less wealthy neighbours to vie with them, in appearance at least, and to hide behind a new front of cut stone the old houses, which had been built of larger and smaller rubble-stones, kneaded together and consolidated with plenty of mortar. This joining, not much to be trusted at any time, was quickly loosened and dissolved by the terrible earthquake. The whole fell together. Among the many singular instances of wonderful preservation which occurred in this calamity, they tell the following. The owner of one of these houses had, exactly at the awful moment, entered the recess of a window, while the whole house fell together behind him; and there, suspended aloft, but safe, he calmly awaited the moment of his liberation from his airy prison. That this style of building, which was adopted in consequence of having no quarries in the neighbourhood, was the principal cause why the ruin of the city was so total as it was, is proved by the fact that the houses which were of a more solid masonry are still standing. The Jesuits' College and Church, which are solidly built of cut stone, are still standing uninjured, with their original substantial fabric unimpaired. But whatever may be the cause, the appearance of Messina is most oppressive, and reminds one of the times when the Sicani and Siculi abandoned this restless and treacherous district, to occupy the western coast of the island.

After passing the morning in viewing these ruins, we entered our inn to take a frugal meal, We were still sitting at table, feeling ourselves quite comfortable, when the consul's servant rushed breathless into the room, declaring that the governor had been looking for me all over the city—he had invited me to dinner, and yet I was absent. The consul earnestly intreated me to go immediately, whether I had or not dined—whether I had allowed the hour to pass through forgetfulness or design. I now felt, for the first time, how childish and silly it was to allow my joy at my first escape to banish all further recollection of the Cyclop's invitation. The servant did not allow me to loiter; his representations were most urgent and most direct to the point; if I did not go the consul would be in danger of suffering all that this fiery despot might chose to inflict upon him and his countrymen.

Messina—The Palazzata.

Whilst I was arranging my hair and dress, I took courage, and with a lighter heart followed, invoking Ulysses as my patron saint, and begging him to intercede in my behalf with Pallas Athène.

Arrived at the lion's den, I was conducted by a fine footman into a large dining-room, where about forty people were sitting at an oval table, without, however, a word being spoken. The place on the governor's right was unoccupied, and to it was I accordingly conducted.

Having saluted the host and his guests with a low bow, I took my seat by his side, excused my delay by the vast size of the city, and by the mistakes which the unusual way of reckoning the time had so often caused me to make. With a fiery look, he replied, that if a person visited foreign countries, he ought to make a point to learn its customs, and to guide his movements accordingly. To this I answered that such was invariably my endeavour, only I had found that, in a strange locality, and amidst totally new circumstances, one invariably fell at first, even with the very best intentions, into errors which might appear unpardonable, but for the kindness which readily accepted in excuse for them the plea of the fatigue of travelling, the distraction of new objects, the necessity of providing for one's bodily comforts, and, indeed, of preparing for one's further travels.

Hereupon he asked me how long I thought of remaining. I answered that I should like, if it were possible, to stay here for a considerable period, in order to have the opportunity of attesting, by my close attention to his orders and commands, my gratitude for the favour he had shewn me. After a pause he inquired what I had seen in Messina? I detailed to him my morning's occupation, with some remarks on what I had seen, adding that what most had struck me was the cleanliness and good order in the streets of this devastated city. And, in fact, it was highly admirable to observe how all the streets had been cleared by throwing the rubbish among the fallen fortifications, and by piling up the stones against the houses, by which means the middle of the streets had been made perfectly free and open for trade and traffic. And this gave me an opportunity to pay a well-deserved compliment to his excellency, by observing that all the Messinese thankfully acknowledged that they owed this convenience entirely to his care and forethought. "They acknowledge it, do they," he growled: "well, every one at first complained loudly enough of the hardship of being compelled to take his share of the necessary labour." I made some general remarks upon the wise intentions and lofty designs of government being only slowly understood and appreciated and on similar topics. He asked if I had seen the Church of the Jesuits, and when I said, No, he rejoined that he would cause it to be shown to me in all its splendour.

During this conversation, which was interrupted with a few pauses, the rest of the company, I observed, maintained a deep silence, scarcely moving except so far as was absolutely necessary in order to place the food in their mouths. And so, too, when the table was removed, and coffee was served, they stood up round the walls like so many wax dolls. I went up to the chaplain, who was to shew me the church, and began to thank him in advance for the trouble. However, he moved off, after humbly assuring me that the command of his excellency was in his eyes all sufficient. Upon this I turned to a young stranger who stood near, who, however, Frenchman as he was, did not seem to be at all at his ease; for he, too, seemed to be struck dumb and petrified, like the rest of the company, among whom I recognized many faces who had been anything but willing witnesses of yesterday's scene.

Messina—The Governor.

The governor moved to a distance; and after a little while, the chaplain observed to me that it was time to be going. I followed him; the rest of the company had silently one by one disappeared. He led me to the gate of the Jesuit's church, which rises in the air with all the splendour and really imposing effect of the architecture of these fathers. A porter came immediately towards us, and invited us to enter; but the priest held me back, observing that we must wait for the governor. The latter presently arrived in his carriage, and, stopping in the piazza, not far from the church, nodded to us to approach, whereupon all three advanced towards him. He gave the porter to understand that it was his command that he should not only shew me the church and all its parts, but should also narrate to me in full the histories of the several altars and chapels; and, moreover, that he should also open to me all the sacristies, and shew me their remarkable contents. I was a person to whom he was to show all honour, and who must have every cause on his return home to speak well and honourably of Messina. "Fail not," he then said, turning to me with as much of a smile as his features were capable of,—"Fail not as long as you are here to be at my dinner-table in good time—you shall always find a hearty welcome." I had scarcely time to make him a most respectful reply before the carriage moved on.

From this moment the chaplain became more cheerful, and we entered the church. The Castellan (for so we may well name him) of this fairy palace, so little suited to the worship of God, set to work to fulfil the duty so sharply enjoined on him, when Kniep and the consul rushed into the empty sanctuary, and gave vent to passionate expressions of their joy at seeing me again and at liberty, who, they had believed, would by this time have been in safe custody. They had sat in agonies until the roguish footman (whom probably the consul had well-feed) came and related with a hundred grimaces the issue of the affair; upon which a cheerful joy took possession of them, and they at once set out to seek me, as their informant had made known to them the governor's kind intentions with regard to the church, and thereby gave them a hope of finding me.

We now stood before the high altar, listening to the enumeration of the ancient rarities with which it was inlaid: pillars of lapis lazuli fluted, as it were, with bronzed and with gilded rods; pilasters and panellings after the Florentine fashion; gorgeous Sicilian agates in abundance, with bronze and gilding perpetually recurring and combining the whole together.

And now commenced a wondrous counterpointed *fugue*, Kniep and the consul dilating on the perplexities of the late incident, and the showman enumerating the costly articles of the well-preserved splendour, broke in alternately, both fully possessed with their subject. This afforded a twofold gratification; I became sensible how lucky was my escape, and at the same time had the pleasure of seeing the productions of the Sicilian mountains, on which, in their native state, I had already bestowed attention, here worked up and employed for architectural purposes.

My accurate acquaintance with the several elements of which this splendour was composed, helped me to discover that what was called lapis lazuli in these columns was probably nothing but calcara, though calcara of a more beautiful colour than I ever remember to have seen, and withal most incomparably pieced together. But even such as they are, these pillars are still most highly to be prized; for it is evident that an immense quantity of this material must have been collected before so many pieces of such beautiful and similar tints could be selected; and in the next place, considerable pains and labour must have been expended in cutting, splitting, and polishing the stone. But what task was ever too great for the industry of these fathers?

During my inspection of these rarities, the consul never ceased enlightening me on the danger with which I had been menaced. The governor, he said, not at all pleased that, on my very first introduction to him, I should have been a spectator of his violence towards the quasi Maltese, had resolved within himself to pay me especial attention, and with this view he had settled in his own mind a regular plan, which, however, had received a considerable check from my absence at the very moment in which it was first to be carried into effect. After waiting a long while, the despot at last sat down to dinner, without, however, been able to conceal his vexation and annoyance, so that the company were in dread lest they should witness a scene either on my arrival or on our rising from table.

Every now and then the sacristan managed to put in a word, opened the secret chambers, which are built in beautiful proportion, and elegantly not to say splendidly ornamented. In them were to be seen all the moveable furniture and costly utensils of the church still remaining, and these corresponded in shape and decoration with all the rest. Of the precious metals I observed nothing, and just as little of genuine works of art, whether ancient or modern.

Our mixed Italian-German *fugue* (for the good father and the sacristan chaunted in the former tongue, while Kniep and the consul responded in the latter) came to an end just as we were joined by an officer whom I remembered to have seen at the dinner-table. He belonged to the governor's suite. His appearance certainly calculated to excite anxiety, and not the less so as he offered to conduct me to the harbour, where he would take me to certain parts which generally were inaccessible to strangers. My friends looked at one another; however, I did not suffer myself to be deterred by their suspicions from going alone with him. After some talk about indifferent matters, I began to address him more familiarly, and confessed that during the dinner I had observed many of the silent party making friendly signs to me, and giving me to understand that I was not among mere strangers and men of the world, but among friends, and, indeed, brothers: and that I had, therefore, nothing to fear. I felt it a duty to thank him, and to request him to be the bearer of similar expressions of gratitude to the rest of the company. To all this he replied, that they had sought to calm any apprehensions I might have felt; because, well acquainted as they were with the character of their host, they were convinced that there was really no cause for alarm; for explosions like that with the Maltese were but very rare, and when they did happen, the worthy old man always blamed himself afterwards, and would for a long time keep a watch over his temper, and go on for a while in the calm and assured performance of his duty, until at last some unexpected rencontre would surprise and carry him away by a fresh outbreak of passion.

My valiant friend further added, that nothing was more desired by him and his companions than to bind themselves to me by a still closer tie, and therefore he begged that I would have the great kindness of letting them know where it might be done this evening, most conveniently to myself. I courteously declined the proffered honour, and begged him to humour a whim of mine, which made me wish to be looked upon during my travels merely as a man; if as such I could excite the confidence and sympathy of others, it would be most agreeable to me, and what I most wished,—but that many reasons forbade me to enter into other relations or connexions.

Convince him I could not,—for I did not venture to tell him what was really my motive. However, it struck me as remarkable, that under so despotic a government, these kind-hearted persons should have formed so excellent and so innocent an union for mutual protection, and for the benefit of strangers. I did not conceal from him the fact, that I was well aware of the ties subsisting between them and other German travellers, and expatiated at length on the praiseworthy objects they had in view; and so only caused him to feel still more surprise at my obstinacy. He tried every possible inducement to draw me out of my incognito—however, he did not succeed, partly because, having just escaped one danger, I was not inclined for any object whatever, to run into another; and partly because I was well aware that the views of these worthy islanders were so very different from my own, that any closer intimacy with them could lead neither to pleasure nor comfort.

On the other hand, I willingly spent a few hours with our well-wishing and active consul, who now enlightened us as to the scene with the Maltese. The latter was not really a mere adventurer,—still he was a restless person, who was never happy in one place. The governor, who was of a great family, and highly honored for his sincerity and habits of business, and was also greatly esteemed for his former important services, was, nevertheless, notorious for his illimitable self-will, his unbridled passion, and unbending obstinacy. Suspicious, both as an old man and a tyrant,—more anxious lest he should have, than convinced that he really had, enemies at court, he looked upon as spies, and hated all persons who, like this Maltese, were continually coming and going, without any ostensible business. This time the red cloak had crossed him, when, after a considerable period of quiet, it was necessary for him to give vent to his passion, in order to relieve his mind.

Written partly at Messina, and partly at Sea, Monday, May 4, 1787.

Both Kniep and myself awoke with the same feelings; both felt annoyed that we had allowed ourselves, under the first impression of disgust which the desolate appearance of Messina had excited, to form the hasty determination of leaving it with the French merchantman. The happy issue of my adventure with the governor, the acquaintance which I had formed with certain worthy individuals, and which it only remained for me to render more intimate, and a visit which I had paid to my banker, whose country-house was situated in a most delightful spot: all this afforded a prospect of our being able to spend most agreeably a still longer time in Messina. Kniep, quite taken up with two pretty little children, wished for nothing more than that the adverse wind, which in any other case would be disagreeable enough, might still last for some time. In the meanwhile, however, our position was disagreeable enough,—all must be packed up, and we ourselves be ready to start at a moment's warning.

Messina—Character of the Governor.

And so, at last, about mid-day the summons came; and we hastened on board, and found among the crowd collected on the shore our worthy consul, from whom we took our leave with many thanks. The sallow footman, also, pressed forward to receive his douceur—he was accordingly duly rewarded, and charged to mention to his master the fact of our departure, and to excuse our absence from dinner. "He who sails away is at once excused," exclaimed he; and then turning round with a very singular spring, quickly disappeared.

In the ship itself things looked very different from what they had done in the Neapolitan corvette. However, as we gradually stood off from the shore, we were quite taken up with the glorious view presented by the circular line of the Palazzata, the citadel, and by the mountains which rose behind the city. Calabria was on the other side. And then the wide prospect northwards and southwards over the strait,—a broad expanse indeed, but still shut in on both sides by a beautiful shore. While we were admiring these objects, one after another, our attention was diverted to a certain commotion in the water, at a tolerable distance on the left hand, and still nearer on the right, to a rock distinctly separate from the shore. They were Scylla and Charybdis. These remarkable objects, which in nature stand so wide apart, but which the poet has brought so close together, have furnished occasion to many to make grave complaints of the fabling of poetry. Such grumblers, however, do not duly consider that the imaginative faculty invariably depicts the objects it would represent as grand and impressive, with a few striking touches, rather than in fulness of detail, and that thereby it lends to the image more of character, solemnity, and dignity. A thousand times have I heard the complaint that the objects for a knowledge of which we are originally indebted to description, invariably disappoint us when we see them with our own eyes. The cause is, in every case, the same. Imagination and reality stand in the same relation to each other as poetry and prose do: the former invariably conceives of its objects as powerful and elevated, the latter loves to dilate and to expand them. A comparison of the landscape painters of the 16th century with those of our own day, will strikingly illustrate my meaning. A drawing of Iodocus Momper, by the side of one of Kniep's outlines, would at once make the contrast intelligible.

With such and similar discourses we contrived to amuse ourselves, since the coasts were not attractive enough, even for Kniep, notwithstanding his having prepared everything for sketching.

As to myself, however, I was again attacked with sea-sickness; but this time the unpleasant feeling was not relieved by separation and privacy, as it was on our passage over. However, the cabin was large enough to hold several persons, and there was no lack of good mattresses. I again resumed the horizontal position, in which I was diligently tended by Kniep, who administered to me plenty of red wine and good bread. In this position our Sicilian expedition presented itself to my mind in no very agreeable light. On the whole, we had really seen nothing but traces of the utterly vain struggle which the human race makes to maintain itself against the violence of Nature, against the malicious spite of Time, and against the rancour of its own unhappy divisions. The Carthaginians, the Greeks, the Romans, and the many other races which followed in succession, built and destroyed. Selinus lies methodically overthrown by art and skill; two thousand years have not sufficed to throw down the temples of Gergenti; a few hours, nay a few minutes were sufficient to overwhelm Catania and Messina. These sea-sick fancies, however, I did not allow to take possession of a mind tossed up and down on the waves of life.

At Sea, Tuesday, May 16, 1787.

My hope of having a quicker passage back to Naples, or at least of recovering sooner from my sea-sickness, has been disappointed. Several times I attempted, at Kniep's recommendation, to go up on deck; however all enjoyment of the varying beauty of the scene was denied me. Only one or two incidents had power to make me forget awhile my giddiness. The whole sky was overcast with a thin vapoury cloud, through which the sun (whose disk, however, was not discernible) illuminated the sea, which was of the most beautiful blue colour that ever was seen. A troop of dolphins accompanied the ship; swimming or leaping they managed to keep up with it. I could not help fancying that in the deep water, and at the distance, our floating edifice must have seemed to them a black point, and that they had hurried towards it as to a welcome piece of booty and consumption. However that may be, the sailors did not treat them as kind guides, but rather as enemies; one was hit with a harpoon, but not hauled on deck.

The voyage from Messina to Naples.

The wind continued unfavourable, and by continually tacking and manœuvring, we only just managed not to lose way. Our impatience at this only increased when some experienced persons among the passengers declared that neither the captain nor the steersman understood their business. The one might do very well as captain, and the other as a mariner——they were, however, not fit to be trusted with the lives of so many passengers and such a valuable freight.

I begged these otherwise most doughty personages to keep their fears to themselves. The number of the passengers was very great, and among them were several women and children of all ages; for every one had crowded on board the French merchantman, without a thought of any thing but of the protection which the white flag assured them from the pirates. I therefore represented to these parties that the expression of their distrust and anxiety would plunge in the greatest alarm those poor folk who had hitherto placed all their hopes of safety in the piece of uncoloured and unemblazoned linen.

And in reality, between sky and sea this white streamer, as a decided talisman, is singular enough. As parting friends greet each other with their white waving handkerchiefs, and so excite in their bosoms a mutual feeling—which nothing else could call forth—of love and affection divided for a while, so here in this simple flag the custom is consecrated. It is even as if one had fixed a handkerchief on the mast to proclaim to all the world, "Here comes a friend over the sea."

Revived from time to time with a little wine and bread, to the annoyance of the captain, who said that I ought to eat what was bargained for, I was able at last to sit on the deck, and to take part occasionally in the conversation. Kniep managed to cheer me, for he could not, this time by boasting of the excellent fare, excite my energy; on the contrary, he was obliged to extol my good luck in having no appetite.

Wednesday, April 15, 1787.

And thus mid-day passed without our being able, as we wished, to get into the Bay of Naples. On the contrary, we were continually driven more and more to the west, and our vessel, nearing the island of Capri, kept getting further from Cape Minerva. Every one was annoyed and impatient; we two, however, who could contemplate the world with a painter's eye, had enough to content us, when the setting sun presented for our enjoyment the most beautiful prospect that we had yet witnessed during our whole tour. Cape Minerva, with the mountains which abut on it, lay before our eyes in the brilliant colouring of sunset, while the rocks which stretched southwards from the headland, had already assumed a bluish tint. The whole coast, stretching from the Cape to Sorrento, was gloriously lit up. Vesuvius was visible; an immense cloud of smoke stood above it like a tower, and sent out a long streak southwards—the result, probably, of a violent eruption. On the left lay Capri, rising perpendicularly in the air; and by the help of the transparent blue halo, we were able distinctly to trace the forms of its rocky walls. Beneath a perfectly clear and cloudless sky glittered the calm, scarcely rippling sea, which at last, when the wind died away, lay before us exactly like a clear pool. We were enraptured with the sight. Kniep regretted that all the colours of art were inadequate to convey an idea of this harmony, and that not even the finest of English pencils would enable the most practised hand to give the delicacy of the outline. I, for my part, convinced that to possess even a far poorer memorial of the scene than this clever artist could produce, would greatly contribute to my future enjoyment, exhorted him to strain both his hand and eye for the last time. He allowed himself to be persuaded, and produced a most accurate drawing (which he afterwards coloured); and so bequeathed to me a proof, that to truly artistic powers of delineation, the impossible becomes the possible. With equally attentive eyes we watched the transition from evening to night. Capri now lay quite black before us, and, to our astonishment, the smoke of Vesuvius turned into flame, as, indeed, did the whole streak, which, the longer we observed it, became brighter and brighter; at last we saw a considerable region of the atmosphere, forming, as it were, the back ground of our natural picture, lit up-and, indeed, lightening.

The voyage from Messina to Naples.

We were so entirely occupied with these welcome scenes, that we did not notice the great danger we were in. However, the commotion among the passengers did not allow us to continue long in ignorance of it. Those who were better acquainted with maritime affairs than ourselves were bitterly reproaching the captain and his steersman. By their bungling, they said, they had not only missed the mouth of the strait, but they were very nigh losing the lives of all the passengers intrusted to them, cargo and all. We inquired into the grounds of these apprehensions, especially as we could not conceive how, during a perfect calm, there could be any cause for alarm. But it was this very calm that rendered these people so inconsolable. "We are," they said, "in the current which runs round the island, and which, by a slow but irresistible ground-swell, will draw us against the rugged rocks, where there is neither the slightest footing, nor the least cove to save ourselves by.

Made more attentive by these declarations, we contemplated our fate with horror. For, although the deepening night did not allow us to distinguish the approach of danger, still we observed that the ship, as it rolled and pitched, was gradually nearing the rocks, which grew darker and darker upon the eye, while a light evening glow was still playing on the water. Not the slightest movement was to be discerned in the air. Handkerchiefs and light ribbons were constantly being held up, but not the slightest indication of the much desired breath of wind was discernible. The tumult became every moment louder and wilder. The women with their children were on the deck praying, not indeed on their knees, for there was scarcely room for them to move, but lying close pressed one upon another. Every now and then, too, they would rate and scold the captain more harshly and more bitterly than the men, who were calmer, thinking over every chance of helping and saving the vessel. They reproached him with everything which, during the passage up to this point, had been borne with silence—the bad accommodation, the high passage money, the scanty bill of fare, his own manners—which, if not absolutely surly, were certainly forbidding enough. He would not give an account of his proceedings to any one; indeed, ever since the evening before he had maintained a most obstinate silence as to his plans, and what he was doing with his vessel. He and the steersman were called mere money-making adventurers, who having no knowledge at all of navigation, had managed to buy a packet with a mere view to profit, and now, by their incapacity and bungling, were on the point of losing all that had been intrusted to their care. The captain, however, maintained his usual silence under all these reproaches, and appeared to be giving all his thoughts to the chances of saving his ship. As for myself, since I had always felt a greater horror of anarchy than of death itself, I found it quite impossible to hold my tongue any longer. I went up to the noisy railers, and, addressed them with almost as much composure of mind as the rogues of Malsesine. I represented to them that, by their shrieking and bawling, they must confound both the ears and the brains of those on whom all at this moment depended for our safety, so that they could neither think nor communicate with one another. All that you have to do, I said, is to calm yourselves, and then to offer up a fervent prayer to the Mother of God, asking her to intercede with her blessed Son to do for you what He did for His Apostles when on the lake Tiberias. The waves broke over the boat while the Lord slept, but Who when, helpless and inconsolable, they awoke Him, commanded the winds to be still; and Who, if it is only His heavenly will, can even now command the winds to rise. These few words had the best effect possible. One of the men with whom I had previously had some conversation on moral and religious subjects, exclaimed, "*Ah, il Balarmé! Benedetto il Balarmé!*" and they actually began, as they were already prostrate on their knees, to go over their rosaries with more than usual fervour. They were able to do this with the greater calmness, as the sailors were now trying an expedient the object of which was, at any rate, apparent to every eye. The boat (which would not, however, hold more than six or eight men) was let down and fastened by a long rope to the ship, which, by dint of hard rowing, they hoped to be able to tow after them. And, indeed, it was thought that they did move it within the current, and hopes began to be entertained of soon seeing the vessel towed entirely out of it. But whether their efforts increased the counteraction of the current, or whatever it was, the boat with its crew at the end of the hawser was suddenly drawn in a kind of a bow towards the vessel, forming with the long rope a kind of bow—or just like the lash of a whip when the driver makes a blow with it. This plan, therefore, was soon given up. Prayer now began to alternate with weeping—for our state began to appear alarming indeed, when from the deck we could clearly distinguish the voices of the goatherds, (whose fires on the rocks we had long seen), crying to one another, "There is a vessel stranding below." They also said something else, but the sounds were unintelligible to me; those, however, who understood their patois, interpreted them as exclamations of joy, to think of the rich booty they would reap in the morning. Thus the doubt which we had entertained whether the ship was actually nearing the rocks, and in any immediate danger, was unfortunately too soon dispelled, and we saw the sailors preparing boat-poles and fenders, in order, should it come to the worst, to be ready to hold the vessel off the rocks—so long at least as their poles did not break, in which case all would be inevitably lost. The ship now rolled more violently than ever, and the breakers seemed to increase upon us. And my sickness returning upon me in the midst of it all, made me resolve to return to the cabin. Half stupefied, I threw myself down on my mattress, still with a somewhat pleasant feeling, which seemed to me to come over from the Sea of Tiberias, for the picture in Merian's Pictorial Bible kept floating before my mind's eye. And so it is: our moral impressions invariably prove strongest in those moments when we are most driven back upon ourselves. How long I lay in this sort of half stupor I know not, for I was awakened by a great noise overhead; I could distinctly make out that it was caused by great ropes being dragged along the deck, and this gave me a hope that they were going to make use of the sails. A little while after this Kniep hurried down into the cabin to tell me that we were out of danger, for a gentle breeze had sprung up; that all hands had just been at work in hoisting the sails, and that he himself had not hesitated to lend a hand. We were visibly getting clear off the rocks; and although not entirely out of the current, there was now a good hope of our being able to make way against it. All was now still again overhead, and soon several more of the passengers came below to announce the happy turn of affairs, and to lie down.

The voyage from Messina to Naples.

When on the fourth day of our voyage, I awoke early in the morning, I found myself quite fresh and well, just as I had been at the same period of the passage from Naples; so that on a longer voyage I may hope to get off free, after paying to the sea a three days' tribute of sickness.

From the deck I saw with no little delight the island of Capri, at a tolerable distance on our lee, and perceived that the vessel was holding such a course as afforded a hope of our being able ere long to enter the gulf, which, indeed, we very soon afterwards accomplished. And now, after passing a hard night, we had the satisfaction of seeing the same objects as had charmed us so greatly the evening before, in a reversed light. We soon left this dangerous insular rock far behind us. While yesterday we had admired the right hand coast from a distance, now we had straight before us the castle and the city, with Posilippo on the left, together with the tongues of land which run out into the sea towards Procida and Ischia. Everyone was on deck; foremost among them was a Greek priest, enthusiastic in the praises of his own dear East; but who, when the Neapolitans on board, who were rapturously greeting their glorious country, asked him what he thought of Naples, as compared with Constantinople? very pathetically replied, "*Anche questa è una città!*" (This, too, is a city.)

We reached the harbour just at the right time, when it was thronged with people. Scarcely were our trunks and the rest of our baggage unshipped and put on shore ere they were seized by two lusty porters, who, scarcely giving us time to say that we were going to put up at Moriconi's, ran off with the load as if with a prize, so that we had difficulty in keeping them in view as they darted through the crowded streets and bustling piazzas. Kniep kept his portfolio under his arm, and we consoled ourselves with thinking that the drawings at least were safe, should these porters, less honest than the poor Neapolitan devils, strip us of all that even the very breakers had spared.

END OF TRAVELS IN ITALY

.

Lightning Source UK Ltd.
Milton Keynes UK
UKHW010943281222
414514UK00004B/237

The natural son; a novel; in two volumes. Translated from the French of M. Diderot, ... Volume 2 of 2

Denis Diderot

PRINT EDITIONS

Eighteenth Century
Collections Online
Print Editions

Gale ECCO Print Editions

Relive history with *Eighteenth Century Collections Online*, now available in print for the independent historian and collector. This series includes the most significant English-language and foreign-language works printed in Great Britain during the eighteenth century, and is organized in seven different subject areas including literature and language; medicine, science, and technology; and religion and philosophy. The collection also includes thousands of important works from the Americas.

The eighteenth century has been called "The Age of Enlightenment." It was a period of rapid advance in print culture and publishing, in world exploration, and in the rapid growth of science and technology – all of which had a profound impact on the political and cultural landscape. At the end of the century the American Revolution, French Revolution and Industrial Revolution, perhaps three of the most significant events in modern history, set in motion developments that eventually dominated world political, economic, and social life.

In a groundbreaking effort, Gale initiated a revolution of its own: digitization of epic proportions to preserve these invaluable works in the largest online archive of its kind. Contributions from major world libraries constitute over 175,000 original printed works. Scanned images of the actual pages, rather than transcriptions, recreate the works *as they first appeared.*

Now for the first time, these high-quality digital scans of original works are available via print-on-demand, making them readily accessible to libraries, students, independent scholars, and readers of all ages.

For our initial release we have created seven robust collections to form one the world's most comprehensive catalogs of 18th century works.

Initial Gale ECCO Print Editions collections include:

History and Geography
Rich in titles on English life and social history, this collection spans the world as it was known to eighteenth-century historians and explorers. Titles include a wealth of travel accounts and diaries, histories of nations from throughout the world, and maps and charts of a world that was still being discovered. Students of the War of American Independence will find fascinating accounts from the British side of conflict.

Social Science

Delve into what it was like to live during the eighteenth century by reading the first-hand accounts of everyday people, including city dwellers and farmers, businessmen and bankers, artisans and merchants, artists and their patrons, politicians and their constituents. Original texts make the American, French, and Industrial revolutions vividly contemporary.

Medicine, Science and Technology

Medical theory and practice of the 1700s developed rapidly, as is evidenced by the extensive collection, which includes descriptions of diseases, their conditions, and treatments. Books on science and technology, agriculture, military technology, natural philosophy, even cookbooks, are all contained here.

Literature and Language

Western literary study flows out of eighteenth-century works by Alexander Pope, Daniel Defoe, Henry Fielding, Frances Burney, Denis Diderot, Johann Gottfried Herder, Johann Wolfgang von Goethe, and others. Experience the birth of the modern novel, or compare the development of language using dictionaries and grammar discourses.

Religion and Philosophy

The Age of Enlightenment profoundly enriched religious and philosophical understanding and continues to influence present-day thinking. Works collected here include masterpieces by David Hume, Immanuel Kant, and Jean-Jacques Rousseau, as well as religious sermons and moral debates on the issues of the day, such as the slave trade. The Age of Reason saw conflict between Protestantism and Catholicism transformed into one between faith and logic -- a debate that continues in the twenty-first century.

Law and Reference

This collection reveals the history of English common law and Empire law in a vastly changing world of British expansion. Dominating the legal field is the *Commentaries of the Law of England* by Sir William Blackstone, which first appeared in 1765. Reference works such as almanacs and catalogues continue to educate us by revealing the day-to-day workings of society.

Fine Arts

The eighteenth-century fascination with Greek and Roman antiquity followed the systematic excavation of the ruins at Pompeii and Herculaneum in southern Italy; and after 1750 a neoclassical style dominated all artistic fields. The titles here trace developments in mostly English-language works on painting, sculpture, architecture, music, theater, and other disciplines. Instructional works on musical instruments, catalogs of art objects, comic operas, and more are also included.

The BiblioLife Network

This project was made possible in part by the BiblioLife Network (BLN), a project aimed at addressing some of the huge challenges facing book preservationists around the world. The BLN includes libraries, library networks, archives, subject matter experts, online communities and library service providers. We believe every book ever published should be available as a high-quality print reproduction; printed on-demand anywhere in the world. This insures the ongoing accessibility of the content and helps generate sustainable revenue for the libraries and organizations that work to preserve these important materials.

The following book is in the "public domain" and represents an authentic reproduction of the text as printed by the original publisher. While we have attempted to accurately maintain the integrity of the original work, there are sometimes problems with the original work or the micro-film from which the books were digitized. This can result in minor errors in reproduction. Possible imperfections include missing and blurred pages, poor pictures, markings and other reproduction issues beyond our control. Because this work is culturally important, we have made it available as part of our commitment to protecting, preserving, and promoting the world's literature.

GUIDE TO FOLD-OUTS MAPS and OVERSIZED IMAGES

The book you are reading was digitized from microfilm captured over the past thirty to forty years. Years after the creation of the original microfilm, the book was converted to digital files and made available in an online database.

In an online database, page images do not need to conform to the size restrictions found in a printed book. When converting these images back into a printed bound book, the page sizes are standardized in ways that maintain the detail of the original. For large images, such as fold-out maps, the original page image is split into two or more pages

Guidelines used to determine how to split the page image follows:

• Some images are split vertically; large images require vertical and horizontal splits.
• For horizontal splits, the content is split left to right.
• For vertical splits, the content is split from top to bottom.
• For both vertical and horizontal splits, the image is processed from top left to bottom right.

THE

NATURAL SON;

A NOVEL,

IN TWO VOLUMES.

TRANSLATED FROM THE FRENCH OF

M. DIDEROT,

Author of the Nun, James the Fatalist, &c

VOL. II.

LONDON·

PRINTED FOR T. N. LONGMAN
PATER-NOSTER ROW

1799.

THE

NATURAL SON.

LETTER XXXIII.

Ah! where is my dear Dormeuille, my only confolation and fuppoit. In fpite of the diftance that feparates us, Ah! let your friendly affection folace my wearied heart, which unpitying Deftiny has again overpowered with a new and dieadful calamity. I am born to be mifeiable, and to become a toiment to all my fiiends. Are you

not

not already tired of my lamentations ?
And will not your friendſhip murmur
at being thus continually taxed, till you
can ſcarcely avoid ſhuddering with
horror, and weeping with compaſſion ?
As long as we continue ſurrounded by
proſperity and happineſs, 'tis natural
we ſhould be always beloved But,
alas ! the unfortunate have very few
friends Dormeuille, I do not include you in this cenſure No, I am
too well acquainted with your virtues

After my promiſe of writing on my
arrival, you will have felt much uneaſineſs at the length of time that has
elapſed, without receiving any intelligence of me. Would to God, my
dear friend, that negligence on my part
were the only cauſe of this deficiency
When you have read this letter,
you will know the new misfortune that
has occaſioned it. I will deſcribe
every

every incident of my journey to you
at length, for to your friendship they
cannot be uninteresting, and to me it
will afford some relief, to unbosom my
affliction

When I declared my last resolution
to you, I perceived how severely it
affected you, and I was therefore determined to spare you the pain of
parting It was a sacrifice that cost
me the greatest efforts, and, even at
the moment of my departure, I could
scarcely resist the impulse of my heart.
The very idea of seeing you no
more, seemed to rob me of every faculty. I felt throughout my frame a
kind of melancholy horror, which the
silent darkness of the night encreased.
I must have yielded to the desire of
embracing you once more, had not
George hurried me away.

I made him ride with me in the
carriage, the time being very short

that

that I should have it in my power to see him, and it being necessary to prepare his mind for his change of situation, and fortify him against the grief of losing for ever a master he loved You will easily imagine this separation afflicted me no less than him, but I concealed my sorrow, because I was certain he would never have consented to quit me, had he seen what was passing in my heart.

I forgot myself, however, for a moment, when speaking of the uneasiness I had caused him I was running over all the past events of my life, my infancy at Richard's, the happy illusion I there enjoyed, the innocent pleasures of that delightful age, which we ever recal with transport, my education at the house of my father's friend, the great care his affection bestowed on me, the loss I sustained by his death, the misfortunes that followed

loved that event, and the difcovery of
my birth which completed my mifery.
The recital of thefe circumftances,
which I felt a pleafure in prolonging,
melted me by degrees till I fhed a
deluge of tears.   The worthy George
participated my emotions, and frequently feizing my hands, preffed them
with tendernefs, and wept.

This affecting fight of my aged at-
tendant in tears, gave me the live eft
fenfation of grief, but it was a grief
mingled with a foothing thrill of pleafure

I endeavoured to confole him by
reprefenting the happy and peaceful
lot that awaited him in your houfe.
" My dear George," faid I, " we
are about to feparate for a very long
time, but you will have an excellent
mafter in my ftead.   The Count of
Dormeuille will love you as well, and
render you far more happy   In lieu

of having grief conftantly impreffed
upon his brow, his character is extremely amiable, and his fweetnefs of
temper, and gaiety of difpofition,
never vary. Every one loves him,
every thing around him breathes the
moft perfect contentment He is a
kind mafter, a good landlor¹, an affectionate fon, a zealous friend, and
a tender hufband With him you
will be happy, but with me your lot
would have been far from comfortable. Perhaps, foured by long continued misfortunes, I might become
tyrannical.—Perhaps I might become
the fcourge of your old age" George
anfwered, fmiling, " Oh¹ no, Sir,—
you become a bad mafter ? No, that
is impoffible. Your fault would rather be too much kindnefs, and too
eafily believing other men as fincere,
and as good as yourfelf. But that is
not the queftion——Do you then
imagine,

imagine, Sir," faid he, after a paufe, " that I could ever confent to leave you? Ah! Sir, you do not know George's heart. Quit you, and attach myfelf to another?—Oh! no, my heart can never change in that manner. Monfieur de Dormeuille has, doubtlefs, many virtues, fince you have chofen him for your friend, but had he a hundred times as many, it would be impoffible I could ferve him, if to do that I muft leave you Could he ever make me forget my good mafter? Could I expect to be happy and contented with him, when I muft give up the hope of ever feeing you more? No, Sir, my life would be very miferable—I fhould be quite inconfolable. I have ferved you, Sir, and loved you, ever fince you were born, for it was I who brought you every thing that was fent you at Richard's, and if I have feemed ig-

noiant

norant of many things, it was only
becaufe I faw you wifhed to conceal
them from me. I am refolved, Sir,
to end my life in your fervice I promifed the Marquis D'Offan never to
leave you, and now you are going to
live in a monaftery, I will go there
too. They will receive me as a fervant, and I want nothing more than
my board, for all my wifh is to live
with you. Perhaps I may be more
ufeful to you than any other perfon;
for who knows fo well the caufe of
your unhappinefs, and how to confole
you in your grief?

"Such, Sir, is my determination.
I concealed it from you hitherto, and
fuffered you to believe I would accept
the Count's kind offer, but it was
merely to avoid being counteracted
in my defign. Though you intended
to bequeath me 20,000 livres, you
fee I have not the leaft need of them;
but,

but, I have some very poor relations:
be so kind as to divide that sum
among them, and then, instead of one,
you will make ten persons happy "

Judge, my dear Dormeuille, of my
astonishment, and my gratitude, for
this proof of George's friendship.
" Ah '" said I, as I embraced him
with transport, " I should be less
miserable when consoled by your kind
offices "

I could not cease admiring his devotion to me, or telling him how
much I was pleased with it. How
sweet to my afflicted heart, were the
expressions of friendship and attachment of this worthy man ' They
seemed to afford me a healing balm,
my destiny appeared less shocking,
and I felt a gleam of consolation to
my grief. Surely, to know we are
beloved, is the most soothing delight that can warm the heart,

or heal the bosom of wounded sensibility.

Blind that I was! I was embracing
a phantom of hope, while I stood
on the edge of the precipice of
despair.

After some days travelling, I found
the carriage so fatiguing, that I determined to take my passage in a vessel
bound for Spain. At first the ocean
afforded me innumerable objects of
meditation, from which I experienced
the happiest effects. The sky was
serene, the sea tolerably smooth, and a
favourable wind wafted us with rapidity through the waves. The vast
uniformity of the surface, the hollow
and melancholy roar of the ocean, the
azure firmament it seemed to reflect,
and which formed a vault over all this
boundless desart, composed a sublime
and awful picture, which filled me
with a mixture of horror and veneration.

tion. Though I was affected by the general sadness that prevailed around me, this was attended with no heart-felt pang, and by leading me into pleasing reveries, it maintained that soothing tranquillity, which George's friendship had shed over my whole moral frame.

This tranquillity, the effect, per-haps, of the weak state of a mind al-most worn out by grief, continued till the evening preceding our arrival, when we had a total and sudden change of weather.

The sky was overcast with dark clouds, which, gathering by degrees, almost converted day into night The sea became high, a dreadful roar seemed to come from the land, and was re-e-choed from the rocks with increasing terror, accompanied by the most violent howlings. While the raging winds threatened our vessel with destruction,

the

the rigging was every moment breaking, the fails tearing, the waves rifing
mountain high, then fuddenly falling
with a deftructive crafh   Sometimes
our fhip was laid down by a fea, or
pitching and rolling with the utmoft
violence, fometimes carried up to the
clouds, then as fuddenly ingulphed
between the waves.

During this dreadful tempeft, every
one expected inftant deftruction   The
captain himfelf was unable to conceal
his uneafinefs, and it was eafy to difcover in his countenance and manner,
that little hope of fafety remained.
Sailors, officers, paffengers, every one
was in the greateft confternation,
every one was addreffing prayers and
vows to heaven.

Though your unfortunate friend,
alas! had little reafon to regret the
lofs of life, yet he felt feverely agitated
at the firft afpect of approaching
death,

death. I remember a moment, when
ftruck by a heavy fea, and believing
myfelf inevitably loft, I cried out with
anguifh, "Oh! my mother! Oh!
my friend! Muft I then no more
embrace you"

Yet, how can I reconcile this emotion, with the defign of which you
prevented the execution, or that of
quitting for ever, all that is dear to
me in life? My friend it is impoffible
to account for all the contradictions
of the human heart. Reafon itfelf
does not acquaint us with all its fecret
folds.

The next moment, however, I
made up my mind, and could have
contemplated the moft violent convul-
fions of nature, with cool and tranquil
admiration, had not the objects by
which I was furrounded, harrowed up
my very foul. Many were playing
to

to God for one day more, to take
their laſt farewel of their affectionate
wives, whom they had not ſeen for
more than five years.   Others im-
plored his mercy to their children,
who would now be deſtitute of ſupport   But what affected me moſt
tenderly was a girl about fifteen years
old, in whom I felt extremely inte-
reſted, not only on account of her
beauty, but ſtill more for her ſoftneſs
of manners, and her affectionate attention to her father, a venerable
old man of ſixty.   She held his
hand conſtartl; between her's, ſpoke
to him with the greateſt tender-
neſs, and endeavoured to give him
hopes of ſafety.   The old man wept
as he received the careſſes of his lovely
girl.   He had no hopes of living
to any remote period, ſhould he
eſcape the preſent danger, but the
idea that his young and beautiful
daughter

daughter would shortly be plunged in all the horrors of an untimely death, overpowered him with grief The fight of this old man, and this charming girl affected me severely. My eyes were constantly fixed upon them. I participated their sufferings, and when the cruel waves, that each moment deluged the deck, invaded this interesting group, I was petrified with the cold that affailed the father, and diftracted with the anguish that tore the bofom of the daughter. Though reduced to extreme debility, she used her utmoft efforts to wipe, to warm, and to confole her aged father. Alas! she was not long able to continue her tender cares. A heavy fea carried away the part of the veffel to which they held, and a moment afterwards I beheld them ftruggling with the waves, and dafhed againft the pointed rocks.

What

What a picture for the heart of fenfibility! It was a dreadful fight, which my nature could not fupport   As I turned from it with horror, another object almoft equally affected me. George was on his knees, with his hands joined, fervently ftretched towards heaven.   Each moment he pronounced my name with that of the fupreme difpofer of events, to whom he was praying for me.—Such complicated emotions of grief, and of defpair, bewildered my mind and exhaufted my ftrength.   I could neither complain nor weep   An awful depreffion paralyzed all my powers, and I could fcarcely extend my arms or cry out, " George! come my dear George, and embrace your mafter for the laft time."—He was advancing towards me, and ftretching out his hand, when, on a fudden, the veffel went in pieces with a horrid crafh, and men and

and women the worthy George, and the moſt unfortunate of men, all—all were ſwallowed up.

Oh! inexorable Nature, why, why is thy anger to me alone implacable? Why haſt thou re-animated me, after ſo many misfortunes? Why ha'ſt thou reſtored me to life, to give me a thouſand cruel deaths each day of my exiſtence?

From the moment I was plunged in the ſea, I loſt all ſenſation, and became inconſcious of every thing that happened during two days. When I firſt opened my eyes, I faintly diſcovered that I was in a cottage, ſtretched on a mean bed, and attended by a woman and two men. All my faculties were ſo diſordered, and ſo weakened, that I had no diſtinct ideas, and every object preſented itſ it to my mind diſtorted and confuſed. My firſt emotion was to call out "George, George,

George, is it you, George?" The
woman then approached my bed, and
said to me in Spanish, " My good
Sir, recollect yourself, and recal your
reason You are just saved from ship-
wreck, and brought to the cottage
of us poor people, and there is no
George here."   By degrees I seemed
to regain strength, and then perceived that neither of the two men
was George, as I had believed during
my delirium.   The one was a poor
Spanish peasant, the husband of the
woman, the other I instantly recollected to be one of the failors   When
he told me that we alone had escaped,
the idea that George was lost, struck
me with sudden horror.   Ah ! what a
cruel pang of grief I felt at this intelligence.   " George, then, is no
more," said I, " that worthy fellow,
who loved me so affectionately, and
so generously devoted his whole exiftence

iftence to my fervice! Dormeuille, I
was quite miferable   " I his George,
Sir," faid the failor, " whom you are
lamenting, well deferved your friendfhip. If you knew all"——" What
do you mean?" faid I,—" I fhould
grieve you too much, Sir," faid he.—
" No matter," replied I, with impatience, " finifh what you were about
to fay" Ah! Dormeuille, this laft
trait alone was wanting to increafe my
affliction Can you believe it?—But
you know that he loved me more than
he loved himfelf. That worthy, that
admirable fellow, pointed me out
to all the failors, an hour before we
were loft, and on his knees entreated them to do every thing in
their power to fave me, affuring them
they would be more richly recom-
penfed than they could imagine. In
fhort, my dear friend, animated by
the eloquence of his generous heart,

one of the failors followed me through the waves, among the other victims of the storm, and inatched me from the hand of death at the hazard of his own deftruction.

What attachment! what heroifm! In his laft moments when every man concenters all his faculties on his own prefervation, that virtuous fervant forgot his approaching fate, to think only of his mafter! Such fortitude is amazing! Great God! Now that he repofes in thy bofom—Ah! may thy juftice grant him all the felicity heaven can afford.

I continued feveral days with the good peafants, together with my deliverer, till I was completely re-eftablifhed. It would be impoffible to exprefs all I owe to their cares and attentions. I have given the failor a letter addreffed to you, which he will deliver in a month or two. I intreat

you

you to recompenfe him for his courage. As for myfelf, I have too little
reafon to be fond of life to be able to
appreciate his fervices Your friendfhip alone will affix to them all the
value that is due and do not, I entreat you, forget the poor Spanifh
peafants, who fo difintereftedly fhared
with me their black bread.

Such, my friend, is the narrative
of my voyage. It would acquaint
you, were you not already too well
convinced of it, under what hoftile
ftars I have the misfortune to be born.

What fufferings, what grief, what
cruel privations from my earlieft infancy ! There is not a wretch, not an
old man on the verge of the grave,
who has experienced fo much affliction, or fo difturbed the air with fighs,
or watered the path of life with fuch
bitter tears. Alas ! My faculties have
fuffered greatly from this continued depreffion,

preffion, and an infupportable languor
drags me to the grave. My dwelling
is ever marked by melancholy and
filence.

I am now in a monaftery of Car-
thufians, which I found near the cottage of my hofpitable peafants. The
peaceful life of thefe monks is fuited
to the temper of my foul, whofe chief
want is tranquillity and repofe. The
father abbé received me in a very
obliging manner. No doubt he read
my misfortunes in my countenance,
for I obferved him melt with compaffion as he looked at me. At firft
he objected to my youth, and, like a
wife man, whom long experience has
matured, he was defirous that, previous to taking the folemn oath, I
fhould become acquainted with the
full extent of the duties I was about
to contract. But neither the aufteri-
ties of a religious life, nor the fatigues
of

of conftant praying, could fhake my
refolution, and very fhortly an indiffoluble bond will unite me with thefe
Cenobites, without a hope of ever feeing you, my dear friend, nor of ever
feeing——

Oh! my friend, what dreadful
thoughts invade the happy lethargy
that foothed my misfortunes, and lulled
my heart to reft.—I am quite exhaufted.—Adieu, my deareft friend.

P S. I have added to this letter
the requifite particulars of George's
lofs, for the fatisfaction of his relations Go to thofe good people.
Carry them the fum I had intended
for that moft worthy man, and which
he gave up to them Tell them what
a virtuous relative they have loft, that
they may endeavour to refemble him.
Who would not wifh to poffefs a
mind like that of George?

Do

Do not omit to enquire concerning the family of Richard, and that of Mathurin, and most assiduously observe the minutest circumstance that may give you any information relative to the situation of my mother. Let your letters be full of these accounts. They will now be more interesting to me than ever.

Once more adieu, my dear Dormeuille 'Tis with regret that I finish this letter. I wish I could write to you for ever.

LETTER XXXIV

DORMEUILLE to his FRIEND.

THE history of your voyage has affected me extremely I could not

read

read it without the most mournful reflections on the injustice of that deftiny, which delights in tormenting,
with so much fury, the man most
worthy of unmixed happiness. After
the cruel privations you have ever suffered, you still possessed one voluntary
self-devoted companion, who was following you into your retirement, and
would have consoled you for all your
sufferings. Yet of this comfort you
are deprived by an unforeseen calamity.
Ah! how sincerely I regret that worthy servant, the good and virtuous
George, who loved his master with
so uncommon, so affecting an attachment. Yet, in spite of all his good
qualities, inexorable Death has swept
him away This event, while it re-
cals to my mind all the misfortunes
you have, in swift succession, experienced, convinces me more than ever,
that the good things of this world are

but

but weak and bending reeds, on which
we ought never to rely

My friend, the sufferings that op-
press you fall also upon me. Your
situation gives me the greatest pain.
You must, however, acknowledge that,
although so rudely handled by fortune,
you ought, in some measure, to blame
yourself for it. Why thus fly from
your friends, from true and sincere
friends, who were anxious to alleviate
your affliction, and offered you, with
their hearts, all the happiness they
could bestow? You feared disturbing
our tranquillity Unjust friend ! Is it
then possible for you to disturb the
happiness of those who love you, and
who even find delight in partici-
pating your sufferings? True friendship never flies from the aspect of mif-
fortune. You know how many substantial reasons I opposed, though in
vain, to your romantic ideas. I flatter

ter myself you are now convinced of your error, and that you regret the slighted offer I made you with so much sincerity In the dwelling of Friendship you would have found that frankness and constancy, those soothing sympathies of confidence and love, where the slightest glance speaks with an animated eloquence, which the pen must ever coldly pourtray. But these are fruitless wishes and superfluous regrets.

Notwithstanding the pain you give us, and which I believe I shall never forgive, I have devoted myself to every object that can interest your feelings. I shall give you an account of my proceedings, which I am convinced will afford you some consolation in your melancholy solitude.

In the first place, I gave the two children you called your play-fellows the little presents you desired. They received them with irexpressible joy

and

and fatisfaction, but they wanted very much to fee you again. and afked repeatedly where you were. When they found all their prayers and folicitations were in vain, they grew very impatient, and even ill-humoured, and cried bitterly all the time I ftaid   Though I promifed you fhould foon come and fee them, they were ferioufly angry with me, and would fcarcely fuffer me to fteal a kifs when I took my leave.   Their parents are very poor. I therefore gave them fome affiftance, and, by feveral legal fteps I took for them, have been fortunate enough to terminate a law-fuit, which has for many years been undermining their little fortune.

George's relations were the next objects of your bounty   They were in a ftate of wretchednefs, which is now fucceeded by joy and abundance. Accept, my dear friend, all the bleffings

fings thefe unfortunate people poured
forth upon your name　They affured
me, that every night they will addrefs
their prayers to heaven for your happinefs. God grant, their wifhes may
be fulfilled! Their change of fortune
affected me in a lively manner　They
could fcarcely believe their fudden
riches, and continually looked at each
other, as it were, to fee whether it
was a dream.

From thence I paid a vifit to Richard. Here my heart was affected
by new fcenes, though of a very different nature from the laft. Your
liberality and beneficence were unable to confole this family for the misfortune of lofing you for ever　That
idea made them miferable. They
were all in tears at once・Henry,
Richard, Margaret, Lewis, James,
Cecily, Blanche, and Annette　My
dear friend, thefe good people are

moſt affectionately fond of you   When
I gave them your flute and your pea-
ſant's working coat, they at firſt ſhewed
great pleaſure, but, at the recollection
of the ſcenes theſe objects recalled,
they again ſhed tears, though leſs bitterly than before.   They talked long
of your infancy, of the pleaſure you
ſeemed to enjoy in living with them,
and the friendſhip they had always
felt for you   " Alas '" ſaid Richard,
" why did the Marquis D'Oſſan take
him away ? With us he was happy,
but from the firſt moment he entered
into the world, he has only known
grief and misfortune.   Would it not
have been far better to have left him
in total ignorance of his birth ? He
would then have conſtantly regarded
us as his father and mother, his brothers and ſiſters, and we ſhould always have loved him as much as if he
were our own child."

The

The little Cecily is to be married in a month. How she grieved that you could not be at the wedding! I promised, however, to fill your place, though I could easily perceive, by her manner of thanking me, that it would by no means be the same thing. You perceive, my dear friend, how dear you are to this worthy family. Indeed I cannot wonder at it. Who-ever knows your value, must grant you the first place in his friendship and esteem.

After quitting Richard, what do you suppose was the next object of my attention? You will easily guess. How was it possible I should not de-sire to know your worthy mother, whom your letters have rendered so interesting to me, and whom you have made me love by every thing you have said of her? I had also another motive. I was certain it would not

be

be indifferent to her to receive certain intelligence of a fon fhe loves fo
tenderly, and fiom whom fhe had
been fepaiated in fo diftreffing a man-
nei. I hoped alfo by this ftep to
procure a fund of happinefs foi your
filial affection   All thefe motives induced me to fet out foi Cleimont.

But as I was unacquainted with
the Maiquis, how could I introduce
myfelf? This was a great embairafs-
ment to me.   At firft innumerable
difficulties prefented themfelves, till,
by long reflecting on them, a veiy
fimple means fuddenly occuried, which
I eventually employed.   I contiived
to ariive rather late at night, and then
prefented myfelf as a traveller who
had loft his road, begging hofpitality
for the night, and not doubting but
the politenefs of the inhabitants of the
caftle would prolong my ftay as much
as would anfwer my intention.   For-

tunately

tunately, the night was very bad and ftormy, and a moft heavy rain, which was fucceeded at intervals by a dreadful wind, rendered my fituation apparently very pitiable.

The Marquis was gone to ftay a couple of days at the town, and the Marchionefs being in bed, the fervants refufed to difturb her I entreated and fupplicated long in vain. At length an old houfe-keeper undertook to mention me to the Marchionefs, and her anfwer being favorable, I was received.

Figure to yourfelf how I was delighted, when fortune thus feconded my enterprize. Not a fingle obftacle now oppofed me, and I was fure of as long an interview as I could defire. Next morning I afked for liberty to return my acknowledgements in perfon to Madame de Clermont for the kind hofpitality fhe had afforded me.

C 5 She

She received my thanks with that en-
gaging modefty, and that goodnefs
of heart, you have fo often praifed,
and which appear to form the bafis of
her character She was alone What
a favorable opportunity ' Yet I dared
not reveal the fecret I came to declare. Having exhaufted all I had to
fay, I remained filent, and at a lofs
how to prolong my interview Her
prefence affected me unaccountably,
and the fear of fhocking her feelings,
and caufing fome unforefeen misfortune, by intelligence fo unexpected,
robbed me of the power of fpeech.
I am certain fhe obferved my em-
barraffment, for I perceived a fuffu-
fion on her cheek. At length I took
courage. As foon as fhe learnt my
pretended miftake of the road, and
the fubject of my journey, fhe fcreamed, and almoft fainted. Fortunately,
however, no one came, and fhe foon
partly

partly recovered from the effects of the surprize. I saw this tender and virtuous mother alternately change colour, grow pale, cast her eyes downwards, and weep She dared not either look at me, or utter a single word But as I expected this timidity, or rather disconfidence, I had brought with me all your letters relative to your history, which I shewed to her. Being then convinced that I was really your bosom friend, and acquainted with all your secrets, she granted me her confidence, and sought no longer to conceal her maternal tenderness and concern. What charming sensibility, what amiable sweetness she possesses! Ah! my friend, I thought myself thoroughly acquainted with her by your letters. But I have seen her, and find you had but imperfectly described her excellencies.

C 6

When

When her firſt emotions had ſub-
ſided, ſhe was very anxious to learn
the ſtate of your health, and particularly what had happened to you ſince
your cruel ſeparation. I anſwered all
her enquiries fully and accurately, excepting one *attempt*, which, as it would
have given her much pain, I ſtudi-
ouſly concealed. When ſhe heard of
the ſudden decline of your health, of
the effect her letter produced on your
ſenſibility, and the reſolution you had
formed in conſequence, to ſeparate
yourſelf for ever from the world ſhe
cried out, with the ſrongeſt emotion,
" My God, how wretched am I!"
All my endeavours to conſole her
were in vain, and even my promiſe
to keep up a conſtant correſpondence
with you, afforded her no relief. She
abandoned herſelf to all the bitterneſs
of ſorrow, and liſtened to nothing but
despair.

defpair Fortunately her children came in, and interrupted us. It was the hour of their firft vifit to wifh their kind mamma a good morning. When they appeared, fhe ftifled her tears and her grief, and careffed them with the moft tender fmiles Ah! how affecting a picture is a virtuous mother furrounded by a lovely off-fpring!

She prefently faid to them, in the fofteft voice, " Go, my dears, and leave me a little while." The three little cherubs then left us, and we re-fumed our converfation.

The impreffion fhe had juft re-ceived from the interruption feemed fo beneficial to her ruffled fpirits, that I endeavoured to continue its effect as long as poffible by the turn of my converfation And how could I better fucceed in this, than by re-lating to her all the virtues and per-fectios

fections of her unfortunate fon ? his
feeling and compaffionate heart, his
fweetnefs of difpofition, his amiable
manners, his knowledge, his talents,
and the good actions he continually
performed virtues for which every
one who knew him loved him ? She
liftened to me with the moft lively
intereft, and anfwered me in a tone
of voice peculiarly expreffive of maternal affection, " His virtues are
known to me, but thev only add new
motives of felf-accufation. Alas !
Can fuch a mind be a martvr to continual wretchednefs and mifery ?"

" You, fir," fhe refumed, after a
moment's paufe, " You, whom he
loves fo tenderly, and whom he has
fo much reafon to love, will furely
not abandon him His fenfibility,
which fo often mifleads him, requires
a wifer guide, and his affectionate
heart demands an object on which to
fix,

fix. This is the only happiness that remains to the unfortunate. May he find it in you. Too long oppressed by misfortune, he has no longer sufficient strength of mind to conduct himself alone. Support him when he totters, and receive his secret griefs in your sympathifing bosom. Continue always to love him, for he deserves your esteem. May your kind and soothing friendship afford him those consolations which his retirement demands; and may he never be deprived of that blessing. Abandoned to himself, grief would soon destroy him; but supported by a friend like you, he may yet taste a thousand pleasures which he might otherwise never know. Ah! Sir, I intreat you do not desert him. Above all, endeavour to inform me, as often as prudence will permit, of every thing that concerns

him,

him, but, for God's fake, let me not
heai of him by any one but yourfelf"

My anfwer to this difcourfe, procured me the moft affecting acknowledgements But, when I told her I
would change my refidence, to live
near her, and form an acquaintance
with the Marquis, in oider to fee her
moie frequently without myftery or
danger, fhe was agitated with the
moft lively emotions, and fcarcely
knew how to exprefs her gratitude.

I endeavoured to take advantage of
this ftate of her mind, to gain fome
intelligence regaiding your fifter, but
in va'n She entieated me never to
mention the fubject to her again.

Such was in part my converfation with your worthy mother, that
moft amiable and moft interefting of
women. As to her own condition,

it

it is as happy as it can be with a husband so little suited to her cha-racter. He treats her with that re-spect which her sex, and her uncom-mon virtues demand. His jealousy, of which he soon perceived the in-justice, did not continue long, for, the conduct of his faithful wife, is pure from every imputation, and she is universally respected and beloved. When virtue is constant and unerring, it triumphs over the feeble powers of suspicion and jealousy. Do you remember the fable of the young girl chaining a lion?—The allegory is fine, and its accuracy apparent. She now seems to have very little to com-plain of from her husband. He is not much with her, and passes the day, either in hunting, or in the town. During his absence she remains in undisturbed tranquillity with her chil-dren, which, to an affectionate mo-ther

ther, is the happieſt mode of employ-
ing her time. Shake off, then the
anxiety you felt for her, and taſting
the unmixed pleaſure of loving her
as ſhe deſerves, imagine you behold
her charming, her angelic form, conſtantly ſurrounded by her lovely off-
ſpring.

Her children often ſpeak of you,
and aſk why you never come and play
with them. You may eaſily imagine
theſe recollections are very pleaſing
to Madame de Clermont, and as her
huſband is never witneſs of their enquiries, ſhe ſeeks not to repreſs them,
but takes a pleaſure in continuing to
talk of you. Sometimes ſhe makes
her little girl play the air you were
ſo fond of, and to which you com-
poſed an accompaniment. On theſe
occaſions this worthy mother ſeems
to hear her little girl's voice, with additional fondneſs, and to recal, with
ſecret

fecret delight, all the careffes, all the little attentions her children received at your hands.

I fhould have continued longer to enjoy the fociety of a lady, who interefted me on fo many various accounts, had not decency obliged me to limit my ftay at Clermont to a fingle day. But I departed in the hope of returning more than once, when you will often become the fubject of our converfation. May this idea enable you to fupport an eternal flavery, on which I cannot reflect without horror.

Adieu, my dear friend, and be affured I will do all in my power, to realize the hopes of Madame de Clermont.

P. S. I did not forget Mathurin. His little family are all extremely happy, but I think he would be ftill happier, if you could now and then

come

come to fee him   Thefe good people regret you fincerely.   They have
not forgot that to you they owe their
life, and all the comforts they enjoy.

———————————

LETTER XXXV.

WHAT pleafure, my dear Dormeuille,
your letter has given me ! Ah ! how
often did I read it, and bedew it with
the tears of fenfibility and joy.   You
have, then performed the journey I
fo much wifhed   This inftance of
affiduity, is a new proof of your
friendfhip, whic far from being
difmayed at my griefs and misfortunes, only becomes more zealoufly
                                active,

active, and more tenderly affectionate.

You have feen my mother, and fhe
talked of me. Her expreffions of
kindnefs are very foothing to me,
but tell her to give herfelf no uneafinefs concerning my prefent condition Affure her I am not unhappy, and that the idea of having the
moft amiable, the moft virtuous of
mothers, will alone fuffice to make
me completely bleffed.

My dear Dormeuille, are you not
enchanted with this adorable mother ?
You muft acknowledge it is uncommon to find fo much beauty and intelligence, fo much genius and fweetnefs, united in one woman. There is
a certain indefcribable charm in every
thing fhe fays or does, which, as it
were, pervades her whole character,
and infpires every one with refpect
and love.

I can-

I cannot then be furprifed at the interest fhe excites in you, or the facrifice you are about to make to be her neighbour   I know I am in fome degree the caufe of your determination, and this idea delights me.   It would, if poffible, increafe my attachment to you.

You affure me that my mother is happy.   I fear you are flattering me ? How is it poffible, that defpicable Marquis fhould fo fuddenly have changed.   Can a regard to juftice ever influence a depraved heart ? No, the fact, I imagine, is, that his indifference induces him to leave the objects that furround him, quiet and undifturbed.

What you fay of the children, at once pleafes and affects me   I am very fond of thofe dear little creatures.   Faithful emblems of innocence and truth, their careffes may

be

be received with confidence, while those of men, alas! are too often perfidious.

Yes, I remember with transport, the moments I have passed with Madame de Clermont's children, sometimes joining in their innocent diversions, as if I had been their little playfellow, sometimes supplying the place of their mother, in the cultivation of the happy dispositions they have received from nature.

I joined in their amusement with a heart-felt interest, and was more attached to the objects they delighted in, than to my own pleasures. The strength of my affection was astonishing. Alas! I felt, without knowing it, the secret ties by which Nature had united us.

What delightful sensations they awakened in my bosom! When I beheld them so lovely and so gay,

when

when I faid to myfelf, "Thefe children then are happy," I participated
in the enjoyment which their ignorance of any other ftate feemed to
render fecure. Strangers to anxiety
and pain, they abandoned themfelves,
without referve, to that facred fentiment of joy and pleafure which commences with our earlieft wants, or,
rather, with exiftence itfelf.   We im-
bibe it with our milk, and it grows
ftronger by continually repofing on the
breaft of her who gave us life.   Ah!
Why muft fuch tranfporting thoughts
be mingled with fo many bitter forrows and vexations?

Her reflections regarding whatever
may render my future deftiny more
happy, are judicious, and natural to a
mind which is conftantly feeking to
benefit every one who has the good
fortune to know her. She feems to
be well acquainted with my heart, for
                                    fhe

she speaks of your friendship as one of my most lively enjoyments. Yes, Dormeuille, my thoughts are ever occupied with you, and you are a principal object in all my reveries. Your image constantly accompanies me, and often consoles me in my afflictions. I often trace back the time to the commencement of our friendship, and recal the pleasure we both enjoyed in communicating to each other our most secret thoughts. I remember our mutual hints and advice relative to our various pursuits and literary studies, given with such disinterested enthusiasm, and received with such pure satisfaction, the eagerness with which we quitted our companions to be together and enjoy each other's company, because we only found in each other that harmony of sentiment, that unison of character, which alone forms real friendships,

and

and proves to mankind there is no
true felicity but in the union of
the heart. Imagination revives our
difputes relative to the arts and fciences, which you difcuffed with fo
much genius and candor. I renew our
ruftic walks and the facred enthufiafm that animated us when contemplating the works of nature. Thefe
fweet remembrances often bid the tear
of pleafure trickle down my cheek.
Who would imagine that, imprifoned
in a folitary chamber, where every
thing wears the afpect of melancholy
fadnefs, I fhould fometimes tafte the
moft exquifite enjoyments? No, Dormeuille, there is no prifon fo dark
and gloomy that friendfhip cannot illuminate, no condition fo miferable,
on which her confolations cannot fhed
a healing balm.

LET-

LETTER XXXVI

Che più d'un giorno è la vita mortale,
Nubilo, breve, freddo, e pien di noia;
Che più bella parei, ma nulla vale?

What else is life but winter's dismal day?
  How short, how clouded, cold, and full of
      grief,
And tho' at first some joys it may display,
  We soon but pant for Death's sad last relief

I AM extremely grateful for your
kind folicitudes concerning my fituation: but if your fenfibility gave
them birth, your reafon fhould have
diffipated them, and have led you to
difcover, in my filence, grounds rather of tranquillity than of fear. I
have as yet faid nothing of my religious mode of life. Is not this a
fufficient proof that, inftead of having
the effect you attribute to it, I have

D 2   thence

thence experienced no painful impressions? In fact, it has occupied my
mind but little   for alas! I have
spent more time with my friends than
in the discharge of my newly-con-
tracted duties   How then, my dear
Dormeuille, could you, who are so
well acquainted with my character,
imagine I was tormented by secret
pains, caused by repentance? Naturally frank and communicative, my
heart has too much pleasure in declaring to you every feeling it expe-
riences, to be capable of concealment.
Do you not know how incapable I
am of disguising my sentiments?
When I am unhappy, you have observed a thousand times that every
thing takes the impression of my sufferings, even my very smile of pleasure. My pen would then in vain
attempt to express sentiments of tranquillity and happiness, and the gayest
                                        I could

I could present would, in spite of my endeavours, assume a gloomy air of sadness and of mourning.

Be assured then, my dear friend, the bonds I have voluntarily received afford me no cause of affliction. On the contrary, I find in these peaceful retreats a thousand consolations to my sorrows My mind grows stronger in the bosom of nature, and my heart indulges in uninterrupted reflections on those I love and esteem.

I confess, however, that when I first entered my cell I experienced a kind of cruel shuddering. The recollection of my misfortunes suddenly returned, and I wept and sighed bitterly at my unhappy lot—But soon your letters administered the balm of consolation, and I felt how much the sorrow of having lost my friend might be softened by the sweet remem-

D 3

brances he had impreſſed upon my heart

Having thus reccovered the exerciſe of my reaſon ſufficiently to view objects in their true colours, my condition began to appear a ſource of felicity for every wiſe man, and of conſolation for the unfortunate. In fact, what more can be deſired than a life of purity and frugality, where, freed from the ſtorms of ambition and the diſtractions of vanity, we may enjoy, beneath the primitive cloathing of the patriarchs, their ancient innocence and their uninterrupted happineſs?

I do not view this condition with a religious eye, for every virtuous man will ever be worthy the favors of heaven. But I diſcover in it every thing that can aſſiſt the practice of ſound philoſophy, every thing that

can

can unfold and preserve the moſt important virtues. In the world, we are
carried away, in ſpite of ourſelves,
by innumerable corruptions, whereas
here we behold nature pure and uncontaminated. Removed from luxury
and intemperance, which are the moſt
dangerous ſources of vice, we may
eaſily ſatisfy our few wants, and thus
circumſcribed within ourſelves, and
freed from the ſolicitations of deſire,
what impure ideas can the mind ever
be tempted to indulge? Each vice
would periſh of itſelf in ſolitude, were
it poſſible it could find admiſſion
there. Every thing that ſurrounds
the individual gives ſtrength to the
love of virtue and to every thing that
can add true dignity to man, and, by
teaching him to think, ſhows how
many inexhauſtible pleaſures lie hidden in the ſecret receſſes of the ſoul.
The man who knows how to live ab-

ſolutely

folutely alone, and totally deftitute of all communication with his fpecies, would be perfect. He would know no privation, and, like the Grecian fage, he might fay, " I carry all I have within me "

Yet I defire not this perfection. I prefer even the torments I fuffer to the greateft pleafures, that indifference affords. Friendfhip is my only good. Alas! I only preferve her bleffings moiftened with tears, and the more fhe forces me to weep, the more I love and cherifh her delights.

LETTER XXXVII

Oh ' My friend, how unaccountable is the human heart! Of all the wonders, the world exhibits, this is the

moft

moſt aſtoniſhing. How it changes
from one moment to another! The
fluttering butterfly cannot be more in-
conſtant—a ſhrivelled leaf is leſs the
ſport of the ruſtling winds

But what means this preamble?
you will ſay My friend, you will
not eaſily imagine. During the interval of more than a month, that
has elapſed ſince you heard from me,
what ſtrange events have taken place!
Liſten to my tale, and compaſſionate
the moſt unfortunate of mankind.

I fondly imagined I had at laſt
found, in this tranquil retreat, that
peace, I had ſo long ſought in vain.
No longer uneaſy concerning the fate
of my mother, and happy in a con-
templative life, where I might give a
free looſe to my thoughts, and collect all the grand truths of nature, I
often ſaid to myſelf, " This alone is
true happineſs," and I purſued its plea-
D 5   ſures

fures without referve. In the intervals between the hours of prayer I retired to my cell, and abandoned myfelf to the reveries, you know my habit
of indulging.   What a crowd of ideas
fucceffively filled my mind, paffing
and repaffing with extreme rapidity,
always in ftrange diforder and confufion.   Made up of the recollection of
all I had ever done or thought, the
beginning and the end often exchanged
places, yet all was interefting.   'Twas
a paftime that afforded me a real delight.

I was fond alfo of recollecting the
objects of my early ftudies   Though
not poffeffed of a fingle book, the fea
having fwallowed up every thing I
poffeffed, yet I have fcarce loft any
part of what I have ever learnt. Thus
I felt the advantage of a good education, and the importance of reading
few and well-chofen works.   A rapid

and

and extensive perusal of books often
fatigues the mind, without rendering
it productive, whereas a well-selected
course of study, accompanied with
much reflection, unfolds the intellect
naturally and without effort, and renders it rich and fertile, almost without intending it.   What a pleasure it
was to me to run over in my mind
my Homer, my Virgil, my Plutarch,
and the charming Rousseau! I always
seemed to have them with me, and
to be actually conversing with those
great men   Yet I recurred most frequently to Rousseau, because, in his
sublime and charming thoughts, I
found that harmony with nature, which
evinces a purity of mind, and that amiable philosophy, which, laying down
the truth with a union of strength and
sweetness in apparently unstudied language, at once instructs and fascinates
the heart.

Such

Such was the manner in which I
paffed my days I was not, as you
perceive, deftitute of pleafure, and
I was able to tafte fufficiently of
variety, to continue all its attrac-
t've delights. As you love to hear
the minuteft particulars that concern
your friend, I fhall not omit any thing
that can intereft you.

One day in every week we have
liberty to walk in a wood fituated
behind the monaftery, where we
are all allowed to converfe together. In lieu of joining the other
friars, I generally walked alone, and
feated myfelf in a grotto, formed by
the hand of nature, in a large mafs of
grey rock, fituated in the fartheft re-
cefles of the wood, and forming the
limits of the territories belonging to
this community. The picturefque
form and appearance of this grotto,
and the beautiful manner in which it

is ornamented within, were particularly pleasing to me. Shells of every form, disposed without order or regularity, are bordered with a beautiful moss, whose verdure add new lustre to their varying hues. Pyrites and Stalactites, in every variety of form, embellish this peaceful retreat with their brilliant chrystallisations, and presents innumerable objects of meditation and of pleasure. A luxury of delight almost inebriated me to extasy, as I reposed in this favorite grotto, reclining on its mossy floor, and indulging freely in my reveries, while listening to the melancholy murmurs of a rill that filters through the roof, and divides into innumerable chrystals all the variegated productions that smiled around me.

My custom of repairing to this spot had attached me to it, and none but myself ever visited it. My soul seemed

ed as it were to reside there, and I
regarded it as my peculiar property.
Every thing I there beheld consti-
tuted my treasure When I perceived a new plant spring up, I watered it with care, and rejoiced at
seeing my little wealth increase If I
discovered a nest of birds in the foliage of a neighbouring bush, or in a
hollow among the rock I protected
them against birds of prey, by concealing them with branches of trees.
I carried bread for the young, and
watched their growth, and my pleasure encreased as they advanced.
They were new companions for the
poor solitary inhabitant of cell, and
finding in my little domain, liberty,
abundance, and hospitality, they continued to be my guests,

" Nor winged their airy flight away "

No sovereign ever contemplated
his boundless territories with so pure
a plea-

a pleafure, fo fweet a delight, as that with which I viewed my plants, my infects, and my birds

Alas! why was I not content with this unmixed happinefs, the moft folid blefling, Nature can afford to man? A foolifh wifh has deprived me of it, and I have loft it, perhaps for ever.

You cannot, my dear Dormeuille, forefee what is to follow all this long defcription. I weary your patience, but I fear to incur your cenfure, and I am defirous to delay its feverity as long as poffible What will my friend fay to my weaknefs? I tremble to anticipate your reply —No matter —we ought always to fhew ourfelves fuch as we really are Franknefs is the firft virtue in the code of friend-fhip.

Walking one day in the neigh-bourhood of my grotto, and contem-plating

plating the beautiful rural cottages, and
country houses around, I found my
view limited to the eastward by the
rocks that terminated the wood. I
climbed them with difficulty, and at
length gained their summit, where I
beheld, in all its extent, the finest
prospect the eye of man can behold.
Smiling and luxuriant meadows extended to the base of the steep and
distant mountains, whose frowning
aspect formed an awful contrast to the
plain   A range of rising grounds
spangled beautifully with field flowers,
skirted the gloomy forests, and fertile
pastures, and innumerable villages
were dispersed around, at small distances from each other, the whole
terminating with a view of the sea.
whose waves chased each other with
melancholy murmurs to the shore

But the dell at the bottom of the
valley pleased me most, because more
within

within the reach of the eye. Great
maffes fcarcely admit more than a
general glance at their wild and favage
magnificence, while the fcenery of a
home profpect, folicits minuter examination, and attaches the heart by the
interefting pictures it exhibits. My
eye repofed with delight on the rich
and beautiful verdure, and the flocks
that were feeding in tranquillity in the
extenfive paftures, watered by rivulets
of pure and liquid chryftal These
ftreamlets fkirted with their meanders
the neighbouring hills, and foftly
murmuring along their ftony bed,
among interweaving branches, or
filently gliding along the heath, united
in a vaft lake, in the midft of which
is a fmall ifland crowned with a
rich clufter of trees, prefenting to
the eve, all the delights of fhade and
verdure. A little farther is a garden
richly

richly stocked with fruit trees, and a
house of simple and ancient architecture. By the tower, at one of the
extremities, I imagined it to be a convent, and was confirmed in this opinion, by observing several nuns,
dressed in black, come out into the
the garden. The similarity of their
condition to my own, rendered them
extremely interesting to me, and my
eye pursued them through the various
walks, while innumerable reflections
and conjectures on their motives for
having thus quitted the world, their
parents, and their friends for ever,
pressed upon my mind. Presently
after I saw a crowd of young women,
of whose most charming figures I could
only snatch a hasty glance, as the rapidity and variety of their motions, did
not admit of my fixing my eyes long
on any in particular Some of them
were

were gathering flowers, fome amufed themfelves by purfuing their companions through innumerable winding paths, and fome went arm in arm, dancing and finging, while others walked gravely along, and feemed engaged in ferious converfation I viewed with inexpreffible delight, this moving picture of youthful gayety, which exhibited the moft uncorrupted innocence in all its purity. But fuddenly another train of ideas threw a gloom over my mind. This youthful band, faid I, but refembles an aviary of birds, fluttering and murmuring at the flavery that enchains them Ah! how they feem to delight in a momentary interval of liberty, whofe rarity increafes its value! Its duration is fhort, and it is limited by a fevere and inexorable regulation. Can pleafure be thus obfe-

obsequious? can she come and go at
the command of monkish auste-
rity?

One of the young people now
separated from her companions, and
entered the orchard that lies between
the garden and the hill on which I
was placed. She took a few turns,
and then sat down at the foot of a
tree. Her pensive air, her noble
and modest mein, attracted my attention, and engrossed my thoughts
from every other object. Why, said
I, does she thus prefer solitude to the
society of her young companions?
what secret grief preys upon her
mind?—I was lost in a train of reveries, and one gloomy idea was succeeded by another of still darker horror. I immediately began to imagine this young creature was the most
unfortunate of women, though ten

minutes had not elapfed fince I firft
beheld her, and all I knew of her was
her figure and her drefs, for as fhe
fat nearly fronting the convent, I had
not yet become acquainted with her
features Do not wonder, my dear
friend, at what I tell you. The firft
want of a tender and feeling heart,
when overwhelmed with misfortune,
is not to meet the fmiles of the
happy, but to weep with thofe who
are as wretched as ourfelves, becaufe
the melancholy ideas they infpire,
enable our hearts to expand with fympathy. We even create imaginary
diftrefs, when we cannot find the
children of misfortune around us.
The fight of pleafure fhuts up the
avenues of fenfibility, and encreafes
our fufferings, but the profpect of
grief dilates and confoles our hearts.
Such was, doubtlefs the caufe of my
reveries, but their impreffion was fo
ftrong,

ftrong, that I could not reprefs my defire of feeing the countenance of her who had already excited fo lively an interefl in my heart. This, however, appeared very difficult to accomplifh, as the orchard was furrounded by a very high wall, and there were no other means to fee over it, than ftanding on the rocks where I was fituated. Every where elfe the ground was flat and low. However, I changed my fiuation, and wandered from one part of the wall to another, purfuing it through all its windings, till at length I perceived a fmall mount on which I placed myfelf, exactly oppofite to the young perfon I wifhed to obferve, and at fo fmall a diftance from the tree where fhe fat, that had fhe fpoken I mufl infallibly have heard her voice. Her face was concealed behind an impenetrable veil, and I long waited in expectation

tion of fome favourable moment She
was reading with fuch profound attention, that fhe did not even make the
flighteft motion, till the bell founded
for us to retire, and the Father Abbé,
who paffed near me, faid to me,
" Brother, it is time to go in " I
obeyed, though not without a fecret
murmur at the inviolable order.

When I had re-entered my cell, all
my thoughts were engroffed by this
beautiful votary of folitude.—But, how
do you know fhe was beautiful, you
will fay ?—Dormeuille, you know my
fertile imagination Yes, her figure
was conftantly before me, contemplating a book, with the moft undeviating attention. My curious eye
ftill feemed to run over all the charms
of her perfon, her robe of perfect
white, which exhibited fo much tafte
and fimplicity, her beautiful hand, her
elegant fhape, her noble and gracious
mien,

mien—but, as my imagination could
not be reftrained by the veil, it ventured to raife it, and difcovered the
moft beautiful countenance, and fweeteft features, the moft amiable of her fex
could poffefs.   Could this idea be an
error? Was it probable any thing common fhould be found among fo many
perfections? Such contradictions, 'tis
true, fometimes exift, but they are extremely rare.   The laws of fymmetry
and harmony, are preferved in all the
works of Nature, particularly in regard to women, in whom every fpecies of beauty, and of deformity, is
claffed in the moft diftinct manner.   It
appears to me, that there is a mode of
exiftence peculiar to each caft of countenance.   A fine woman does not
drefs, or fpeak, or move, fhe does not
even ftick a pin, or tie a ribband like
other women   The confcioufnefs of
beauty, or that of wanting it, gives
                              a cha-

a character to each action of her life.

But I pursued this train of consequences still farther. Her unremitting attention to her book, led me to conclude its subject was far from trifling, and I thence inferred, that her mind and understanding were of a superior rank, and that no frivolity could harbour in her bosom. I pleased myself by arguing, that with these qualities, sweetness of temper, and the most amiable sensibility, were congenial.

You will laugh at my chimeras. Had they never been realized, I would also laugh at them.—But, let me finish this dreadful confession.

Every thing I observed in this young lady, awakened a tender interest in my bosom. She even caused in me a more than ordinary dejection, because, added to my own af-

flictions, I felt thofe by which I imagined her oppreffed Perhaps, faid
I, fhe has but lately entered the convent, and this reclufe and monotonous
life, is ill-fuited to her active mind.
To live continually under the direction of an auftere governefs, and pafs
her days with thofe, whofe characters
do not harmonife with her own, and
muft appear at beft but frivolous—
To do every thing precifely according to the prefcribed rules of the order, and not to tafte of pure liberty,
even at the moments devoted to its
enjoyment, can all this compenfate
for perpetual banifhment from her
paternal roof? Ah! no. She de-
plores the lofs of a kind father, and
a tender mother. Perhaps, fhe de-
plores fome friend of her early infancy, whom fhe faw with each returning day, and in whofe bofom fhe
repofed

repofed all her feelings, or a brother, whofe fondnefs for fo lovely, fo beautiful a fifter, was proved by all the attentions of the moft affectionate attachment Unfeeling parents! How can you thus confent to facrifice all that fhould be dear to you, to futile prejudices, a thoufand times more poifonous to the heart, than they can ever be ufeful to the mind. Reflect, that whatever your children learn from ftrangers, without your aid, but weakens thofe fentiments of which Nature has formed the bonds of family affection, and without which neither virtue nor happinefs can exift.

I fhould never have done, were I to relate all the reveries that fprang from thefe ideas. Such is the wandering and excurfive humour of the folitary mind, that I purfued them

E 2 anew

anew each day, and at night they often interrupted my slumbers. The more I reflected, the more I was convinced of their truth, nor could my self-love admit a belief, that an object so enchanting, was not worthy the love and esteem of the whole world.

In the mean while I was anxious again to behold my female philosopher, and ascertain the truth of my conjectures. But for this I was obliged to wait a week, Oh! how long and tedious this period appeared! At length, however, it elapsed, and I hastened to my observatory, almost at the same hour as before. After waiting a few minutes, she again appeared in the garden, walked directly to the orchard, and returning to her former place, at the foot of the tree, resumed the same employment. She was veiled as before, and, though this cir-

circumstance afflicted me much, the
second view of her excited in me a
moft tender interest, and agitated me
with ftrange emotions I watched
with unremitting attention, every motion fhe made, and when, for a moment, fhe ceafed to read, and feeming
to reflect on the contents of her book,
looked towards me, I trembled, caft
my eyes downwards, and concealed
myfelf by ftooping behind the wall.
I could not conceive the caufe of thefe
fears and trepidations, which to me
were entirely new fenfations. From
time to time I ventured to raife myfelf, though not quite upright, or endeavoured to diftinguifh her through
the plants that covered the wall. Still
fhe continued intenfely bent upon her
reading, with the moft profound and
unremitted attention. The more I
obferved her, the more I was convinced of the truth of my dreams, and

E 3   was

was delighted to find them verified. One circumstance in particular confirmed the favourable opinion I had formed of her character.

Hearing on a sudden a plaintive bleating, which seemed to come from the extremity of the orchard, exactly opposite to me, she started up, and ran towards the spot from whence it procceded Fortunately that spot was very near me, and I could distinctly perceive every thing that passed. She there found a little lamb, limping along, and dragging after it a long branch of hawthorn. The poor animal's leg was covered with blood, and it seemed, by its moans, to be in extreme pain, till her beneficent hand relieved its anguish. It seemed to be consoled by her cares, and turned its head towards its benefactress, in an affecting manner, as if wishing to relate to her all its sufferings.

fufferings. She drew the thorn from the poor little creature's foot, with the utmoft gentlenefs, then led it to a neighbouring fountain, wafhed its wounds, and gathering fome leaves and herbs, bound them on the part with a piece of linen which fhe tore from her handkerchief. How her compaffionate care of this poor lamb affected me! Ah! faid I, what a kind heart fhe poffeffes! while the emotions fhe awakened, moiftened my eyes with delicious tears. I was animated with a pleafure, an extafy I know not how to defcribe. Never did I feel fuch fenfations before

The animal finding himfelf relieved, licked with expreffions of gratitude, the hand that fuccoured him. I could not take my eyes from this lovely fcene, till—the deteftable bell again deftroyed my happinefs, and, full of bitter anguifh at its intrufive

E 4   orders,

orders, I turned my unwilling fteps towards the lonely cloifter

I now, for the firft time, confidered my duty as a burden, and beginning to feel all the torments of repentance, my cell appeared to me a dungeon or a tomb

To be thus buried and immured at my firft expanfion into life!—Eternal, indiffoluble vows!—Oh! fatal and fhort-fighted determination!—— But how vain are all retrofpective regrets! She who gives birth to thefe feelings, ought rather to prevent them rifing in my bofom.   Had I not fought an afylum of repofe in this fequeftered dwelling, fhould I ever have beheld the object that has deftroyed my peace? But I am now more than ever a ftranger to the tranquillity I purfued. Every thing is become a fource of pain, except—Alas! I know not what I write.

I began

I began to feel fo great an internal commotion of contending paffions, that I was at a lofs to conceive this new labyrinth in which my heart feemed to be involved. A burning heat violently agitated my frame, nor could I continue a moment at reft. My accuftomed meditations no longer pleafed and foothed me, fleep and repofe were fled, and I paffed both day and night, in rapidly traverfing my little prifon What a contraft between this infupportable agitation, and the fweet abfence of care in which my days had hitherto glided on! Yet, the mere fight of a woman has caufed this fudden change! Where then is the manly refolution I ought to poffefs — Fool that I was! I attempted to become a philofopher, and I find myfelf but a child I dared to judge of other men before I was acquainted even with myfelf.

E 5   My

My thoughts, alas! were now engroffed by the young female, whom I
thought fo kind, fo good, and poffeffed of every virtue and every charm,
although I had not yet even beheld her
face. I was fatisfied, however, with that
which my imagination had pourtrayed.
That countenance I feemed continually to behold, while abandoning myfelf entirely to thefe thoughts, I fat
upon the ground, leaning my head
againft a ftool, and covering my eyes
with my hands. How many tears
have I not fhed in this poftuie, which
feemed moft adapted to the oveiflow-
ings of my heart. I had no one in
whofe fympathifing bofom to repofe my
cares, and I poured them forth to the
idol befoie whom I proftrated myfelf.

But, what will my dear friend think
of this new weaknefs? I anticipate the
reproaches, your cold reafon will dictate to your pen.

" Aftei

" After having recently made a vow to devote yourfelf to a religious and holy life, thus fuddenly to fall in love! and with whom? with a woman, of whom you have as yet, but obfcurely beheld the external form? Do you even know who fhe is? And were fhe an angel in virtue, and in every perfection, is it poffible you fhould ever be able to fpeak a fingle word to her? For what then can you hope?"

For heaven's fake, my dear friend, be more indulgent to the paffions of human nature. More irrefiftible than the moft boifterous winds, they fafcinate and fubdue the heart, and no human force is capable of oppofing them. Can he who fleeps in perfect fecurity from the ftorm, impute blame to the unfortunate wretch who falls a victim to its fury? Ah no. He will rather beftow on him his compaffion.

E 6

I re-

I refume my ftory.   You will eafily imagine I now began to murmur at the laws which held me thus impri- foned.   What would I not have given for permiffion to go out for a fingle moment? But to wait a whole week appeared impoffible.   What then muft I do?   Love rendered me ingenious. I went to the father abbé, and told him that having a violent head-ache, I wifhed to walk out a little.   He replied, that he could not refufe me what appeared fo neceffary to my health.

What a happinefs! I believe I fhould have embraced the good old monk, but that my gratitude would have excited his fufpicions. I therefore thanked him in a moderate manner, and then haftened to my obfervatory.

Though I was yet a ftranger to the pains of love, I foon began to feel them feverely.   Perfidious urchin!—
The

The cup with which he intoxicates us is always delicious at firſt, though he ſoon forces us to ſwallow the moſt bitter draughts.

I waited in vain during ſeveral hours, but no one appeared. Great God! What misfortunes did I not torture myſelf by imagining. Sometimes fearing ſhe was ill, I addreſſed the moſt fervent prayers to heaven for her recovery, and would have ſacrificed half my life to have ſpared her the ſlighteſt pain. Sometimes I imagined ſhe had quitted the convent, and was returned to her family. This idea tormented me ſtill more than the former, for it left me totally deſtitute of hope. I did not, however, too eaſily admit the truth of theſe conjectures, and flattered myſelf, her abſence only proceeded from a rule ſimilar to that of our own monaſtery, which did not permit us to go out

every

every day. "To-morrow, perhaps," said I, " I fhall be more fortunate " I returned full of this hope, which fomewhat cheered my fadnefs, and rendered my difappointment lefs infupportable.

In my way I paffed near my favorite grotto, which I entered. But alas! I no longer found that foothing pleafure in folitude, which exifts but when the paffions are at reft. The birds approached me, and lighted near my feet, as I had accuftomed them, but my heart refufed them its former intereft, for it demanded an object, whofe fenfibility might anfwer its tender emotions with mutual attachment.

I re-entered my cell full of affliction, and abforbed in profound melancholy. Alas! my dear friend, how frequently did I reflect on your kindnefs and compaffion. What would I not have given to have had you with me,

me, and to have told you how wretched I was ! To a heart oppreſſed with
grief how foothing is the balm of con-
fidential friendſhip !

The next day I repeated my application, under the ſame pretext, and
now I no ſooner arrived at the accuſtomed ſpot than I perceived—yes,
I perceived the moſt beautiful, the
moſt adorable object all nature can
exhibit. She advanced ſlowly, with a
deeply-reflective air, and took her favorite ſeat under her accuſtomed tree.
I now felt happineſs again to dawn
upon my ſoul and thrill through every
vein. As it ſpread throughout my
frame, it ſeemed to revive me, as the
dew of heaven re-animates a plant,
drooping under a too fervid ſun.

" Do I then again behold thee ?"
ſaid I, with tranſport. " My fears were
all chimerical. Oh ! heaven ! Oh !

protector

protector of the wretched ' may she long repofe in yonder manfion, and may this tree, of whofe fhade fhe is fo fond, and where I can behold her without danger, ever continue to be her loved retreat "

Though fhe ftill wore her veil, I found in this privation new reafon to admire her , for it feemed to indicate an extreme modefty, which enhanced the charms of her beauty. Love is equally ingenious in creating imaginary pleafures as in producing unfubftantial pains. In fhort, I was convinced fhe was a perfect beauty, and poffeffed of every attraction in the moft exquifite degree I confidered her as an angel, and loved her with fenfations and emotions, I had never before experienced Never did mortal infpire me with fuch celeftial extafy.

This time fhe had no book her fole employment was reflection Her
thoughts

thoughts feemed to be extremely interefting, for fhe was profoundly engaged in meditation. She was, however, fuddenly roufed from them by
the little lamb, who had perceived her
from a diftance, and came running
up to its benefactrefs, renewing its expreffions of gratitude I was pleafed
with the animal's lively remembrance,
which made me love it fo tenderly,
that had I been near enough, I fhould
have kiffed it with tranfport.

After careffing it with great fweetnefs, and holding it clofely embraced
for fome minutes, fhe rofe. At that
moment I felt extremely agitated, particularly when I perceived that fhe
turned into a path, which brought her
very near me. At every ftep fhe
took, my heart rebounded with joy,
and thrilled with the trepidations of
fear. My bofom heaved with palpitation, and my lips were unable to
articulate

articulate a fingle word —But what violent emotion did I feel when— Oh! how can I defcribe it?—when her veil caught upon a branch, and I faw—yes, I faw the moft beautiful, the moft adorable of human features. —I then entirely loft the command of myfelf, and fcreamed with joy and admiration.—She heard me, turned her eyes towards me, obferved my agitation, (fhe was not above twenty paces from me) made an involuntary movement of furprize, blufhed, and returned, with an affrighted air, to the convent.

Ah! What comfort this view adminiftered to my afflicted heart! By degrees I recovered myfelf. Had my emotion continued, I fhould have funk under its violence. When I recovered the ufe of my reafon, I argued thus with myfelf. "Why fo much agitation? How can fo fweet

a look

a look affect me more terribly than thunder itfelf?—Surely my fenfes are deranged I intereft myfelf in this young creature, becaufe fhe feems to poffefs the moft uncommon charms. But why can I not think of her without experiencing fo much pain? Is it poffible that her approach fhould have excited fuch difturbance in my breaft? This, then, is that love which, as yet, I have only read of in romances The ills of lovers hitherto appeared incredible and ridiculous.— Alas! how unjuft were my cenfures, when I attempted to judge of what was totally unknown to me."

When I re-entered my cell, I locked my door, as if I had been afraid of being feen, or my foolifh paffion were written in my countenance. Certain that I was then free from interruption, I abandoned myfelf to all the vehemence of my emotions.

My

My ideas followed each other with a rapidity that prevented my pausing upon any. An inconceivable confusion disturbed my mind. One moment her form floated before my eyes, the next she vanished from my view. Then the tree, the book, the lamb, presented themselves. This perturbation of my thoughts, this strange incoherency of sensation, gave me some uneasiness, and I imagined my poor brain had suffered a fatal revolution. Fortunately, I soon recovered myself, and my ideas became clearer and more fixed. Then I seemed exclusively to behold the object I adored, and felt the soothing pleasure of contemplating her alone. My enthusiasm was now no longer chimerical, since her features were known to me. Can you believe it? They were nearly similar to the picture my imagination had drawn. The same eyes, the

same

fame mouth, the fame caft of countenance. Ah ! Dormeuille, how a-
dorable is her form ! Could you but
behold her, even you would not refufe her the tendereft regard. You
would no longer be a cold and indifferent philofopher. Her very looks
are fafcinating, and how attractively
amiable is her fmile ! An angelic
fweetnefs is pourtrayed in her countenance, and foftened by a fhade of
melancholy that evinces a moft tender
fenfibility of heart Such a woman
cannot love with flight attachment:
but who is the mortal that can de-
ferve her heart ?

I tafted an inexpreffible pleafure in
thinking of her, and reflecting on her
virtues, on the graceful majefty of her
deportment, the elegance of her fhape,
the charming fimplicity of her drefs,
her beautiful hand, her delicate foot,
her clear complexion, varied with a

gentle

gentle glow, with which fome hand
divine feemed to have adorned it, her
fine black eyes, her hair, that curled
with enchanting negligence . and when
I had completed the enumeration of
all her beauties, I repeated it again
and again   In this manner I paffed
the greater part of the night, which
was by no means one of the leaft
happy of my life.   But of all the delights thefe thoughts procured me,
the moft exquifite was—a miracle, you
would believe of no one but myfelf.—You know how fond I always
was of drawing, and that it was one
of my favourite amufements,   During
my amorous reveries, I took my pencil from time to time, and endeavoured to pourtray the adorable features that continually prefented themfelves to my imagination.   But I was
always difgufted with my performance, becaufe I could not give it all
the

the beauty of the original. Once, however, I felt infpired by a facred tranfport—a celeftial ray illumined my imagination, and I produced upon the paper the true image of her who is the arbitrefs of my deftiny ; and, as if fome God had guided my hand, I drew that angelic figure fo perfectly accurate, that I fell upon my knees before the work of my own hand, abforbed in love and veneration, as if I had been in the prefence of the original.

When this firft enthufiafm had fubfided, I again examined my work, and found the refemblance equally ftriking. I was myfelf highly aftonifhed at it, as it had not coft me half an hour's application Love had, for once, lent me genius and talents.

Ah! how dear this portrait was to my heart. I could not ceafe to contemplate it—and to declare to it all

that

that I ought to conceal from the whole world. I wrote behind it thefe words, " Oh how I adore thee," and having hung it on the favorite tree, I haftily withdrew.

I then repaired to my obferva-tory behind the wall, and, waiting for the moment of her appearance, I felt a violent trepidation, which in-creafed whenever I looked towards the tree, while innumerable appre-henfions at once oppreffed me   Had I been feen by any one, or had any other young perfon approached the tree before her, I was ruined — " What effect," faid I, " can this por-trait produce ?—Will fhe contemplate it with pleafure or indifference ?"— What cruel perplexity !—At length fhe came—but accompanied by one of her youthful friends.   What a mis-fortune ! As they advanced how my heart beat—they entered the orchard— they

they approached the tree—my palpitation became violent—fortunately, her
friend ftopped to obferve a plant, while
fhe approached alone, with downcaft
eye, and a more reflective air than
ufual When fhe came to the foot of
the tree and faw the portrait, what
aftonifhment fhe feemed to exprefs!
At length fhe looked towards me, and
perceived me, for I know not how
I had ventured to fhow myfelf more
openly than before My emotion
feemed forcibly to ftrike her, fhe
blufhed and turned pale alternately,
and her eyes became wild —But when
her friend came up to her—Heavens! what was my happinefs! when
I faw her quickly fnatch the picture
from the tree, and with an air of myftery put it in her pocket. Her
friend was uneafy at her fudden pale-
nefs, and enquired the caufe, but fhe
feemed to make her an evafive anfwer,

and they foon after returned to the convent.

I cannot defcribe to you, my friend, all the happinefs I felt at this delicious moment What I had obferved, was highly favourable to my paffion, her emotion at beholding the portrait, her hurry to fnatch it from the tree, her concealing it from her young com-panion——Certainly, faid I, fhe can-not then have beheld me with total indifference   Yet how is it poffible a fingle look fhould produce fuch an effect?—'Tis true my own heart yielded to as flight an attack, but fhe —fhe is an angel, whom to fee is to be enamoured with her beauty, and to be fafcinated by her charms. But am I, (the moft miferable, the moft melan-choly of mankind) am I formed to be beloved by the moft beautiful, the moft perfect of all nature's works—Yet notwithftanding all the ardors I

fhou d

should have convinced me of my error,
I could not prevail on myself to disbe-
lieve, what so exquisitely flattered me.
No, it was impossible not to prefer a
pleasing error to a destructive truth.
Doubtless she perceived in my countenance the marks of a tender heart,
and the expression of the love she had
awakened in me. Perhaps we breathed that sympathy of sentiment, which
causes those who feel it, to reciprocate
each other's sensations and affections,
even at first sight. Ah! were my
hopes but true, I should be the happiest of mortals —But I may at least
aspire to be her friend. for though
she is the most perfect of womankind
and I but a mere man, yet my heart
is full of that tenderness and sensibility which alone can love for ever, or
form the happiness of the object of
its affections.

F 2   Though

Though my heart overflowed with these transporting ideas, this delightful train did not continue long. Happiness, alas! is but the ephemeral phantom of a moment.

My dear friend, I have not seen her since, though more than a week has elapsed. Often have I repaired to my observatory, yet always in vain, and what drives me to despair, she no longer comes out to walk; for I have carefully observed all the young boarders, and I know her person too well not to distinguish her from them all. What then is the cause of this long absence? Why totally abandon a tree that formerly gave her so much pleasure? Is it inconstancy? No, I cannot believe it. Or has the portrait displeased her? Was this gentle declaration of my attachment, in her eyes, a blameworthy indiscretion?——There is no idea however fleeting, but comes to torment my mind in this uncertainty.

Oh! my dear Dormeuille, how miserable is my lot! Oh! inexorable fortune! 'Twas not enough to be totally deftitute of parents and relations, but, to fill up the meafure of wretchednefs, I am deftined to fuffer the moft infupportable of all evils, that of loving without the leaft hope of return.

No, my friend, you cannot imagine to yourfelf how much mifery this fatal paffion caufes me. I tafte not a moment's repofe, and I feel my health daily decline.

Adieu my dear friend. You fee all my weaknefs, but you know my extreme fenfibility. Grant me at leaft a little indulgence, a little tendernefs Give me, however, your candid advice, for I have the greateft need of it My reafon feems totally deftroyed.

Reflect

Reflect for your friend on his wretch ed condition, but do not speak of it to any one

Once more adieu. I dare not read this letter; a kind of shame prevents me from dwelling on its contents

---

LETTER XXXVIII

WHY is not your advice, my dear Dormeuille, as practicable as it is just? —But it is too late to preach reason to me. Love is become completely my tyrant, and carries me irresistibly away. What human power can resist his omnipotence? Ah! my dear friend, I am now supremely happy— I have seen her—I have spoken to her—She loves me—She has told me it Yes, she has repeated the tender sounds

But I must pause, that I may relate what I have to communicate with some degree of order.

When I wrote last, I was oppressed by an almost insupportable melancholy A secret affliction violently agitated me, a burning fever insensibly consumed me, and my very existence became a burthen, for I was deprived of all that could render it happy or supportable In vain did I seek for objects to divert my afflicted mind from its anguish, which had entirely driven sleep from my pillow. Alas ! cried I, in the utmost despair, has she then for ever abandoned her dwelling—and shall I never behold her more ?—No one, who has not loved —no one, who has not experienced a similar privation, can conceive the heart-distracting misery I suffered.

F 4   One

One night, after having been tormented by the moſt horrid dreams, I aroſe in a ſtate of wildneſs, and ſtood at the window, where the freſhneſs of the air, and the gentle ruſtling of the foliage, ſomewhat calmed the emotions that diſturbed my ſoul. But a profound dejection ſtill remained, and all my thoughts were on her, who was the cauſe of my miſery. Ah! ſaid I, ſhe, ſhe is now at reſt. No paſſion chaſes tranquillity from her breaſt, peaceful, and undiſturbed, becauſe none but the pains of love are truly inſupportable. Oh! moſt beautiful, moſt adorable of women, may you never feel the pangs that tear my heart aſunder No, I would not even that you ſhould love me as I love, for then you would be wretched like myſelf, and your peace is more dear to me than my own Ah! could I remove far from you every care, and

every

every pain. Ah! could I fpare your heart the anguifh of a fingle figh.

I could not refift the defire of going laft night into the orchard. What happinefs I promifed myfelf in vifiting the favourite tree, in fitting beneath its foliage, in the very fpot—Yes, my heart palpitated at the idea.

I paffed through the long extended galleries of the monaftery, and opened innumerable doors, then traverfing the garden and the wood, I climbed the wall, and at length arrived in the orchard. As I advanced, what was my aftonifhment when I difcovered by the light of the moon, a young female dreffed in white, and walking to and fro At firft I could not difcover whether it was her, but hiding myfelf in the fhade behind fome rofe trees and rafpberry bufhes, I obferved her with the greateft anxiety and impatience. — She advanced flowly

F 5   towards

towards me—approached the tree—
ftopped there—and then looked at it
with a ftedfaft eye.—At length I recognized her figure—Ah! what fenfations I experienced?   I could fcarcely refrain from quitting my hiding
place.   My heart forced me away—
yet my fears again reftrained me.   I
now faw diftinctly all her features
the moon, that reflected a filver
light on every object, gently illu
mined her ftill fofter features, and decorated her beauties with a pallid
luftre —But why does fhe come out
fo late?   Alas! faid I my conjectures
were too juft.   Yes, fome fecret agony
difturbs her mind and drives fweet
fleep from her pillow.   But hark,—I
am near enough to hear her fpeak, and
perhaps I fhall learn from her own lips,
all the forrows that afflict her.   Yes,
'tis no idle curiofity that prompts me.
If I am defirous of knowing the fource

of

of her grief, 'tis but with the hope to
share, if not alleviate her affliction

After contemplating the tree for
some minutes, she cast her eyes upon
the earth and sighing, resumed her usual
seat in profound silence, which to my
impatient curiosity appeared extremely
long I listened with unremitting attention, scarcely daring to breathe lest
I should lose a single word she might
utter. If the wind did but agitate the
foliage I was in despair I conjured all
nature to be silent, lest any interruption
should oppose my tender wishes—At
length I heard a deep sigh. "Great
God!" said she, "how unfortunate,
how wretched am I!" These were
were the first words I ever heard her
pronounce, and it would be impossible
to describe the effect they produced on
me. What a soft enchanting voice!
What a plaintive tone !—I was at once
transported with pleasure and dis-
tracted with the bitterest grief—An

inde-

indescribable sympathy made me participate all her various emotions, and every word she uttered penetrated my very soul To every sigh I sighed responsive, when she cast her pensive eye on the earth, I was unable to raise mine, and when she looked up to heaven for its pitying aid, I united in the imaginary prayer and ejaculation In short all her sensations were mine, and I seemed animated by the same heart that beat in her bosom.

"Alas!" she resumed, "how pitiable is my lot!—must I then endure every evil at once Oh! my heart! How many pangs thy sensibility causes me to suffer!—Oh! fatal sensibility—without thee my life would peaceably glide on in uninterrupted felicity like this serene and tranquil night How sweetly the soft brilliancy of yon orb soothes my soul!—How her melancholy aspect awakens each tender sentiment, and inclines

inclines to meditation! Lefs dazzling than the fun, the eye may contemplate her luftre without pain and the innumerable ftars that twinkle around her, compofe a more magnificent and a more pleafing picture than the unvarying azure of the fineft day.

"This folemn, this awful filence, declares all nature is at reft. I alone, perhaps, am deprived of the benefits of repofe Yet how neceffary to my diftracted bofom! Alas! how I envy the happy indifference of my young companions! their hearts are awake only to friendfhip, they are, as yet, infenfible to every other care "—

She then took from her pocket the portrait I had hung upon the tree, and viewed it with tendernefs —Ah! my friend, figure to yourfelf the agitation I felt and the happinefs I enjoyed, at this interefting moment.

"Yes,"

" Yes," faid fhe, " this is certainly my refemblance With what exactnefs he has delineated it! He has deigned then to think of me.—Ah! if he did but love me!—But why fhould this ftrange idea take poffeffion of my heart? How is it poffible that the mere fight of a man, whom I do not know, fhould thus agitate me?—Yet there was fomething in his countenance that affected my fenfibility, and caufed a continual emotion in my heart. I dare not fee him more. my agitation would betray me—Ah! cruel neceffity!"—

Thefe tranfporting words had fo powerful an effect on me, that I could not contain the violence of my joy, and, without reflecting on the danger, I flew to throw myfelf at her feet

She fcreamed with terror, turned pale, and almoft fainted away. " Be not alarmed," faid I, feizing her trembling hand, " 'tis your friend, your

most

moſt tender friend."—At length ſhe recoveied. But ſhe daied not either ſpeak to me or meet my eyes. " Why theſe feais ?" ſaid I, " am I not he whom you condeſcend to love ? Be-lieve me you aie very dear to me ; your abſence has driven me to deſpair, and I am only come to appeaſe my giief by the pleaſure of at leaſt be-holding the ſcenes, you ſo often adoin. I have had the happineſs of hearing your avowal—Ah! may our ſenti-ments ever be the ſame "

She fixed her eyes on me and wept. A tear trickled down her cheek, and I kiſſed it away with my lips.—' Ah!" ſaid I, heſitatirg with confuſion, " thus, thus let me ever obliterate the traces of your grief" She tiied to ſpeak, but love, timidity, and modeſty agitated hei ſoul, and the woids died away upon her lips.

Her

Her silence afflicted me, and I ventured to tell her so. At length she replied with a feeble and trembling voice, "Have you not already heard too much?" "Ah! yes," answered I with transport, "that single sentence was enough."

I arose and seated myself beside her, half intoxicated with joy and transport. —I seemed no longer to dwell upon the earth.

I could now contemplate her without reserve. Never had she appeared half so beautiful. At every look I discovered in her countenance some delicacy of feature that had hitherto escaped me, or the marks of some sentiment, ever flowing in new and varied expression from her heart. The gentle reflections of the moon encreased the charming freshness of her complexion, and rendered the melancholy of her countenance still more affecting.

What

What an interefting figure! who could have beheld her without emotion? Her eyes almoft continually fixed upon the earth, her fmile, in which pleafure and fear were contending, the enchanting found of her voice, the tender accent of every thing fhe uttered, every circumftance that regarded her, even her name filled me with rapturous delight. She is called Sophia. Ah! what a charming name! Surely there is fomething celeftial in the found!

When we had continued together fome little while, a mutual confidence naturally arofe. The hearts of thofe who love, foon coalefce in every point of union. That fentiment by which they are allied feems to declare, they are formed for each other, and they can no longer refufe the pleafure of mutual communication.

Thus

Thus it was that we gave and received a reciprocation of delight, in talking of our attachment, and of every thing that was interesting to us both. I told her what an irresistible passion she had excited in me from the first moment I beheld her, and that it had totally destroyed my peace I described the uneasiness her melancholy had caused me, the reveries and afflictions that succeeded, the extasy with which I had delineated her portrait and her charms, and in short, all the emotions she had excited in my breast This conversation was long, and I often repeated the circumstances that swelled my passion, for I delighted to multiply the expressions that best pourtrayed my emotions I then pressed her hand to my bosom, saying with vehemence, "Ah! Sophia, how I love you! Yes, I love you alone, and this is the first time I ever felt this

tender

tender paffion. Before I knew you, I
thought friendfhip the primary fentiment of the heart, and I confidered
the empaffioned fondnefs of lovers,
as the delirium of folly. In fact, fuch
it frequently is. But you have taught
me, it may fometimes be natural and
dignified, and that it is even a too
feeble homage for fuch an union of
beauty and virtue. Doubtlefs you
merit infinitely more, but he who
could pay you an adoration worthy of
your perfections, muft be more than
man. Ah! Sophia, believe me I
feel all the love of which a mortal is
fufcepable, and which can never be
obliterated from this heart, whofe fenfibility and affection have caufed me
fuch cruel pangs.

" This attachment will mark the
deftiny of my future life, I am now
incapable either of happinefs or mifery, of pleafure or pain, but through
you,

you. If you cease to love me, I shall cease to exist, but if you are as constant as you are lovely, ah! then I shall be the happiest of men. Tell me, then, my charmer, can you always love me?"

She fixed her eyes upon me, smiled, and in a tone of voice, which love rendered still more affecting, " Yes," said she, " I will always love you, I swear it in the presence of him who can read every heart, of him who knows that mine is governed by sentiments of the purest and most constant sympathy "

No language can express all I felt at this extatic moment. To lie at the feet of Sophia, to breathe the same air that kissed her lips, to press her lovely hand to my bosom, and hear her confess she loved me !—Ah! why did not that night continue for ever?

Ou·

Our happiness made us forget the rapid flight of time, and believing we had but just met, we were astonished at the unwelcome appearance of the dawn. Sophia perceived it first, and exclaimed, " we are ruined '"—— " Ah !" replied I, " in such society, my charming Sophia, how is it possible not to forget all nature—to me you are more than the whole universe besides "

But we had no time to lose. 'Twas the hour when the nuns were to go to prayers, and had one of them appeared in the garden —how dreadful would have been our situation ! We therefore parted abruptly till the following night, and I hastened to my wall, from whence I could still observe her in safety. There my eyes pursued her till she entered the convent, nor did a single step or motion of her lovely form, escape my observation. Every thing

that

that regarded her, interested me even to emotion I contemplated the glow of the morning reflected from her robe, to which it gave a faint roseate hue, somewhat resembling the beautiful tint that adorned her lovely cheeks Before she entered the convent she turned back. It was only to see me once more. Ah! how grateful did I feel for that tender look!

During the first moments that followed this delicious night, I was transported with pleasure. I felt relieved from a heavy burden, and I fancied no one could be so happy as myself. Yet this happiness did not ensure me constant peace, or undisturbed tranquillity. Sometimes it was so extreme as to be converted into pain, merely from excess of pleasure I paced to and fro with agitation—I spoke with vehemence, my eyes gazed wildly around,

at

at every moment I exclaimed, with admiration, " How beautiful! how lovely! how adorable!" and my emotions were so violent, that I was obliged to sit down to recover my self-command

Then I felt the most cruel anxiety for the pain my happiness might cost my Sophia. She had told me, that as she had an apartment to herself, no one would perceive her absence, and that she was so beloved by all the nuns, that they suffered her to go out by night as well as by day, so that it was enough if we were not actually seen together. These reasons, though sufficient to quiet my apprehensions, yet did not set my heart at rest Ah! how could I enjoy the peace of security, when the severest pangs might afflict, her I loved.

The next day was that, appointed for all the monks and nuns to walk out. I repaired to my obfervatory, but no longer beheld my Sophia alone or in the orchard, but walking in the garden with feveral other young people. She would not come there alone during the whole day, becaufe, as we underftood each other, fhe feared we might be obferved. How whimfical in their fears a e lovers' from the di-ftant they have declared their paffion they feem to think all the world may read it in their faces.

My firft care was to examine by her countenance whether her heart was at eafe She feemed to enjoy the calm repofe of happinefs, and I tafted without alloy the pleafure of contemplating her beauty.

Had I not known her true motive, I fhould have fufpected her of coquetry, for fhe poffeffed the moft ftriking fu-periority over every thing fhe approached. Her drefs was ftill more

simple

simple than usual, though I thought I could discover a more minute attention to its adjustment, and more of those beautiful though fascinating elegances which give taste to the figure, without adding ornament to the dress, or charms to the person, but which exhibit the picture of beauty with a finer composition and prove that true beauty, " when unadorned, is then adorned the most." She exceeded her companions in height, and her grave and majestic air, though destitute of haughtiness, and tempered with sweetness, gave her the appearance of a divinity surrounded by her nymphs, who seemed to approach her with respectful veneration. At a little distance they laughed and danced, and played about, as was natural to their age ; but when they returned to Sophia, and took her arm, when they

fixed their eyes on her, and liftened to
her converfation, they inconfcioufly
adopted her ferious manner and tone
of voice. Their fteps became flower,
their air lefs fprightly, and in fhort,
when in her prefence, they were totally
different from themfelves. The virtues of Sophia form a kind of electric
atmofphere around her, whofe divine
influence purifies and transforms every
object. With what delight did I contemplate its effect! Oh! Sophia,
Sophia! how fhall I declare all
the praife you merit, all the admiration and love your various excellencies awaken

When night returned, my happinefs was renewed, and though I could
not have conceived it poffible it fhould
increafe, our fecond interview was
thoufand times more delicious than the
former. We had now no referve or
reftraint,

reftraint, and we feemed to have been acquainted for many yeais Our love was pure, our hearts feemed fpontane-oufly to unite, and we abandoned ou-felves without controul to the expan-five overflowings of mutual confi-dence.

Nothing can charm the mind or fafcinate the heait like the reciproca-tion of that true love, whofe fincerity and franknefs fupeifede the defire to pleafe, becaufe they cannot defcend to its cold piecifion, and becaufe mutual fondnefs excludes all fubordinate con-fiderations. The love which can in-vent fine-turned phiafes and flowing periods is not the affection that fpings uncontaminated from the heait.

When I defciibed to Sophia what kind of lovers women in the polite cicles of fafhion defiied, fhe could fcarcely comprehend me She replied, " Thofe women then do not wifh to

G 2   be

be fincerely loved." "Yes," faid I, "'tis they who wifh it moft, not from the impulfe of nature, but merely for the pleafure of fhowing their power and exhibiting their flaves When coquetry renders the heart infenfible, the language of fentiment is no longer intelligible, its accents become an empty found, and nothing but wit can give pleafure. Such women muft be amufed, but to love or adore them would be a profanation.

"Ah ! moft adorable Sophia ! may we for ever love as Nature prompts the heart—with unreferved franknefs, and unerring conftancy. The fympathy of fentiment is the firft characteriftic of love. Let us not *endeavour* to be amiable, and we fhall always be lovers.' After having long converfed on this fubject, Sophia was defirous to know every thing that concerned me, the manner in which I paffed my time, my ftudies, my amufements. "I wifh," faid fhe, " to know thefe particulars, that my imagination may follow you every moment of the day For when you are abfent, all my employment is to think of you."

She afked me what induced me at fo early an age to enter on fo auftere a life. " Ah!" faid I, " let us defer a hiftory that would plunge me once more into the bitternefs of grief. 'Tis but a moment fince I began to tafte unmixed happinefs. Ah ' let me enjoy my felicity without interruption."

We continued together, this night, a fhorter time than on the preceding, and we returned early, in order to avoid fufpicion. Sophia had gained the confidence of all the nuns of her convent, and therefore enjoyed almoft perfect liberty. Yet there was no doubt, but if fhe abufed it, fhe would be immediately deprived of it

and,

and then what would be my interest!
These arguments were too powerful
to be resisted, I therefore submitted
without a murmur.

My dear friend, what happiness I
how enjoy! Each night I see my dear
Sophia, each night I drink a thousand
pleasures from her animated eyes, and
receive a thousand enjoyments from
her conversation, of which the remembrance charms away the tedious intervals of absence.

Never do I cease to have her image
before me. It accompanies me at all
times, and I seem still to be conversing
with her. All she has said repasses in
my imagination, and appears so full of
the charms of good sense, sound judgment, and acute observation, that I
am improved by her remarks, and delighted with her uncommon elegance
of thought. Oh, Sophia! how can I
describe

defcribe the innumerable perfection.
lavifhed on you by Nature?

I fhall fee her again to-night What
are the joys of angels to thofe my Sophia can impart.

LETTER XXXIX.

My dear friend, what agitation I feel
while I write this letter ! Never did I
experience fuch a tumult in my breaft.
How my hand trembles !--I can fcarcely guide my pen.

What I am about to communicate
will aftonifh you fo much, that were I
not to relate all the circumftances, you
would not believe it poffible.

Oh fatal love ! in what an abyfs of
wretchednefs haft thou plunged me!
—Oh, my Sophia, my Sophia !—I

G 4　　　fhudder

shudder at the thought —Alas! how was it possible to foresee it ?—Hear my tale, my dear Dormeuille, and pity your unfortunate friend

You know how tenderly I loved Sophia. Yes, I loved her with all the passion, with all the sensibility, of which my heart was susceptible. She absorbed as it were all the energies of my soul, and fixed my tenderest affections Sophia was to me the most beautiful, the most lovely, the most adorable object, nature could exhibit among all her works. But this sentiment was as pure as her who excited it; and was so sanctioned by virtue, that I cherished and gave a loose to it in the temple of prayer itself Sometimes I even dared to speak of my Sophia to the Deity. " Great God!" said I, with enthusiasm, " surely she is the most virtuous of thy crea-

tures,

tures, and deferves, next to thee, to receive the homage of mankind "

I was happy, becaufe I was loved by Sophia If I received pleafure from feeing her, fhe was no lefs re-joiced at the renewal of our interviews. Her eyes declared the truth of this affertion, and fhe affured me of it in fo perfuafive and captivating a man-ner, that thofe interviews were the moft delicious moments of my life. Yet my enjoyments had nothing to render them remarkable to a ftranger; and many a cold heart would regard them as perfectly infipid. To us it was enough, that we were together, and fometimes we paffed confiderable in-tervals without uttering a word. To lie at the feet of my Sophia, to recline my head upon her knee; fometimes to receive from her lovely hand a gentle fqueeze, and view her lovely face, were to me a fupreme

G 5 delight.

delight. The moſt poliſhed eloquence could not have ſurpaſſed this expreſſive ſilence. Words were formed but to amuſe the cold and indifferent, lovers have another language, more varied and energetic, which conveys with more fidelity all the ſhades of tender paſſion. The tongue has but one mode of ſaying, *I love*; but the eyes can vary the ſame ſoft aſſurance with every momentary glance.

Theſe ſilent interviews were often firſt interrupted by the charming Sophia. Sometimes ſhe deſired me to relate how I paſſed my time when we were not together, a requeſt with which I complied the more readily, as it was but deſcribing the conſtant effect of my paſſion. She perceived by what I ſaid, that not a moment paſſed but ſhe engroſſed my thoughts, and this always procured me a repetition of her careſſes, except when I had been

been idle, and neglected my studies,
which she urged me to pursue with
affiduity She even set me a task herself, which I engaged to perform;
such as translating passages of the English or Italian poets. I brought my
work in the evening, and at the feet
of my tutress received her praises or
her censures. When I had performed
well, a kiss was my reward, otherwise
I was threatened with a frown. I took
care, however, to render that cruel
punishment very rare, and Sophia
read my productions with confiderable
candour and indulgence

With what ardour did not the hope
of pleasing my Sophia inspire me for
my studies! With what delight did I
not listen to her applause! Her opinion
was the more interesting, as she has a
cultivated mind, and often makes observations on style, which prove her
to possess an exquisite taste. I was

charmed

charmed to perceive, my beloved poffeffed talents fo uncommon in her
fex, for without thefe, no attachment
can be permanent.   So numerous are
the charms neceffary to feed the infa-
tiable cupidity of love.

Oh, my Sophia! my too lovely
Sophia! thy energetic and cultivated
mind, thy acute judgement, thy eminent virtue, are worthy of an eternal
affection   Alas! notwithftanding the
prejudices that oppofe our union and
condemn our paffion, notwithftanding
the torments it inflicts on me, I feel
that it will continue till I fhall ceafe to
exift.

Sometimes, yet very rarely, fhe
permitted me to talk of herfelf, and I
then enumerated her charms with all
the impaffioned fondnefs of a lover.
The exquifite turn of her features, the
gracefulnefs of her deportment, the
goodnefs of her heart, the elegant
polifh

polifh of her converfation, her extenfive knowledge, her matured judgement, her never-failing activity of
mind, her extreme fenfibility; in
fhort, every feature fhe poffeffed, and
every fyllable fhe uttered, were alternately the objects of my admiration.
I often repeated thefe remarks, tho'
accompanied with that heartfelt tone
of tendernefs which gives to the fame
words an unceafing variety of expref-
fion The fubject to which I moft
frequently recurred was her fympathiz-
ing care and attention to the little lamb,
which had communicated to me fo
much pleafure. But the modefty of
Sophia foon prompted her to interrupt
me. She would often fmile at thefe
defcriptions, and then enumerate a
long train of faults, which fhe declared fhe poffeffed, " For," faid fhe,
" I muft bring you back to reafon,
when I fee you abandoning her
dictates.

dictates. Tho' your wandering imagination has created a seducing phantom of perfection, 'tis for me to dissipate the illusion, and present myself before you in my true colours, that you may be accustomed to my imperfections, and feel towards me only such sentiments as, being consistent with truth, may be expected to be permanent "

I replied to this severe morality by the tenderest caresses. 'Twas the only manner in which I could prove to my Sophia the truth and sincerity of my passion, notwithstanding the illusory exaggeration of which she accused me.

When I recal to mind those innocent delights, I am melted with the tenderest emotions, and tears of pleasure trickle down my cheek. Alas ! why do not these delicious moments last for ever.

The

The laft time my unhappy deftiny permitted me to enjoy them, I was far, very far from fufpecting they were foon to ceafe. One evanefcent trifle had given birth to them, and another trifle deftroyed our future hopes The real fource of the moft important events, is often infignificant in every thing but its confequenc s.

Some wild flowers had grown around my grotto, whofe fimple co-louring appeared to me fo charming, and their fragrance fo delicious, that I made a nofegay of them for Sophia. She received it with kindnefs, and was defirous of feeing the fpot from whence they were gathered. I was pleafed and gratified by her wifh, and thought it an additional proof of her attachment. But as it was impoffible for her to climb the wall, we looked for a more eafy paffage, and after a fhort fearch, difcovered, at one of the

extre-

extremites, a breach, covered with hawthorn and brambles, which I eafily removed. I then took my Sophia in my arms, and, with this lovely burden arrived at the grotto. She entered it, and examining every corner of it, expreffed herfelf much delighted The moon, which was at the full, darted directly into this little retreat, and being reflected by the fhells, and refracted by the pyrites and ftalactites, produced a foft yet brilliant illumination —" What a charming fpot!" faid Sophia, " How I love its fimplicity, and the coolnefs of the air we breathe. Let us fit down, the night is not far advanced, and here we may pafs a few agreeable moments."

We feated ourfelves on a moffy bench, I had formed, and on which I was accuftomed to purfue my meditations " This," faid I, " is the fcene where I paffed all my leifure

hours

hours before I knew you. Here I lived in perfect folitude—here, deprived of the fociety of a fingle being that poffeffed fenfibility, my heart attached itfelf to the plants I cultivated, and the birds that hovered round me."
—" Oh! my dear friend," replied fhe, with tender emotion, " how this fimplicity of tafte charms me! It is a proof of a virtuous heart, the very heart for which mine has always panted. Ah! yes, I am more and more convinced by the fimilarity of our ideas and taftes that we were formed for each other. Before I loved you," faid fhe, taking my hand, and gently preffing it to her bofom, " like you, my heart could fix on nothing but the works of Nature."

I related to my Sophia the pangs fhe had caufed me, and the tears I had fhed on her account in this grotto, where fhe now made me fo happy.

She

She replied with a moſt lovely ſmile, " My dear friend, I wul endeavour in future to ſpare you theſe afflic- tions "—" That," ſaid I, " will be very eaſy, you have only to love me always.'—" Then," ſaid ſhe, " no- thing will be to me a greater plea- ſure."

The night was now advanced, and, notwithſtanding the pleaſure of being with my Sophia, I began to be uneaſy at her ſtay within the precincts of our monaſtery. A preſentiment I could not account for, tormented my boſom, and I was the firſt to urge her depar- ture. She felt the neceſſity of ſepa- rating, but as we quitted the grotto, " Ah!" ſaid ſhe, " Allow me for a moment to walk among theſe fine trees, doubtleſs you have often en- joyed ſweet repoſe beneath their re- freſhing ſhade." When we had taken a few turns in the wood, I reminded

her

her of the too urgent reasons for sa-
crificing our present gratification, to
our permanent security."—" Yes,
my dear friend," said she, " indeed
we must part, it would be dangerous
to continue together any longer, and
particularly in this wood. Let us go.—
But I see your monastery through the
trees, before I leave you, let me just
behold the window of your cell How
sweet it will be to recal its image to
my mind, in the long interval when I
must bear your absence "—" Ah !
my Sophia !" said I, " all the proofs
of your love affect me most tenderly ;
but to what dangers do not your
wishes expose us ?"—" I only ask,"
said she, " for one momentary
glance."

I obeyed, though I shuddered
at the danger. It was surely a secret
presentiment of the events that were
about to follow. Ah ! my Sophia !
my

my lovely Sophia! thou yieldedit with out diſtruſt to the pureſt ſentiments of innocence Ah! 'tis that very inno-cence which has ruined us.

Purſuing a viſta of thick trees, we approached the building, and Sophia ſatisfied her curioſity—that fatal cu-rioſity which it was but too natural for her to feel —Great God! what tears it has already coſt us! what ſtill greater anguiſh awaits our break-ing hearts!

As we were about to return, we heard a door open at the end of the walk, and from that door a monk was ap-proaching us.—This ſight was a death-blow to me, and Sophia ſunk ſenſe-leſs in my arms. We had not a ſin-gle moment to loſe. I covered her with my cloak, whoſe enormous am-plitude was now extremely uſeful, and haſtily carried her to my cell. 'Tis true, I ran the riſk of meeting other

friars,

finals, but it was the only means of safety left. Fortunately I saw no one, and I saved the innocent, at least for a few moments.

God of all goodness! deign to assist my endeavours to protect her for ever from the rude attacks of misfortune

I carefully shut myself in, and hastened to revive the unfortunate Sophia. Alas! In what a state did I behold her! Her eyes were closed, and the paleness of death was upon her countenance.

My dear friend, all the afflictions I have ever suffered, are nothing compared with what I felt at this overwhelming moment.

I pressed her to my bosom, and endeavoured to recall her expiring warmth but, all my endeavours were in vain, and I felt the deepest despair. At length she began to shew signs of life,

life, and foon after faid, in a low and
extremely faint voice, and with an accent that proved fhe had not yet recovered the poffeffion of her fenfes,
" Oh ! dear Mother Abbefs, forgive
me—indeed I was not to blame."

By degrees her reafon returned,
fhe opened her eyes, and gazed round
her with an air of wildnefs " My
dear Sophia," faid I, in a foft and low
voice, " take courage, you are no
longer in danger. 'Tis your friend
who folds you in his arms. Do you
not know me?" She caft her eyes
towards me, but made no reply.
What an affecting languor ! I could no
longer reftrain my tears, yet they
were fweetened by mingling with thofe
of my Sophia

Our hearts were mutually foothed
by thus weeping in unifon, and fhe
afked me if any hope was left. I endeavoured to afford her that confolation,

tion, though not a fingle ray cheaied my own bieaft. I placed her on a feat, and opened my dooi foftly, to obferve if any one was in the gallery. Alas ! 'twas the houi foi going to prayers, and from that moment there were lanterns in every dormitoiy till daylight. How could we pafs, without being feen The whole monaftery was in motion, every momert I heaid fome one walking by, and though I conftantly watched, in order to feize the firft favourable moment, all was in vain, and day appearing, oui misfortune was irremediable.

How can I defcribe our mutual defpair!—What could we do ? what was to become of us ? what innumerable evils crowded upon our minds ? 'Twas a dreadful profpect, on which I could not bear to paufe. I endeavouied to drive it from my mind, in oider to employ all its energy

gy in confoling my Sophia. What
chimeras did I not imagine, to palliate
the horror of my fituation! At firft
fhe would not liften to me, but poured forth tears and lamentations, and
abandoned herfelf to the moft violent
defpair. At length, however, my
affectionate expreflions and careffes
calmed her mind, by foftening it with
tendernefs. I know not how I gained
eloquence enough, to reprefent her
new fituation in fo feducing a light,
and perfuade her that none could be
more adapted to her virtues, or fo favourable to her happinefs. This converfation, which was too long to be
related in a letter, produced a very
ftriking effect upon the mind of Sophia She folded me in her arms,
bathed me with tears, and faid with an
ardour I had never witneffed before,
" Oh! my friend, you are the moft
virtuous of men, I adore your worth,
and

and truft to your protection to preferve the facred depofit of your Sophia's honour." She took my hand,
knelt down, and made me do the
fame, then raifing her eyes to heaven,
" Oh my God," faid fhe, in a low
voice, " thou who readeft every
heart, and knoweft our innocence,
what crime can we commit in living
together? Thou haft given us a heart
of fenfibility, and we love each other;
we alfo love virtue. Ah! protect the
tender bond by which we are united,
and which will ever retain its unal-
terable purity."

There was fomething heavenly in
her countenance, that at once gained
my affent, and made me adopt the
chimerical idea of fecurity, in which
I had lulled her fears.

" My adorable Sophia," faid I,
" if the moft fincere, the moft tender,

the moft conftant love, can fulfil the
wifhes of your heart, be affured that
in this peaceful retreat nothing can be
wanting to your happinefs." She anfwered with confidence, " He whom
I love has a virtuous heart, and I
have no uneafinefs concerning my future lot. Could I pafs my life with
you, and be unknown to the whole
world befide, I fhould have no other
wifh to gratify. But how can I reflect on the caufes that may difcover
us, without fhuddering at our danger,
and then, what will become of you,
my dear friend ? 'Tis not for myfelf I
fear "

I faid every thing I thought adapted
to pacify her uneafinefs, and affured
her, no one ever entered our cell's,
not even the domeftics, and that they
ferved our provifions through a hole
made for that purpofe in the wall

or

of our antichamber*.—" Come," said she, " let us drive away all melancholy thoughts, and I shall taste, without alloy, the happiness of living with the only object of my wishes—But, my, dear friend, let us be ever faithful to virtue, for, without that, there can be no happiness upon earth.

" Above all," said she, " Ah! supply the place of my dear mother—and—" the violent palpitation of her bosom, deprived her of the power of finishing the sentence. My imagination readily subjoined the word *father*. Alas! I was mistaken. " Yes my Sophia," said I, " you will find in the love I bear you, (the purest that ever warmed the breast of man) a firm protection to your honour, and all the consolation you stand in need of. Yes, we will console each other

* The cell of a Carthusian Monk, consist of several divisions

H 3

for

for the misfortune of being thus separated for ever from our parents.

She knew not then all the force of these words, nor was I acquainted with the afflictions of her heart. There was a kind of reserve and restraint in our emotions, not unusual between lovers. Alas! our hearts were too much in unison, and Nature gave them a secret presentiment of the real ties that so closely united them. But we attributed to love alone our tender affection.

Thus passed this first day. At the fatal hour when we had met the preceding evening in the orchard, Sophia sighed, fixed her eyes upon me, and wept I had great difficulty to divert her from the afflicting remembrance that oppressed her, and I perceived by her countenance, how much her modesty revolted at the idea of unavoidably passing the night with a man. On this

this subject, however, I satisfied her, by obferving, that it was our cuftom to fpend almoft the whole night in the church. "That will be the time," faid I, "for you to take your reft, and as for me I will fleep in a chair, or on a bed I will contrive to make with my cloaths

With this fhe was fomewhat calm ed, and, at my folicitation, confented to take fome repofe. I then attended divine fervice, which, having omitted the preceding evening a fecond ab- fence might have given rife to enqui- ries after my health, that might have been fatal to us.

At my return Sophia was afleep. She had paffed the preceding night, and the whole day, in the cruelest agi- tation, which had fo exhaufted her ftrength, that fleep at length triumphed over her affliction. What a charm- ing, what a heavenly figure ! Yet her

unpa-

unparalled beauty was softened by an impression of grief that pierced my very soul. Her breath was short and unequal, and sometimes she moved her head and arms, in a manner that proved how little her mind was at peace. Soon afterwards she awoke, and perceiving, for the first time, a man by her bed-side, she was seized with sudden alarm, but at length she recovered from her fears, and seemed to have benefited by repose.

To her new situation she could not reconcile herself so suddenly, and notwithstanding her endeavours to conceal from me what she suffered, by an appearance of tranquillity, I could plainly discover her uneasiness. Alas! what pains did I not employ to confole her under the weight of her afflictions! I observed her, with anxious minuteness, to discover the cause of her uneasiness, and employed the ten-

derest

derest expressions and most delicate
attentions love could suggest, to sooth
her. I endeavoured to divert her
sorrowful thoughts by displaying to
her mind all the pleasures we might
enjoy in the purest and most sacred
union. " What can be more delightful," said I, " than to be continually in the presence of the object
we love, without interruption or privation, far from a corrupt world,
where innumerable prejudices abro-
gate the most sacred laws of friendship, and the mask of virtue is used
as a means of rendering imposture
successful? My Sophia, if we do but
love each other, if our happiness depends on the reciprocations of sentiment, the most limited space will to
us be a boundless universe, and we
shall adorn it with every thing desirable in nature, by enriching it with

H 4   the

the moſt tender love and the cloſeſt
friendſhip."

She united in all theſe marks of
affection, and I had even the pleaſure ſometimes to behold a ſmile enliven her languiſhing features Yet
her accuſtomed melancholy ſoon returned, and it was neceſſary to renew
my conteſt with its baneful power.
When we were together, Sophia could
conquer it, but when my duties called
me away, I found her cheeks, on my
return, always pale, and her eyes
ſwelled and inflamed with weeping.
I perceived, that beſides the concern
ariſing from her preſent ſituation, ſhe
had ſome other internal affliction, of
greater weight and more exquiſite
ſenſibility. It might have been eaſy
to have learned its cauſe, had it not
been my only wiſh to chaſe all melancholy thoughts from her mind.
                                    Alas!

Alas! 'tis this delicacy that has undone me, and I am the victim of the
tender fentiments that reign within my
breaft.

Thefe contefts, at once productive
of pain and pleafure, continued during fome days. At length fhe became calmer, and her health, which
had fuffered fiom continual grief, returned. The rofes that bloomed upon
hei cheek again revived and expanded,
her eyes renewed their luftie, and the
amiable and chafte Sophia, convinced,
hei virtue was not in danger of a fall,
experienced no longer the torments
of continual feai Ah! how delicious
was the change to my aching heart.

Encouraged by this happy effect
of my cares, I took pleafure in mul-
tiplying them with increafing delicacy and tendernefs. Our condition
now appeared fupremely bleft. I was
unable to imagine a moie enchant-

H 5   ing

ing felicity, and all my prayers were that it might endure for ever.

From the moment when I beheld my Sophia rise at early dawn, more beautiful and lovely than Aurora herself, to the close of the day, when we were obliged to separate, I tasted the inexpressible pleasure of her society. I loved without the least fear of interruption or separation, for it was already a week since we had been together, and there was no appearance of discovery or danger.

I have often heard it said, that Love feeds on contradictions and sorrows, and that he expires as soon as he enjoys continual and unalloyed pleasure. This can only be true of those lovers who pursue an illusive happiness. As long as they view their chimeras but with the rapid glance of the unobservant passenger, they are delighted with fancied excellencies, but as soon

as they approach too near, they are
aftonifhed at having fo long lavifhed
their affections on fuch undeferving
objects Not fo the lovers, whom
reafon unites in fympathy of foul and
fimilarity of character, whofe thoughts
are in conftant unifon, who love more
tenderly as they become more intimately acquainted, and who receive
from each other all the intellectual
pleafures and enjoyments they are capable of tafting Yes, I embraced
happinefs itfelf when I held my Sophia in my arms, or preffed her lovely
hand to my bofom: when, converfing
in gentle whifpers to avoid notice, I
infenfibly approached her lips, or
felt the foft breath of her mouth
upon my cheek Sometimes I even
dared to kifs her, though Sophia
rarely permitted fo great a favor;
and its privation was the more
eafy to inflict, as her prefence infpired

H 6   me

me with an invincible timidity, and
the flighteft look was to me an abfo-
lute command   To her wifhes alone
I liftened, and for her fatisfaction
would have rifked throwing the uni-
verfe into confufion.   But this abfo-
lute fubmiffion to her will arofe from
my knowledge of her wifdom and her
virtues.   To her I left the guardian-
fhip of our happinefs, becaufe fhe beft
knew how to fulfil the important
charge.

Ever attentive to render our happinefs permanent, and fearing that a
life of uniformity might become fatal
to our love, Sophia gave it all the
charms of variety   I continued to
purfue my ftudies, which fhe regulated and participated. In thefe, though
fhe always furpaffed me, I was never
jealous of her fuperiority.   If I related to her fome fact of hiftory, repeated fome ftrain of eloquence, or
explained

explained fome difcovery of philofophy, her judicious obfervations proved,
fhe had much better ftudied and conceived the author, and thus fhe at once
aftonifhed and informed me   Sometimes I extracted a paffage from Petrarch or Taffo, which we both tranf-
lated.   But what a difference did our
performances exhibit ' She feized all
the beauties of the original with an in-
fallible fidelity, and adopted them in
her tranflation with additional elegance, always preferving the graces
and fentiments of the orginal.   The
ftudy of her charming productions
improved my own, and I enjoyed her
fuperior excellence with exquifite delight.   My very exiftence was fo
clofely united with that of my Sophia,
that her various perfections produced
the fame effect as if they had been
my own   My whole foul but breathed,
as it were, in her's.

At

At other times we varied our amusements with drawing.   She painted several of the most picturesque and
charming views we could discover
from my window, and with her pictures
I embellished our happy, peaceful retreat.

At another time she drew my portrait.   " I will try," said she, " whether Love will bestow as much genius
and talent on me as on you."   " That
is impossible," cried I   " What could
he add to all the endowments you
have received from nature ? Ah ! Sophia ! should all the powers of heaven combine, they could never form
a beauty that could compare with
yours."

She smiled at my enthusiasm, and
took her pencil.   Her lovely hand,
equally skilful and charming, executed
the work in a moment, and produced
a most accurate resemblance.   It was

added

added to the other pictures, and hung
by the fide of that of Sophia With
what pleafure did we behold our labours ! Often did we melt into delicious tears, when contemplating thefe
drawings, and reflecting on the ideas
the yrevived.

Forgive me, my dear Dormeuille,
if I am tedious on this interefting fubject. Alas ! the unfortunate have no
other refource but perpetually to recur
to their paft happinefs. Ah ! how
can they tear themfelves from the
fweet remembrance ?

Oh, my charming Sophia ! whither
are our happy moments fled ? Thofe
moments, when we might without
fear or reftraint abandon ourfelves
to all the fympathies of love , when
the pure and delicious pleafure of beholding you made our days glide too
rapidly away, and converted our frugal meals into feftivals of enjoyment.
Oh !

Oh! delights of innocence! Oh! luxurious frugality of the golden age, whither are ye departed?

Thus did we pass two months in uninterrupted happiness, when this enchanting dream, like the vapour of the hills, vanished in a moment. Never will the events of that fatal day be effaced from my imagination, when my imprudent passion made me forget the sacred duties, Sophia herself had imposed or me. The idea haunts me without intermission, and each reflection but renews my torture

One morning, when I returned from prayers, Sophia had just awakened from her slumbers, and appeared a thousand times more fascinating than I had ever beheld her. Her eyes sparkled with heavenly fire, and were still more animated by the lively carnation of her cheeks, and the lovely smile that sported on her lips, that

lovely

lovely and enchanting fmile, which is
at once the child and parent of pleafure "I have been dreaming of you,"
faid fhe, in a more impaffioned tone
of voice and manner than fhe had ever
addreffed me before, "your image
has difturbed my fleep, and your expreffions of tendernefs made me feel
the happinefs afforded by mutual love."
Strongly affected by thefe words, agitated by a ftrange emotion I am incapable of defcribing, and feduced by
the moft fafcinating, the moft irrefiftible attractions, my lips feemed fpon-
taneoufly to unite with thofe of my
Sophia. Ah! what a delirium of joy!
what an intoxication of pleafure! I
forgot all Nature but the angel, the
divinity I embraced, and feemed tranf-
ported to the heaven of heavens in her
arms.

But foon I beheld my lovely Sophia with more anxious folicitude.
She

She wept, she dared not even raise her
eyes to meet mine. I endeavoured to
console her by assuring her that I alone
was criminal, and that if she had
yielded to passion, her mind at least
was innocent   She conjured me to be
silent, hid her face with both her hands,
and shed a torrent of tears   This sight
tortured my very soul.   At length she
drew from her pocket a gold box, on
which she long fixed her eyes with a
smile of bitterness, and then in a tone
of the profoundest affliction sighed out,
" Oh, my mother !"

The sight of this box, in spite of all
my firmness, threw me into a violent
palpitation , for which, however, I
could discover no reason, though I
endeavoured to pacify and conceal my
emotion in the presence of Sophia.
Throwing myself at her feet, I exclaimed, " Oh, my Sophia ! what torments
your affliction makes me endure !
Alas !

Alas! I wished to make you happy,
I had no defires but thofe which
feemed to animate your own bofom,
till a moment of weaknefs has undone
me, and I have become a fource of
mifery to you, inftead of happinefs.
Ah! 'tis impoffible you fhould ever
love me more, and nothing remains
for me but to refign my exiftence, and
take refuge in the tranquillity of the
grave.

She was affected with my defpair,
and her angelic foul forgot her own
forrows, to think alone of thofe under
which fhe beheld me finking.

" I ceafe to love you!" faid fhe,
with foftnefs, " Oh! 'tis impoffible!"
" Ah! if you love me ftill," faid I,
" difpel, I conjure you, the deep
defpair, your countenance betrays. Are
you not ftill my Sophia?—Are you
not ftill the lovelieft and tendereft of
women? Do you not ftill feel that
angelic

angelic goodnefs in your bofom,
whofe characteriftic foftnefs beams
through all your perfon ? Can a fingle
fpot deftroy all the luftre of virtue, and
rob it of all its purity ?"   " I believe,"
faid fhe, " I have ever poffeffed fome
goodnefs, and fenfibility of heart,
but, alas ! can thefe qualities, which
are indifpenfable duties, and fcarce
merit the name of virtues, obliterate
my crime ?

" Oh ! my God !" faid fhe, " I
have committed a dreadful fin, but I
was at leaft innocent of any evil intention, and never will repeat the offence.
Oh ! grant thy forgivenefs to the
inexperience of an unfortunate peni-
tent, who will endeavour to appeafe
thy juft difpleafure by a life of recti-
tude and virtue.

" My friend," fhe added, " our
crime is great, but God knows the
weaknefs of our nature, and perhaps

we

we may atone for it by a pure and fpotlefs life Let us then forget the paft, and may a courfe of undeviating virtue efface the dreadful remembrance from our hearts "

A chafte embrace fealed the facred engagement, ever to refpect the boundaries of virtue, and then our tranquillity returned

I now enquired, " What might be the contents of the gold cafket, to which fhe feemed fo particularly attached, and which fhe had fo conftantly concealed ever fince we had lived together ?" " It contains," faid fhe " an important fecret. I have concealed it from you till this moment, becaufe I would not difturb the tranquillity you feemed to enjoy by melancholy tales But 'tis no longer in my power to hide the myftery ; and I muft communicate to you all my misfortunes."

She

She opened it—Oh! how I fhudder at the thought!—it contained—yes, it contained—a medallion—precifely fimilar to that I wear.

At the fight of this medallion, which was to me more dreadful than thunder,—I fank fenfelefs on the floor

When I began to recover, I perceived Sophia by my fide, holding a fmelling-bottle to me, herfelf deeply agitated and afflicted at my fituation.

When my powers returned, I once more fixed my eyes on the picture, and became certain, I was not deceived. The form and fize, the myfterious cypher, every thing proved that the lovely the tender Sophia was—my fifter!

The firft idea this excited in me, after my recovery, was that of the moft exquifite delight, for my mind was then engroffed by the pleafure of having found my fifter. Ah! my dear

friend,

friend, forgive this transport. This sentiment rendered me inacceffible to every other reflection. A thoufand times I tenderly embraced my Sophia, a thoufand times I preffed her to my bofom, without uttering a single word.

Sophia beheld me with aftonishment. At length, fomewhat more tranquil, " Ah!" faid I, " my Sophia, you will prefently know what gives me fo much happinefs."

As I uttered thefe words, I took from my bofom the medallion I wore, and prefented it to Sophia. Ah! how fhall I defcribe her emotions, which were equally ardent with my own. Again I embraced her, and preffed her to my bofom, calling her by the tender name of fifter. She called me her dear, dear brother, and our tears mingled upon our cheeks. Ah!

Ah! what delicious tears! the firſt
offspring of fraternal love!

But ſoon the moſt dreadful reflections affailed our minds and deſtroyed
on all our happineſs, when we reflected
the dreadful crime we had committed!—How could we depict to our
imaginations all its complicated horror?—I was thunderſtruck with the
thought—my eyes were rivetted to
the ground, and my limbs, petrified
with terror, refuſed to ſupport me —
I dared not raiſe my eyes, left they
ſhould meet Sophia's.—Alas! how
could I behold her, who was at once
my miſtreſs, my wife, and—my ſiſter!

This depreſſion continued ſeveral
hours, a period during which I was
inſenſible to every thing that paſſed
around me. Again the image of my
Sophia returned full upon my mind,
and the pain her ſufferings cauſed me,
awakened

awakened me from my lethargy. At length I ventured to look round At firft, not finding her, I was in the utmoft alarm, till I obferved her lying on the floor, her head reclined on the bed, pale, fenfelefs and without motion, and veiled in the folds of the curtain

Tremblingly I approached her—and endeavoured to fpeak—but in vain—and fhe was equally unable to hear as I to articulate.

We continued long fpeechlefs. For a confiderable time I fcarcely dared to take the hand of Sophia, and then their mutual preffure was the only language we employed to communicate the tender emotions of our hearts. By turns feeble and timid, or animated and ftrong, tender or energetic, they imparted the delight of a union fo long defired, but combated by the dreadful confcioufnefs of our crime, to

which this difcovery had given a ftill
deeper horroi. 'Twas a language
that impreffed me with a lively picture of every thing my Sophia felt,
and my heart anfwered iefponfive to
her emotions in the fame expreffive
manner. I endeavoured to overcome
her grief by the foothing folicitudes
of friendfhip, and at length, after innumerable fruitlefs attempts, I had
the happinefs to fucceed. The amiable Sophia, by degrees, recovered
her tranquillity. At firft fhe ventured
to turn towards me, then raifed hei
eyes to behold me, fmiled at me, and
no longer rejected my careffes.

At length love triumphed over
every other fentiment, and when I
beheld my Sophia's lovely countenance I became lefs impreffed with my
crime, while the tranquillity fhe feemed to have recovered relieved me
from a depreffive weight of grief.
" Alas !"

"Alas!" said I, "but a moment
ago we consoled ourselves for our
criminality by our resolution to atone
for it by a life of strict virtue: Can
it then have changed its nature by
this discovery? 'Tis true we have
committed a crime without intending
it, and therefore we were not guilty
of all its atrocity. 'Twas rather a
misfortune, which it was impossible
for us to avoid, since we were not acquainted with each other's history.
Let us then, though without impiously
denying our criminality, endeavour to
obliterate its horror, and enjoy the
consolations held out to us by heaven."

Sophia was too much abashed and
confused to reply, but I could perceive by her eyes that her soul was at
rest, though modesty forbid the confession.

The reflection, however, that I was
her brother, sometimes triumphed

over every reserve, and she spoke to
me with frankness of our unfortunate
condition. I endeavoured to prolong
these conversations, in order to chase
from our thoughts every sentiment
foreign to this mutually interesting
subject. She requested me to relate
to her minutely all I knew relative to
our birth, and every thing that had
happened to me from my infancy.
I complied, and communicated all I
had hitherto discovered, and you will
readily conceive, my friend, how lively
an interest she took in the narration.
With what attention she listened to
the tale! With what sensibility she
participated the pleasures and pains I
had experienced! She transported herself, as it were, to the time and place
I described, and was equally affected
by them with myself. She was extremely gratified with my endeavours
to discover her and my mother, but
when

when she heard that I had enjoyed the happiness of beholding that angelic woman, ah! how can I paint her emotions! Embracing me in the tenderest manner, " Oh! my dear brother," said she, " have you then indeed seen my mother? Say, is she happy?" I thought it wrong to shock her acute sensibility, which had already suffered too much, and therefore told her she was—happy. Alas! when I pronounced that word, what anguish did I feel!—But Sophia fortunately did not perceive my uneasiness.

It was necessary also to conceal from her the motives that induced me to enter on a religious life. I assured her, that grief at not being able to find my sister, and my forlorn and insulated existence in the world, were the only causes of my forming that resolution.

I wished,

I wished, in my turn, to know the history of Sophia, and she replied to my enquiries as follows.

" I have very little to inform you of. At first, like you, educated in a village, and afterwards shut up in a convent till the moment when our acquaintance commenced, I have had little opportunity to know any thing of the world. I have only lived with pious nuns and abbesses, and a few young persons who were boarded at the convent, and who all love me affectionately.

" Alas! I am too unworthy of their esteem But my heart is innocent, and this is all the consolation I enjoy.

My childhood passed without much pain or pleasure, and equally unagitated by sorrow or desire. Fortunately I received from Nature a happy and contented disposition, and while I

submitted

submitted to the employments imposed on me, and learned what I was
defired to learn, the pleasure of walking in the garden, and talking and
laughing with my young companions,
was sufficient to render me com-
pleatly happy.   But when the en-
creasing sensibility of my heart began
to unfold, and exhibited objects under new points of view, the amusements of childhood no longer delighted me, and I began to reflect.
Then, whatever surrounded me, excited my mind to action, and interested my feelings, and the works
of Nature imparted new pleasure to
my heart   The flowers that adorned
our garden, the trees that shaded me
with their friendly foliage, the birds
that flew above my head, the animals
that shared my caresses, all communicated a sensation hitherto unknown.

I 4   When

When my reafon became more matured, this general affection, which
at firft extended to every object attached itfelf more particulaily to an
abbefs who had the charge of my
education, and was entrufted with the
fecret of my birth   Though fhe was
a woman advanced in years, her extreme kindnefs, her uncommon good
fenfe, the fweetnefs of her difpofition, and her amiable temper, made
me forget the difference of our ages.
I felt a fincere affection for her, and
often quitted my companions for her
fociety, becaufe with her I found a
fource of pleafure more equal and
more fuited to my tafte, and her converfation delighted me the more, as
fhe always faid precifely as much on
every fubject as could inform or intereft me.   I fat by her with my
work, and while we employed ourfelves in fewing, fhe would relate
                                    ftories

ſtories which conveyed a pure and in-
ſtructive moral, or pointed out the
advantages of the ſolitary life to which
I was condemned. One day, without
reflecting on the conſequences, ſhe
told me the hiſtory of a young man,
who had ſuffered great misfortunes
becauſe he had quitted his parents, who
lived in a village in peaceful and
happy obſcurity. After weeping bitterly at this affecting ſtory, I aſked
her why I was not ſuffered to remain with my parents This queſ-
tion embarraſſed her. She perceived
her indiſcretion when it was too
late, and her evaſive reply only increaſed my curioſity. From that
time my deſire to know my relations
increaſed continually, and at length occupied all my thoughts. My young
companions ſometimes went to paſs
ſeveral days with their families, and,

at their return, all their converfation was the pleafure and happinefs they had enjoyed. My God ! faid I, when will it be my turn to tafte thefe delightful enjoyments ? Does not my mother love me ? Alas ! I know her not. Ah ! my dear mother, how happy fhould I be, had I but the power to return your love !

" Thefe reflections, which I always made to my good mamma, (for fo I always called the mothei abbefs) affected her, and fhe embraced me with tears. This was a new caufe of aftonifhment to me, and I continually tormented her with innumerable queftions, which fhe never fatisfied.

" When my underftanding was more matured, and mamma thought fhe might fpeak to me on this interefting fubject without danger, fhe declared the horrid fecret of our birth, and confided to me the cafket

you

you now fee, together with the medallion it contains. My God! what
floods of tears I fhed at this affecting
tale!

" From that moment a fixed melancholy has taken poffeffion of my
mind. The idea that I fhould never
behold my mother and my brother
rendered me extremely unhappy. Heaven has at length taken pity on my
affliction, and has difcovered to me
my brother, but alas!——"

" My dear fifter," faid I, embracing her, " let us think no more
of our misfortunes: we are the involuntary caufe of them ourfelves,
but our hearts are virtuous, and fhall
ever continue fo."

Our fraternal affection reftored peace
to our minds, and for a time infured
its continuance. We refumed our
ftudies, our tranflations, our philofo-
phical converfations, and our draw-

ing, to which natural hiftory was now
added   I brought her fhells from
my grotto and plants from the hills
within the territory of the monaftery
I told her their names, and explained
their ftructure, and our days paffed in
the happieft occupations.   Often fhe
made me repeat the hiftory of my
youth, and enter into the minuteft
details, or defcribe the flighteft fenfations I had experienced, affuring
me, every thing that concerned me,
was interefting to her.

You will readily conceive the friendfhip of my dear Dormeuille made no
trifling figure in thefe converfations,
Ah! 'twas one of our moft interefting and moft pleafing topics   I cannot defcribe to you the delight my
Sophia took in talking of you   Every
day we read fome of your letters together, nor did we ever finifh them
without tears of pleafure.

The

The fubject to which fhe moft frequently recurred was my journey to
Clermont   Eveiy thing that related
to our worthy mother was extiemely
interefting to the good, the tender
Sophia.   When I defciibed the countenances and tempers of the childien,
fhe almoft fancied herfelf among them,
and longed to embrace them.   She
would often afk me, with tears, whether
Madame de Clermont ever thought
of her daughter.   " Ah, Sophia,"
replied I, " how is it poffible fhe
fhould not think of you conftantly?"

Thus paffed our days, in mingling
our mutual griefs and pleafures, oui
thoughts and feelings, and all the little attentions that aie dictated by fraternal love   Ah ! my friend, how
delightful is that affection when pure
and exempt fiom envy   'Tis the
firft fentiment of which nature has
rendered man fufceptible, to teach
                                him,

him, from his earlieft infancy, that our greateft happinefs is friendfhip.

I have always had a bad opinion of brothers who do not love each other. 'Tis an affection which can only be extinguifhed by the growth of vicious paffions.

Had this mode of life continued without interruption or change, we fhould then have known true and permanent felicity. No pleafures can be compared with the enjoyments that continually occupied our moments. They were pure, they were heavenly, and if Sophia received a kifs in the midft of our employments or converfations, 'twas always the kifs of pure fraternal love. But alas! this enchanting phantom of happinefs foon vanifhed, and I am deftined never to tafte of any durable enjoyment. Scarcely from the moment of my birth have affliction and forrow ever

quitted

quitted me, nor do I doubt they will
purfue me to the grave.

My Sophia, my amiable Sophia,
began to be reftored to happinefs,
and I was fatisfied with my condition. Only at the intervals when I
was obliged to quit her, I felt a fecret uneafinefs at the greatnefs of
our danger. But in her prefence
every difmal idea vanifhed, and I only
felt the moft exquifite, the moft unalloyed pleafure.

One day I obferved her more melancholy than ufual, but attributing it
to fome paffing reflection, I endeavoured rather to divert her thoughts
than to difcover the caufe of her dejection, which, however, increafed
daily, and at length became extreme.
One morning I found her in tears,
and unable to anfwer me but in fobs,
which, however, fhe ftruggled to fup-
prefs. Whence could this fudden
change

change arife? Alas! a croud of horrid images preffed upon my imagination. At length I learnt the dreadful
fecret, that my Sophia would in a few
months become a mother!—

'Tis impoffible either to defcribe
or to conceive the fhock this fatal
news produced on my whole frame.

For a long time I fat motionlefs
and unable to fpeak, infenfible to every
thing but the ftifled fobs of her whom
I fcarcely dare to name

Great God! to what misfortunes
am I ftill deftined. To find the moft
dreadful torments in the tender fentiment from which happinefs moft fpon-
taneoufly arifes! in paternal love itfelf! Great God! what a complication of mifery!

This, alas! was a fatal blow to all
our hopes. How was it poffible to
fave ourfelves from fo great a danger?
What was to become of our unfortunate

nate offspring, or of the lovely and ten
der Sophia herself?—Ah! why should
the most amiable of human beings perish, a victim to a momentary error?

Sophia was equally convinced with
myself, that our destruction was in-
evitable, and it was now impossible to
calm her despair   Two months have
we continued in this state of anxiety
and horror, which it is impossible to
pourtray. The time will come when
we shall live in daily expectation of the
dreadful event—an event I cannot
think of without shuddering   Yet we
are destined to bear these terrors during several months to come. What an
age of misery !—yet how short a period ! Thus are all our days embit-
tered, thus are they marked by misfortune and despair   Great God!
perhaps that period will terminate our
tender union,—perhaps we shall be
separated for ever —consigned to unfeeling

feeling judges!—Ah, my Sophia, muſt I then be the cauſe of thy deſtruction—I! thy brother, thy friend?—

Adieu, my dear Dormeuille. Expect to hear ſome dreadful news. Ah? my good friend, what pains do I not cauſe you! Yes, 'tis pity you ever knew me.

LETTER XL.

'Tis now two years, my dear Dormeuille, ſince I have been able to write to you. You muſt have ſuffered great anxiety for me, and I have ſhared your uneaſineſs. But the moſt inſurmountable obſtacles have rendered my ſilence unavoidable. It requires the greateſt precaution to convey my letters

to

to you · and the man to whom I con-
figned them being dead, it demanded
confiderable time to gain the confidence of his fucceffor.

I anticipate the objects of your en-
quiry, and you fhall be fatisfied. What
a hiftory I have to relate to you ! But
do not communicate them even to
Leonora She would perhaps believe
me criminal, when in fact I am but
unfortunate.

At the time when you received my
laft, I was in a ftate, my pen is unequal
to pourtray. The moft diftracting
anxiety tormented me day and night,
leaving me not a moment's repofe.
Yet I was conftrained to appear at
eafe, in order to relieve Sophia of part
of her affliction. Alas ! I held out to
her the foothing picture of hope, while
defpair filled all the receffes of my
foul. My attention and folicitude,
alas ! produced but little effect. She
replied

replied not to my reasonings, and continued whole hours with her eyes fixed on the ground, or weeping bitterly. Thus had I not only to endure my own affliction, but to console the despairing Sophia, which was far the most arduous trial of my fortitude. Her health visibly and daily declined, her cheeks grew pale with continual weeping, her eyes lost their enchanting vivacity, a settled melancholy obscured them; and the paleness of death characterized all her features.—And to me alone she owed all this agonizing wretchedness.

Our misfortunes were now at their summit, for even the communications of sympathy were denied. Sophia passed her days and nights in tears, and the anguish I felt was such, that to me death would have been a welcome relief, had I not feared to leave my Sophia destitute. For I possessed not

fortitude

fortitude equal to fupporting her heart-
rending afflictions.

I had no interval to give vent to
my grief, except when I was obliged
to attend divine Service, and on thefe
occafions I unburdened my foul of
all its accumulated fufferings. This
was generally in the night, and the
obfcurity of the building, the mournful hymns of the other friars, and the
difmal ideas arifing from the folitude
in which I had left Sophia, every
thing fwelled the tide of forrow, to
which I could then abandon myfelf
without obfervation or controul

The important period was now advancing with rapid ftrides, and we had
already entered the laft month, the
commencement of which chilled me
with horror. I endeavoured however
to fuppref my anguifh, that I might
render my too unfortunate Sophia all
the

the affiftance fhe needed, and which fhe could only receive from me. I was now about to be called to the difcharge of the moft important of duties, for which it was neceffary I fhould qualify myfelf. With this alone I was fully employed. Alas ! how could I without horror contemplate the danger to which fhe would foon be expofed? How could that delicate form, which affliction and defpair had almoft exhaufted, fupport the cruel pains fhe was about to undergo, with no other affiftance than mine? I endeavoured to ftrengthen my fortitude and courage, and even confirmed it with fome illufory reflections. In misfortune, the moft powerful remedy is a conviction that we are able to extricate ourfelves from our difficulties.

You remember that phyfic and furgery, particularly anatomy, were always my favourite ftudies. Hitherto they

they had only formed my amufements:
I had then no idea of the important
benefit and utility I fhould one day derive from them. I endeavoured to
recollect all I had once learned relative
to thefe fciences, and particularly
every thing applicable to this important occafion. All this I arranged
in my mind, and conftantly reflected
on it, endeavouring to forefee every
accident, and to remember the means
of preventing the evil confequences
that might follow. What phantoms
did I not purfue? I was in want of
every thing, yet I imagined that I
poffeffed all the knowledge I required, and perfuaded myfelf that,
aided by Nature, my fmall acquirements were fufficient. Yet this confidence, perhaps, ought not to be
entirely attributed to too elevated
an opinion of my abilities. It
arofe wholly from a defire to repair
the

the misfortune I had caufed, and hence I placed all my hopes in the fuccefs of this undertaking, and conftantly drove from my mind every thing that could diminifh my confidence. 'Tis true, this was an error, but to that error I owed a degree of fortitude highly beneficial to us both. What efforts do not love and friendfhip enable us to perform!

Thus encouraged by hope, I looked forward with lefs apprehenfion and terror to the approaching event. At length the dreadful moment arrived. " 'Tis now the time," faid I, " to render myfelf worthy of the tender name of father, and to expiate an involuntary error by ufeful virtues."

'Twas midnight, when my Sophia was attacked by the pains of child-birth. Alas! her inexperience and timidity made her believe her laft hour was at hand.

Each

Each moment I thought I was about to lofe her for-ever.—Great God! what could I do? What was to become of us? Unable to call for affiftance!—What a wretched fituation! Never did human being experience greater mifery.

Judge of my defpair, when I was each moment in expectation of beholding my Sophia expire in my arms.

Great God! on what dreadful conditions haft thou granted and preferved my life!

But foon what a happy change! At length fhe opened her eyes, and the blood began to circulate with more freedom. My Sophia was reftored to life, and with her I feemed myfelf again to revive.

Alas! My hopes again fuccefsively vanifhed and returned, and then again abandoned me. — Ah! what dreadful uncertainty and fufpence!

Thus it is that Fortune ever fports with our wifhes, and before fhe throws us down the precipice of defpair, arrefts us for a moment on the edge of the abyfs, feems to pull us back from deftruction, threatens us anew, and makes us each moment anticipate our fate.

At five in the morning, the bell rang for the firft mafs. Its chilling found re-echoed through the filent obfcurity of the night, and with ominous voice appalled my very foul. Sophia feemed to awake fuddenly at the hollow knell, raifed her hands towards heaven, and in a half-extinguifhed whifper, " Alas!" faid fhe, " I am unworthy to partake in that holy ceremony "

The fymptoms however ceafing I attended this awful fummons, fervently

to

to invoke the Deity to be merciful to my Sophia, in the approaching hour of trial.

But what was my aftonifhment, when at my return fhe prefented the child to me! It was a daughter. Paternal love now took entire poffeffion of my heart. I received it in my arms, and kiffed it repeatedly, while Sophia beheld me with tears of pleafure. 'Twas an angelic look that drew me clofer to her, and our kiffes and our tears mingled on the innocent face of our child.

" Almighty God," faid Sophia, " grant thy protection to this helplefs little babe. Ah! may her too finful mother long preferve her from every evil, and defend her from the ftigma fhe has never merited.

" Ah! ceafe," faid I, " my dear Sophia, to think yourfelf criminal; Surely heaven has made you a mother,

that

that you may efface that fault by the moſt important virtues. You will henceforth be the chaſteſt, the beſt of mothers· And who can better deſerve the favour of the Almighty?"— " Yes," ſaid ſhe, " I will endeavour to fulfil thoſe moſt ſacred, and moſt pleaſing of all duties "

We gave our child Madame de Clermont's name, and called her Louiſa.

I was now conſtantly employed in the requiſite attentions both for the mother and the child. Long before the event, I had provided myſelf with every thing neceſſary. Under pretext of a wound in falling down ſtairs, I had procured ſome linen, and as I was intimate with the friar who had the care of the infirmary, he had given me a key of the diſpenſatory, that I might myſelf take what I wanted. As to fuel, very little

was

was diftributed to us, though it was
winter, and therefore I went every
night to collect fome in the coppice
of the monaftery, by which means I
procured more than we wanted Of
broth we had fufficient, as I could
order as much as I chofe, and my in
difpofition was fo trifling, that it was
not thought neceffary I fhould be
placed in the infirmary, or my provifions diminifhed in quantity, either
of which would have been fatal to
our wifhes.

Thus was I enabled to furnifh Sophia and her child, with every neceffary, and became at once her
nurfe, her doctor, and her cook.

Sophia's diftrefs had now difap-
peared, and was fucceeded by the
fweeteft of enjoyments. With what
eagernefs I endeavoured to procure
every thing her health required! With
what pleafure I witneffed her reco-

very,

very; with what delight did I fee her fuckle the little Louifa. To me it formed the moft angelic picture, all nature could afford.

The firft time fhe held her to her breaft, fhe bent down her head, kiffed its eyes with a timid air, and a fudden glow covered her cheek, yet a foft fatisfaction foon mingled with her fears, and at length overcame her modeft fcruples.

My Sophia foon afforded me the fatisfaction of perfect convalefcence; and appeared more beautiful than ever. Her eyes poffeffed greater animation, her complexion was more florid, and her features acquired a certain air of matronly grandeur that excited my warmeft admiration.

Her maternal cares now occupied all her moments, and made her forget her paft misfortunes. Happinefs dwelt in her heart, and ferenity in her coun-

countenance.   I participated her
tranquillity, and felt that I was the
happieft of men.

Some narrow fouls may think the
fatisfaction we both enjoyed, rather
deferving of cenfure than of praife.
But you, Dormeuille, know that fuch
fentiments are the pure dictates of
nature, your philofophy is rational,
and accordant with the human heart.
How is it poffible it could be virtuous not to love our child, or not to
feel enchanted at having her in our
arms, and beholding her innocent
face? In fhort, ought not paternal
love, ever to prevail over every other
fentiment.

The care and education of Louifa
now engroffed all our thoughts. Not
only our love for her made us anxious to fpare her every pain, and to
fee her always happy, but our fituation rendered this precaution necef-

fary to our fafety, for we were obliged
to keep her as quiet as poffible, that
fhe might not betray us by her cries
In this we have hitherto been wonderfully fuccefsful, and fhe has never
given us caufe for much anxiety.
Whenever the unavoidable evils of
infancy give her pain, Sophia takes
her in her arms, and redoubles her
cares. She diverts her with fome attractive object, or hufhes her in her
bofom Fortunately the child at no
time cries loud, and it appears from
experience, as well as from reafon,
that the eafieft way of keeping children quiet, is to make them happy.

It was neceffary to our fafety that
Louifa fhould not learn to talk, and
therefore, as foon as fhe began to articulate, we only fpoke in whifpers.
This lovely child is now near two
years old, and cannot yet fpeak a
fingle word. She always expreffes
herfelf

herfelf, however, with great intelligence by figns. If fhe is in pain fhe
looks grave, and throws herfelf into
the arms of her mother, if fhe is
pleafed, this is eafily perceived by the
moft lovely fmile, when fhe kiffes
her mother or myfelf, and pats our
cheeks with her little hands, we interpret thefe tender careffes as a proof
that fhe loves us and is happy, and I
often fpread my bed-cloaths on the
floor, for her to jump and dance upon,
as is natural to her age. Thus have
we hitherto avoided danger Oh!
may we ever continue to efcape de-
tection.

Yet I cannot help often feeling
fome uneafinefs at our fituation. Could
it but endure for our whole lives, it
would leave us nothing elfe to wifh for.
But how many caufes might produce
a fatal revolution in our affairs, and
then what would become of the dear

K 5   Louifa?

Louiſa? Oh! my Louiſa, perhaps one day you will have too much reaſon to curſe your father for giving you exiſtence.

While I am now writing, Louiſa is ſleeping peaceably beſide her mother. What a charming picture! 'Tis Virtue and Innocence embracing each other.

My dear friend, this lovely child is already diſtinguiſhed by uncommon graces. Her amiable manners reſemble thoſe of her mother, and her countenance has the ſame enchanting ſoftneſs. Yeſterday, when ſhe ſaw me writing, ſhe took my pen, and ſmiling archly, made the ſcribbling you will obſerve on another part of the paper. You muſt conſider this as a billet-doux from my daughter.

Preſently after ſhe raiſed herſelf up at the window, and ſaw the tops of ſome trees, which ſhe pointed at to ſhew

shew me; and then sighed deeply. This sigh tenderly affected my Sophia and myself, and we took her in our arms, and kissed her. Ah! my friend, may heaven preserve her, and make her happy, when we are both no more! But even then what will be come of her? What a source of anxiety and fear.

You, my dear Dormeuille, who are a model of friendship, will never forget my dear Louisa, nor her angelic mother. Should any accident happen to your friend, may these unfortunate beings find a solace in your protection.—Adieu my dear Dormeuille.

Our

Our youthful monk wrote various other letters to his friend, containing the moſt intereſting accounts of the progreſs and education of the child, but circumſtances of a peculiar na-ture prevent our publiſhing them at preſent. We ſhall extract from them a hiſtory of all the misfortunes, the two lovers experienced in their cell, a ſituation no leſs extraordinary than affecting to every one who is endued with a heart of ſenſibility or the milk of human kindneſs.

Wholly occupied with their child, they at length forgot the error to which ſhe owed her birth, and while they watched her growth and the de-velopement of the charms ſhe had received

received from nature, they received
from her a thousand tender careffes, by
which the innocent little creature con-
foled them for their pains, and made
them happy by the warmth of her
affection. How could they feel their
forrows and afflictions while the future
and the paft were alike abforbed in the
love of Louifa? and what unfeeling
breaft could blame the pleafing il-
lufion?

In the mean while Dormeuille,
very uneafy at the fituation of his
friend, was anxious to refcue him
from the danger that threatened him.
In concerting his plans and projects
for this effect, he thought it neceffary
to relate every thing that had paffed to
Madame de Clermont, who had been
fome time a widow, and might now
freely exert herfelf for the fafety of her
fon. This hiftory had the moft
powerful effect on her mind. She was
inconfolable

inconfolable at hearing of the dreadful crime her fon and daughter had committed, yet could not reproach them with an act into which they were gradually and almoft inevitably drawn againft their will. She confulted with Dormeuille, and each took the preparatory fteps they thought moft effectual. As foon as they had raifed the fum they judged neceffary for the enterpiize, Dormeuille fet off with a determination to refcue, thofe unhappy victims of misfortune from the convent, whatever might be the confequence. But he arrived juft two days too late.

The next cell to that of Julius and Sophia had continued uninhabited feveral years, but at length a Spanifh monk named Don Manuel de Armas was lodged there, and by him they were difcovered.

About

About this time the child was very
ill, and in great pain with her teeth.
Sophia exerted all her powers to pacify
her and prevent her from crying, wrap-
ping her up in her gown, to stifle the
noise, rocking her in her lap, and careffing her in the tenderest manner, but all
in vain.   Don Manuel, who heard her
cries, at first thought himself mistaken,
as he could not imagine it possible a
child could be found in the cell of a
Carthusian monk.   He listened, however, more attentively, and heard distinctly the cries of a child, which he
concluded, by the interruption of its
complaints, to be lulled by a woman.
Thus convinced of the fact, and listening but to the voice of fanaticism, he
went immediately to the father Abbé,
and declared the dreadful secret. but
the latter totally disbelieved the information, as absolutely inconsistent
with probability, and ordered Don
Manuel

Manuel to preserve the most profound secresy on the subject, in order to avoid incurring any scandal on the order.

This fanatic, however, was unfortunately too confident of the truth of his deposition, and being highly indignant at the disbelief of his assertions, now eagerly sought new proofs of their truth. He therefore listened with a barbarous avidity, and was soon satisfied.

At night, while Louisa was asleep, Julius and Sophia sometimes conversed, though always in a low voice. But as the separation of the two cells was not very thick, and somewhat cracked, Don Manuel could distinguish articulate sounds, whose contrasted tones convinced him, there was a woman in the cell. Delighted at this second discovery, he returned in triumph to the Father Abbé. The good father, however,

again

again affured him it was impoffible, and that he muft be miftaken. "No," replied Don Manuel, with firmnefs, "I am certain of the fact. But why, my good father," faid he, "do you doubt the teftimony of my fenfes? Can I be miftaken in moft diftinctly hearing the voice of a child and of a woman?" — "My fon," anfwered the Abbé, "we ought always to diftruft evil impreffions." — "What I have faid," replied he, "is truth and fact, and you may eafily convince yourfelf of it I never anticipate a truth to the difadvantage of any one. On the contrary, I am extremely flow in admitting fuch, and can only believe it when conviction is forced upon my mind.—Father, your doubts of my veracity offend me, and I will be revenged."

Thus inflamed with anger, Don Manuel returned in hafte to his cell, and

and immediately wrote an account of what had paſſed to the Inquiſition.

In the mean time, the Abbé, fearing there might be ſome truth in Don Manuel's account, or that this young fanatic might do him ſome injury, that might cauſe him to repent of his incredulity, determined to examine the cell of the unfortunate Julius, it being cuſtomary for the Father Abbé to have a key to every door in the monaſtery.

What a ſcene now preſented itſelf! Sophia was ſitting with the innocent Louiſa in her arms, endeavouring to pacify her under the pain ſhe ſuffered. Julius was intent upon them both, and keenly affected at his inability to alleviate their miſery.

It is ſcarcely poſſible to deſcribe either the ſurprize of the Father Abbé or the horror and deſpair of the unfortunate couple. They both threw
themſelves

themfelves at his feet, and endeavouring to fpeak, yet unable to utter a
word, prefented him the child. Tears
were the only language that found
vent, and though the good father was
at firft highly incenfed againft them,
the fight of the interefting and tender
Sophia, and her helplefs infant, foftened
his aufterity with an emotion of pity,
and he even fhed tears of compaffion.
Julius, encouraged by this proof of
goodnefs of heart, related, in a fimple
manner, all his misfortunes, and fo
interefted the good father, that his
philofophic mind now only beheld the
conduct of thefe young people as a
weaknefs that excited his commifera-
tion. " Alas !" faid he, " indeed I
pity you. Would to God I could
fave you from the punifhment that
threatens you, but 'tis entirely out of
my power to ferve you. The duties
of my office oblige me to treat you
with

with a severity, without which my own life would be in danger. I fear the Inquisition is already informed of every thing. You must fly this very night I will myself open the gates for you, but that is the last benefit I can confer."

The worthy Abbé withdrew, his heart overwhelmed with grief, for he foresaw the misfortunes that must await them.

What a blow to the unfortunate Julius and Sophia ! They had now no hope of safety but in flight, and without money or means of conveyance how could they hope to escape a pursuit, which could not fail to be speedy and effectual. How was it possible Sophia should walk sufficiently fast with the incumbrance of a child, and where could they expect to find an asylum, or to meet with persons sufficiently compassionate to afford

ford them hofpitality, or ferve them
with affiduity, with no other motive but
mere humanity? It was Sophia herfelf
who made thefe difcouraging reflections. Alas! how could her natural
timidity fupport the idea of flying
like a criminal, and being treated
with every humiliation. Thefe fears
Julius did his utmoft to obviate. As
he was very ftrong, he faid he would
carry the child, and even Sophia herfelf,
and they were certain at leaft of that
fupport which charity refufes not to
the loweft of mankind. "As to hu-
milition," faid he, " 'tis impoffible
my Sophia fhould ever experience any.
Are not your virtues ftamped on every
feature? Who that beholds you would
not be impreffed with the moft facred
refpect? "There," they will fay, "is
an unfortunate family," and then they
will be melted with our condition.
Yes, I will carry my wife, my fifter, my

daughter

daughter, every thing that is dear to me, and we shall find, under the roof of my friend, an asylum, which the arrows of misery cannot invade."

Thus did this unfortunate and benevolent young man indulge the emotions of his heart, always mistaking his wishes for possibility, while Sophia listened to him with a sort of placid and implicit confidence. " Great God !" said she, " could we but save our dear child ! My dear Julius, how much more should I still love you"——

She was interrupted by a dreadful noise at the door, which being presently burst open, two men tore the unfortunate Julius from the arms of his Sophia, from whom he refused to part, till superior force overcame him, while two others seized the mother and her child, and conducted them all to the prison of the Inquisition.

They

They were lodged in fubterraneous dungeons, fix feet long, by four broad, and feven high, built of rough ftone, grown black by age, whence the moft unfeeling inhumanity had excluded every avenue of light, and only admitted the air by indirect openings in the wall, to prolong the fufferings of its victims. Such were the horrid dwellings of this unfortunate pair, rendered ftill more defponding by feparation from each other.

The wretched ftate of their minds cannot be defcribed. Julius, thus removed from his dear Sophia and his infant daughter, probably for ever, abandoned himfelf to the moft violent defpair. Sometimes agitated with rage, he traverfed his narrow prifon with hafty fteps, beating his forehead with agony; fometimes he caft himfelf precipitately on his bed of ftones, invoking death or annihilation, fince

he

he had now no hope ever again to behold his Sophia or his child.

Sophia, too much depreffed to be
violently agitated, feated herfelf on
one of the projecting ftones of her
dungeon, holding her Louifa in her
arms, and ftrove to pacify the terrors
of the child at the horrid darknefs of
her prifon.   This tender mother, re-
gardlefs of her own fate, was appalled
with horror at the cruel deftiny that
awaited her child and its unfortunate
father.   Excefs of grief deprived her
of the power to weep, or even to
complain, yet fhe ftruggled to fupport
and foothe her helplefs child.   All
the nourifhment that was brought her
was bread and water, and of that but
a very fmall quantity.   But fhe willingly deprived herfelf of what was
neceffary to her own fupport that her
tender infant might fuffer lefs feverely.

It

It would melt a heart of ftone to hear the tale of Sophia's fufferings or the hiftory of her days in this horrid dungeon, where her fole employment was to foften the lot of her innocent child. Having now no difcovery to fear, fhe taught her to fpeak, and to pronounce the name of her father. She told her a variety of little tales to amufe her, and to affuage the terrors of an imprifonment fhe fo little deferved. Their dialogues foon became extremely interefting. but we muft haften to relate events by which the fate of this wretched family was decided.

Julius, having for a time abandoned himfelf to his affliction, began to examine whether any means remained to fave the unfortunate mother and child, of whofe fufferings he was the caufe. His firft idea was to gain the man who brought him his food.

But these men, accustomed to the
sight of human misery, are acccf-
sible to no feelings but those of
avarice, and our unfortunate prisoner
had no means to interest him but his
tears and afflictions His endeavours,
therefore, were totally fruitless. At
length he threw himself at his feet,
and supplicated him, by all that could
influence the heart of humanity, to
inform him where Sophia was imprifoned. " And if I tell you." replied
he, with a brutal voice———" You
would confer on me," interrupted Ju-
" lius, the greatest obligation. I have
nothing to give you myself, but I
have a friend who is rich, and I will
write to him to recompenfe you "—
" Well," said he, " she is in a dungeon
that way,' pointing towards the left,
" but there is a wall five or six feet thick
between you And pray of what use is
it to tell you ?—For you need never
hope

hope to see her any more."—"What do you mean?" said Julius. "Oh," replied he, "my humanity prevents me from telling you."—"For God's fake tell me," said Julius, "I would know the full extent of my misfortunes" "Well, if I must then, in a few days the holy tribunal will fit to try you, and they fay there is no hope of pardon."

Wretched as were his reflections, he dreaded refigning himself to them for a moment. "What," said he, with indignation, "shall my Sophia perifh by the hand of an executioner? No. As long as I have any blood left in my veins, fhe fhall not die."

After reflecting for a fhort time on various projects, he determined to attempt making his way through the walls, and then to efcape with Sophia and the child. It was a fcheme which required an Hercules to accomplifh;

but

but when love and friendſhip prompt to action, we rarely compaie our ſtrength with oui undertakings. Theſe motives are more powerful than Hercules himſelf.

Fortunately he was poſſeſſed of a ſtrong knife, which had not been taken from him, and which he now converted into a ſaw, by rubbing it on the hardeſt of the ſtones. He then uſed it to detach from the door a ſtrong iron bar, two inches thick, which, as many others ſtill remained, could not very eaſily be miſſed, particularly as the dungeon was extremely daik.

Julius now fell to work with the moſt unremitting activity. The enormous ſize of the ſtones, their extreme hardneſs, the cement, indurated by time, the great thickneſs of the wall, all yielded to his powerful exertions. He did not reſt a moment night or day;
and

and to fave time, eat his black bread while he was at work. " Alas!" faid he continually, my Sophia is wretched, fhe is threatened with the moft horrid of deaths, and it is in my power to fave her." Thus he urged himfelf to redoubled efforts of un-ceafing labour.

When he had confiderably advanced in his labor, he found his ftrength fuddenly forfake him, and was obliged to fit down to reft himfelf. " Great God," cried he, " affift me !—Oh! enable me to fave the virtuous Sophia. Grant me but this, and difpofe of me as thou wilt. Sophia at leaft has not deferved her misfortunes. Oh ! grant that fhe may live to preferve her helplefs child !"

He arofe, and returned to his work with renewed ardour. Though the leaft delay increafed his alarms, yet,

L 3   not-

notwithstanding his truly heroical
courage, he did not advance so rapidly
as before, and the stones seemed heavier
and more difficult to separate

At length his indefatigable perse-
verance accomplished the Hercu-
lean labour, and pierced the wall,
when passing through the aperture, he
perceived, by the glimmering of a
sepulchral lamp suspended to the roof,
a female lying on straw, with a child
by her side. His heart palpitated
violently as he heard her groan, and
approaching her, he recognized Sophia, whose alarms at the noise were
converted into a joyful surprize as
soon as she beheld her Julius.

Their sensations at meeting in
such a situation, and after so long a
separation, can only be conceived by
those who are endued with the most
exquisite sensibility.

The

The pleasure they mutually received was, alas! but of short duration. Sophia, whose tender frame could ill contend with the humid and infected air, or the total privation of day-light, and all the afflictions that harrowed up her soul, was almost in a dying state. Her features were so altered, that they alone would scarcely have enabled Julius to recollect her. Her pale and haggard cheeks, her sunken eyes, and her feeble voice, rendered her a dreadful picture of sickness. At first she was somewhat re-animated at seeing him, but she soon sank again into her desperate condition. She beheld him, as it were, with a dying countenance, and pointed to her child, whom she recommended to his unremitting tenderness.

"Oh, my Sophia!" said he, "must I then lose you at the very moment when I was about to save you! Oh! cursed

L 4

fana-

fanaticifm! Oh! infernal prejudices of barbarous and unfeeling hearts!

"What, have the monfters refufed you every affiftance? Are the minifters of God totally deftitute of humanity?" "Alas!" faid Sophia, "they have given me nothing but black bread and water, and with the greateft difficulty have I procured this lamp. I folicited for it, to remove the horror which a perpetual darknefs excited in my child." "What monfters!" faid Julius, "but let us efcape from their power, my Sophia. Take courage, we fhall yet be able to cheat them of their victims"

Having haftily informed her by what means he had penetrated the wall that feparated them, he affured her that in a few hours it would be eafy to pafs in the fame manner the outer wall, and immediately refuming his maffy tool, he began to break

break his way on the side towards which he conjectured the street to be, —when in the midst of his labours he heard the door of Sophia's dungeon open, and two men entered. "Great God!" cried he, throwing himself on the earth, "we are then irretrievably lost!"—"No,—no," said one of the strangers, "you are saved. 'Tis your friend, who is come to rescue you from the hands of your cruel persecutors."

He soon recognized the voice and countenance of Dormeuille "Ah," said he, "this joyful surprize is too much!" They embraced again and again, and Sophia was once more animated with joy at beholding the friend of the father of her child.

It has already been said that this kind and sympathetic friend had intended to carry off the three unfortunates

nates from the Carthusian Monaftery, had he not arrived too late.
From the moment he had learnt
their new misfortunes, he had been
exerting the most powerful interest to
procure their pardon , but being unable to succeed in this object, he had
bribed several of the domestics who
were employed about the prisoners,
and had thus procured access to his
friend.

Having said this in as few words as
possible, he urged them immediately
to depart, and they all drove off with
the speed of lightning in a post-chaise,
that waited for them a few paces from
the prison.

Thus they travelled with the greatest rapidity into Switzerland, where,
under the protection of liberty and
toleration, secured by the wisest laws,
they lived in happy peaceful affection,

no longer dreading the vengeance of bigotry and fanaticism.

A small house in a fertile valley, and surrounded by the most beautiful hills, became their happy retreat. They arrived late in the evening, and the next morning Dormeuille came to prepare them for the visit of a stranger. 'Twas Madame de Clermont, who had quitted her native country, together with her children, to live with this unfortunate family.

It is unnecessary, it is impossible to describe their meeting. 'Tis a picture which imagination will draw for the heart of sensibility.

Determined not to quit his friend, Dormeuille inhabited a neighbouring mansion, where his Leonora long continued to enliven this little circle, and to enjoy unmixed happiness. The closest friendship united them all in the bonds of reciprocal affection, and they

they spread benefits and contentment among all the unfortunate individuals who surrounded them.

Thus liberated from the immediate pressure of danger or calamity, the minds of this unfortunate couple had leisure to recoil upon themselves, and though no external object interposed to destroy the most delicate tissue of earthly enjoyment, yet conscience reproached them with a crime which nothing could obliterate from their imagination.

Sophia, after an interval of ten years of negative happiness, or rather of melancholy content, was removed to a private receptacle for lunatics, and this event, added to the constant reflection that he was the cause of all her misfortunes, preyed so continually on the morbid sensibility of Julius, that Dormeuille, one day surprised at

his

his late rifing, when on a vifit at his manfion, found him in his chamber, weltering in the blood, his own hand had fhed.

He left on the table a letter to the following effect

" Forgive, my dear Dormeuille, the weaknefs of your unfortunate friend. Were it in my power to contribute to the happinefs of a fingle human being, perhaps it were a crime to quit my ftation. But I can no longer bear to live among mankind, merely to make them wretched, and myfelf to linger in defpair.

" If I commit an offence in with-drawing from a life of mifery, which perhaps the Almighty intended as a punifhment for my errors, pray to heaven, my dear friend, to grant me

its

its forgivenefs and its mercy   Above
all, take care of my lovely Louifa,
fhe alone could attach me to life : but
alas ! even to her I fhould have been
only a fource of misfortune   To you
I bequeath the legacy of my duties and
relations in life, and the fame care
you have always beftowed on myfelf,
you will doubtlefs not refufe extending
to a daughter who is dearer to me
than my own happinefs. Alas ! my
wife, my fifter, my mother—Oh ! I
can no more—Adieu."

Such were the fatal confequences,
fuch the additional crimes refulting
from that criminal indulgence of
the paffions, for which it is too often
alleged

alleged as an apology, that it may continue undifcovered, and be compenfated by marriage.

FINIS.

Milton Keynes UK
Ingram Content Group UK Ltd.
UKHW031328270823
427564UK00016B/455